Augsburg College
George Sverdrup Library
Minneapolis, Minnesota 55454

HARVARD HISTORICAL MONOGRAPHS

Published under the direction
of the Department of History
from the income of the
Robert Louis Stroock Fund

Volume LXXIV

MICHAEL P. FITZSIMMONS

The Parisian Order of Barristers and the French Revolution

HARVARD UNIVERSITY PRESS
Cambridge, Massachusetts, and London, England   1987

Copyright © 1987 by the President and Fellows of Harvard College
All rights reserved
Printed in the United States of America
10 9 8 7 6 5 4 3 2 1

This book is printed on acid-free paper, and its binding materials have been chosen for strength and durability.

Library of Congress Cataloging in Publication Data

Fitzsimmons, Michael P., 1949-
    The Parisian order of barristers and the French Revolution.

  (Harvard historical monographs ; v. 74)
  Bibliography: p.
  Includes index.
  1. Lawyers—France—Paris—History. 2. France—History—Revolution, 1789–1799. I. Title. II. Series.
KJV173.F57   1987   349.44'36'0922   86-19519
ISBN 0-674-65464-1 (alk. paper)   344.43600922

KJV
173
F57
1987

To Theresa

Contents

Preface		ix
1.	The Order of Barristers under the Old Regime: 1774–1789	1
2.	The Onset of Revolution: The Dissolution of the Order of Barristers, May 1789–December 1790	33
3.	A New Era: January 1791–July 1792	65
4.	The Impact of the Terror: August 1792–December 1794	90
5.	Regroupment: 1795–1799	111
6.	The Promise of Reconstruction: 1800–1804	130
7.	A Hollow Victory: 1804–1815	154
	Conclusion	193
	Appendix A. Members of the Order of Barristers at Paris in 1789	203
	Appendix B. Parisian Barristers to the Parlement Who Assumed Positions in Civil Courts in Paris	219
	Appendix C. Parisian Barristers to the Parlement Who Assumed Positions in District Courts outside Paris	221
	Appendix D. The Order of Barristers: Individual Portraits	223
	Notes	228
	Bibliography	281
	Index	295

Preface

The Parisian Order of Barristers (Ordre des avocats) began to interest me at a relatively early stage of my graduate career. I was especially impressed by the questions that their experience raised for the historiography of the French Revolution.

Most historians have portrayed barristers largely as a professional group that played an important role in the Revolution, arguing that they were representatives of the interests of the bourgeoisie. Even scholars with such disparate views as Georges Lefebvre and Alfred Cobban were alike in depicting barristers as the vanguard of the "revolutionary bourgeoisie." Lefebvre wrote about "the lawyers, who represented and guided the bourgeoisie," while Cobban stated that "the revolutionary bourgeoisie was primarily the declining class of *officiers* and the lawyers and other professional men." Thus, most historians contended not only that barristers were politically engaged, but that as an occupational group they generally supported the Revolution. Yet an initial reading of memoirs and other works by the Parisian *avocats au Parlement* suggested that this was not necessarily true. It was obvious that such assessments were based primarily on the composition of the National Assembly rather than on any analyses of the legal profession itself. I became convinced that there was a clear need for a study of the legal profession from within—on its own terms rather than from deductions based on the membership of Revolutionary assemblies—and I was astonished to find that none existed; indeed, Philip Dawson's *Provincial Magistrates and Revolutionary Politics in France, 1789–1795*, a study of *bailliage* magistrates, was the closest analogue and virtually the only study of any legal occupational group below the level of the *parlementaires*. At almost the same time, however, Lenard Berlanstein's *The Barristers of Toulouse in the Eighteenth Century, 1740–1793* appeared, and his findings, which centered largely on the Old Regime, strengthened my conviction that an analysis of the profession during the Revolution should be done.

Several factors made Paris the logical choice for the study. The size of the Order of Barristers there was an obvious consideration; with over six hundred members in 1789, the Order of Barristers in Paris was the largest and most important body of barristers in France. The appearance of Berlanstein's book reinforced my decision in this regard. Although the example of Toulouse may or may not have been typical, it became clear that after his careful study an examination of any other provincial town would be of only marginal value, and that an analysis of Paris offered a much more useful counterpoint. As I began the project, however, I quickly discovered that while Paris offered advantages as the site for the study, it also had an enormous liability. The fires set during the Paris Commune in 1871 had annihilated much important documentation. The burning of the Hôtel de Ville had destroyed the birth and death records for the city. The fire at the Palais de Justice had consumed the Bibliothèque des avocats, which contained not only the records of the Order but also the papers of several avocats au Parlement. It had also destroyed the court records for the city of Paris, and another blaze claimed the archives of the Council of State, which deliberated on the reorganization of the Order.

Concerned about whether the topic could be researched properly, I went to France for four months to explore the sources. The collection of *tableaux des avocats* preserved at the Bibliothèque des avocats in Paris, which had apparently been out of the library at the time of the fire, was a crucial starting point. The tableaux precisely defined the Order and provided full names and addresses of its members; it also corroborated other references that used no first name or employed the title "citizen." The importance of the tableaux became even clearer when a comparison with the list of avocats au Parlement in the *Almanach Royal* revealed the unreliability of the latter compilation. The *Almanach Royal* of 1789, for example, incorrectly listed as members of the Order twenty-five men who did not belong to it and omitted sixty-seven men who did.

As a result of the increased role of the government in judicial affairs during the Revolution and the Empire, official documents in the Archives Nationales yielded considerable information. The records of the Ministry of Justice in the BB series were particularly helpful, especially the BB^5 series, which offered much biographical information for both the Revolution and the Empire, enabling me to reconstruct the activities of many barristers after the abolition of their Order. To a lesser extent, the D^{III} series provided similar biographical material up to the year 1795, and the F^7 series presented a chronicle of the barristers' problems during the Terror. Finally, the Bibliothèque du Sénat possessed a collection of working drafts of the Council of State on the project to reorganize the Orders of Barristers under the Empire. I came back to the United States convinced that the study I envisioned could be written.

Although on subsequent trips to France I tried to be as thorough as I could in my research, the incendiaries of 1871 had created gaps that could not be overcome. To give but one example, I would have liked to examine the social background of members of the Order more thoroughly, but the lack of documents in the reconstituted état civil at the Archives de Paris et de l'ancien Département de la Seine and in the notarial records in the minutier central at the Archives Nationales precluded it. For those who may wonder why this study is neither quantitative nor prosopographical in nature, one reason is that the sources were not extensive enough to sustain either approach with any degree of methodological validity. Despite these limitations, I believe that a credible body of evidence exists through which one can draw conclusions about the Parisian Order of Barristers.

As I developed the subject, I was struck by the dichotomy between the barristers in the National Assembly and those who continued in the profession in Paris. It became apparent that the barristers in the Assembly were not necessarily representative of their colleagues who remained in practice. After August 4, the National Assembly, whose membership included several men from the Order of Barristers at Paris, operated under a dynamic of its own, and was propelled by the vision of a new France. One of the most prominent features of the Assembly's conception of this new France was an implacable hostility toward privilege and corporate bodies and, as part of its effort to remake the French nation, the Assembly suppressed the parlements and abolished the Orders of Barristers.

Rather than rallying to the Revolution, most of the members of the Order of Barristers in Paris who still practiced law could not understand the attack launched on the traditional structure and institutions of French society by the National Assembly. In Paris the abolition of the Order left the majority of its members disappointed and disillusioned. Most of the men who had constituted it took one of three steps. Some retired from practice altogether, some left the profession to embark on administrative or judicial careers, and still others continued the practice of law in the new courts.

This book is primarily concerned with men in the last category. Only by concentrating on the men who continued to practice can one best examine the reaction of the members of the legal profession to the changes wrought by the Revolution. Far from welcoming the actions of the National Assembly, they were dismayed by them and even attempted to circumvent the abolition of their Order. They did not subscribe to the new ideals for France asserted by the National Assembly. Instead, they remained imbued with an Old Regime consciousness of *état, corps,* and *ordre,* and continued to adhere to the corporate ethos of their profession, which had been categorically rejected by the National Assembly. In fact, the men from the Order who remained in practice spent much of the period of the Revolution and the Empire trying to undo the impact of the National Assembly's actions on their profession.

In discussing these men, I refer only to those who formed the unofficial coalition maintained after the Order's abolition in 1790. They were bound together by shared traditions and assumptions and acted in a somewhat unified fashion. This group, and not the entire Order of 1789, constituted the Order after 1790, and that is how I use the term. For the men who remained committed to the profession, the problems raised by the Revolution were not settled in 1791, 1794, 1795, or 1799; they were resolved only in 1811 with the reestablishment of their Order. The nature of the resolution underscored the change between the Old Regime and the Napoleonic administration in the structure of the French state and in its relation to a professional group. Indeed, the experience of the legal profession during this era challenges several prevailing assumptions about the development of the professions in France.

I owe a debt of gratitude to many people for their assistance and encouragement. During my undergraduate years John Hanahan and Anselm Biggs, O.S.B., instilled in me intellectual discipline and a respect for scholarship. At a later stage in my academic career, Joan W. Scott guided this study. It also benefited from the comments of Lamar Cecil, John Headley, and Donald Reid. George Taylor not only offered thoughtful ideas, but also provided support and encouragement at a difficult time. Similarly, I would like to thank Gerhard Weinberg for his interest and support. Frederick Behrends was also unstinting in his moral support. Lenard Berlanstein kindly and unselfishly offered advice and suggestions. Jan Goldstein helped me to resolve a difficult organizational problem, and her insightful comments immeasurably strengthened the work.

In Chapel Hill the staff of the Wilson Library was at all times unfailingly helpful, especially the Interlibrary Loan and Humanities Divisions. Patrick Wreath offered encouragement from an early point in my graduate career and continued to do so even as he vainly battled the disease that ultimately killed him. The friendship of Tom Conner made the vagaries of graduate school and much else infinitely more bearable.

During my trips to France countless archivists and librarians facilitated my research. I would especially like to thank M. Michel Bouille and M. Jean Paul Hubert of the Archives Nationales, M. Albert Tropenant and M. Michel Brichard of the Bibliothèque des avocats à la Cour d'Appel in Paris, and Mlle. Nicole Villa, formerly of the Bibliothèque Nationale and currently at the Louvre, for their help; all of them were extremely generous and courteous. The staffs of the Bibliothèque historique de la ville de Paris and the Bibliothèque du Sénat were very kind in providing assistance. Furthermore, in the floating community of American and British scholars in Paris, I was most fortunate to enjoy a vintage year. The friendship of Mike Broers, Rory Browne, Cheryl Danieri, Donald English, Joe Mandel, and Anne Quartararo was not only a source of fellowship, but also contributed to a cordial sense of shared purpose.

I am happy to acknowledge the assistance of the Georges Lurcy Trust for a grant that made much of the research in Paris possible, and the University of North Carolina for a university teaching fellowship that expedited the writing of this study.

The Department of History at Rice University provided a congenial working environment. I would especially like to thank Charles Garside, Jr., Francis Loewenheim, Allen Matusow, Richard Smith, and Albert Van Helden. I would also like to thank Elizabeth Suttell and Elizabeth Hurwit, of Harvard University Press, for their help in the preparation of this book.

Finally, although I am grateful to everyone heretofore mentioned, the following acknowledgments are of a deeper sort. Kenneth Margerison taught me the French Revolution as an undergraduate and initially encouraged me to pursue graduate study. This was not possible at the time that I graduated, and his efforts to boost my sagging spirits during a hiatus in which I was eight thousand miles away performing essentially involuntary military service will never be forgotten. Moreover, as prospects in the historical profession deteriorated during that period, he conscientiously informed me of it. After I decided to undertake graduate study anyway, he continued to encourage me, as he has to the present.

The assistance and support provided by Alan Forrest to a neophyte in the archives in Paris far exceeded the normal bounds of academic courtesy. The friendship that has developed since has enriched me in more than merely a scholarly manner, although my enthusiasm for and understanding of French history have been considerably abetted over numerous meals and gallons of coffee consumed together in Paris, Manchester, Chapel Hill, and Houston. His careful reading of the manuscript in its various forms considerably improved it, and his constant encouragement assuaged some disappointments.

Finally, I owe the deepest debt of gratitude to my wife, Theresa, who suffered no mean amount of personal hardship during the preparation of this book. It is a debt that can only be acknowledged rather than repaid, and I could not possibly express it in any satisfactory way; I only hope that she knows how grateful I am.

The Parisian Order of Barristers and the French Revolution

1 / The Order of Barristers under the Old Regime: 1774–1789

> All of your subjects, Sire, are subdivided into as many different corporate bodies as there are different callings [*états*] in the Kingdom: the clergy, the nobility, the sovereign courts, the lower courts, the universities, the academies, the trading companies, all of which produces, in every part of the State, extant corporations that one can consider as links in a great chain, the first of which is in the hands of Your Majesty, as head and sovereign administrator of all that comprises the body of the Nation.
>
> *Remonstrance of the Parlement of Paris*
> *March 12, 1776*

This characterization of France presented to Louis XVI by the Parlement of Paris in opposition to Turgot's Six Edicts succintly conveys the nature of French society under the Old Regime. From the guilds of different trades up through the three estates of the realm, the French polity was a collection of corporate entities so multitudinous that the examples offered by the Parlement do not even begin to indicate their diversity and totality.[1] The governing ideals of this social construct were *état, corps,* and *ordre,* concepts which were frequently overlapping and interchangeable. These terms embraced the values, assumptions, and spirit of the corporate framework of Old Regime society.[2]

One of the elements of this myriad of corporate entities was the Order of Barristers (Ordre des avocats) at Paris, the organization formed by the barristers to the Parlement (avocats au Parlement) of Paris. In the eighteenth century the services of a barrister were needed most often at the appellate court level, and the Parlement of Paris was preeminently the high court of justice in France. Its domain was enormous, covering more than one-third of the kingdom. It heard cases on appeal from the 164 lower courts and from the far more numerous seignorial courts within its direct jurisdiction. Since it was the foremost court of the land, it is not surprising that the barristers to the Parlement of Paris comprised the largest single body of avocats in all of France. In 1789 there were 605 barristers affiliated with the Order of Barristers at Paris, nearly triple the number associated with the next most prominent parlement of the realm, that of Toulouse, where there were 215 barristers.[3]

After the magistrates themselves, the barristers were the most critical group in the operation of the Parlement. The disruption caused in the Parlement by the occasional strikes of the barristers in the eighteenth century testified to their importance in the administration of justice. But if the barristers were important to the Parlement, the reverse was also true. The barristers' affiliation with the Parlement not only formed the basis of their professional identity, but also governed many other aspects of their lives as well. A barrister's affiliation with the Parlement often determined his politics, his intellectual interests, and perhaps even whom he married or where he lived. Being an avocat au Parlement encompassed much more than a knowledge of law. It represented a way of life so prestigious that many men became avocats au Parlement for this reason alone, with no intention of ever practicing law.

The professional function of the barrister was to present his client's case to the court, either through oral arguments or in writing. In principle, the avocats were closely linked to the attorneys *(procureurs)*. In every lawsuit that a barrister handled he worked with an attorney representing the party and, insofar as a procureur could file some written briefs on behalf of his client, their duties overlapped. The convergence of the two professions was further reflected in Paris by the fact that they were linked through the confraternity of Saint Nicholas, a spiritual and mutual aid society founded in 1342.[4] In reality, however, sharp corporate and professional differences divided the two professions, and the barristers sought to distance themselves from the attorneys as much as possible.[5] Only the barrister could present oral arguments before the courts, and in written briefs only he could argue points of law or legal precedent, whereas the procureur could concern himself only with procedural matters or points of fact that might work in favor of his client. The barrister considered himself the jurist or legist and disdained the duties of the attorney as little more than clerical.[6] One could not be an avocat and a procureur concurrently, and barristers viewed with great displeasure the practice of changing from an avocat to a procureur.[7] The barristers also demonstrated their desire to distance themselves from the procureurs by the termination of their participation in the confraternity of Saint Nicholas in 1782.[8] Not only was there a professional divergence between them, there was also a disparity in prestige; the profession of avocat carried more esteem than did that of procureur. The profession of barrister, for example, did not derogate a noble under any circumstances, while that of procureur, if not practiced before a parlement, did.[9] More formally, in ceremonial matters, which were of some importance in the Old Regime, avocats always took precedence over procureurs. Finally, the fact that each group had its own separate professional organization understood the differences between them; the attorneys had the Communauté des procureurs as their professional organization while the barristers had the Ordre des avocats.[10]

Whereas the term *communauté* (as well as *corps*) connoted an officially established corporation, the barristers continually emphasized that their Order was not a formally constituted corporation. Strictly speaking, this was true, for the Order did not hold letters patent from the king, the essential legal requirement for recognition as a corporation.[11] Instead, the barristers asserted that their Order was an association of individuals freely united in a common discipline for the practice of their profession.[12] Even if it was not juridically ratified, however, the corporate nature of the Ordre des avocats was an established fact that was apparent to all, particularly in Paris.[13] The Order limited membership only to barristers who passed a probationary period, much like an apprenticeship. Moreover, it had its own unwritten regulations and discipline, its own exclusive rights and privileges, its own patron saint, Saint Nicholas, and it met each May 9 to attend Mass as a body and to elect a new leader. Thus, it did not differ in any significant respect from legally accredited occupational corporations in France.

Why, then, were the barristers so adamant in disclaiming formal corporate status for their Order? It stemmed from their insistence upon the independence of their Order, which they saw as indispensable to the free exercise of their profession.[14] The barristers argued that the unique nature of their profession, which required clients to confide totally in them, and occasionally entailed the passing of such confidences to the barrister of the opposing party, meant that it was imperative for them to have the exclusive determination about whom they would accept as colleagues. They asserted that they alone should have the authority to deal with all questions affecting the interests of the

Order, particularly disciplinary matters.[15] To have acknowledged the Order as a corporation would have implicitly admitted the possibility of royal control and undermined their claim to such prerogatives. But by defining the Order as a free association of individuals united simply by a common discipline and an elected leader, the barristers emphasized its autonomy and deflected arguments for external regulation. The Crown seems to have acceded to the barristers' sensitivity on the matter. The degree of sovereignty accorded to the Order in Paris is evident in the fact that the Order of Barristers appears to have been almost entirely outside the jurisdiction of the Paris police.[16] Infractions involving members of the Order seem to have been handled not by the police but by the Order itself. Police reports in Paris apparently were often careful to note whether or not a barrister was a member of the Order, presumably because those who were not were more vulnerable to police action.[17]

While each parlement had an Order of Barristers, the structure and regulations of the various Orders differed slightly from parlement to parlement. At Paris, before an aspirant could apply for membership in the Order, he had to have completed his law studies.[18] There were two means of fulfilling this requirement. One method was through the universities, where he could enroll in the law school at the age of sixteen.[19] At the university he followed a three year course of study that involved instruction in Roman law, canon law, and French law. In his first year the student studied the *Institutes* of Justinian and at the end of this first year took an examination on it. The test was a prerequisite for the *baccalaureat* and did not in itself confer any degree. In the second year the curriculum consisted of additional study in Roman law as well as canon law. At the end of the second year the student argued a thesis and took his baccalaureat, which gave him the title *Bachelier ès Lois*. In the third year of study, he was required to study French law and could choose between Roman law or canon law as his other area of study. At the conclusion of his third year the student had to argue publicly a thesis before acquiring his degree and receiving the title *Licencié ès Lois,* after which he could present himself to the Order of Barristers. University training was the most common method of legal education and the law schools had large enrollments under the Old Regime. The University of Paris, the largest and most prestigious, averaged about 646 students each term between 1770 and 1778.[20] Schools in the provinces enjoyed strong enrollments as well. There were twenty-two universities in France in 1789, and all of them offered a course of study in law.

The second method of meeting the requirement for a legal education was to become a clerk to an attorney and to read and study law during this apprenticeship. The clerkship was a less common route, and a more difficult one, because the clerk had to provide for his study time while maintaining a heavy work schedule.[21] But after studying prescribed legal texts, such as the *Institutes*, an aspirant could take a degree examination which, if passed, qualified him as a Licencié ès Lois and allowed him to present himself to the Order for consideration. Many who pursued their law studies in this manner felt that they had an additional advantage because their apprenticeship taught them procedure while their independent study grounded them in jurisprudence.

The state of legal education in the French universities of the eighteenth century was very low, plagued by a variety of problems ranging from virtually nonexistent academic standards to venality. The memoirs of Etienne Denis Pasquier, who became a magistrate in the Parlement of Paris in 1787 and who pursued his law studies at the University of Paris in the 1780s, convey the laxity of standards. Pasquier wrote that he took up the study of law without giving much attention to it, and that he attended the lectures only rarely. Instead, with two of his friends, he went riding, engaged in fencing, or took dancing lessons. Moreover, he stated that he did not feel that he had lost much by doing this rather than attending classes.[22] Students could inscribe themselves at the beginning of a school term, skip lectures altogether, and then purchase "certificates of study" that attested to their presence at the classes and enabled them to take the degree examinations. The fact that professors received various fees from each student who earned a degree provided additional incentive for relaxing academic standards.[23] Abuses became so rampant at one institution, the University of Cahors, that the government closed it in 1751, and the University of Reims was particularly noted for the ease with which one could purchase a law degree after a short residence period.[24] The poor quality of legal education at the universities was well known and was a source of embarrassment to the legal profession. One authoritative legal text complained that "the knowledge that one learns today in these public institutions is hardly sufficient to prepare a jurist" and added that "it would perhaps be desirable if one could reform the course of [legal] studies at the universities on a new plan, or at least give degrees only to those whom they know are capable of learning; this would be easy to recognize with a little zeal and attention."[25]

One result of the conditions prevalent in the law schools was that the

Order assumed part of the task that it believed the universities had abdicated. In lesser jurisdictions a barrister could begin practice almost immediately after receiving his law degree and taking an oath in which he pledged to observe the edicts and regulations of the court where he intended to practice.[26] But to become a member of the Ordre des avocats at Paris it was not enough simply to possess a law degree; this was but a starting point.[27] For this reason the origin of a law degree was not an issue of importance in seeking admission to the Order. It did not matter whether an aspirant had graduated from the law school of a university or whether he had emerged from the study of an attorney to take his degree.[28] The essential requirement to be met was the satisfactory completion of a long and compulsory probationary period *(stage)*, a large part of which was devoted to correcting any deficiencies in a candidate's legal education. The probationary period, which was governed at Paris primarily by a decree of the Parlement of May 5, 1751, lasted four years and was thus longer in duration than the course of study at the universities. It was designed not simply to evaluate a candidate's academic abilities, but also to ascertain if he possessed the personal qualities deemed desirable for a member of the Order. These included, among others, diligence, sobriety, discretion, and intelligence.[29]

To begin the *stage* the candidate presented himself to the Order, where a senior member of that body took the necessary information from him and verified that he was eligible to commence the probationary period. French law required the candidate to be a Catholic, while the Order demanded of him, in addition to the law degree, a known and fixed domicile in Paris, a set of furniture, the possession of prescribed legal texts, and the payment of an initiation fee.[30]

The requirements of the *stage*, like the statutes of the Order itself, were unwritten. At all times one had to demonstrate and maintain a demeanor and appearance proper to a man of the law. In addition, throughout one's probationary period one had to attend a series of discussions *(conférences)* held by the Order for its probationary members. The discussions treated legal questions of both a philosophical and practical nature and were intended not only to judge a candidate's aptitude and application, but also to compensate for the inadequacy of the universities. The discussions were always presided over by a senior member of the Order and sought particularly to acquaint the candidates *(stagiaires)* more thoroughly with Roman law, which the avocats considered the basis of all jurisprudence, and which they believed was insufficiently taught in the universities.³¹ The discussions were highly regarded by most of the probationary members, and in later years some barristers would refer to themselves as students of senior members of the Order.³² The conférences were supplemented by attendance at the audience of the Grand' chambre, the most important chamber of the Parlement, in which all of the cases presented were oral pleadings. In these audiences the stagiaire did not learn jurisprudence as much as the custom and usage in effect in the Grand' chambre, as well as tactics and techniques for pleading. Unlike the discussions, presence at these sessions was not mandatory, but the probationary barristers were strongly encouraged to follow them. Pierre Nicholas Berryer, who became a noted pleading barrister, called the audiences "the most instructive school" of all and considered attendance at them to have been one of the most valuable aspects of his *stage*.³³ Similarly, although it was also not required, during the period of his probation, a stagiaire could attach himself to the office of a barrister to learn and perform routine legal duties. He did not have the right, however, to sign his name to any work he prepared during this period. The satisfactory completion of the probationary requirements by the stagiaire had to be certified by six barristers designated by the president of the Order. Only after the successful conclusion of the probationary period was the candidate listed on the Register of barristers (Tableau des avocats) as an avocat au Parlement. If for any reason the Order found a candidate unacceptable, it could deny him admission without having to offer any explanation. This was an issue of importance to the Order because absolute control over its tableau was a prerogative the barristers deemed essential.³⁴

The exceptional requirements for membership demanded by the Order, which unlike the regulations of the law schools could not be circumvented or evaded, commanded respect from barristers in lower courts and conferred upon the Order a degree of authority.³⁵ When barristers in lower courts within the Parlement's jurisdiction asked the *avocat général* of the Parlement to settle questions of usage and custom or to adjudicate professional disputes, the avocat général often turned to the head of the Order at Paris for guidance.³⁶ The strict standards for entry also served to promote an extremely strong sense of esprit de corps among the men who formed the Order. To be a member was considered a sign of both talent and probity, and one's inscription in the

Order united him in a bond of common trust and respect with his colleagues.³⁷

The extremely strong role played by the Order in the professional formation of the barristers runs counter to the standard interpretation that sees the profession on the Continent emerging primarily from a university milieu. With the corruption in legal studies at the universities, the effort to define the legal profession — the delineation of intellectual activity, the determination of what was accepted as knowledge, the formation of professional standards and outlooks — came much more from the Order than from the university. In this sense the development of the legal profession in France, despite some overlap with the university, is more analogous to the English model of evolution outside of the university than is generally supposed.

Moreover, the legal profession evolved much more independently of the state than most other professions in France.³⁸ While the state did attempt to regulate legal education, there was no royal legislation regarding the profession of avocat between 1693 and 1774, and of the sparse legislation concerning it between 1774 and 1789, none directly affected the practice of the profession. Indeed, while many of the professions in France developed through cooperation or collaboration with the state, the Order developed in a much more autonomous fashion, so much so that at times, as in the Maupeou parlement or Lamoignon reforms, it was in direct and fundamental opposition to the Crown.

Finally, the crystallization of professionalism began much earlier than in the late eighteenth and early nineteenth centuries. Through the medium of the Order, the first phase of professionalization — association — was established by the eighteenth century, and from an early point in the eighteenth century, in fact, the Order had virtually all of the attributes usually associated with a "profession."³⁹

Membership in the Ordre des avocats alone enabled a man to claim the title of avocat au Parlement and clearly distinguished him from the other categories of barrister in Paris. One such group, unique to Paris and a legacy of the Maupeou parlement, was the avocats *du* Parlement. When he had been confronted with a strike by the barristers at the time of the establishment of the new courts, Maupeou had created one hundred positions of avocat du Parlement and assigned them to one hundred procureurs of the Parlement. They had had the right to perform both procedural and pleading duties in the courts. Although the avocats du Parlement were suppressed after the recall of the Parlement of Paris, the term continued to be used occasionally up to the Revolution. The avocats *en* Parlement was a second and much larger category; it was comprised of men who had a degree in law but were not members of the Order, and who therefore could not practice in the Parlement itself. The appellation was given to those barristers outside Paris who exercised in the lower courts within the Parlement's jurisdiction. Often the title was assumed by men who had a law degree but did not practice or who held other employment. Finally, the term was also applied to barristers in Paris who were not members of the Order, either because they had not successfully completed the probationary period or because they had not applied for admission, and of whom there may have been as many as five hundred in Paris at the end of the Old Regime.[40]

Once a barrister was inscribed on the Tableau des avocats as a member of the Order he received certain privileges. First, only the avocats au Parlement could practice before the Parlement itself.[41] Moreover, since they could practice in any court that fell under the Parlement's jurisdiction, members of the Order did not merely practice at the Parlement, but at the Châtelet and various other courts. As a result, there was not any kind of corporate rivalry between barristers in the sovereign court and those of the lesser courts, as was the case at Toulouse.[42] There was, however, a sharp division between those barristers who were on the tableau and those who were not. The advantage for the litigant in retaining a barrister to the Parlement was that an avocat au Parlement could handle a case in the first instance and then, if necessary, take it to the Parlement on appeal as well. This would save the litigant the time, trouble, and expense of having to find and retain another barrister, who would then have to familiarize himself with the case before he could argue it on appeal. Other privileges for those inscribed included exemption from all personal service, such as service in the militia.[43] Finally, the twelve most senior members of the Order at Paris were granted the right of *committimus,* a privilege that conferred the right to bypass all inferior courts and to present a case directly to the Parlement in the first instance.[44] Far less tangible, perhaps, but nonetheless of great importance, was the fact that these men derived considerable professional and social prestige from their affiliation with the Parlement. Professionally, there was a great distinction in being attached to the highest and most powerful court of the realm. In the words of one member of the Order: "Although the functions of barristers are more or less the same in all courts, at the same time those functions are more or less honorable in proportion to the dignity of the place where one exercises them; those who have taken their oath in the Parlement or some other superior court have a more distinguished rank than those who have taken their oath only in an inferior court."[45]

Professional pride manifested itself on ceremonial occasions, when members of the Order were accorded the right to wear a scarlet robe while barristers not affiliated with the Parlement wore a black one.[46] There was also a high degree of social prestige involved in the Order's close association with the Parlement. This aspect alone attracted many individuals who took up the profession of avocat au Parlement not as a livelihood, but simply for the social distinction attached to it. Such men were referred to by their colleagues as *avocats ad honorem,* and one contemporary estimated that approximately half of the Order fell into this category.[47] The practice of law had long been regarded as a gentleman's profession, and those associated with the law believed that to practice it meant that one could live nobly. Contemporary treatises continued to lend support to this idea, calling barristers *demi-noblesse* because their exemption from the militia gave them one of the privileges of the nobility, if not its legal status; similarly, the *Encyclopédie méthodique* deemed their status one of "personal nobility."[48] Christophe Jean François Beaucousin, who was "intensely interested in bibliography in the way others are interested in paintings or medals," typified the avocat ad honorem. Although inscribed on the Tableau des avocats in 1752, he "spent more time collecting manuscripts and old books than practicing or studying jurisprudence." He continued his studies until the Revolution and earned a significant reputation for himself in the field of bibliography.[49]

While many of the men in the Order who did not exercise the profession sought its prestige, there were others who also did not practice law but nonetheless belonged for professional reasons. Louis Nicolas Clement de Malleran, for example, had been accepted into the Order in 1737, and in 1764 had been appointed professor of French law at the University of Paris. Although his appointment would have precluded the active practice of law, he continued to be a member of the Order. Not all of the law professors belonged to the Order, but those who did joined in the belief that such professional contacts with their colleagues in practice helped to improve the quality of jurisprudence in the courts.[50] Similar considerations were doubtlessly responsible for the membership of David Houard, formerly a prominent barrister to the Parlement of Rouen and the author of several noted works on the laws and customs of Normandy, who joined the Order in 1785, the same year he was named to the Académie royale des belles lettres.[51]

In addition, the challenge of a career in Paris drew accomplished barristers from all parts of France to Paris to affiliate with the Ordre des avocats. Those barristers who had been members of provincial Orders did not have to undergo the probationary period, but they could not maintain any seniority they had previously acquired and had to accept an inscription date based solely on their arrival in Paris. Felix Julien Jean Bigot de Préameneu had been inscribed at the Parlement of Rennes in 1767, but with the help of the Rohan family, which encouraged his move and used its influence to assure him clients, he moved to Paris and was inscribed there in 1779. François Placide Nicolas Ferey had achieved a notable reputation at Beaumont in Normandy and then at Evreux, and gave up fifteen years of seniority at the Parlement of Rouen when he became associated with the Order at Paris in 1770. Others of note included Raymond de Sèze, one of the most important barristers of the Parlement of Bordeaux, who was inscribed at Paris in 1784, and Pierre Louis Lacretelle, who came to Paris from Nancy in 1778.[52] These men all earned an enviable professional reputation after their arrival in Paris, but for others the transition from the provinces to Paris was much less successful. Etienne Polverel, who enjoyed some success at the Parlement of Bordeaux, gave up twenty-one years of seniority when he moved to Paris in 1780. Louis Robin de Mozas sacrificed ten years when he came from Grenoble in 1781.[53] Neither of these men, however, established any sort of professional reputation for themselves after they came to Paris. One informed observer of the Parlement, for example, became aware of Robin de Mozas's presence in the Order only in 1784, after Robin de Mozas published a brief *(mémoire)* in which some suspected Linguet had collaborated.[54] Similarly, of course, the Order also lured young men just beginning their careers who felt that the opportunities Paris offered were greater than those available in their native region.[55]

Entry into the Order at Paris did not mean, as has been claimed, a complete ban on all other outside activity by members, although the Order at Paris was more strict in enforcing limits on outside endeavors.[56] There were collateral duties that one could perform, but they were strictly regulated in accordance with the Order's conception of the profession. One could not, for example, hold another full-time occupation and be a member of the Order at the same time. The Order justified this restriction on the grounds that the defense of clients was a full-time commitment in itself, requiring not only intense study for the preparation of a case, but also entailing that the barrister be at a client's disposition at all times to provide moral support or to meet any other needs the client might have. Furthermore, the Order regarded the profession of avocat as incompatible with the possession of most venal offices because the duties that these offices necessarily involved infringed upon the freedom "which is the heart of the profession of barrister." The profession of avocat was also considered inconsistent with posts encompassing tasks that the barristers regarded as beneath them or to which fees were attached, because such positions derogated the nobility of the profession.[57] Under no circumstances, then, could one be an avocat and a procureur concurrently, nor could a barrister act as a clerk *(greffier)* in any jurisdiction. Still, however, the barristers claimed an affinity with the magistracy and viewed their profession as a necessary first step to the exercise of such functions. The Order therefore allowed its members to act as judges or to fulfill other positions in the various seignorial jurisdictions in and around Paris; in fact, virtually all of the *baillis* and *lieutenants* in the seignorial courts in the Paris region were barristers to the Parlement and were generally the more prominent and successful members of the Order.[58] Such outside duties, however, were clearly regarded as subordinate to one's obligations as a barrister, and any conflict between them was not tolerated. Thus, Louis Le Roy quit his position as a *lieutenant* in the bailliage du Palais "in order to devote himself entirely to his profession."[59] The individual's identity as an avocat au Parlement took precedence over all other activities, and if such activities interfered with or reflected unfavorably on the profession of barrister, he could be removed from the Order.

Because of its large size, the Order rarely met as a body. Instead, it was divided into twelve benches *(bancs)* or sections, each corresponding to one of the pillars of the great hall of the Palais de Justice. Each section had its confidential bench *(banc affidé)*, and the prospective barrister first presented himself to one of these sections for consideration rather than to the Order as a whole. The system of benches, however, was not centrally regulated. No procedure existed for apportioning barristers to different benches, and by 1781 such an imbalance had developed between the benches that the Order reorganized itself. In an effort to distribute the number of barristers more equally, the reorganization divided the Order into ten columns that were largely equal in size.[60] The creation of the columns was for organizational purposes only and did not abolish the tradition of the benches, which continued to be used as meeting places. Subsequent tableaux specified both to which bench and to which column an individual belonged. At the head of each column were two colleagues elected by the members of the column whose duty was to examine the prospective candidate upon his entry into probation, and to ascertain that he met the specified requirements. The heads of the columns were also charged with scrutinizing the conduct of the candidate during his period of probation, and with holding the conférences that were a component of the probationary term. The heads of the columns, along with the former leaders of the Order, formed an unofficial council for the Order.

All of the columns together met to form the entire Order, which was under the direction of a president or *bâtonnier,* so named because of the long baton that he carried on ceremonial occasions. The Order met each May 9 in the Tournelle, the chamber of the Parlement that heard criminal cases, to elect the president, whose term of office was one year. With the assistance of the heads of the columns and the former presidents, the bâtonnier was charged with drawing up the Tableau des avocats and ensuring that it was printed. He also presided over meetings of the Order called for disciplinary proceedings, and was the head of the chapel for the barristers. In addition to the bâtonnier, there was also a dean or *doyen,* but this was merely an honorific title conferred upon the most senior practicing member of the Order, and did not involve any responsibilities or duties. Similarly, a barrister who had been inscribed on the tableau for twenty or more years consecutively could take the title *ancien avocat.*

Virtually the only other reason for which the entire Order would meet was to deal with matters of discipline, and even then such sessions were reserved for the most serious cases. The punishment that could be imposed on a barrister for an infraction took one of three forms: a reprimand, a temporary suspension from practice, or disbarment, and it was only in the event of the last that the Order as a whole would be convened. Normally, disciplinary matters were handled by the president in conjunction with the council formed by the deputies of the columns. This group received and investigated complaints, which could come from clients, judges, or colleagues. If a sanction appeared warranted, then this body would deliberate and pronounce the penalty, which could include disbarment, in which case the two deputies representing the column to which the affected barrister belonged expelled him. The disbarred barrister had the right to appeal the decision by asking for a meeting of the entire Order. There he had the right to be heard once more, after which the entire Order decided his punishment definitively.[61] The decision was communicated to the Parlement, which almost invariably concurred in it and issued a decree ordering all of the procureurs and other personnel of the Parlement to cease all professional contact with the barrister.

Disciplinary action appears to have been invoked more to preserve the image or internal harmony of the Order than for any other reason. In 1778 a client made an allegation against the barrister Louis François Feval over the manner in which Feval had handled some money, but the Order determined that Feval had not acted improperly and took no action. In general, however, it seems that complaints by clients against their barrister were rare.[62] Most often the Order acted against members who became too personally involved in a case and attacked either the opposing barrister or perhaps the opposing barrister's client too harshly. Such excesses posed a dual threat to the Order. Externally, they damaged the image of *pureté et délicatesse* that the Order wished to project.[63] Internally, they threatened the bond of trust and respect that united the barristers, thereby placing in jeopardy the stability of the Order itself. For these reasons, then, the Order could not afford to overlook such incidents when they occurred. Thus, on July 29, 1776, the Order suspended Louis Claude Rimbert for the duration of the Parlement's session that year and ordered him to retract his statements at the next opportunity in court for his intemperate remarks during an audience on July 17. Similarly, on August 28, 1777, it suspended Paul Laurent Dodin until the following January 1, after the Parlement complained about the tone and content of a written brief he had filed against his client's adversary.[64]

Both of these incidents were confined to the court and therefore had only limited impact. If, however, a barrister launched such an attack publicly, potentially affecting the Order's public image or the standing of the Parlement, the Order reacted much more severely. In 1777 Etienne Mallet was disbarred when a consultation bearing his name was published in conjunction with a brief that he had not authored, which was a slanderous diatribe against a Mme. de Saint Vincent. The latter went to court and won a judgment from the Châtelet ordering that the mémoire be suppressed. The Order summoned Mallet and upon investigation discovered that Mallet, who was elderly, infirm, and almost senile, had signed the consultation without reading it, for which he had been paid three hundred livres. Despite the circumstances and a pathetic plea from Mallet, who had been a member of the Order for more than forty years, he was disbarred.[65] In 1778 the Order disbarred Claude André Dassy for publishing a brief that contained a scathing attack upon the Parlement and the magistrate who had rendered an unfavorable decision against his clients, the Baron and Baroness de Bagges.[66] Such an action not only threatened the public image of the Order, but also, in appealing to public opinion, implicitly debased the position of the Parlement as the highest arbiter in France, and was therefore dealt with severely. The most well-known disbarment of the period, that of Linguet in 1775, although intertwined with political issues, revolved largely around his publication of a brief in which he bitterly attacked his colleague Jean Baptiste Gerbier.

The details of these episodes are less important than the fact that in each one the act of publication threatened the Order's public image. The Order knew that Mallet was elderly and had been deceived, and Dassy was a well liked and respected colleague, but their actions endangered the impression of professionalism and probity that the Order wished to project and therefore could not be tolerated.[67] Indeed, in its effort to preserve this ideal the Order extended its disciplinary authority to embrace activities completely removed from the confines of the courtroom. In 1779, for example, one young barrister received a six-month suspension for acting as a second in a duel in which one of the participants had been killed.[68] The Order's influence on the lives of its members was pervasive, encompassing not merely their professional conduct but their general comportment as well. The leadership of the Order once expressed it in the following terms: "When we have been inscribed on the Tableau, we have agreed to submit ourselves to the judgment of our colleagues on even the most trifling accusation that will be brought against us, to walk always on the straight and narrow path of virtue, [so] that no suspicion could arise on our ministry, and to consent to be sooner sacrificed as innocent victims to the honor of our Order than to remain with integrity that would seem to be under a cloud."[69]

The decisions of the Order could not be appealed to any outside authority, for the exclusive right of the Order to discipline its members was a strongly enunciated and jealously guarded prerogative.[70] In the disbarment of Linguet, the Parlement, for reasons that will be discussed later, had briefly sided with Linguet and implicitly contested the exclusive right of the Order to discipline its members. The action provoked much resentment among the members of the Order and represented one of the only periods in this era when the barristers and the Parlement were in serious conflict. Ultimately, however, the Parlement concurred in Linguet's disbarment and reaffirmed that the Order alone could discipline it members. This claim, along with the Order's insistence on no outside accountability concerning those whom it chose not to admit after the probationary period, served to underpin the barristers' contention that they alone were masters of the tableau, a contention that masked a far greater degree of self-determination than was at first apparent. Not surprisingly, then, it was precisely in these two areas that the Order was subject to the greatest criticism.[71] Its decisions could appear autocratic and left the Order open to charges of arbitrariness in its selection and disciplinary procedures. But the barristers contended that these two mechanisms were the means by which the Order could instill and enforce the professional qualities necessary among its members. Moreover, they argued that only those who exercised the profession could truly understand and appreciate its values, which was why the Order alone should wield such authority.[72] There can be little doubt about the barristers' success in asserting these arguments and maintaining the Order's independence. Aside from the Linguet episode, the authority of the Order to select and discipline its members was never seriously challenged. Its operations were almost completely untrammeled by the Crown, so that the Order controlled both private bonds among its members and its public image completely. Like the corporate nature of the Order itself, its autonomy was never publically acknowledged by either the Order or the Crown, but was nonetheless an undeniable reality.

As a public service the Order at Paris offered free legal consultations for the poor.[73] A board of six members of the Order, assisted by the probationary barristers, provided free consultations once a week. It appears, however, that the aid was more effective in giving the Order an opportunity to evaluate the stagiaires who were obliged to appear there than it was in meeting the needs of the poor, for in December,

1787, André Jean Boucher d'Argis, a judge at the Châtelet, founded the Association for Judicial Benevolence (Association de bienfaisance judiciaire), the stated purpose of which was to provide free legal services for the needy and to indemnify those among the poor who were acquitted in court.[74] Had the efforts of the Order been adequate, the association would probably not have had to concern itself with the first objective; moreover, the presence of several barristers to the Parlement in the association's membership implies that they regarded the aid offered by the Order as insufficient. Finally, the fact that the association was quite active, handling over three hundred cases in 1788 and in early 1789, seems to demonstrate that there was a need that the Order failed to meet.[75]

A distinctive feature of the Ordre des avocats at Paris was that it possessed its own library. It had been founded in 1708 with a bequest from the barrister Etienne Gabriac de Riparfonds, who wished to see it used for the professional enrichment of his colleagues and as a place of instruction for younger and probationary barristers. The library opened on May 5, 1708, and it was at this time that the conférences for the probationary barristers began. In the early years the discussions were very successful, attracting not merely the stagiaires, who were required to attend, but also high officials of the Parlement, the bâtonnier, and several senior avocats au Parlement to debate proposed legal questions.[76] An unspecified incident in 1725 led to a suspension of the conférences, but they were resumed in mid-century and continued uninterrupted thereafter, although they were followed almost exclusively by the probationary barristers.[77] The library depended completely upon the Order of Barristers for its existence and maintenance. The Order earmarked a large portion of the fee paid by the candidates when they began their probationary period for the support of the library, and this was its main source of income, supplemented by a few other sources; by 1789 the library had an operating income of several thousand livres.[78] Since so many aspects of the Order as an entity were unofficial or unacknowledged, and since it gathered as a body only infrequently, the library was the most tangible symbol of the Order's existence; it would later provide an institutional base for the reestablishment of the Order. The Order took much pride in it and the Bibliothèque des avocats grew in the course of the century as barristers left books and legal briefs to it. In 1778 one member of the Order estimated that the library contained ten thousand volumes, while a second contemporary placed the total holdings of the library in 1789 at approximately forty thousand volumes. Whatever the size of its collection, by 1789 it was unquestionably among the most important libraries of Paris.[79]

Such, then, were the official structure and operation of the Order, but there were further informal divisions within it as well. In accordance with the judicial procedures of the Parlement, there were three categories of barristers to the Parlement: the *orateurs* or *plaidants*, the *écrivains*, and the *consultants*.

The orateur or plaidant pleaded cases orally in the audiences of the Parlement, particularly in the Grand' chambre. The oral pleading in the Grand' chambre was a formal and closely regulated affair of protocol and ceremony.[80] Visitors to Paris often attended its audiences, and one avocat au Parlement recalled with pride how they "attracted foreigners of distinction."[81] They were also followed by Parisians, and a barrister's reputation, particularly outside of professional circles, often rested on his abilities in the Grand' chambre. One senior member of the Order advised younger barristers not to attempt to plead a case in the Grand' chambre too early in their career because the atmosphere there could be very intimidating, and he warned that a clumsy performance could adversely affect a young barrister's reputation.[82] A young barrister's first appearance in the Grand' chambre was a rite of passage that truly marked his initiation into the profession and provided him with some clue to the future course of his career. Berryer, for example, recalled that when he finally received his first opportunity to plead in the Grand' chambre he became quite nervous due to the oppressive silence both during and after his pleading, wrongly believing it was the result of some shortcoming in his presentation of the case; the tension was so great for him that he fainted afterward and had to be carried out of the chamber. Eustache Antoine Hua was so encouraged by his first effort in the Grand' chambre that it banished his doubts about whether or not to remain in the profession.[83] The oral pleading allowed the barrister to show not only his legal scholarship but also his rhetorical abilities. This mode was quite demanding in terms of preparation, and those who were skillful in pleading were highly respected by their colleagues.[84]

The écrivains were those barristers who prepared written briefs *(instructions)* for clients for use primarily in the chambres des enquêtes, which considered only cases presented in written form. The opposing barristers would "communicate" by submitting for each other's inspection and use the documents associated with the case. Each barrister would then examine the documents and cite legal precedents that favored his client. Once the opposing barristers agreed to terminate the arguments, a reporter prepared a draft summarizing the opposing positions that the judges used to reach a decision. It was this aspect of a barrister's work that most clearly overlapped that of a procureur, but a procureur could not present case law; he could argue only the facts of a case and not its jurisprudence. Although this method of practice was perhaps less respected professionally than pleading, it gave a barrister the chance in the *instruction* to show the depth of his knowledge in a way that pleading precluded.[85]

The *consultants* comprised the third and most diverse type of practice, which could range from assisting in minor family matters to resolving complex legal questions. In less important affairs, such as preparing a marriage contract or drafting a will, the consulting barrister's duties could conceivably overlap those of a procureur; these were tasks that the plaidants or écrivains could assume as well. But the *consultants* were also sought out to resolve such difficult legal matters as conflicts between local custom and law, and the like. It was this aspect of their duties that separated them from the other two categories of barrister. Quite often they were utilized by colleagues for advice in preparing a case, leading the *Encyclopédie méthodique* to use the analogy of the *avocat consultant* providing the arms while the *avocat plaidant* made use of them.[86] The consulting barristers, who were supposed to devote themselves to long and considerable study of the law, were acknowledged as the most scholarly and learned of all barristers and were widely respected; one barrister referred to the *consultants* as "the Newtons of the bar."[87] Consulting was often an activity assumed by many pleaders to prolong their career when their voice was no longer strong enough to sustain the rigors of the plaidoirie, and normally the title of *consultant* was assumed only in the later stages of one's career.[88] One member of the Order, however, Pierre Paul Nicolas Henrion de Pansey, a distinguished scholar and author whose talents were regarded as exceptional, devoted virtually his entire career to being a *consultant.* He pleaded only once in his career, winning a case for an escaped slave; for the remainder of his time as an avocat au Parlement he practiced entirely as a *consultant.*[89]

The members of the Order took particular pride in the fact that success in their profession was predicated upon ability and talent rather than background, and it was not an idle boast.[90] It is not surprising, then, that the degree of professional success among the barristers to the Parlement varied widely. The most successful avocats au Parlement were on retainer for important figures or institutions, such as churches, towns, or universities, and their reputation was so great that they were sought after in major cases and could therefore choose which ones they wanted to handle. Such a level of success was attained by only a small percentage of individuals in the Order, men like Jean Baptiste Treilhard and Jean Blondel, who were among those on retainer to the Royal General Farm, or Guy Jean Baptiste Target, whose clients included the comte d'Artois and the University of Paris.[91] These men were assured of a fixed or regular income, a steady practice, and doubtlessly other considerations as well.

Behind this group came a larger collection of mostly younger men who did not yet have significant retainers, but who might be on retainer for a less important client or have an independent practice of their own. Pierre Nicolas Berryer, to give but one example, was on retainer for two ecclesiastical chapters at Brioude and Bourges but also had an important practice in feudal and business affairs.[92]

The least successful barristers, larger yet in number, were those who were almost entirely dependent on the procureurs for cases and simply made themselves available in the Parlement. Underemployment or unemployment was such a problem that some barristers could not even attain this level and had to turn elsewhere. Jules Paré, who had been inscribed on the tableau in 1782, took work in Danton's office of avocat aux conseils, and Jacques Nicolas Billaud de Varennes worked there occasionally as well. Marguerite Louis François Duport-Dutertre was regarded as talented but was unable to attract many cases and sought, apparently unsuccessfully, a position in the offices of the police.[93] We know of these individuals primarily because of their subsequent careers, but surely they were not unique. It must be remembered, however, that overarching the varied levels of success among the avocats au Parlement was the much more pervasive and important fact of membership in the Order itself, which acted as a unifying thread. It meant that the most successful members of the Order would feel more in common with its least successful members than they would with any barrister not belonging to the Order, irrespective of the latter's level of success.

Although there were different degrees of success in the profession, the barristers to the Parlement of Paris, like those at Toulouse, do not appear to have possessed very much professional ambition.[94] As at Toulouse, the underemployed barristers did not resort to unethical methods to gain clients; perhaps, like Paré and Billaud de Varennes, they simply sought employment elsewhere. Moreover, for those who were able to maintain themselves in the profession, a large and busy practice does not seem to have been a major goal. Berryer mentions that a case in which he was involved early in his career concerning the former Indies Company was in itself enough work to occupy fully a young barrister, but, he claimed, the demands of this case did not preclude him from taking a second major case as well.[95] It appears that most barristers to the Parlement handled only one case at a time and that the intensity or volume of work was not very great. Jean Baptiste Gerbier, who was acknowledged as the most skillful pleading member of the Order, pleaded a maximum of only four or five cases per year between 1783 and 1788, the year of his death.[96] During this period his reputation was at its zenith, and he could have accepted many times this number had he wished to do so. The discussion of the profession of avocat in the *Encyclopédie méthodique* underscored the lack of ambition when it mentioned as a privilege of the profession that the barrister had the freedom to practice when he pleased and where he pleased.[97] To the barristers, this pace of work contributed to the nobility of their profession and separated the barrister from, for example, the businessman, who had to devote virtually all of his time to business affairs. Indeed, the industrious barrister aroused more bemusement than admiration among his colleagues. Louis Claude Rimbert, who was noted for the exceptionally heavy workload that he carried in the less important seven o'clock sessions of the Parlement, was regarded as an oddity by his fellow barristers. Because most of them disdained these cases, only a small number of barristers pleaded at the seven o'clock session.[98] Given the fact that underemployment was a problem in the profession, such derision is rather surprising and shows that the attraction of a career at the bar was more the prestige it conferred than the opportunities it offered.

Another feature of the profession of avocat au Parlement in the eighteenth century is that despite the high cost of justice at the parlements, a career as a barrister does not seem to have been particularly lucrative. The barristers claimed that their profession lavished more honor than revenue on those who practiced it, and there seems to be some truth to the assertion. Because the barristers to the Parlement at Paris refused to give a receipt for their honorariums or even to itemize their charges on written consultations for clients, however, one can rely only on a small amount of indirect evidence.[99] In written briefs, the barrister's fee was based on the amount of work done as reflected in the number of pages in the brief, and criticism of barristers stemmed not from the fee itself but from the practice by some barristers of writing in large handwriting in order to inflate their fee. In 1790 an anonymous pamphlet appeared whose author claimed to have been a litigant ruined by the expense of his case at the Parlement. Although he chastized the barristers for the tactic mentioned above, and denounced their refusal to account for their fees, he also spoke of them with a tone of respect quite in contrast with the remainder of his pamphlet. He spoke of the enlarging of handwriting in order to extract a larger fee as incompatible with the honor and dignity of the profession. He praised the profession for its nonvenal nature, adding that "it demands qualities which are not sold."[100] In what is otherwise a long and bitter attack upon the cost of justice before the Parlement, its treatment of the avocats is notable for its brevity and moderation, and seems to indicate that barristers were among those least responsible for the expense of justice at the parlement.

A second and perhaps more telling indication is the fact that Brissot, who was unremittingly hostile to the Order of Barristers, complained in a pamphlet against them not that the barristers made too much money, but that they did not earn enough, which he regarded as one of the factors responsible for the low quality of men in the Order.[101]

Another example is provided by Eustache Antoine Hua, who was inscribed in 1785 and enjoyed some success in the profession before the Revolution, and who mentioned in his memoirs that in 1788 he had an income of fifteen hundred livres. While this was by no means negligible and would have allowed him to live comfortably, it was not, by Old Regime standards, a substantial income.[102] Keeping in mind that there were not enough lawsuits to sustain the number of men in the Order, it is probable that professional fees for less important cases would have remained low because of the abundance of barristers available to handle such litigation.[103] Most of the cases tried were relatively minor ones involving such matters as seignorial rights or benefices, and the most important cases that came before the Parlement were almost certain to be taken by prominent barristers. In other parlementary towns a career at the bar was not very financially rewarding, and it appears to have been true at Paris also.[104] The larger jurisdiction of the Parlement of Paris and the availability of a greater variety of cases because of Paris's role as a financial center were more than offset by the high number of barristers practicing there. Occasionally a grateful client might bestow a large honorarium upon the barrister, but it would probably happen only in major cases and appears to have been quite exceptional.[105] This again seems to indicate that it was primarily intangibles such as prestige or the opportunity for renown, rather than the potential earnings, that attracted men to the profession of avocat au Parlement.

The social background of the barristers to the Parlement is quite difficult to trace and, because of the state of the sources, cannot be done in any systematic fashion, but it can be said that members of the Order ranged from nobles to men of artisanal background.[106] Neither of these two elements appears to have been very common, however, and most of the avocats au Parlement seem to have had bourgeois origins. In the 1780s, particularly after the publication of Brissot's pamphlet against it, the Order occasionally came under attack for allegedly discriminating against and refusing to accept men from artisanal families, but it is difficult to determine conclusively the validity of these accusations. On the one hand, several members of the Order had artisanal antecedents, and, as Brissot's biographer notes, the reasons for his rejection from the Order were due more to his temperament and personal shortcomings than to anything else.[107]

On the other hand, the absolute authority of the Order to decide whom to admit certainly carried the potential for discrimination, and many of the men with known artisanal backgrounds were admitted in the 1780s, perhaps in reaction to criticisms of the Order. Moreover, it is clear that there were factors that militated against men from artisanal backgrounds, so that apart from any possible policies of the Order at Paris, a career in law seems to have been an intimidating prospect for such men. One study, in fact, has shown that sons of artisans comprised fewer than 1.5 percent of the students enrolled in two law schools in France in the eighteenth century. Such apprehension on their part may not have been groundless; in 1772 students in the law school at Besançon went on strike because the son of a master wigmaker had been admitted.[108] Finally, the structure of the profession would have been an impediment. The four year probationary period imposed a delay before one earned a regular income, and during this time the probationary barrister had to pay fees and purchase legal texts and other items, such as a barrister's robe. Even after the successful completion of the probationary period, a young barrister to the Parlement often needed additional time to establish himself.[109] While some artisanal families could perhaps incur the expenses a legal career entailed, in all probability, most could not. In many respects, then, membership in the Order was a luxury few sons of artisans could afford, and it may have been for this reason, as much as to any possible policies of the Order, that there were few men from artisanal backgrounds in the Order.

In France the prohibition against clerics practicing in lay courts, which had been pronounced by the Fifth Lateran Council, had not been enforced. As a result, the profession of barrister was open to clerics as well as laymen, and the Order of Barristers at Paris included priests in its membership, although they were few in number. In order to practice the ecclesiastics had to remain subject to secular jurisdiction in the event of misconduct, and could not have themselves transferred before a judge of the Church. Moreover, they were not allowed to handle criminal cases since they could result in the death penalty. Priests who had taken monastic vows were not allowed to enter the profession because the barristers believed that the vow of obedience taken by the monk was incompatible with the independence of the bar.[110]

One of the most conspicuous features of the Ordre des avocats in the late eighteenth century is the extent to which it considered its interests as being inextricably bound with those of the Parlement. When Maupeou instituted the new courts in 1771, for example, he did nothing to disturb the rights and privileges of the barristers.[111] In spite of this precaution, the barristers, who had stopped work when the Parlement had gone on strike, continued to refrain from practicing even after the new courts were installed. The government waged a campaign appealing to the barristers' professional values, but it soon resorted to more forceful tactics as well.[112] In May and June 1771 the procureurs were suppressed and replaced by one hundred avocats du Parlement, who were authorized to perform the tasks done formerly by the procureurs and avocats separately. This act, along with the perception that the reform might not be merely temporary, caused many barristers to reconsider their opposition to the new court. Moreover, Maupeou exerted pressure on the highly respected barrister Jean Baptiste Gerbier to force him to appear before the new court, correctly calculating that Gerbier's defection would lead many others to follow him. Gerbier's sister had been imprisoned for Jansenist activities, and Maupeou conditioned her release upon Gerbier's agreement to practice in the new court. Gerbier submitted, and in November 1771 he led a group of over two hundred barristers, including such prominent men as Anselme Joseph D'Outremont, François Denis Tronchet, and Simon Nicolas Henri Linguet, for the opening of the Maupeou parlement. Most of those who resumed practice did so out of fear of financial ruin, and the capitulation of Gerbier offered them an opening. At the same time, however, a large segment of the Order refused to follow Gerbier's course and continued to remain out of the court in sympathy with the Parlement. The result of the split was a complete cessation of the activities of the Order; there was no tableau from 1771 to 1774, and the term of the president elected in 1771, Nicolas Lambon, was extended by default. No new barristers were accepted into the Order during this period either.

In November 1774, after the death of Louis XV and the exiling of Maupeou, Louis XVI recalled the former Parlement. The avocats du Parlement were removed, the procureurs were restored, and the barristers who had remained out of the Maupeou court resumed practice. Nevertheless, the Maupeou parlement left sharp strains in the Order, strains that ran along two main lines. First, there was a conflict among the men who had practiced before the Maupeou court. Imposed upon this was the ill will between those who had practiced and those who had not, with some of the latter, led primarily by Guy Jean Baptiste Target, wishing to take reprisals on the former. Both conflicts, however, had the barrister Gerbier at their center.

Tensions culminated in 1775 with the disbarment of Simon Nicolas Henri Linguet, an exceptionally complicated episode that will be only briefly described here.[113] Linguet was a rash man whose pleadings and briefs were sometimes intemperate, a quality that offended many of his colleagues. In 1773, after a government prosecutor had refused to have a brief called by Linguet read, Linguet attacked him in a pamphlet, drawing a warning from the Maupeou court that he be more circumspect in the future. In late 1773 the comtesse de Béthune retained Linguet to handle her case against the marquis de Béthune and the maréchal de Broglie. The marquis sought Gerbier to take his case, but

Gerbier refused to accept it when he learned that Linguet would be his adversary, and M. de Broglie did not succeed in his efforts to persuade any other barrister to handle it. This led to a decree by the court stating that it had not intended to deny Linguet the practice of his profession. Despite this statement, however, the barristers continued in their opposition and met to discuss the problem. They agreed on a measure by which Linguet would refrain from pleading for one year, but Linguet would not consent to this. After Linguet's refusal, an official assembly of twenty-four barristers met on February 1, 1774, and decreed a one year suspension against him. In response, Linguet published a pamphlet entitled *Réflexions pour M. Linguet, avocat de la comtesse de Béthune*, in which he bitterly attacked Gerbier and the members of the assembly who had acted against him. The legitimacy and action of the assembly were very questionable, but Linguet's response so offended the barristers practicing before the Maupeou court that they convened under the bâtonnier Lambon and suspended Linguet. The court endorsed the measure on February 11, 1774, when it declared that he would be removed from the tableau. Later in the year, Louis XVI abolished the Maupeou parlements and recalled the former Parlement. Linguet appeared before the Parlement in January 1775 to ask for his reinstatement. The Parlement, eager to punish those who had practiced before the Maupeou parlement, annulled the decree of February 11, 1774, and authorized Linguet to resume practice.

Prior to this, however, on December 22, 1774, the deputies of the benches had met and provisonally decided that they would not have any professional contact with Linguet and said that this was equivalent to an anticipated disbarment. The council furthermore claimed that this deliberation superseded that of February 11, 1774, so that the Parlement's reversal of the latter meant very little when it occurred. On January 26, 1775, Linguet was admitted to the Order but was refused permission to read a prepared statement; at the meeting, the Order backed the council and decreed Linguet's disbarment. On January 27 Linguet appealed to the Parlement to overrule the Order, so that what had originally been a quarrel between Linguet and the members of the Order had come to pit the Order against the Parlement over control of the Order's tableau. Shortly after this, on January 30, Linguet published a second pamphlet, *Supplément aux réflexions pour M. Linguet, avocat de la comtesse de Béthune*. This work was even more inflammatory than his previous effort and denounced the entire

Order. It concluded by demanding that the disciplining of members be removed from the Order and that the Order be made subordinate to the Parlement, but it was so bitter and extreme that one neutral observer characterized it as "a tirade in which the author seems to have totally lost his head."[114] Moreover, the Parlement was beginning to have serious reservations about embroiling itself in a major dispute with the Order simply for the sake of Linguet. On February 4 Lambon and several other barristers presented themselves to the Parlement to condemn the work, and the Parlement concurred, ordering that Linguet be disbarred. Linguet again resisted the ruling, and in an attempt to convince the Parlement to reverse itself, pleaded before the Parlement in early March 1775. But on March 29, 1775, the Parlement confirmed the punishment and Linguet was definitively disbarred.

In backing Linguet against the Order, the Parlement had been seeking to punish Gerbier, whom it held responsible for leading so many barristers into the Maupeou court. Gerbier had temporarily stopped practicing when the Parlement was recalled and had worked surreptitiously to bring about a reconciliation between himself and the magistrates of the Parlement. His success in this endeavor largely accounts for the Parlement's reversal of itself when it pronounced the disbarment of Linguet. At the same time, Gerbier was also the target of some of his colleagues who had stayed out of the Maupeou court, and who held him primarily responsible for the defection of so many members of the Order. Some of them considered attempting to remove Gerbier from the tableau, but ultimately they did not make the effort. It was, however, an added stress for the Order at the time that the proceedings against Linguet were in progress, and the dissension that resulted from the Maupeou parlement did not dissipate quickly.[115] Ironically, the strife had come about because of the Order's original solidarity with the Parlement, a solidarity that had been broken only under great pressure. The resentment shown toward those barristers who had practiced in the Maupeou court demonstrates the seriousness with which the members of the Order regarded the Order's affiliation with the Parlement. Although personal and professional jealousies played a role in the discord that followed the recall of the Parlement, it is also apparent that the Order regarded an attack on the Parlement as an attack on itself, and that in participating in the subversion of the Parlement the men who had appeared before the Maupeou court had betrayed the Order. The Order was never more divided in the years before the Revolution, but these conflicts had largely receded by the later 1780s. One galvanizing factor may have been the periodic attacks upon the Order, particularly Brissot's pamphlet *Un indépendant à l'Ordre des avocats, sur la décadence du barreau en France,* published in 1781. It is an indication of the Order's concern for its public image that the work seems to have caused some consternation in the Order; pamphlets were written in response to it and there may even have been an attempt to have it suppressed.[116] A few pamphlet attacks on the Order continued through the decade, but they did not disturb the avocats au Parlement, nor did they strike a responsive chord with the public.[117] Tension within the Order decreased throughout the 1780s so much that Gerbier was elected president in 1787.

In 1787, with the renewal of political conflict between the Crown and the Parlement, the barristers again gave the latter their support. When the Parlement was exiled to Troyes, the avocats au Parlement did not go to participate in sessions that were to be held there, a step that might have prolonged the magistrates' exile by helping to continue the administration of justice. They even closed their offices in Paris and went on strike in support of the Parlement, an action that caused considerable hardship for some of them.[118] And again in 1788 the barristers helped to defeat the judicial program of Lamoignon that sought to reduce sharply the judicial and political powers of the Parlement.[119] As a body, the barristers followed the Parlement's political lead, and they continued in their allegiance to the Parlement up to the time of the Revolution.[120]

The identification of the barristers with the Parlement was evident not only in their politics but in their intellectual interests as well. The barristers considered themselves hommes de lettres, and members of the Order were proud of the fact that one of their colleagues, Guy Jean Baptiste Target, had been named to the Académie Française in 1785, partly on the strength of some of his important legal briefs.[121] It is clear, however, that the barristers' intellectual outlook and pursuits were framed largely by their affiliation with the Parlement and by their professional role within it. One result was that they effectively excluded themselves from many of the ideas of the Enlightenment, a divergence that is particularly clear in the contrasting views of the Parlement. While most of the philosophes considered the Parlement of Paris to be a selfish and reactionary institution, the barristers were among its most ardent defenders; two of the most famous apologies for the Parlement were the work of members of the Order. Louis Adrien Le Paige wrote *Lettres historiques,* in which he attempted to trace the lineage of the Parlement back to the popular assemblies convened before Clovis, thus serving to reinforce the Parlement's political pretentions; a subsequent work that praised the role of the Parlement in France, *Maxims du droit public française,* was principally the work of two barristers to the Parlement, Claude Mey and Gabriel Nicolas Maultrot.[122] Similarly, in 1784 Armand Gaston Camus, in his position as a royal censor, used his authority to prevent publication of a work highly critical of the Parlement and its political claims. Camus noted that the book sought "to downgrade the Parlement" and to support the peerage and, citing the "damaging effect" that the work could have, recommended against publication.[123]

Their allegiance and devotion to the Parlement was not the only factor that separated the barristers to the Parlement from many of the precepts of Enlightenment thought. The barristers' professional and intellectual framework was grounded in existing law whereas the philosophes believed in natural law, which stressed a well-regulated and self-evident order of things. In accordance with this notion they regarded existing law as an obstacle to the establishment of natural law because of its irrationality and advocated its total restructuring in order to achieve the universal and inalienable rights that natural law prescribed.[124] Most of the Parisian barristers, with the exception of occasional figures such as Pierre Louis Lacretelle, could not accept such a doctrine. One contemporary observer touched on the gulf between the barristers and the philosophes when he wrote that "the barristers of Paris are the born enemies of the men of letters because the latter, more philosophical, go back to principles and tend to simplify questions; moreover, they sacrifice the authority of old books to the authority of reason."[125] This does not mean that the avocats were entirely uncritical defenders of the legal system of France. They recognized that it was deficient in many respects, but they believed that reforms had to be made within the context of correcting faults in existing law rather than abolishing it.

As a consequence of their attitude, those barristers who were interested in reform were far more equivocal in their approach to it than were the philosophes. In the field of law reform, for example, the issue of capital punishment is illustrative. Most of the philosophes, following Beccaria, were opposed to capital punishment and wished to do away with it altogether. But this view of the philosophes contrasts sharply with the stance of François Michel Vermeil, a member of the Order who in 1781 published a pamphlet entitled *Essai sur les réformes à faire dans notre législation criminelle*.[126] In it he proposed that heresy not be regarded as a capital crime, but he advocated the death penalty for a host of other offenses, even recommending some brutal standards of punishment for certain categories of crime, including the burning alive of arsonists and the blinding and torture of those convicted of parricide. Vermeil's interest in the subject of law reform was exceptional, however, and the lack of interest among members of the Order of Barristers at Paris underscores the fact of how little involved barristers were in the field of legal reform. Although it was the largest and most distinguished body of barristers in France, only one other member besides Vermeil, Pierre Louis Lacretelle, achieved any sort of reputation for his efforts in this area.

Most of the barristers avoided the subject of reform altogether and instead limited themselves to treatises on aspects of existing law, such as feudal law or religious questions.[127] Other barristers undertook works broader in scope but still restricted themselves largely to their professional field. Antoine Gaspard Boucher d'Argis revised Ferrières's *Dictionnaire de droit et de pratique* and was also one of the most prolific contributors to the *Encyclopédie*, but his contributions were almost all on the topic of law and legal institutions. Diderot, in fact, was so displeased with Boucher d'Argis's discussion of natural law that he wrote an entry of his own under a separate heading.[128] The narrow concentration of the avocats au Parlement upon professional matters separated them from the more speculative and reform-minded philosophes.

There was a further divergence between the avocats au Parlement and the precepts of the philosophes as well. Several of the barristers to the Parlement served as royal censors in the field of jurisprudence during this period. In 1789 more than one-third of the censors in jurisprudence were barristers to the Parlement, including some of the most distinguished and successful members of the Order, such as Camus, Blondel, and Blanchard de la Valette.[129] These men were respected by their colleagues, and there is no reason to believe that their position as censors was peculiar or that it invoked the disapproval of their fellow barristers. Indeed, these men were proud to occupy such a position and took its duties quite seriously.[130] And, as the incident with Camus demonstrates, they did not hesitate to use the post to stifle views that were not in accord with their own. Even allowing that censorship was largely benign and ineffective, the very fact that the barristers to the Parlement were associated with such a position reflects a mode of thought fundamentally opposed to that of the Enlightenment.[131] This is particularly true when one considers that the post of censor was not materially rewarding; it was an unpaid office that conferred only social status and a pension after twenty years of service.[132] Clearly, it represents an intellectual outlook much more closely aligned with that of the Parlement, which itself condemned sixty-five books between 1775 and 1789.[133]

One study of reading habits of various occupational groups under the Old Regime suggests that barristers all but ignored many of the more significant works and some of the most important figures of the Enlightenment. Not a single avocat au Parlement in the sample studied possessed a copy of either *Emile* or *Nouvelle Héloïse*, for example, and many other works of the philosophes were notably absent as well. Although the methodology of this study has been attacked, one cannot dismiss its findings out of hand. On the contrary, the barristers' aversion to much of the Enlightenment is underscored in the fact that the Bibliothèque des avocats did not contain the works of Diderot, Rousseau, Voltaire, Mably, Raynal, Helvétius, or Condillac.[134] It is clear that the avocats au Parlement at Paris were firmly rooted in the Old Regime, and there is little in either their writings or their actions to indicate that they were in any way broadly sympathetic to the ideas advanced by the philosophes. Rather, their political and intellectual perspectives had much more of an affinity with the Parlement than with the Enlightenment.

At the end of the Old Regime, then, affiliation with the Ordre des avocats encompassed much more than an attestation that one was proficient in law; this was but one aspect of that affiliation, albeit one in which the barristers took great pride. The Order, however, was much more than a professional association; the corporate ethos transcended purely professional concerns, so that corporatism and professionalism should not be viewed as interchangeable concepts. Membership in the

Order was far more pervasive, constituting a central element in the lives of those comprising it. Their association with the Parlement and their professional role within it, through the medium of the Order, defined their political outlook, shaped their behavior and intellectual interests, and often affected even where they lived and other considerations.[135] Moreover, it conferred great prestige upon them, affording the avocats au Parlement a favorable niche in the corporate structure of Old Regime society.

2 / The Onset of Revolution: The Dissolution of the Order of Barristers, May 1789 – December 1790

> The National Assembly, wanting to establish the French Constitution on the principles it has just enunciated and declared, irrevocably abolishes the institutions that were injurious to liberty and equality of rights. Neither nobility, nor peerage, nor hereditary distinctions, nor distinctions of orders, . . . nor any corporations or decorations requiring proof of nobility or presupposing distinctions of birth, nor any superiority other than that of public officials in the performance of their duties exists any longer . . .
>
> There is no longer any privilege, nor any exception to the law common to all Frenchmen for any part of the nation or for any individual.
>
> There are no longer any *jurandes*, nor corporations of professions, arts and crafts . . .
>
> *Preamble to the Constitution of 1791*

The most distinctive achievement of the French Revolution was the destruction of the corporate framework of the Old Regime. The consensus that sustained the attack upon corporations came into existence largely on the night of August 4, 1789, when a stratagem designed to pacify the countryside acquired a momentum of its own and became an emotional and extensive assault on privilege. In its aftermath the National Assembly launched a comprehensive attack on privilege and corporate bodies, which ultimately led to the abolition of the Ordre des avocats. The Assembly, however, could not communicate its moral imperative to groups outside itself; as a result, there were two dynamics operating in France in 1789 and 1790. On the one hand, the National Assembly, infused with a sense of vision and purpose after August 4, reorganized the nation in pursuit of its new image of France. On the other hand, apprehensive individuals and corporate bodies outside the Assembly were still governed by a countervailing traditional mentality of état, corps, and ordre. The dichotomy is particularly apparent in the

Ordre des avocats at Paris, since seven of its members sat in the National Assembly. The two dynamics will be examined separately. First, the avocats au Parlement as participants in the events of 1789 and as deputies in the National Assembly will be considered; this will be followed by an examination of the response of the avocats au Parlement outside the Assembly to the action of their former colleagues in the Assembly.

Most members of the Order reacted favorably to the decision to convene the Estates-General, although their reasons varied. Some, with the memory of the Parlement's exile to Troyes and the "coup d'état" of the Lamoignon measures still vivid, saw in the Estates-General an opportunity to curtail the despotic powers of the monarchy. Similarly, some of the more senior barristers recalled the experience of the Maupeou parlement and likewise viewed the Estates-General as a salutary check upon ministerial or royal despotism. Others saw in the Estates-General a new outlet for their talents, a forum that would be even more prominent than the Parlement.[1] In these halcyon days few, if any, could foresee that the movement to curb royal despotism would evolve into a complete rebuilding of the nation.

In 1789 barristers to the Parlement had a prominent role in political activity in Paris. The decree of January 24, 1789, regulating elections for the Estates-General specified that the inhabitants of towns would assemble by corporation. For Paris, however, the Crown established a completely separate procedure, with assemblies not grouped along corporate lines, but formed by subdividing the city into sixty districts.[2] Thus, the barristers of Paris did not meet as a body, which would have diminished their importance by making the Ordre des avocats but one of many corporate bodies competing for attention. Instead, their potential influence became far more pervasive as each avocat au Parlement met in his respective district. Other factors made the barristers important in electoral assemblies not only in Paris but in the provinces as well. With the electoral assemblies classified by estates, barristers did not have to contend with the nobility in the gatherings. Many barristers had attained recognition beyond the confines of the Palais de Justice as a result of their professional activities in the Parlement and, consequently, were more well known than most other members of the assemblies. Furthermore, their profession, with its emphasis on oratorical ability, gave them a special advantage: they were among the most skillful and experienced in public speaking and could formulate and articulate, better than most, the grievances and aspirations of the Third Estate. In addition, the conditions of eligibility for participation in the assemblies were more stringent in Paris than in the provinces, disenfranchising many apprentices and journeymen.³ Consequently, the assemblies were more homogeneous than would otherwise have been the case, and therefore less prey to conflicts between the interests of the popular classes and the middle classes, conflicts that might have weakened the position of the barristers. Finally, the structure of their profession gave the avocats au Parlement more leisure time — which could be devoted to political activities — than was available to many members of the Third Estate.

The predominance of the barristers to the Parlement in the political process at Paris first became apparent in the selection of electors for the Third Estate in April 1789. In a further exemption from the decree of January 24, the Crown allowed the Third Estate in Paris to choose a larger number of electors and to send additional deputies to the Estates-General. Because of these special provisions and a controversy between the Lieutenant of Police and the Provost of Merchants over which body would supervise the elections, the elections were not held until late April, much later than elsewhere in France. Due, perhaps, to inexperience and a fear of popular violence, the turnout for the elections in Paris was low: out of approximately 150,000 eligible voters, only 11,706 participated, and in one district, Saint Victor, only 24 persons voted.⁴ Ultimately, the assemblies chose 407 electors for Paris. The strong position achieved by the avocats au Parlement can be seen in the fact that of the 407, 68 were members of the Order in 1789, so that over 16 percent of the electors of Paris were avocats au Parlement, a percentage much higher than their representation among eligible electors.⁵

Due to the geographically rather than corporately based electoral procedure, in Paris, perhaps more than elsewhere in France, avocats au Parlement played an important role in the activities that preceded the convening of the Estates-General. Electors made up over 11 percent of the Order in 1789, and when the electors convened on April 26 they named barrister to the Parlement Guy Jean Baptiste Target as their president and another member of the Order, Armand Gaston Camus, as vice-president. On April 27, when the electors selected the committee for the drafting of the *cahier*, eight of the thirty-six members chosen were barristers to the Parlement.⁶ The growing ascendancy of the avocats au Parlement disquieted some other elements of the Third Estate. Following the choice of electors for the Third Estate, a pamphlet critical of the large number of avocats selected appeared. It expressed suspicion about their commitment to reform and questioned their value as representatives of the Third Estate. Referring to the choice of electors, the author wrote: "This surprise in balloting, which went in favor of speakers of their type in every district, is very dangerous for the well being of the Third, because the corps des avocats adheres to a judicial system whose abuses they know and are afraid to reform, since it would endanger their état; therefore the greatest abuse of our present constitution will be perpetrated, to the disadvantage of the nation, by representatives who would be concerned only with the interests of their corps."[7] The author's criticism grew even sharper in a second pamphlet published after the selection of the committee for the drafting of the cahiers in which he denounced the "esprit de corps" among the men selected to draw up the cahiers.[8]

The basis for such suspicions was understandable. The avocats au Parlement were strongly attached to both their Order and profession. Their close affiliation with the Parlement minimized the sense of conflict with the other two estates, particularly the nobility.[9] Indeed, one member of the Order recalled that some of the barristers had viewed the calling of the Estates-General as an opportunity to take revenge on the Crown for its actions against the Parlement. Others had considered the Estates-General advantageous for personal or career opportunities.[10] Few apparently viewed it as an occasion to assert the interests of the Third Estate.

The critcisms contained in these pamphlets prompted a defense of the barristers in which the author, also anonymous but claiming to be an avocat, argued that the barristers were worthy representatives of the Third Estate.[11] He asserted that the privileges of the Order were a bulwark for all of society against despotism. Financiers, men of letters, and merchants, he said, were greater friends of authority than barristers, and the legal community had been chosen according of the rules of the election. Although he conceded that the barristers owed their ascendancy in part to their rhetorical abilities, he intimated that they had not spoken against the views of the Third Estate, and argued that it was to this estate's advantage to have skilled orators presenting its cause. He did not, however, specifically equate the interests of the avocats with those of the Third Estate.

The defense evoked a rejoinder that again denounced the number of barristers selected as electors, claiming they had acquired a degree of representation entirely disproportionate to their corps, leaving the rest of the Third Estate underrepresented. In part, the dispute centered on different ideas of representation. The barrister argued that members of his profession could represent other interests, as they did professionally, because of their skills. The critic, however, demanded real representation based on knowledge and conviction. The pamphlet questioned the commitment of the avocats au Parlement to reform and asserted that they had opposed some progressive measures in the debates on the cahier, in particular, recognition of the sovereignty of the nation and a declaration of rights. Above all, the tie between the avocats and the Parlement rankled the author: "you are suspect to us because you are slavishly devoted to the Parlement, which itself is suspect to us; because your corporate mentality stifles in you all concern for the general welfare; because in place of searching for the truth, you work only to obscure it from others and to mislead them."[12]

The controversy is noteworthy because it raised the issue of the commitment of the avocats au Parlement to the Third Estate at the very beginning of the Revolution. It is evident that to contemporaries one of the most striking characteristics of the Order was its strong attachment to the Parlement. After the ruling in 1788 by the Parlement that the Estates-General would meet as it had in 1614, the Parlement had become the focus of the Third Estate's resentment; one's attitude toward the Parlement became a touchstone of one's commitment to the cause of the Third Estate, so that the barristers' unshaken fidelity to the Parlement made them suspect. The ascendancy of the barristers to the Parlement in the events surrounding the convening of the Estates-General and their role in the formulation of the cahier of Paris were therefore viewed with growing apprehension by other members of the Third Estate.[13] To be sure, the fears of their supporters were justified if one assumed a static relationship between occupation and political position; the events of 1789 were to show, however, that the political process itself shaped the attitudes and actions of those involved in it, and barristers to the Parlement were no exception.

The strong position that the barristers had achieved in the political activity surrounding the convening of the Estates-General culminated in the election of deputies to the Estates-General. The suburbs of Paris had been allotted sixteen deputies, which meant that the Third Estate's delegation was eight. Of the eight elected, two of them, Guy Jean Baptiste Target and Jean Jacques Lenoir de la Roche, were avocats au Parlement. Of the seven men selected as alternates, one, Jacques Joseph Dartis de Marcillac, was a member of the Order in 1789.[14]

By the decree of March 28, 1789, the city of Paris had been accorded forty deputies for the Estates-General, which meant, of course, that the Third Estate would provide twenty of the deputies for Paris. Of the twenty who were chosen, five were avocats au Parlement. The Third Estate also elected twenty alternate deputies, of whom eight were members of the Order in 1789.[15] Of these eight, one, Jacques Delavigne, assumed a seat in the National Assembly on February 1, 1791, in replacement of a deputy who died. He was the only alternate deputy from the delegation elevated to the position of deputy.

With the city and suburbs combined, avocats au Parlement comprised 25 percent of the Third Estate delegation from Paris, a percentage that even surpassed the profession's showing in the selection of electors. Moreover, again taking the city and suburban delegations together, barristers to the Parlement comprised 33 percent of the alternate deputies. The dominance of the avocats au Parlement was indisputable.

It is not merely the percentage of barristers to the Parlement chosen that is significant, but also their identity. All of the barristers chosen as deputies, with the exception of Lenoir de la Roche, were extremely well established in the profession. Although they were often overshadowed by fellow delegates Bailly and Sièyes, who of course were not barristers, most of them came to command the respect of their fellow representatives in the Estates-General, with Target and Camus in particular enjoying some influence.

Because of the tardiness of the elections in Paris, the Parisian delegates arrived belatedly at the Estates-General. At the time of their arrival, the Estates-General was in a state of complete paralysis on the issue of verification of powers. From the beginning, then, the barristers to the Parlement who were deputies found themselves in a difficult situation, one entirely different from what they had expected. They began their duties not in a spirit of deliberation or consultation, but in an atmosphere of crisis and confrontation. They were in daily contact with men from all parts of France and were continually dealing with issues of great national importance. As deputies, they were immediately subjected to new ideas and pressures and placed in an environment where corporate or local loyalties seemed to have little place or importance. The same was true for those deputies not from Paris, since many of them, according to one member of the Assembly, had never before left their province.[16] Whereas their former colleagues at the bar could return to their activities in the courts and follow the Estates-General from their vantage point as avocats au Parlement, those who became deputies were forced to consider issues in a broader national context. In the course of their duties they met a far greater range of individuals and acquired a much higher degree of political consciousness than did their former colleagues who remained in the Order. The events of May and June, specifically, brought the deputies together in a sense of common purpose and blurred local, provincial, or corporate differences and loyalties. As they entered the political sphere, then, the barristers to the Parlement who were deputies developed new perspectives and values that superseded many of their traditional allegiances. They became representatives of the political interests of the Third Estate.[17]

The deadlock in the Estates-General ended only in late June when Louis capitulated to the idea of a National Assembly and ordered the clergy and nobility to meet with the Third Estate. In July 1789 the Assembly formed the Committee of the Constitution, comprised of eight members, to draft a constitution for France.

Political apprehension continued to build in Paris in late June and early July, however, because of suspicions regarding royal intentions toward the National Assembly. A sharp rise in the price of bread and problems in provisioning the city exacerbated the disquietude. Tensions reached a climax on July 12, with the news of the dismissal of Necker the day before, and culminated in the storming of the Bastille. The aftermath of the fall of the Bastille drew many barristers more deeply into urban affairs.

During the crisis a complete collapse of municipal government had occurred. Most duties had been handled by the electors of Paris, but the resolution of the crisis brought their authority into question, with some of the districts no longer willing to take orders from them. As a result, by the end of July, under a plan submitted by Bailly, who had been named mayor of Paris, a new body composed of 2 men from each district, 120 in all, was elected. It became the municipal government and met for the first time on July 25. Of the 120 members elected, 23 were avocats au Parlement.[18] Furthermore, the 2 vice-presidents selected to serve under Bailly, Moreau de Saint-Méry and Delavigne, were both members of the Order.

The municipal assembly of 120 proceeded to form several standing committees to deal with such critical problems as policing and provisioning the city. The committees removed such a large number of men from the assembly, however, that it decided on August 1 that each district could name a third representative to the body, raising its number to 180. Of the 60 new members elected, 14 were avocats au Parlement, so that 37 of the 180 individuals comprising the municipal assembly were barristers to the Parlement.[19] As a consequence, by August 1789, through their representation in the National Assembly and the municipal assembly, barristers to the Parlement were an important element in both local and national affairs for Paris.

The National Assembly, saved from threatened dissolution by the upheaval in Paris, continued work on the drafting of a constitution. But news of serious disorders in the countryside confronted the Assembly with a far more pressing problem than the formulation of a constitution: the pacification of the peasantry. The attempt by the Assembly to settle the uprising led to the highly important and emotional meeting of August 4, which provided the Assembly with the principles that thereafter guided it.

From its beginnings the rural crisis had placed the Assembly in a quandary. The Assembly could not settle the situation by force without undermining its authority, and any effort to deal with the issue through legislation would have divided the Assembly sharply by forcing it to decide whether or not seignorial rights were a legitimate form of property.[20] To forestall a crisis, members of the Breton Club devised a strategy whereby the duc d'Aiguillon, one of the greatest landowners in France, would propose the voluntary renunciation of feudal rights and dues in return for compensation for rights pertaining to land. During the evening session of August 4, however, the vicomte de Noailles, who would not have been affected by the action, made a similar proposal before Aiguillon could speak. Nevertheless, Aiguillon seconded the motion and offered some additional ideas, and both recommendations were quickly and easily adopted. Contrived or not, Aiguillon's action had an electrifying effect on the National Assembly, which for most of the previous three months—ever since its original convocation as the Estates-General—had been hindered by a narrow adhesion to privilege and prerogative. The resolutions were heartily applauded and launched the Assembly into an emotional and unrelenting condemnation of privilege, which in turn brought forward a spirit of what might be called the sublimity of the nation—a belief that the nation should henceforth be a source of equity and should be the focus for the highest ideals and conduct of its members.[21] The nation emerged as a unifying force transcending the corporate identities and privileges that had hitherto prevailed; the inequity of privilege was discarded for the equity of laws common to all, which would form the basis for a community of citizens. Some calculation and jealousy undoubtedly underlay actions that evening, but a much stronger sense of renewal and altruism was also present. The Assembly sought to regenerate the state—to blend all individuals into it equally by discarding the privileges that had so fragmented the polity. In the conviction that private interests and aspirations could be subordinated to the higher good of working for the benefit of the nation as a whole, for several hours delegates from all estates and virtually all regions spontaneously relinquished a wide variety of rights and privileges.[22] Proprietary rights in judicial office was one of the renunciations offered by the judiciary during the session, and there was also a commitment made to the free administration of justice.[23]

In the following week, from August 5 through August 11, the Assembly sought to transform its pledges into a formal decree. While the intoxicating idealism generated on the evening of August 4 could not be completely sustained, it is nonetheless clear that the emergence of the ideal of the sublimity of the nation had infused the Assembly with a powerful sense of identity and purpose. The impact of the evening can perhaps best be seen in person of the marquis de Ferrières, a conservative noble deputy representing Saumur who had been one of the recalcitrant deputies whom Louis had had to order to join the National Assembly on June 27. On August 7, however, in the midst of the drafting of the decree, de Ferrières wrote to a constituent about the significance of August 4. He said that it had produced something that twelve centuries of the same religion, the same language, and the habits of common manners had not been able to achieve—the reconciliation of interests and the unity of all France toward a single objective, the common good of all. Then, without mentioning the National Assembly specifically, but unmistakably referring to it, he told his correspondent of the session "creating, so to speak, a new solemn covenant, and, from this very moment, acquiring an irresistible authority, and a might that will inevitably rise above the other powers."[24] His letter is remarkable, both as a succinct and explicit articulation of the distinct dynamic of the sublimity of the nation under which the National Assembly would henceforth operate, and as an indication of the resolve with which it would assert its new vision of France.

The meeting of August 11 dealt with resolutions concerning the free administration of justice and the abolition of proprietary rights in judicial offices. At the beginning of the discussion several members of the Assembly proposed that from that moment the free administration of justice in France be established, and this was quickly followed by the offer of many judicial officers to abandon the proprietary rights of their offices. Then Mirabeau, who had not been present at the session of August 4, made a speech in which he advocated a far more comprehensive plan of reform, challenging the Assembly to consider not merely the judges but also the auxiliary professions in the judicial system, such as the bailiffs, sergeants, attorneys, and barristers.[25] He proposed that each individual be allowed to plead his own case in the courts, and also that he not be forced to utilize bailiffs, attorneys, and other subalterns. He could not offer any specific proposals for implementation, but he urged the Assembly to investigate his ideas. Shortly afterward protests from other deputies apparently interrupted Mirabeau's speech, but not before he had extended the range of the Assembly's concerns. In suppressing the seignorial system the Assembly had committed itself to a "new judicial order," which essentially involved the eradication of venality and the free administration of justice. Mirabeau, however, called not only for these reforms, but for a total revision of the judicial system.

The Parisian avocat au Parlement Target responded to Mirabeau's speech first. He began disingenuously by forcefully declaring himself equally opposed to venality, an opening that made venal offices such as that of procureur the focus of attention while removing from consideration that of avocat, which of course was not venal but had been specifically included in Mirabeau's address. In an apparent effort to limit change in the judiciary, Target concentrated on venality, vehemently denouncing it as a component in the system of justice. He cautioned against acting too quickly to reorganize the judicial system because such hasty action could lead to chaos in the courts.[26] Target's speech carried the day, for apart from commitments to the free administration of justice and an end to venality, the decree approved by the Assembly on August 11 left the scope of judicial reform unspecified.

When the Committee of the Constitution presented its ideas for judicial reorganization to the Assembly on August 17, however, it was clear that in the aftermath of August 4 it had interpreted its mandate quite broadly. Its proposals marked a radical departure from the established system of justice in France. Among the committee's recommendations were the implementation of jury trials in criminal cases, the abolition of the death penalty except for murder and treason, and the creation of a commission to revise completely the criminal code. It not only called for the end of venality and proprietary rights in the judicial system, but also endorsed the idea of the election of judges. On the subject of the parlements, the committee did not make a specific recommendation that they be abolished, but it was implicit because the report made no provision for them in the court system envisaged. The committee's report posed a direct threat to the barristers' profession by proposing to strip them of their monopoly on pleading rights and of their right to form an Order. The proposal was contained in section II, article 8 of the report, under the heading of civil matters. "Each party will have the right to plead his case himself if he finds it convenient, and finally, so that the profession of barrister will be as free as it should be, the barristers will cease forming a corporation or an Order, and any citizen having made the studies and passed the necessary examinations for practicing the profession, will have to answer for his conduct only to the law."[27] The proposal was not absolute and appeared to offer the barristers a loophole. In retaining the need for training and demonstrated skill, the committee offered the barristers some control over their profession. Although the Order would be dissolved, some organization would be necessary to monitor the screening process stipulated in the article. And who would be better prepared to administer studies and examinations in law other than trained barristers? The clause therefore tempered the proposed abolition of the Order. Although it would no longer have its monopoly on cases nor powers of discipline, it potentially represented a way for the Order of Barristers to continue its existence in much the same way as before.

Bergasse, who presented the project to the Assembly, realized that the recommended changes went far beyond what most of the deputies had expected, and admitted that the committee "proposes to you an order of things absolutely different from that which has been established for so long among us."[28] The Assembly applauded Bergasse's presentation and ordered that it be printed. Since it was occupied with the debate on the Declaration of the Rights of Man, the Assembly took no action on the measure and sent it back to the committee for further consideration.

Without question, however, the report represented a remarkable downturn in the fortunes of the profession of avocat au Parlement. Not only was the continued existence of the parlement in danger, but the report posed a serious threat to the avocats' profession. It was a development that could not have been anticipated, for there was not widespread sentiment against the profession of avocat. On the contrary, insofar as many cahiers asked that defendants in criminal cases be allowed the right to legal counsel, one can view opinion of the profession as favorable.[29] Moreover, had there been considerable resentment against avocats it is unlikely that so many of them would have been elected to the Estates-General. In those instances where the cahiers did find fault with the legal profession, their criticisms were usually made against the procureurs rather than the barristers.[30] Even after the night of August 4, the barristers to the Parlement outside the Assembly could not necessarily have foreseen this step. After August 4 action against venal offices could be expected because the Assembly had specifically addressed itself to the problems of venality and proprietary rights in the judicial system, but neither issue applied to the barristers to the Parlement. What, then, was the basis of the proposed encroachment upon the profession of avocat? It is clear that, in the aftermath of August 4, the National Assembly, acting on the ethos of the sublimity of the nation that had emerged that evening, was mounting a comprehensive attack on privilege.

Notwithstanding the occasional pamphlet that appeared, most of which, as with Brissot, seem to have been the work of unsuccessful aspirants to the Order, it is doubtful that the barristers' monopoly on pleading rights was an object of wide indignation. Conducting a legal defense was a task undoubtedly beyond the abilities of most of the populace, and legal costs, which in the case of the barristers were not exorbitant, were nonetheless high enough to put recourse to legal action beyond the means of most elements within French society.[31] Thus, the courts were inaccessible and distant institutions, and the issue of who possessed pleading rights in them was of little consequence to the great mass of the population. The Assembly was therefore not subject to any popular pressure to strip the barristers of their monopoly on cases or particularly of their right to form an Order. This attests to the fact that the National Assembly was concerned with the principle of privilege, rather than merely with selected privileges, such as feudal obligations, that were objects of widespread displeasure.

Under the Old Regime, law had been subordinated to privilege, but on the night of August 4 the National Assembly repudiated privilege as a superintending principle of society and sought to supersede it with the more unifying norm of the sublimity of the nation. The instrument for this norm would be laws common to all, but if law was to be the organizing principle of society it could not be the preserve of a few — for the ideal to have any meaning, recourse to the law by all members of society was imperative. Sagnac observed that the night of August 4 created the nation, as uniformity of law gave a nucleus to what had previously been only a territorial unity tenuously fused by privilege.[32] Indeed, the fundamental redefinition of the state that occurred that night — the supplanting of privilege by laws common to all — affected the legal profession more profoundly than any other group, because the role of law henceforth became central to the political system's definition of itself. In its report, then, the first one made after the night of August 4, the Committee of the Constitution was not limiting itself simply to specific renunciations made that evening; it was seeking to implement the mandate of the sublimity of the nation by attacking privilege comprehensively.

The National Assembly had been considering the Declaration of the Rights of Man when Bergasse delivered the committee's report on the judiciary. The Assembly promulgated the declaration on August 26 and then returned to consideration of the Constitution. On August 29, however, Mounier, in the name of the Committee of the Constitution, proposed that the new judicial order be the last issue considered.[33] Taking precedence over it were such issues as the principles of monarchical government and the organization of the legislature, the executive branch, and the military. The heart of these matters was whether or not the king should receive the power of an absolute veto. The monarchical element in the Committee of the Constitution — Mounier, Lally-Tollendal, Clermont-Tonnère, and Bergasse — favored the creation of an upper and lower chamber, as in England, and the right of the king to have absolute veto power. But on September 10 the Assembly decisively rejected the concept of an upper house and voted to form a single house legislature. The next day, in a compromise, it gave the king a suspensive rather than an absolute veto. The defeat of most of their proposals caused Mounier and most of the other monarchists from the Committee of the Constitution to resign and led to the formation of a new committee on September 15. Four original members of the committee—Sièyes, Talleyrand, Lally-Tollendal, and Le Chapelier—remained and were joined by Thouret, a barrister to the Parlement of Rouen; the Parisian barrister to the Parlement Target; Demeunier, a secretary for the comte de Provence and also a member of the Paris delegation; and Rabaut de Saint-Etienne, a Protestant minister from Nimes.[34] It was these men who would subsequently give further consideration to the organization of the judiciary as well as other constitutional matters. The new committee retained the agenda recommended by Mounier and deferred action on the judiciary.

The change in membership of the Committee of the Constitution ultimately resulted in an alteration of the plan for the judiciary, although the decision to defer consideration of the judicial system meant that the amended plan did not appear until several months later. In December 1789 the committee issued a new set of proposals for the judiciary that was far more favorable to the profession of avocat.[35] The reasons for the change are unclear, but the addition to the committee of Target, who had sought to exclude the profession of avocat from the reforms proposed in August 1789, and of Thouret, another avocat au Parlement, may have played a role. In a brief explanation of the plan Thouret noted that the committee had significantly revised Bergasse's project, but he reassured the Assembly that the committee nevertheless remained fully committed to the idea of a total restructuring of the judiciary.[36] In its revised report the committee called explicitly for the suppression of the parlements as well as all other existing courts. But on the recommendations regarding the profession of avocat the new report was far less severe than the one presented by Bergasse; it stated that each citizen would have the right to defend his case himself, whether in a written brief or through oral pleading. At the same time, it said nothing about the dissolution of the Order or about exam requirements for individuals to practice law. The new report represented a compromise whereby the committee addressed the problem of privilege by removing the barristers' monopoly on cases in the courts, but otherwise left the profession undisturbed. The elimination of committimus and all other jurisdictional privileges stripped the Order of the most important of its remaining privileges. The bill thus envisaged the profession continuing largely as it had previously, though devoid of its privileges and deferring to litigants who wished to handle their own case. In the final analysis the new report would have allowed the profession to exist in the new judicial system with only minor changes.

The Assembly ordered that the report be printed and annexed to the written record of the proceedings *(procès-verbal)*, but it did not begin to debate the issue until March 1790. The deputy Thouret reported the bill to the Assembly, and his opening discourse left no doubt that one of the facets of the judicial system with which the committee had been most concerned was privilege, and that the barristers' monopoly on cases had been a component of the problem. Thouret asserted that the committee had in its report achieved a complete equality in justice and had abolished "the hindrances to the freedom of personal defense."[37]

When debate began, however, the critical issue was not the future of the legal profession or any other individual disposition, but the scope of the reform itself. Some deputies were extremely reluctant to break completely with several hundred years of legal development and tradition, arguing that a major reform of the existing order was sufficient and that it was not necessary to destroy it altogether. Jacques Antoine Marie de Cazalès put forward a motion by which the Assembly would decide whether the existing judicial order would be destroyed or only reformed, and asked that the Assembly spend at least three days considering the issue. His suggestion produced a tumult in the Assembly, and he withdrew it when the president of the Assembly, Rabaut de Saint-Etienne, pointed out that the constitutional aspects rather than the structure of the judiciary had to be considered first. But as soon as Cazalès withdrew his motion, Pierre Louis Roederer, a deputy from Metz, said that the Assembly ought to decide immediately whether or not the present judicial system would be restructured entirely. This led to an angry exchange during which another deputy asked for a reconsideration of Cazalès's motion, and the session ended with the Assembly defeating Cazalès's measure and decreeing the complete reconstitution of the judicial system.[38] For the judiciary, then, it was this vote, as much as the night of August 4, that sounded the death knell of the Old Regime.

Following the decision to reorganize the judiciary, debate did not resume until March 29. The first speaker, Jean Louis Viefville des Essarts, a barrister from Laon, had published a pamphlet critical of the project drafted by the Committee of the Constitution; he began by arguing against the complete restructuring of the judiciary, asserting that the financial burden of reimbursing venal officeholders would be too great. This part of his presentation was ruled out of order, since the Assembly had already decreed that the judicial order would be entirely restructured. When the Assembly asked Viefville des Essarts to continue with the second part of his discourse, he then implicitly pleaded for the right of barristers exclusively to handle cases by arguing against the freedom of individuals to defend their cases. He expanded upon the ideas presented in the pamphlet and disputed the notion of each individual being allowed to defend his own case in the following terms: "If all citizens are admitted without distinction to plead their cases, their insults, cries and injustices will profane the sanctuary of the law. Will the two litigants bother to inform themselves about the law? Will they not try to catch each other in error? Therefore, one ought not to permit each person to defend his case in writing and especially not orally; or else such an action will in effect suppress ministerial offices, since their functions would not be necessary, in which case it would be necessary to give them an indemnity on their services."[39] Viefville des Essarts's discourse sought to alter altogether the dimensions of the plan as it affected barristers. On the one hand, he presented reasons against the limited measure proposed by the committee for removing the barristers' monopoly on handling cases in the courts. On the other hand, he tried to link the profession of avocat to other judicial offices in an attempt to gain some sort of settlement if the Assembly proceeded with the action. The Assembly had recognized the principle of compensation for the suppression of an office; Viefville des Essarts sought to extend the principle from the office itself to the functions it involved. He claimed that establishing the right of each individual to handle his own case would in fact amount to a suppression of the profession of barrister, so that some indemnification was due. Here was an opportunity for the Assembly, by a simple extension of an already established principle, to provide some compensation to members of the legal profession. Yet it ignored Viefville des Essart's recommendation; for the remainder of the debates his suggestion was never again mentioned. The failure of his proposal underscores the fact that the National Assembly considered the barristers to be the possessors of unwarranted privilege. Where there were property rights involved, even in the case of an acknowledged abuse such as venal offices, the Assembly acted to protect those rights through reimbursement. But where it encountered privilege that was intangible — intangible in the sense that no capital outlay had been committed for it — it acted with less consideration and provided no compensation, even when, as with the barristers, the privilege was crucial to the continued existence of the group that held it. As a consequence, the barristers' monopoly on litigation was to disappear without an indemnity.

Other deputies in the Assembly did not want to see the mandate of the sublimity of the nation affirmed on August 4 interpreted so narrowly, and sought, ultimately successfully, to enact it in a much broader fashion. Until this time, the National Assembly, in its consideration of the judiciary, had concentrated almost exclusively on the aspect of privilege in its attack on the traditional paradigm of privileged corporatism. Several deputies, however, wished to do away not merely with privilege, but also with the corporate framework that had supported it. One prominent member of this group was Jean Baptiste Charles Chabroud, who spoke to the Assembly on March 30. Chabroud, a barrister from Vienne, criticized his colleagues for their propensity to build a judicial system that in structure was similar to the old one, a series of ascending jurisdictions. He berated the Assembly for its timidity in planning a new judicial order and told it that "it was hardly worth changing the decorations if the scene was to remain the same." He was particularly critical of permanent, fixed courts, especially courts of appeal, which he believed would adhere to a corporate rather than public mentality.[40] Not only did Chabroud attack the concept of permanently established courts because of their narrow corporate outlook, he also claimed that their existence would encourage litigation, which in turn would promote discord among the citizenry. In a comment that reflects his concern for the ideal of forging a community of citizens, Chabroud stated that one of the goals of the new judicial system should be to reduce litigation, and he concluded by offering the Assembly an alternative project for the judiciary.

Chabroud's speech and plan, with their more sweeping notion of the manner in which the ethos of the sublimity of the nation and the sentiment for a community of citizens should be interpreted, raised new issues and played a major role in subsequent deliberations. Prior to Chabroud's discourse the Assembly, in its consideration of the judiciary, had dealt chiefly with the problems of venality and privilege. Although it had committed itself to a complete restructuring of the judiciary, it had put forward a system of justice essentially similar to the old. The proposed system rested upon new principles and eliminated the privileges and abuses of the former, to be sure, but in structure it was quite similar to the Old Regime edifice. The revised report of the Committee of the Constitution, for example, clearly implied that the Order of Barristers would continue to exist, even if its privileges did not. But Chabroud challenged the Assembly to do more. He told his colleagues that simply to eradicate privilege was insufficient; they also had to treat the problem of corporate bodies that had been the guardians of privilege. Even stripped of their privileges, the continued existence of corporations would mean a furtherance of particularism, to the detriment of the greater well-being of the nation.

Chabroud's presentation, which was heartily applauded and which the Assembly ordered printed, challenged the profession of avocat au Parlement on several counts. First, he implicitly called into question the continued existence of the Order of Barristers because it could be seen as precisely the type of corporate body that Chabroud claimed would concern itself with its own particular interests rather than the general welfare of the nation. Second, the presence of an Order of Barristers at permanent court sites served, in Chabroud's view, to encourage litigation and dissension rather than making litigation an action of last resort. Furthermore, the incentive for litigation spawned more barristers and attorneys; as Chabroud said, "it is war that produces warriors."[41] He saw the relationship between lawsuits and barristers as symbiotic, and thus called for fewer barristers and fewer cases in what was by far the most explicit challenge posed to the avocats. Finally, Chabroud's recommendation of only one degree of jurisdiction also represented a threat to the profession of avocat au Parlement. The services of a barrister were utilized most often at the appellate level, and the Orders of Barristers were all attached to the parlements, the highest appeal jurisdiction. The establishment of only one degree of jurisdiction, rather than the three in existence under the Old Regime, would largely obviate the Orders of Barristers, since there would be no specific appeals court of superior jurisdiction. Thus, both implicitly and explicitly Chabroud argued for the destruction of the Orders of Barristers as a measure for the public good. This once again brought before the Assembly the issue of the dissolution of the Orders, a matter not presented by the Committee of the Constitution after it had revised Bergasse's report.

Although Chabroud's recommendations were perhaps ultimately not as decisive as those of Thouret or Adrien Duport, his ideas played a significant role in the configuration of the new judiciary.[42] His concept of only a single degree of jurisdiction, for example, became a feature of the new judicial system. In addition, the bureaux de paix et de conciliation, created by the Assembly with the purpose of settling disputes before they went into litigation, appear to be based on Chabroud's idea. His views also became influential on the issue of avocats. The next day, March 31, Lanjuinais noted in a speech that one principle before the Assembly was the need to diminish the number of barristers, a precept that had never been elucidated in any plan or principle of organization prior to Chabroud's speech.[43]

By this time the Assembly was beginning to feel overwhelmed by a surfeit of plans and recommendations for the judiciary. Besides that offered by the Committee of the Constitution, there were plans being circulated by Sièyes, Adrien Duport, and Chabroud, as well as by several other deputies. Immediately after Lanjuinais spoke, the deputy Bertrand Barère took the floor. In an attempt to provide both a focus and a common ground for the competing plans, Barère suggested a set of propositions that should guide the Assembly in its consideration of the new judicial order. His agenda, which the Assembly adopted, concentrated primarily on the use of juries, the number of jurisdictions in the new judicial system, the selection and duties of judges and other officers of the court, and whether a high court of review would be established. It did not include the matter of whether the profession of avocat would be preserved.[44]

Throughout the spring of 1790 the Assembly debated and decided most of the matters concerning the new judicial system and then awaited the new project from the Committee of the Constitution incorporating them. Early in July 1790 the committee began to present its work to the Assembly for approval, and one of the first sets of proposals submitted pertained to judges and their conditions of eligibility in the new judicial system. Although the articles concerned judges, most of the debate centered on the profession of barrister, the only group other than judges that was eligible for judgeships in the new judiciary. One objection concerned the use of the term homme de loi, to which Demeunier responded that the committee had utilized that term rather than *avocat* because the Assembly had not yet decided whether the Orders of Barristers would be preserved. His reply carried the clear implication that to employ the term avocat would prejudge the question, and Thouret added that the committee had chosen to use only generic expressions in the articles of the Constitution.[45]

On the same day, July 5, the Assembly passed an article that granted each citizen the right to handle his own case. In Bergasse's original report this proposal had been linked to the dissolution of the Orders of Barristers, but the article was introduced in terms that said nothing about barristers. Instead, it simply stated, "In all civil or criminal cases the pleadings, reports and judgments will be made public; and each citizen will have the right to defend his case himself, whether orally or in writing."[46] Most of the debate on the recommendation concerned the former aspect, the openness of court proceedings. There was little discussion of the latter disposition, although an amendment to grant any citizen the right to defend any other was defeated.[47] No mention was made of Viefville des Essarts's proposal; the Assembly adopted the article exactly as it had been presented, so that the barristers' monopoly on litigation disappeared without compensation.[48]

The Assembly completed most of the work establishing the basic structure of the new system for civil law on August 16, but the legislation, which was approved by the king on August 24, did not include any specific measure concerning barristers. At the same time, the Committee of the Constitution, acting in concert with the Parisian delegation, was preparing a separate plan instituting the new system of justice in Paris.[49] In the course of preparing this legislation, at least one deputy who appeared before the Committee of the Constitution argued for the preservation of barristers. Antoine Omer Talon, formerly a judge in the Parlement of Paris and the Châtelet, presented a comprehensive plan for a judicial system for Paris. He prefaced his presentation with a defense of the professions of procureur and barrister, and warned that litigants in the new court system could be victimized by unscrupulous individuals if these professions were not preserved.[50]

After its deliberations with the Paris delegation and others, the committee presented its plans for Paris to the Assembly on August 25. The two key elements in the judicial organization for Paris were the establishment of a justice of the peace in each of the forty-eight sections of the city and the setting up of six district courts in Paris. Louis Simon Martineau, from the Parisian delegation, opposed the high number of justices of the peace, but his objections failed to persuade the Assembly, which approved the measure.[51]

More controversial was the proposal for six district courts in Paris, for the Paris delegation strongly supported a single court of twenty judges for Paris. It argued that to have several courts would depart from the guidelines on the number of courts per department under the new system, that there was no more reason to fear a single court of twenty judges than six courts composed of five judges each, and finally that the *gens de loi* would be too distant from the jurisdictions of the courts. The committee, with Thouret reporting, rebutted the first point by saying that the number of courts among the departments was already unequal, and the second by asserting that judges in different courts would not have the opportunity for daily contact as would those in a single court, and that the lack of contact would keep them from constituting a parlement-like body. On the third issue the committee argued that Paris, in spite of its vastness, was not an obstacle to the proper execution of the duties of the people of law. The committee claimed that its plan was necessary to maintain the constitutional uniformity of the appeals process, to guard against the rise of a great judicial corporation that could become a surrogate parlement, and to prevent jealousy of Paris by other cities, which had to follow the law of August 16. Nevertheless, Louis Simon Martineau, an avocat au Parlement in the Paris delegation, vigorously resisted the proposal, and his arguments reveal a direct concern for the interests of the Order: "The six proposed courts will be infinitely harmful to the city of Paris. As for the issue of great judicial corporations, there is no reason to fear them since judges are elected for only six years. In the system that you have proposed, it will be impossible for a man of law to go defend a client in a court other than that of his arrondissement, unless you give the attorneys and barristers carriages."[52] Martineau did not receive any support from the six other avocats au Parlement in the Paris delegation, and his appeal for special consideration drew a sharp rebuke from Barnave, who said that the Assembly had not destroyed abuses in order to let them hide out in Paris. Barnave called for approval of the committee's plan with no exceptions or deviations from the Constitution, and the Assembly adopted the proposal for six district courts, as well as the remaining articles presented by the committee.[53] The legislation meant that the Order of Barristers would not be able to exist as it had previously because there would be no single court to which it could attach itself. Henceforth, there would be six discrete and equal tribunals for Paris rather than one court for the entire city.

On September 2 the committee presented its articles on the eligibility requirements for hommes de loi to be elected as judges. In the course of the session, a discussion of attire for members of the new judiciary led several members of the Assembly to raise the question of whether the hommes de loi should wear an official costume in the performance of their duties. After overruling an attempt by Martineau to postpone consideration of the issue, the Assembly decided that since the hommes de loi were in the service of the public, any point of difference between them and the public, including the formation of an order or corporation, ought to be forbidden to them.[54] In accordance with this decision, the Assembly approved an article that read "The men of law, previously called barristers, who can no longer form any order or corporation, will not have any special costume in their duties."[55] This was one of the last issues decided in the legislation establishing the new system of civil law in France, and it meant the complete abolition of the profession of avocat as it had existed in France for hundreds of years. The barristers had previously lost their monopoly on litigation; now their Order, their distinctive costume, and even their title of avocat disappeared. There was nothing to distinguish barristers from the litigants in the new courts.

Why did the Assembly take these actions? Jean François Fournel, a member of the Order at the time of its abolition, claimed that the measures had been recommended by some members of the Parisian Order of Barristers. According to Fournel, a split existed in the Committee of the Constitution between one faction that wanted to abolish the Order of Barristers, as well as the term avocat, and another that wanted to preserve the profession as it was, with its rights and privileges, in the new court system. Fournel asserted that some members of the latter group approached some of the barristers of the Order in Paris for advice. Those approached allegedly prepared a written response in which they claimed that the profession of barrister would be virtually meaningless under the new system because it did not allow for sovereign or superior courts to which the profession could be attached. The full text of their opinion, as given by Fournel, was as follows:

One should consider us in two aspects: under that of *barristers,* and under that of *barristers to the Parlement.*
 The dissolution of the parlements takes away from us the latter. As for the

former, it can only have meaning as long as there are sovereign courts to which we can transfer our name, our attributes and our prerogatives; but the new judicial organization leaves no place for *such courts*. It recognizes only wretched courts of first instance that will work in relays with each other for appeal cases. These courts will be the ones that will confer upon us the quality of *barrister;* therefore, each of these many courts that will cover the face of France will become the home of a new bar.

These bars will be furnished with a large number of men who, without any idea of our principles and discipline, will debase our honorable duties, and degrade them of their nobility. These same men, however, will be bent upon honoring themselves with the name of avocat, they will usurp the ornamentation of barristers, they will also want to form *an Order;* and the public, confused by the similarity of name, and which in its natural malignity is always inclined to generalize attributions, will confuse these improvised barristers with those from the old regime. The only way to escape this dangerous *posterity* is to suppress immediately the name and *Order* of *barristers,* and the attributes upon which they depend; let there be no other barristers from the time that we cease to exist.

Alone trustees of this noble calling [état], let us not allow it to be ruined by passing it into hands that would stain it; let us not give ourselves unworthy successors, rather let us exterminate ourselves the object of our devotion, rather than betray it to outrages and affronts.[56]

Fournel contended, then, that the abolition of the Order was not the result of hostile intentions, but the product of an "impassioned devotion" for the glory and memory of the profession of barrister in the face of its legal destruction.[57]

One cannot dismiss Fournel's version out of hand. He remained in the legal profession throughout the Revolution and the Empire, and was named president of the restored Order in 1816; in addition, some events lend credence to his account. First, the revision of the article regarding the Orders of Barristers seems to indicate a split in the Committee of the Constitution. Second, the Parisian delegation worked hard to have a single court established for all of Paris. And third, the dissolution of the Order and the abolition of the profession occurred only after the decree establishing the district courts in Paris. In the final analysis, however, Fournel's account is not convincing. He wrote it when he was sixty-eight years old, twenty-three years after the event had transpired, and his own devotion to the Parlement made him hostile toward the Revolution. More important, his explanation has never been corroborated by any other member of the Order; neither Berryer, Bonnet, nor Hua mention it in their memoirs, and Berryer and Bonnet in particular were closely involved in the affairs of the Order at this time. Furthermore, Fournel did not repeat the account in a subsequent work on the history of the Order during the Revolution.[58] Finally, the apparent spontaneity of the action, and the sense of shock and paralysis that characterized the members of the Order after its abolition, belie Fournel's rendering of the event; the barristers do not appear to have been prepared for what occurred.

One cannot say, however, that the Order fell victim to repugnance on the part of the Assembly for the profession of barrister itself. It is true that the Assembly, as a result of its commitment to the ideal of a community of citizens, did manifest hostility to litigation, which it considered divisive, and that a desire to discourage the initiation of lawsuits guided its deliberations on the new judicial system. But only Chabroud attempted to place the onus for litigation directly upon the barristers, and his attacks on the profession gained no visible support in the Assembly. Indeed, had the Assembly truly felt an aversion toward barristers, it would not have made them eligible for positions in the new judicial order.

Rather, the reasons for the dissolution of the Order were rooted in the Assembly's antipathy for privileged corporatism and its adherence to the ideal of the sublimity of the nation. The Assembly had transcended its original attack on privilege to encompass also the corporate entities that had acted as the agents for privilege and exclusivity, thereby contributing to the fragmentation of the polity.[59] The Order of Barristers, then, could no longer exist even without its privileges; it was precisely the type of institution to which the Assembly was so opposed, and as a result it was abolished.[60] The argument that the Order was not truly a corporate body since it did not have letters patent from the Crown, which was doubtlessly made, would have sounded excessively legalistic and would not have elicited any sympathy from the Assembly. Having done away with the Order, the suppression of its traditional robe inevitably followed, because this attribute contributed to its corporate exclusiveness. The same is true of the term *avocat;* to have retained it would have reminded individuals of the Order that formerly bore the name, so that the appellation of avocat comprised an additional facet of the Order's corporate identity. The rejection of the term *avocat* and the substitution of the more generic *homme de loi* testify to the Assembly's desire to do away with all distinctions between citizens.

The inspiration of the sublimity of the nation explains yet another aspect of the abolition of the Order, and why it arose over the issue of attire for the men of law in the new system. If laws common to all were to be the new basis of society, it could not be the preserve of a few, which is why the Assembly had granted each citizen the right to handle his own case. Beyond this, however, each citizen had to have recourse to the law on an equal footing—litigation was to be only a last resort, and then differences were to be resolved on the merits of the case rather than on the perceived erudition of those presenting it. Henceforth, law was to be the structural foundation for society, and to have allowed barristers to retain their traditional robe would have conferred upon them a distinct advantage. In refusing to allow the men of law to be demarcated from the parties, and especially in emphasizing that the hommes de loi were to serve the public, the National Assembly signified that they should in no way be allowed to dominate the law—they were to be servitors rather than oracles.

It was the paramount importance accorded to law that accounts for the experience of the legal profession diverging from that of other professions during the Revolution. As Foucault noted, there was a tension between the requirements of a profession and the abolition of privileges, and subsequent legislatures were not nearly as severe, for example, in dealing with the medical profession. But law was central to the impulse of the sublimity of the nation in a way that medicine was not. As a result, in the tension between the requirements of a profession and the abolition of privileges, for law the National Assembly acted much more decisively on the latter imperative—the antipathy for privilege—than subsequent legislatures did for the medical profession. Indeed, it was never envisaged to open up the medical profession completely to free practice in the way that law was.[61]

The Assembly's pursuit of the standard of the sublimity of the nation was the linchpin of its effort to reorganize France. The Estates-General had been called to resolve a financial crisis that the Assembly of Notables had failed to end. The failure of the Assembly of Notables had demonstrated the unwillingness of the privileged bodies in France to surrender their privileges, particularly their financial privileges, even in the knowledge that this refusal could result in the virtual paralysis of the state.[62] The inescapable conclusion of many contemporaries was that corporate bodies in France would place their own special immunities and interests above the needs of the nation. Adhesion to prerogatives and entitlements continued at the Estates-General, when the privileged orders attempted to cling to voting by order and resisted uniting in a sense of common purpose to deal with the problems that had led to its convocation. The result of their intransigence was the creation of the National Assembly, and from its inception the Assembly knew that the key to resolving the crisis that had brought it together was privilege. This is why there was such a sense of renewal and regeneration on the night of August 4 when, in its assault on privilege, the Assembly transcended the corporate loyalties dividing it and forged its own sense of identity and purpose.[63] Translating this idealism into concrete legislative measures proved difficult, but the Assembly remained faithful to the attack on privilege that had given it such a sense of cohesion on August 4. Henceforth, in the view of the Assembly, the nation, rather than any corporate body, would provide the focus for an individual's loyalty, concerns, and identification, and it proceeded to reorganize the nation in accordance with this vision. Not limiting itself simply to the most obvious examples, it eradicated all vestiges of privilege and abolished as well the bodies that had supported it.

Seen in this light, the Assembly's actions assume a greater sense of design and consistency. The movement against privilege began in August 1789, continued through 1790 with the reorganization of the Church and, less important of course, the dissolution of the Order of Barristers, and culminated in 1791 with the law of June 14, 1791, the *loi le Chapelier,* which abolished artisanal corporate bodies.[64] Only a few weeks later, in the preamble to the Constitution of 1791, the National Assembly proudly proclaimed that it had abolished privilege and all corporations of professions, arts, and trades.

In the final analysis the Revolution, at least in its critical formative stages from 1789 to 1791, was not the work of any single class or group. Rather, in the institution of the National Assembly, it took the form of a movement transcending such lines; gripped by a sense of the sublimity of the nation, the Assembly committed itself to the ideal of reformulating the French nation in a more equitable manner. This mandate stemmed from the night of August 4, but the Assembly, recognizing that it could not communicate to groups outside of itself the moral imperative that had seized it that evening, instead utilized the more readily communicable medium of Enlightenment discourse, selecting the words and phrases that best suited its purposes as it reorganized the French nation.[65] But even this adjustment failed to close the fissure that the Assembly had opened between itself and much of the rest of

France. Most interests outside of the Assembly affected by its actions, not sharing the vision and sense of purpose that impelled the Assembly, were often not able either to understand or to accept the Assembly's rationale. In no way, however, can the members of the Assembly be accused of cynically promoting their reforms at the expense of their original profession or livelihood, secure in the knowledge that they would never have to return to it and could embark upon new political careers for themselves. By disqualifying themselves from election to the Legislative Assembly, they became the only active citizens in all of France for whom the possibility of a national political role was foreclosed. It is indicative of their altruism, an altruism too often overlooked or denigrated, that they forced themselves to enter the society they had created.[66] The abolition of the Order of Barristers was but one small step in that endeavor.

In order to appreciate the separate dynamics that produced a disjunction between the Parisian avocats au Parlement in the Assembly and those outside it, it is necessary to examine the Order during the years 1789 and 1790. Most of the men who continued in the Order remained attached to it, and to its traditional values of adhesion to the Parlement and consciousness of état, corps, and ordre. They had little sympathy for or understanding of the new standard of the sublimity of the nation asserted by the National Assembly.

For those who remained associated with the Ordre des avocats the elections to the Estates-General and other unrelated events altered their situation significantly. In 1788 Jean Baptiste Gerbier, the premier pleading barrister of the Order, had died. His death was followed by that of Louis Eugene Hardouin de la Reynerie, a brilliant young protégé of Gerbier, in February 1789. The elections to the Estates-General removed many of the remaining foremost barristers from the Order. As a result, some of the younger men who had been in the middle ranks of the bar saw their career situation improve and were able to achieve a more established position than would otherwise have been possible.[67] Furthermore, the situation within the Order in 1789 also meant that some men who were mere probationary barristers received greater career opportunities than would otherwise have been the case.[68] Not only did the younger and probationary members have their career opportunities enhanced but, with the bâtonnier of the Order in the National Assembly along with several senior members, they were allowed to assume a greater degree of responsibility in the Order. It was these men who began to provide much of the direction and leadership of the Order; they worked in a collegial fashion and none of them emerged as the acknowledged or unofficial leader. Nearly all of them were devoted entirely to their practices and avoided any involvement in political affairs, although a few, such as Delacroix-Frainville and Fournel, were members of the municipal assembly in 1789. For others, however, the avoidance of politics was conscious and deliberate. Pierre Nicolas Berryer, for example, was meeting with the administrative bureau of his district on the evening of July 14 when he saw a crowd march by outside with the head of de Launey, as well as those of the Swiss Guard who had been massacred with him, mounted on the end of long pikes. Berryer was so horrified by the scene that he vowed to himself not to undertake any kind of political career and to remain in private life.[69] It was these men who attempted, somewhat hesitantly at first, to lead the Order in the absence of its president and most of its senior members. While the political process assimilated those in the Assembly into the Revolution, the men who remained in practice became not only leaders of the Order, but also its defenders, ultimately even against the Revolution.

The most telling indication of the irresolution that characterized the Order in 1789 and 1790 is its almost complete failure to react to the proposal to abolish it. It appears, however, that several factors were responsible for the barristers' inactivity during this period.

Almost certainly the large number of barristers involved in municipal affairs played a role; the avocats au Parlement had been actively involved in the administration of the city since the July crisis, and these duties required much of their time. On August 30, 1789, the municipal assembly decided that each district should name five deputies to form an assembly of three hundred members, which in turn would name a city council (Conseil de ville) and its officers, as well as organize the various departments of the municipal government. The number of barristers to the Parlement who served in the expanded body amounted to sixty-three, although a few served only briefly.[70] A new provisioning crisis in September, as well as political anxieties stemming from the debates on the constitution and Louis's failure to ratify the Declaration of the Rights of Man and the August Decrees, produced a new crisis in the city and ensured that those active in municipal affairs would be largely preoccupied by such matters. Also symptomatic of the heavy involvement of avocats au Parlement in municipal administration is the fact that virtually all of the ranking municipal officers below Bailly were members of the Order. Jean Baptiste Boullemer de la Martinière was chosen procureur syndic on October 14, and the two procureur syndic adjoints were Bon Claude Cahier de Gerville and Louis Mitouflet de Beauvois; all of them were members of the Order. Other avocats au Parlement occupied key posts as well.[71] As a result, a significant number of barristers were removed from contact with and developments in their profession and absorbed in an endeavor totally outside it.

While many barristers assumed positions in municipal administration, the unrest in Paris or uncertainty in their profession led others to leave the city altogether. Throughout 1789 and 1790 several members of the Order left Paris and returned to their original locality, further weakening the Order at this critical time.[72]

Another factor in the barristers' passivity was that they had a great sense of confidence in their colleagues in the National Assembly and believed that these men would attend to the interests of the profession and not allow the proposed measure to pass. Not only was their president in the Assembly, their colleague Target was, after September 1789, a member of the Committee of the Constitution. The avocats au Parlement doubtlessly felt that their views were well represented and that any efforts on their part were unnecessary or redundant. Besides their own associates from Paris, they were aware of the presence in the Assembly of avocats au Parlement from other areas of France and had nearly the same degree of confidence in these men as they did in their own colleagues. Furthermore, they may have regarded Bergasse's resignation from the committee as largely marking the end of the threat. Even if this was not the case, one must remember that the initial proposal did not appear absolute and seemed to allow the possibility of maintaining the Order in a modified, less formally institutionalized manner.

Only one avocat au Parlement from Paris, Louis René Chauveau, who had been a member of the Order since 1778, went before the Committee of the Constitution late in 1789 to give his views on the proposed measures.[73] In the course of a long, wide-ranging, and forceful presentation, he argued against the recommended abolition of the

Order by stating that it could lead to serious abuses within the profession, asserting that there would be no mechanism for enforcing a standard of conduct among those who would take up the practice of law under the new arrangements. Chauveau stated that abuses could become rampant and concluded that Bergasse, in his plan, had confused liberty with license.

The revised report of the committee that appeared shortly afterward in December 1789 deleted the proposal to abolish the Order. Although this may have encouraged the avocats au Parlement, it did little to revitalize the Order. Uncertainty over its prospects lingered and left the Order in a state of disarray. The younger men attempting to provide direction to it were faced with a totally unprecedented situation and were unsure about what to do, and the withdrawal of many members from practice in Paris further impaired the Order. Indeed, it is symptomatic of the Order's difficulties during this period that by March 1790 a charitable fund run by the Order for widows and orphans of members was completely exhausted because of the failure of most members to make their normal contribution.[74] The strongest sign of indecision and disorganization is that although the Order was still in full and legal existence in May 1790, the annual ceremony for electing a new president was not held, which meant that the Order continued to be without formal leadership. Clearly, part of the uncertainty resulted from the situation of the Parlement, which was operating only in its truncated vacation form and whose suppression was all but certain, but is is also evident that the Order itself was in a weakened and confused state.

During 1789 and 1790 the dichotomy between the Parisian avocats au Parlement in the National Assembly, who were forced to take a broader view of issues as they strove to build a new France, and those outside it, who continued to abide by the traditional consciousness of état, corps, and ordre, became increasingly apparent. The men who remained active in the Order had little understanding of or sympathy for the transformation that their colleagues in the Assembly were trying to accomplish.

A series of pseudonymous pamphlets, which almost certainly emanated from the Order, reflect the division. The first disparaged the work of the Assembly in forging a constitution — the author denounced in biting terms the abolition of the provinces and nobility, as well as what he saw as the degradation of the king and clergy.[75] The schism became particularly evident after the adoption of the new court system and the suppression of the Parlement. In two pamphlets the author upbraided the members of the Order in the Assembly for abolishing the Parlement. In one of the pamphlets he bitterly attacked them, telling them that they would have been better off had they never left their colleagues. He accused them of being rebels and traitors to the king, and claimed that they had disgraced their professional oath.[76]

When the Assembly abolished the Order such feelings intensified. The men who had remained in the Order reacted with dismay, anger, and a deep sense of betrayal. The sentiments of Berryer, expressed many years later, are typical:

> There were, in the heart of the Constituent Assembly, a great number of barristers, all of them noted for their rhetorical abilities and profound knowledge, the elite of all the tableaux of France: from Paris, Tronchet, Target, Treilhard, Camus, Bigot de Préameneu, Hutteau and others; from Rouen, Thouret; from Rennes, Chapellier [sic]; from Bordeaux, the eagles of the Gironde; from Aix, Portalis, Simeon; from Grenoble, Chabroud; from Nancy, Regnier; from Douai, Merlin, etc., etc. One can say that . . . they were there in a great majority. The Order should thus not have lacked defenders who would oppose themselves to its destruction . . .
>
> I have never been able to understand by what surliness the Constituent Assembly decided to abolish it, and even to go so far as to extend the proscription to the very title of a *avocat*.[77]

Fournel likewise reacted with bitterness and anger toward his colleagues in the Assembly and wrote caustically of the Assembly making war on names and titles.[78]

The response of the men in the Order is illustrative of the two separate dynamics operating in France during this period. On the one hand, the National Assembly, infused with a sense of purpose and driven by its new vision of France, sought to eradicate privilege and corporate bodies as it endeavored to rebuild the nation in a more equitable manner. On the other hand, elements outside the Assembly, imbued with a traditional, countervailing mentality of état, corps, and ordre, found the Assembly's motivation and actions incomprehensible.[79] Most of the avocats au Parlement who remained active in the Order in 1789 and 1790 refused to subscribe to the new ideals put forward by the National Assembly. Instead, they remained devoted to the corporate ethos of the Old Regime.

The destruction of the Order left its members confused and disheartened, and quite uncertain about their place in the new judicial system. Although the National Assembly had enacted the organization of the new judicial system, the institutions that would comprise it had not yet been established. A hiatus of three months ensued between the completion of legislation on the court system and its actual implementation. During this time the former barristers were able to examine their situation and consider their future in the new courts.

3 / A New Era: January 1791 – July 1792

> This was one of the first abuses of freedom, that the right [was] left to anyone, without scrutiny, nor any apprenticeship, to practice the liberal professions, especially the profession where confidence should best be proven before handing over the honor of families, the fate of the widow and the orphan.
>
> *Pierre Nicolas Berryer,* Souvenirs

Faced with a total alteration of their professional situation, the former avocats au Parlement had to reconsider their position in the new judiciary. The response of the members of the Order to its abolition generally took one of three forms: most retired altogether rather than practice in the new judicial system, some sought positions in the new judiciary as either judges or commissioners of the king *(commissaires du roi),* while others elected to remain in practice in the new system. This last is the group with which this study is primarily concerned. While embittered at the suppression of the Parlement, the destruction of their Order, and the changes introduced into their profession, the former barristers who remained in practice nonetheless recognized the political legitimacy of the National Assembly and accepted, albeit reluctantly, its arrangements for the judiciary. The compromise, however, was a tenuous one, and by late 1791 and early 1792 the former barristers in practice had revived in an unofficial fashion the corporate ethos of their profession that the National Assembly had rejected.

The abolition of the Order and the suppression of the Parlement were only the most obvious changes confronting the former barristers as they pondered their place in the new judicial system, but the sense of loss resulting from both events was profound. The influence of the Order on their lives had been pervasive, and doubtlessly it was difficult to envision professional life without it. The Parlement had been a focus of their professional concerns, as well as the source of enormous status, and the prospect of practicing in the new courts, which had no more stature than any other court in France, elicited little enthusiasm. Fournel commented bitterly that the former barristers had been "transferred from the most august court of the realm into a refectory of lesser mendicants or into a nun's dormitory."[1]

In addition, the new court system reduced the scope of activity of the former avocats au Parlement. First, the area of jurisdiction under the new court system was reduced, a development that stemmed from the National Assembly's fear of a powerful judicial body and desire to impose administrative uniformity upon France. The department, the foundation for the administrative system, also became the basis for the judicial system. There was a justice of the peace for each canton (each section in Paris), and a civil court for each district. With the single degree of jurisdiction proclaimed by the Assembly, the court of appeal became one of seven district courts closest to the court in which the case was initially tried. In most respects, however, the domain of a district court was confined not merely to the department, but to the district, which was only a portion of the department. Under the former judicial system France had been divided into fifteen jurisdictions based on the sovereign courts, with the Parlement of Paris being the largest and most prominent; under the organization enacted by the National Assembly there were over five hundred district courts with approximately equal areas of dominion. The result, of course, was a sharp reduction in the domain of the courts, and nowhere was this more evident than at Paris, where the jurisdiction available to the former barristers to the Parlement was reduced to a fraction of what it had been formerly (see map). Whereas the members of the Order had previously practiced in an area of jurisdiction encompassing nearly one-third of France, the hommes de loi in the new system practiced in a dominion covering only the city of Paris, and even this contracted domain was divided into six courts. Since the immense area of jurisdiction of the Parlement of Paris had not been able to support the entire Order of Barristers, the new courts could not possibly sustain the same number of individuals.

A second consequence of the single degree of jurisdiction established for the new court system was that from Paris one might potentially have to to go as far as Orléans or Rouen to appeal a case. Under the appeals system established by the National Assembly seven neighboring district courts were designated as courts of appeal. One of them would serve as the court of appeal, but one never knew in advance which one it

A New Era

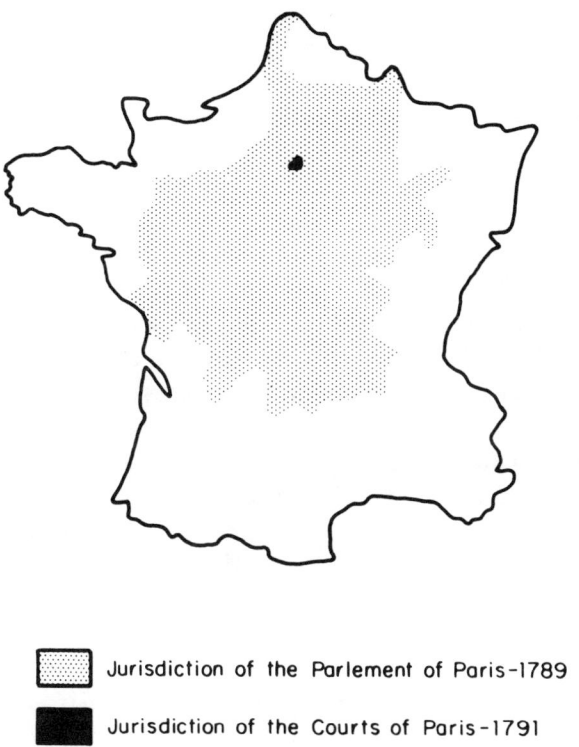

▢ Jurisdiction of the Parlement of Paris-1789

■ Jurisdiction of the Courts of Paris-1791

would be because it was determined by a process of elimination. The appellant first rejected the three courts that he thought would be least sympathetic to his case, and the defendant in turn did the same; the remaining court became the court of appeal. Appeals from Paris were to be handled by the five other courts in the city as well as the district courts of Rouen and Orléans. The rotating system of appeals, and the likelihood of having to travel to Rouen or Orléans to appeal cases under the new judicial system, were features that many of the former barristers found unattractive.[2]

Geographical factors were not the only disadvantages facing the former barristers in the new court system. One goal of the National Assembly, in its effort to implement the ideal of the sublimity of the nation, had been to reduce the amount of litigation between citizens, and the new institutions were oriented toward this goal. First, all parties were required by law to attempt a reconciliation before they could begin a lawsuit. If the individuals lived in the same canton or section, the justice of the peace (*juge de paix*), an elected local official whose function was to conciliate, arbitrate, or judge disputes, handled the conciliation effort. If they were from different sections or cantons, it was referred to a bureau of peace and conciliation attached to each district court. For those instances in which conciliation failed, minor disputes—those in which the amount at issue was less than one hundred livres—went before a justice of the peace, of which there were forty-eight designated for Paris. In any proceeding before a justice of the peace, however, no legal counsel of any kind was to be permitted, in the belief that the propensity of a counsel to exaggerate the claims of his client would impair the process of conciliation.[3] Decisions of the justice of the peace that were eligible for appeal—those involving at least fifty livres—were forwarded to the district court, which was also the court of first instance for more important litigation. Attached to each district court was the bureau of peace and conciliation, whose function was to attempt to adjudicate the dispute before it advanced to actual legal proceedings. The bureau was composed of six individuals appointed to a two-year term, of whom two were to be men of law. The institution apparently enjoyed a high degree of success after it went into operation. Although no information is available on its success rate in Paris because of the destruction of court records in 1871, research on Montpellier suggest that over 40 percent of the disputes there were settled by the bureau before they went into litigation.[4] Although the former barristers would have had no way of knowing whether the bureaus would achieve their purpose, in the aftermath of the abolition of the Order they must have realized that the structure of the new system would further diminish the number of lawsuits available for them to handle.

In addition to geographic and structural changes, there were other developments of importance. The abolition of feudalism, even if not as sweeping as it appeared, marked the end of this institution, which had generated a substantial number of lawsuits in the past, as a source of future lawsuits. Its abolition did not affect all of the former barristers equally, since several of them had diversified their practice and others may not have dealt with feudal matters at all. But those who had built their reputation upon their expertise in feudal law doubtlessly considered their careers ruined. In the same vein, the enactment of the Civil Constitution of the Clergy in July 1790 seemed to represent a needed and thorough reform of the Church in France and appeared to presage a sharp decrease in legal proceedings in this sphere as well, affecting the careers of those men who had centered their practice on ecclesiastical affairs.[5]

Finally, added to all of these considerations was the realization that even in the reduced number of cases ultimately reaching the courts, the former barristers could not be assured that their services would be utilized as before. The end of the barristers' monopoly on litigation through the enactment of the right of each citizen to handle his own case diminished even further the number of lawsuits available. It opened the possibility that in the new courts the former barristers would not be competing against former colleagues from the abolished Order, but perhaps against individuals with little or no training in law — "anyone who presented himself in the arena" was the description of Fournel.[6]

Facing this new situation, the vast majority of the former barristers understandably decided not to remain in their profession. When the new courts opened in Paris, more than four months after the abolition of the Order, only about fifty of the more than six hundred men who had been listed on the tableau of 1789 were prepared to carry on in the new judicial system. Even allowing for the fact that approximately half of these individuals had not originally practiced law actively and had been members of the Order primarily for its social prestige, the attrition was extremely high. Furthermore, according to one of the members of the Order who did remain in practice, those men who continued in the new courts did so reluctantly and with misgivings.[7] For most, the decision to continue the practice of law was based more on dedication to their profession than on loyalty to the Revolution.

The former barristers in practice were not the only ones whose position had been changed by the new situation; individuals seeking entry into the profession were also affected by the transformation that occurred, and many reacted in the same manner — the number of students enrolled in the law school at the University of Paris fell sharply. In the last period before the Revolution for which figures are available, enrollment had averaged 646 students each term, and even in the spring of 1790, after the beginning of the Revolution, which doubtlessly brought some dislocation, the number of students inscribed stood at 376. But in October 1790, the first term after the abolition of the Order, the number of students enrolled fell to 184, a figure less than half that of the spring level.[8] Figures from some of the other law schools in France also reflect a steep drop. The University of Caen, where 229 students matriculated in 1785, fell to an enrollment of 28 in 1790, while the University of Orléans went from 76 in 1785 to 20 in 1790.[9] Again, the reasons for such declines are not hard to discern. For those who had been seeking to gain admission to the Order primarily for the prestige attached to it, the abolition of the Order meant that there was no longer any purpose in studying law. Those who desired to enter into the practice of law were in an uncertain situation, and there was much confusion regarding the Assembly's intentions. The National Assembly had abolished the Orders, but had not made any provisions for regulating the entry of individuals into the capacity of homme de loi, and there was perplexity about the need for taking a law degree.[10] The Assembly had given each citizen the right to handle his own case, but had not stated whether those who did not wish to do so had to utilize the services of an homme de loi. As for those just entering the legal profession, they faced the same constricted availability of cases and all of the other factors that had led so many of the former barristers to the Parlement in practice to leave. Confronted with a confused and entirely new situation, then, most law students and potential law students decided not to pursue a career in the field.

Even before the abolition of the Order, some of its members had begun to establish themselves in new pursuits, such as administration. Many of the avocats au Parlement who had left Paris in 1789 and early 1790 were back in their native area when elections for administrative offices were held, and some stood for and were elected to these positions.[11] A similar phenomenon manifested itself in Paris, but at a later date, because its administrative structure was not legislated until later, so that the election of municipal officers began only in August 1790. Several of the barristers had been active in this sphere because as electors they had been forced to assume many administrative tasks to keep Paris functioning, but the duties had been regarded as provisional until a municipal framework could be established. In the course of the elections, however, most of the individuals who had been in office under the provisional Commune were elected to the posts that they had held.[12] These posts, however, were no longer primarily honorific, ad hoc, or provisional, but a livelihood, a new career, conferring wide-ranging responsibilities and a handsome salary.[13] The assumption of such posts by the barristers involved by consequence their departure from the legal profession. Other barristers, hoping perhaps to position themselves for a possible career in municipal administration, ran for the office of notable, the group from which city councils were formed. Of the 144 men elected, 14 were members of the Order, and of these 14, 3 assumed the duties of administrator in the department of the police.[14] Although there had been some movement out of the profession of avocat au Parlement into such posts prior to the suppression of the Order, the earlier departures had not been significant.

The abolition of the Order provided the real impetus for departure, especially since it coincided with the elections for judgeships in the new district courts. Each district court had five judgeships and four substitute judgeships, and the elections offered a new pursuit to the former barristers, for the law organizing the courts specified that only former judges and hommes de loi, by which was meant former avocats, with five or more years of experience were eligible for the position. Thus, at the very time when the prospects for their own profession appeared to be in decline, a new opportunity opened before them. Indeed, because the judgeships and public prosecutor *(ministère public)* posts were the only occupations for which a legal education and experience were required under the new judicial system, the new positions accorded more closely with their notion of themselves as specialists in law. Thus when the elections for judgeships in the district courts were held in October, November, and December 1790, many of the former barristers to the Parlement sought them. In Paris, sixteen of the thirty district judgeships ultimately went to members of the abolished Order, while seventeen of the twenty-four substitute judges *(suppléants)* who were elected were former avocats au Parlement. This was a remarkable showing, especially since the competition was stiff. The former avocats au Parlement were competing not only against ex-magistrates from the Parlement and the Châtelet for the posts, but also against several distinguished members of the National Assembly. Thouret, for example, who was from Rouen, was elected to a judgeship in Paris, as was Jean François Gaultier de Biauzat, a deputy from Clermont-Ferrand.[15] The Parisian positions alone thereby accounted for a substantial number of members of the dissolved Order leaving the profession.

The assumption of these posts by former avocats au Parlement was not confined to the city of Paris alone. Often the prestige of a career at the Parlement of Paris was such that members of the former Order were elected to judgeships in their native district, despite the fact that they had been gone for several years.[16] Thus, particularly in the Ile-de-France, but also beyond, several members of the abolished Order were chosen for positions in the new courts.[17] Not all of the former barristers to the Parlement accepted the positions to which they were elected, but such individuals were exceptions; most seized the opportunity if it was offered.[18] Ultimately, many members of the suppressed Order at Paris were elected to district judgeships and substitute judgeships throughout France. Because of the incomplete and fragmentary nature of the sources, the precise number cannot be ascertained, but it was at least sixty-seven and probably higher. The elections to the new district judgeships were one of the leading alternatives pursued by former barristers to the Parlement after the abolition of the Order.[19]

A second, and completely unanticipated, development in connection with the establishment of the new judicial system also served to draw several former barristers away from their original occupation. In November 1790, on the eve of the elections for the judiciary in Paris, Jérôme Marie Champion de Cicé resigned as chancellor. Through the intercession of Lafayette, Louis XVI appointed to the newly named post of minister of justice Marguerite Louis François Duport-Dutertre, a former member of the Order who had become active in municipal politics, holding the position of substitut du procureur at the time of his appointment.[20] Duport-Dutertre's tenure as minister of justice shows that despite the abolition of the Order, the corporate spirit and bonds that it had engendered were not so easily dissolved. Duport-Dutertre had moved away from the Order even before its abolition and had become active in municipal affairs. Nonetheless, when he became minister of justice he helped several of his former colleagues who were apparently discouraged about continuing as hommes de loi under the new system. In the new judiciary, the position of commissaire du roi was to have as its function the representation of the king's interests in the court and oversight of the administration of the law; it was an office to which one was appointed by the king, who received nominations from the minister of justice. This was clearly an attractive alternative for those who might have had doubts about practicing as an homme de loi, particularly since it too required a law degree and experience. But while Champion de Cicé was chancellor few members of the Order sought the office.[21] The appointment of their former colleague as minister of justice, however, increased their confidence and encouraged them to pursue the position. Indeed, one aspirant in late 1791 who had been a member of the Order appealed consciously and unequivocally to the connection formed by the abolished Order when he opened his letter to Duport-Dutertre by stating "Permit me to call to mind for you *one of your colleagues from the bar* to whom you have shown some esteem and attachment."[22]

Without question, the link from the former Order was propitious, for during the period he was minister of justice Duport-Dutertre nominated almost exclusively former members of the Order for these positions in Paris. Of the six commissioners of the king in the district courts established at Paris, three were former members of the Order. And when, in early 1791, six provisional courts were formed to deal with the backlog of criminal cases, all of the commissaires du roi appointed were former colleagues of Duport-Dutertre.[23] Furthermore, there was some degree of turnover in the latter positions, and Duport-Dutertre almost invariably named former members of the Order to replace commissaires du roi who went elsewhere.

He also nominated other former Parisian barristers to the Parlement to the position in their native district.[24] In this case also the sources are incomplete and an exact number cannot be determined, but at least twenty men from the abolished Order, and probably more, assumed the position of commissioner of the king in various courts. Along with the elections to the district judgeships, it was one of the other leading alternatives to continuing as an homme de loi favored by former members of the Order at Paris.[25]

Not only did Duport-Dutertre place many of his former colleagues in the post of commissaire du roi, he also brought several into the newly organized Ministry of Justice to serve in administrative positions.[26] All of these positions, whether public posts in the new courts or administrative duties in the ministry, were salaried state places, and the assumption of them meant that former members of the Order would not continue in their original profession, although they would remain in the field of law.

An additional avenue that attracted many former members of the Order as they left the profession was the position of justice of the peace, the elections for which followed those for the district courts. This office was less prestigious than that of district court judge; not only was it inferior in jurisdiction to the latter but, unlike the district court judge, the justice of the peace did not have to possess a law degree to be eligible for the post. Still, the position paid well and it too allowed its holder to remain in the field of law. Of the forty-eight justices of the peace elected in Paris, ten were former barristers from the Order. Other former members were elected as justice of the peace in outlying areas of Paris or in their native canton.[27] Moreover, in Paris twenty other former barristers to the Parlement were selected for the unpaid post of *assesseur juge de paix*. Since neither the justice of the peace nor his assessors could practice as an homme de loi while he held the office, all of these men were also lost to the profession.

In his study of Toulouse, Lenard Berlanstein found that only a small minority of barristers supported the Revolution.[28] His main criterion for identifying those who sympathized with the Revolution was the holding of public office, but even this may overstate somewhat the extent or degree of support for the Revolution. In Paris, at least, the assumption of such posts by former avocats au Parlement should not necessarily be interpreted as a sign of enthusiasm for the Revolution on their part. Rather, their movement into the positions appears to have been motivated as much by personal or professional concerns as by "prorevolutionary" sentiments. Of the sixteen former barristers who were elected to judgeships in the district courts of Paris, eight were members of various Parisian political clubs. Seventeen former members of the Order were chosen as substitute judges, and five of them belonged to clubs. And of the ten justices of the peace from the abolished Order, seven participated in clubs.[29] To the extent that membership in clubs indicates some political involvement in the Revolution, it was an involvement manifested by only a minority of the former barristers to the Parlement. Much of the former barristers' participation, furthermore, was in such conservative clubs as the Club de Valois and the Club de Sainte-Chapelle—arguably, no demonstration of Revolutionary ardor. The evidence, then, though not conclusive, points away from political commitment to the Revolution as a factor in seeking the posts.

It appears instead that professional or career concerns were as significant an element in seeking the posts as enthusiasm for the Revolution. To be sure, some of those who assumed such positions warmly supported the Revolution, but the pursuit of these positions should not be regarded ipso facto as evidence of such sentiments.[30] As practitioners in what had been by far the largest single judicial domain in France, the former barristers to the Parlement in Paris suffered a much greater shrinkage of jurisdiction and dispersal of clientele than any other area.

As much as anything else, the posts held an attraction by offering them an escape from the bleak prospects and utter havoc wreaked upon their profession by the actions of the National Assembly. They offered professional satisfaction (with the abolition of the Order, the judgeships and ministerial positions were the only occupations in France that required a law degree), security, and an ample salary. A district court judge served a six-year term, was eligible for reelection, and in Paris earned 4,000 livres annually. A commissaire du roi served for life and received the same salary as a district court judge. A justice of the peace was elected for a two-year term, was eligible for reelection, and in Paris earned 2,400 livres annually.[31] Whether or not they agreed with the abolition of their Order, then, it is not surprising that the former barristers sought these offices; they seemed to offer much better prospects and a far more secure livelihood than did the new profession of homme de loi.

Another large group of former avocats au Parlement reacted to the abolition of the Order in a different manner. They did not leave the profession to seek an office, but simply retired from practice altogether rather than appear in the new courts.[32] Indeed, according to one member of the Order, this was the most prevalent response among its members after its abolition; a majority of them gave up practice.[33] The reasons for their retirement varied. For some, such as Pierre Angot, the new procedures were the cause, while others, such as Raymond de Sèze, withdrew out of a sense of loyalty to the Parlement. At bottom, however, nearly all of the different motives shared the common trait of a fundamental dislike for the new judicial system produced by the Revolution. Most of the former avocats au Parlement in Paris, to use Berlanstein's description of a similar situation among the barristers at Toulouse,"were 'aristocrats' who preferred to desert the profession rather than support the new judicial order."[34]

When the new courts opened, only about fifty of the former barristers to the Parlement were willing to practice in them. Most of the former avocats au Parlement who decided to continue to practice did so reluctantly and without enthusiasm, and even considered resorting to a strike to demonstrate their unhappiness with the new courts.[35]

Adding to the uncertainty of the former barristers was the fact that the National Assembly did not begin to consider dispositions regarding the occupation of homme de loi until several weeks after the abolition of the Order, further indicating that the action was primarily a spontaneous measure directed against the Order's corporate structure. It is apparent that the Assembly acted in accordance with philosophical rather than judicial concerns, and that afterward it was forced to deal with the consequences of its decision. In November 1790, more than two months after the suppression of the Order, the Committee of the Constitution was still unable to provide answers to questions concerning the role of the hommes de loi in the new courts.[36] It simply responded that the matter would be decided later, and only in December 1790 did the Assembly begin to address itself to the issue.

On December 13, 1790, the Assembly heard a report from Jacques Samuel Dinocheau, a deputy from Blois, on the suppression of ministerial offices.[37] The report called for the abolition of procureurs and advocated the termination of the division of duties between the former professions of avocat and procureur, claiming that the division had been simply a fiscal device that had resulted in unnecessary expense and corporate rivalries. Dinocheau recommended that both procedural and legal duties be performed by the hommes de loi in the new courts. In a proposal that clearly reflects the sentiment for a community of citizens that guided the Assembly, he also recommended the establishment of the office of défenseur officieux, which would allow any citizen to defend the case of any other citizen simply by virtue of the latter's trust and confidence in him. This was designed to give the widest possible latitude to the freedom of defense, and no legal training would be required as a prerequisite. Several deputies in the Assembly, however, were in favor of preserving ministerial officers in order to assure procedural uniformity in the new courts. On December 15, 1790, the Assembly went along with some of Dinocheau's proposals and abolished the procureurs and other lesser offices in declaring the suppression of venal and hereditary ministerial offices. At the same time, it decreed that ministerial offices would be necessary in the new courts, a provision that became controversial because of concern in the Assembly that the establishment of ministerial officers would create a privileged group.[38] There was also concern that creating and requiring these officials would conflict with the Assembly's decision granting each citizen the right to defend his own case.

One of the most effective spokesmen for the establishment of ministerial offices was François Denis Tronchet, the last president of the dissolved Order. On December 16 he spoke to the Assembly and addressed its concerns in arguing for the creation of ministerial officers known as *avoués*. He asserted that some guarantees of procedural uniformity were necessary and that this would not be possible if any citizen could handle the procedural aspects of his case. Tronchet claimed that by limiting the avoué to procedural duties and reserving the right to argue the case to the individual, the creation of the avoués would not infringe on the citizen's right to defend his own case. If, however, a person did not feel capable of arguing his case, he could utilize a défenseur officieux for this purpose or, if he desired, he could authorize the avoué to do it in addition to performing procedural duties. Tronchet's speech was influential, and nearly all of his proposals were included in the law that established the avoués. The law, promulgated on January 29, 1791, mandated the creation of the office of avoué to handle procedural details of a case.[39] It also sanctioned the office of défenseur officieux to argue a case for an individual, orally or in writing, and also gave the avoués the right to do so if expressly authorized by their party. It made former avocats eligible for the position of avoué, along with former procureurs, although few of the former barristers to the Parlement in Paris became avoués, doubtlessly considering it too analogous to the Old Regime profession of procureur.[40]

In establishing the position of défenseur officieux, the National Assembly made law a free profession, with no limitation on practice or qualifying requirements — it could be practiced by anyone. This development further demarcates the experience of the profession of barrister from that of many other professions in France; where most professions developed in close conjunction with the state, that of barrister, far from developing in confluence with the state, was instead "deprofessionalized" by it.[41] Once again, however, the reason is clear — law was central to the ideal of the sublimity of the nation, for it was law that was the source of equity and endowed each individual with his identity as a citizen. Thus, in the redefinition of the state that occurred, it was almost inevitable that the legal profession would be more profoundly affected than any other group.

The legislation of January 29 obviously further eroded the standing of the former barristers in the new judicial system. Under its provisions, former avocats would have to share their duties not merely with individual citizens wishing to plead their own case, but with avoués and défenseurs officieux as well. While procedural functions were reserved for the avoués alone, written or oral legal arguments could now be handled by three groups: hommes de loi, défenseurs officieux, and avoués. Moreover, with the recognition of the office of défenseur officieux, a law degree or even any legal experience was unnecessary to perform these duties and therefore became superfluous. Just as the new judicial system began, then, the proud Old Regime profession of avocat au Parlement was thrown open not merely to former procureurs, but to the public at large. For those former Parisian avocats au Parlement who remained in the profession, the development only served to alienate them further from the Revolution.

The new courts in Paris were installed on January 25 and 26, 1791, and one of the first former barristers to appear in them was Pierre Nicolas Berryer, whose account of the episode reveals the reluctance and misgivings with which the former avocats au Parlement approached the new tribunals. After the reorganization had gone into effect, the National Treasury had been made a defendant in a case called before the Tribunal of the First Arrondissement, where an Englishman named Hartley sued it for 800,000 francs in restitution for a ship captured during the American Revolution. The treasury, for whom Berryer did some work, sought him to take their case and he agreed. Berryer's intention to plead in the new court prompted a visit to his office by two of his colleagues, Nicolas François Bellart and Louis Ferdinand Bonnet, who asked him if it was true that he was going to handle the case in the new court. Berryer's account of the ensuing discussion is not exact, but the experience of the Maupeou parlement and the possibility of a strike were raised because Berryer said he told Bonnet and Bellart that he did not view the measures adopted by the National Assembly for the reconstruction of the judiciary with the same hostility as he had the Maupeou innovations of 1771. Berryer claimed that the national will, as expressed by the Assembly, had more stability than the decision of a ministry.[42] Berryer wrote that Bellart and Bonnet were convinced by his argument and agreed to practice in the new courts at the first opportunity, and that a potential strike was thereby averted, although Berryer recalled that when he made his appearance at the court it was like that of a ghost and raised some unfriendly murmurs. Not all of the former barristers were prepared to concede the points that Berryer did. Fournel, who also continued to practice, mentioned the courts' "illegitimate origin," which, he said, "bore the character of usurpation." Despite this "stigma," Fournel said he and some other former avocats au Parlement were reconciled to the new courts by the good choice of judges for them.⁴³ It is clear, however, that the former barristers' loyalties remained with the abolished Parlement, and that they were unhappy with the system enacted by the National Assembly; additional evidence of their attitude is provided by a satirical newspaper account published nearly three weeks after the opening of the new courts:

> The new organization of the courts has driven insane a large number of hommes de loi, who regularly come to the Palais as if the Parlement still held its audiences. Their delusion is to believe firmly that the proceedings of the new court are a game, that the Parlement is only on vacation, etc. I was recently in the Palais and approached a group of these unfortunates; I no longer had any doubts about their insanity when I heard one of them say to his colleagues: "Have a little patience, my friends, a good old decree from the Parlement will rid us of these scoundrels."⁴⁴

The new courts established in January 1791 were civil courts. In April 1790 the National Assembly had decided that there would be a jury system for criminal cases, but it continued to debate other aspects of the criminal court system. As a result, there was no criminal court whatsoever in operation, since the former courts had been suppressed. As a temporary measure, the Assembly enacted a series of additional articles in October 1790 that gave the civil courts the authority to try criminal cases without juries until the new criminal court system could be established. The backlog of cases in Paris was so great, however, that the six district courts could not process old cases and treat current ones at the same time, so in order to alleviate the problem the National Assembly decreed on March 14, 1791, the establishment of six provisional criminal courts in Paris to handle all cases pending before January 26, 1791, the date of the establishment of the new courts.⁴⁵ The six courts were each comprised of seven judges, with one judge drawn from each of the forty-two district courts in the departments closest to Paris. The tribunals began operation in April 1791 and ultimately dealt with the backlog of cases effectively. Their opening also meant that by the spring of 1791 there were twelve tribunals in operation in the city of Paris alone.

Throughout 1791 the institutions established by the National Assembly in its judicial restructuring of France were put into operation, and members of the former Order of Barristers in Paris were represented in nearly all of them. On November 2, 1790, the Assembly, despite its fear of a Parlement-like judicial body, had agreed upon the necessity of creating a Tribunal de cassation, a high court of appeal that would review the judgments of the district courts. It was divided into a civil section and a criminal section, but was allowed to review only procedural aspects of cases and was not empowered to interpret laws. Although its powers of review were thus sharply limited, it was still an important and respected institution, holding its sessions in the old Grand' chambre. The first elections to the Tribunal de cassation were held in March 1791, and two former members of the Order at Paris, Gilles Boucher de la Richarderie and Jean Philippe Garran de Coulon, were elected as judges. Another former Parisian avocat au Parlement, Gilbert Hom, won election as greffier.[46] At first glance the assumption of the latter post by one of the former barristers to the Parlement seems rather puzzling, since they had generally viewed this office with the same disdain as they did that of procureur, considering it more clerical than legal in nature. It must be remembered, however, that despite the massive changes occurring around them, many of the former barristers to the Parlement still adhered to the mores and values of the Old Regime. Under the Old Regime the post of chief clerk to the Parlement had been quite prestigious, so much so that at times some counselors had resigned their position to become greffier.[47] Under the new judicial organization, the Tribunal de cassation was the court most analogous to the Parlement of Paris, and in this context the position of greffier must have seemed attractive.

Most of the measures concerning the criminal court system had been approved by February 1791, but final legislation on the subject was not completed until September 1791. There was to be one criminal tribunal for each department that would try felonies; lesser crimes were to be handled by a justice of the peace. The criminal court would consist of an elected judge as president; an assistant judge, who was also elected; and judges from the civil courts serving at the criminal court on a rotating basis. The public prosecutor was also to be an elected official, as was his assistant. The elections for positions in Paris were held in June 1791, and former members of the Order were elected to some of them. Other former members were elected to criminal court positions in departments outside of Paris.[48] By the end of 1791 the judiciary decreed by the National Assembly was thus in place. The pursuit of places in it as an alternative to continuing as an homme de loi after the abolition of the Order had brought about a virtual diaspora of the former Order's members. They were scattered in many departments throughout France, and in jurisdictions ranging from that of the canton to the highest court in the land, while only a small minority of the previous membership of the Order remained in practice in the new courts in Paris.

The administrative burden involved in inaugurating a completely new judicial system in France was enormous, and it was exacerbated by the fact that the Assembly's intentions were often not clear because of the vague wording of some of the laws. The introduction of such new terms as *avoué, homme de loi, défenseur officieux,* and others created additional confusion.[49] In the year 1791 alone, the Conseil judiciaire of the Ministy of Justice answered 4,774 inquiries, nearly all of which concerned the new system of justice.[50] Initially the commissaires du roi in Paris were assiduous in scrutinizing the qualifications of individuals who presented themselves in the courts as avoués or as défenseurs officieux, but their efforts to control the entry of persons into the offices were hampered by the wide degree of latitude permitted by the law of January 29, 1791. Thus, several individuals whom the commissioners of the king had sought to prevent from practicing in the new tribunals were nonetheless admitted because of the interpretation of the law given by the Conseil judiciaire.[51]

For those former barristers to the Parlement who, however reluctantly, continued to practice, the transition was easiest in the civil courts, which had been instituted first and where procedural changes were less extensive. The monopoly on litigation enjoyed by the Order under the Old Regime had applied to civil cases, and this previously established position, although abolished, helped the former avocats au Parlement. The records of the courts have not survived, but a published collection based on notes taken before their destruction, as well as contemporary legal journals, show that several of the former barristers to the Parlement practiced regularly in the civil courts.[52] The cases for 1791 that were transcribed or reported show that former avocats au Parlement were utilized in a majority of cases. Although they clearly did not like the new courts, the former avocats au Parlement did come before them, and their presence helped to assure the continuity of justice and facilitated the proceedings; civil cases appear to have been dispatched with few difficulties.

For criminal justice, however, this was not the case. In this sphere the former barristers to the Parlement had not profited from an exclusive right to handle cases, for the Ordinance of 1670 had forbidden counsel to criminal defendants. Furthermore, the freedom of defense accorded to individuals by the Assembly allowed great latitude to defendants in choosing a legal representative, and the results of this became most noticeable in the criminal courts, where ethical and professional standards were often ignored. One reason, perhaps, was that the criminals or defendants chose as representatives individuals whom they had known in their former milieu or someone who had been suggested to them by an associate. Often they were desperate and therefore not selective in choosing a legal representative. Without question several of the persons who entered the courts as défenseurs officieux, hommes de loi, or avoués did not adequately attend to their clients' interests.[53] In an undated report to the National Assembly, the provisional criminal courts reported with obvious concern the following incident:

Recently, a woman that the judicial system found not guilty was brought into one of our courts. At the very moment that her case was going to be tried, her counsel abandoned her. She was given another counsel and told that her case would be judged the next day; there was a delay of only one day, but apparently a day is a century in prison. The unfortunate woman burst into tears, uttered some heart-rending cries and beat her head against the railing while cursing the judges, and the public, witness to this scene, saw her carried out by two soldiers.

The procès-verbal of this incident has been sent to the minister of Justice. But how many others there are who exist and who are not verified by the procès-verbaux! Yes, gentlemen, the abuses have increased, they are constant and up until now we have vainly sought solutions.[54]

One study of the provisional criminal courts has shown that the quality of representation in these courts was not good, with counsel present often in only a minority of cases. Initially, the failure of the counselors to be with their clients caused delay and confusion in the courts, but later the judges simply disregarded their absence and proceeded with the case, which resulted, of course, in the defendant being denied legal counsel altogether. It is apparent that in a period of extensive judicial change the possibilities of implementing an efficient and refined court system were limited, and part of the problem may have been caused by the large number of innovations in the criminal system of justice. The courts themselves were occasionally at fault because they sometimes failed to notify legal representatives of trial dates.[55] Even allowing for these factors, it is apparent that there were serious problems with the professionalism and ethics of the hommes de loi and défenseurs officieux in the criminal courts. When the courts first opened, the commissaires du roi had been unable to prevent the entry into practice of individuals whom they considered unqualified, and their impotence may have emboldened other unprincipled men to enter the tribunals. As early as February 8, 1791, only days after the courts began operation, there was an instance in Paris of a défenseur officieux appearing in court uninvited in an apparent attempt to solicit cases.[56] By late 1791 the problem had reached such dimensions that the commissaire du roi of the First Provisional Criminal Court requested an appointment with the minister of justice to discuss the matter. In his letter he mentioned that complaints were being received from prisoners about some of the counselors and the fees that they were charging clients. Obviously frustrated by his inability to act against them, he asked the minister of justice to consider some kind of action that could be taken against "the speculations of those who practice with contempt the honorable ministry of defender while extorting the unfortunate prisoners of considerable sums as the price for their counsel."[57] Clearly, the integrity of the legal profession was being threatened but, stripped of any power to regulate their profession, there was nothing that the former avocats au Parlement could do to address the situation.

The dishonorable activities of some of the new hommes de loi and défenseurs officieux were in themselves graphic reminders of the dissolution of the Order, but the fact was pressed home in another manner late in 1791. On September 1, 1791, the library of the Order, which had been impounded when the Order was abolished, was taken over by the municipal librarian, Hubert Pascal Ameilhon, and a municipal official, Jacques Joseph Hardy.[58] The library, which had been a point of pride for the Order for nearly three-quarters of a century, was confiscated along with those of various religious communities, although no immediate disposition was made of its contents. With this act the last remaining tangible vestige of the Order disappeared.

Although it did not affect the fortunes of the profession, the transition from the National Assembly to the Legislative Assembly is also worthy of notice because it highlights a feature of the new era after the abolition of the Order — the dispersion of its members as many embarked upon new careers. On September 30, 1791, the National Assembly dissolved and gave way to the Legislative Assembly, which opened on October 1. Of the twenty-four deputies from the Paris delegation, five were former members of the Order.[59] Most of these former members came from judicial posts to which they had been elected in 1790 or 1791, although one of them, Jacques Godard, had continued to practice after the Order's abolition. More significant, an even larger number of former barristers from the Order at Paris were elected from departments other than Paris, nearly all of them also coming from judicial or administrative posts to which they had been elected.[60] In all, thirteen former avocats au Parlement from the Order at Paris, representing seven different departments (including Paris), sat in the Legislative Assembly.

Initial complications had certainly been expected when the new judicial system was inaugurated, but even several months after it had been in place the new judiciary was plagued with problems. The difficulties affected both those in the judiciary as well as those who had continued as hommes de loi, and they made the process of accommodation to the new system more difficult. In March 1792, for example, Jean Guillaume Locré, a former member of the Order and the justice of the peace for the section Bondy, had to stop holding audiences because he did not have enough assistants to continue them. He informed the minister of justice of his difficulties, who in turn notified the minister of the interior. The latter then contacted the municipal administrators, who responded in April by stating that the mayor had been apprised of the problem and that they had urged him to act on it.[61] By this time a month had passed, and one of the key institutions for the administration of justice under the new judicial system had remained at a complete standstill.[62]

This development was confined to a jurisdiction involving lesser suits in one area of the city and, while symptomatic of the complications that arose in the new judicial system and irksome to those affected, it was not a critical problem. Far more serious were the difficulties that manifested themselves in the district courts in Paris, which were broader in jurisdiction and processed more important suits and crimes. For many of the former barristers to the Parlement who had become district court judges, the conditions were trying because of the many demands placed upon the tribunals. In January 1792 Jacques Nicolas Millet de Gravelle, a former avocat au Parlement who was president of the Tribunal of the First Arrondissement, became concerned because there were too few substitute judges in his court since one of his substitutes had been elevated to the position of judge. The minister of justice asked the minister of the interior to convene the electors to choose new substitute judges, but when the latter tried to implement this, administrative problems ensued due to the immaturity of the system. The administrators of Paris notified the minister of the interior that it would not be possible to proceed with the election of substitutes by the terms of the law of August 24, 1790. They argued that the law called for judicial elections to be held only every six years, and that although the law specified that substitutes would be named to the post of judge when the position became vacant, there were no provisions for replacing the substitutes themselves.[63]

Similarly, the commissaire du roi of the Tribunal of the Second Arrondissement wrote to the minister of justice in May 1792 to point out that his court was undermanned. The tribunal was supposed to be composed of five judges, but one of the five was directing a grand jury, one was serving on rotation to the criminal court, and a third had been delegated to a court of appeal for sentences passed by a minor crimes court (tribunal de police correctionelle). Thus, the court was down to two judges, and there were not enough substitutes to replace them. A vacancy had existed previously, one suppléant had been named to the position of judge and a third was acting as a prosecutor.[64] Consequently, only one substitute judge was available for service, which meant that the court would still not have a full complement of judges.

With the courts relying on the substitute judges to assist in the administration of justice, such impasses could only increase the workload of the judges, slow the judicial process, and cause frustration for both the judges and the litigants or defendants. The Legislative Assembly resolved the matter regarding the Tribunal of the First Arrondissement on February 9, 1792, when it passed an emergency decree authorizing the election of two substitute judges to the court. There had been a heavy influx of cases involving counterfeit *assignats* into this tribunal, and the Assembly took the step of authorizing the replacement of substitute judges in order to shore up public confidence in the assignats.[65] Later, on February 18, 1792, Roederer, the procureur général syndic for Paris, acting on the recommendations of the minister of justice and the judges of the civil courts, authorized elections to fill six other vacant substitute judgeships.

In addition to the problems of overwork and insufficient personnel, judges during this period often went unpaid. On January 31, 1792, Millet de Gravelle, the president of the Tribunal of the First Arrondissement, wrote to the minister of the interior to complain that the salary of the members of the court was in arrears. He complained of the insouciance that the directory of the department showed in meeting its financial obligations, and asked the minister to see that this did not happen again in the future. Other former members of the Order who had assumed positions in courts in other departments experienced similar problems.[66]

Despite such irksome conditions, several former barristers to the Parlement continued to seek these posts. In the elections of the substitute judges for the civil courts, more than half of the eight individuals chosen were men who had belonged to the Order in 1789. Others accepted positions in departments outside Paris.[67]

The continued pursuit of judicial positions by former barristers to the Parlement suggests that the situation in their own occupation was difficult, and this was, in fact, the case, for by early 1792 in ways both large and small the Revolutionary calling of homme de loi resembled less and less the proud Old Regime profession of avocat au Parlement. One change introduced was a stylistic one that took place in 1792 with the inauguration of the jury system in the criminal court. Initially, the former barristers tried to plead before the juries as they might have done in the Tournelle. In their pleadings they often cited quotations from noted jurists to buttress their case, but the citations were in Latin, which most of the jurors could not understand. The jurors therefore could not follow the arguments made by the former avocats au Parlement, and as a consequence several of their clients were convicted. When the former barristers realized the problem, they stopped utilizing Latin quotations and the number of acquittals increased.[68] No doubt the development served to confirm the former barristers' already low opinion of the new courts.

Of far greater concern to the former avocats au Parlement was the integrity of their profession as unprincipled individuals entered the courts as hommes de loi and défenseurs officieux, a phenomenon that accelerated during late 1791 and early 1792. A variety of contemporary sources document this and provide a glimpse of the new conditions faced by the former barristers to the Parlement.

On March 30, 1792, Nicolas Orry, a défenseur officieux in Paris, was tried in the Fifth Provisional Criminal Court along with two associates for trying to buy wine from an innkeeper with a counterfeit forty *vol* note from the Maison de secours, a bank established primarily for the poor that issued small denomination notes. In his defense, Orry claimed he did not know that the notes were counterfeit, and he was found not guilty, but the case offers some insight into the changing complexion of the legal profession in 1792.[69] Even though Orry was acquitted of the charge, the very fact that he could have been accused in the first place is evidence of the presence in the profession of men of doubtful character. There was an active trade in counterfeit notes from the Maison de secours, and the fact was well publicized, so that in all probability a prudent person would not have dealt in the notes.[70] By 1792, however, the ranks of défenseur officieux included persons of questionable character, and there were no constraints on their entry into the courts.

This was underscored by an incident in the Tribunal of the Fourth Arrondissement in April 1792. At a conference of the judges of the six courts that was held at regular intervals, the representative for the Tribunal of the Fourth Arrondissement, Jacques Delavigne, himself a former member of the Order, sought guidance from his colleagues on an episode that had occurred there. A man named Truchon, who had been arrested and imprisoned for bigamy and was awaiting trial, appeared in court to practice as a défenseur officieux. His presence prompted a protest from other défenseurs officieux, who did not wish to associate with him. Despite the protest, the judges of the fourth arrondissement took no action to exclude Truchon from their court, basing their inaction on the belief that the law specified that the function of défenseur officieux was completely free and that there were no restrictions on who could practice it, to the extent that the judges believed that not even nonactive citizens could be excluded. The conference agreed unanimously that this interpretation was correct.[71]

Abuses were particularly prevalent in the criminal courts. Individuals entered the prisons to solicit cases and often pressured defendants to enter into agreements with them. One homme de loi was apparently placed on retainer by a gang of thieves to defend any of its members who were caught.[72]

The diminution of ethical standards was not confined simply to the défenseurs officieux and hommes de loi. The avoués, who were also empowered to present legal arguments if authorized by their party, were likewise plagued by unprincipled conduct in the courts. At the conference of judges from the six courts held on February 16, 1792, the representative for the Tribunal of the Fifth Arrondissement denounced an abuse by which the avoués were able to increase their fees to clients, and a subsequent conference on July 8, 1792, was partially devoted to the excessive charges levied by the avoués and défenseurs officieux.[73] In a report on the state of the courts made by the minister of justice to the Legislative Assembly in July 1792 the avoués were singled out for criticism because of the exorbitant charges they were imposing on their clients. The minister suggested that firm measures might be necessary to curtail such activity, but he made no specific proposals in his report.[74]

Additional evidence of the increasing unattractiveness of a legal career is reflected in law school enrollment: by 1792, inscriptions at the University of Paris Law School had dwindled to a fraction of their former levels. In April 1792, for example, only forty-seven students were enrolled, and by July 1792, the number declined to twenty-two.[75] This represented a further threat to the profession, since it was apparent that it would not be able to renew itself in accordance with its former standards.

Confronted with conditions they considered intolerable, the former avocats au Parlement reverted to the corporate ethos of their profession. Those who remained in practice adopted the rules of the abolished Order as their standard and admitted as colleagues or entered cases only with hommes de loi who were willing to conform to them. They deliberately separated themselves from individuals who would not abide by the statutes of the dissolved Order, and refused to have any dealings with them whatsoever. Moreover, they held meetings in which they attempted to regenerate and maintain the spirit of the suppressed Order.[76]

These actions by the former avocats au Parlement evoked criticism. In March 1792 a legal journal that covered the new courts reproached the former members of the Order at Paris for reverting to custom and usage rendered obsolete by the new constitution. Noting that one of the aims of the Constitution had been to "abolish all privilege and extinguish all esprit de corps in society," it accused the former barristers to the Parlement who remained in practice of subverting this ideal. It particularly denounced their refusal to enter into cases with avoués, claiming that the refusal stemmed from the corporate rivalry and disdain they had manifested toward procureurs under the Old Regime.[77] The obvious implication of the article was that the former members of the Order were trying to undermine, if not undo, the work of the Revolution.

It is clear, then, that even before the onset of the Terror the former barristers to the Parlement were unhappy with their professional situation. Although embittered by the destruction of the Parlement, the suppression of their Order, and the changes introduced into their profession, they had nonetheless recognized the political legitimacy of the National Assembly and accepted, albeit reluctantly, its arrangements for the judiciary. When the measures enacted by the Assembly appeared to threaten the integrity of their profession, however, the former avocats au Parlement revived the corporate ethos categorically rejected by the Assembly. Their action clearly and unequivocally indicated that their loyalty lay with their profession rather than with the Revolution, and revealed how tenuous and reluctant their accommodation to the Revolution was. In August 1792, however, this fragile compromise was shattered.

4 / The Impact of the Terror: August 1792 – December 1794

> Notice that the men of law belong to a revolting aristocracy.
> *Danton to the National Convention*
> *September 22, 1792*

Most of the former avocats au Parlement who had continued to practice in the new judiciary had predicated their acceptance of the Revolution upon its legitimacy. Although they did not subscribe to the ideals promulgated by the National Assembly and had attempted to evade its proscription of the corporate structure and values of their profession, most of them recognized the political sovereignty of the National Assembly as valid and accepted, however reluctantly, its reforms. For most of the former barristers, the validity of the Assembly's authority outweighed the resentment they felt concerning the changes its actions had introduced into their profession.

But the overthrow of the king on August 10 nullified this compromise and caused the Revolution to lose its legitimacy in the eyes of most of the former avocats au Parlement; with the Constitution cast aside and the monarch deposed, the Revolution had no legal standing. Berryer's memoirs, which provide the best view of the milieu of the former barristers in this epoch, convey the distress he felt at the sudden downfall of the monarchy. The reaction of several of the former avocats au Parlement who were members of the National Guard on August 10 is also indicative of their monarchism, as is a subsequent unsolicited attempt by many of them to organize a collective defense for the king at his trial.[1]

The fall of the monarchy had ramifications that were professional as well as political for the former barristers to the Parlement still in practice. Under the Old Regime the dispensation of justice had been regarded as originating with the king, for whom the courts acted as agents. While the Revolution made the nation the source of all justice, it nonetheless implicitly accorded the king a major role, a role embodied in the institution of the commissaire du roi, the officer in each court whose function was to act as the king's representative and to oversee the administration of justice. For their entire professional career, then, both in the Parlement and in the new tribunals, the former barristers to the Parlement had had as a basic postulate the belief that the king was an integral part of the judicial system and that the courts were his executors. As a result, for most of them, the dethroning of the king threw into question the legitimacy of the entire judicial system.[2] The Legislative Assembly also recognized this problem and moved quickly to separate any association between the king and the judicial system. On August 14, 1792, it changed the name of the post of commissaire du roi to *commissaire national* and charged the Committee of Legislation with preparing a report on the position. On August 18 the committee presented its report and the Legislative Assembly adopted most of its recommendations. It suspended all of the commissaires nationaux from office and provided for the election of *commissaires du pouvoir exécutif* to replace them. It specifically disqualified for the post of commissaire du pouvoir exécutif, however, all of the men who had been serving as commissaires nationaux on the date the decree was promulgated.[3] In Paris nearly all of the suspended commissaires nationaux were former barristers to the Parlement, and at least one of them was disquieted by the prospect of having to return to private practice. Claude Jean Ferrier, a former member of the Order, fought to retain eligibility for an official post by writing the Legislative Assembly to ask it to reconsider the terms of the exclusion so that those who had served in the provisional criminal courts could be eligible as commissaires du pouvoir exécutif. When his request was unsuccessful, he retired from practice.[4]

In addition to the issue of the legitimacy of the judiciary, developments of the following month were also pivotal in determining the attitude of many of the former barristers to the Parlement toward the new regime. The September massacres repelled them and left them in a state of great consternation. To men whose profession had nurtured in them a belief in due process and the role of law, the massacres were a horror; Berryer's memoirs reflect how deeply he was shaken, and his sentiments are echoed elsewhere.[5] Compounding their philosophical revulsion was a personal element. Three of their former colleagues, all of whom had left the profession to assume administrative or judicial positions in Paris, died in the massacres, while others only narrowly escaped.⁶ The massacres so unnerved some former barristers that afterward they fled Paris.⁷ Moreover, the perceived involvement of the minister of justice, Danton, in the massacres could only have intensified the suspicion of many of the former avocats au Parlement of the new government.

The elections to the National Convention took place in the atmosphere produced by the September massacres. In the previous two legislatures the Parisian delegation had included respected ex-colleagues in whom the former barristers to the Parlement had confidence — Tronchet, Camus, and Target in the National Assembly, and Jacques Godard and Pierre Louis Lacretelle in the Legislative Assembly were men who had enjoyed the esteem and trust of most of the former avocats au Parlement. As one consequence of this, the former barristers, although perhaps disappointed by various measures enacted by the assemblies, were not alienated from the political process itself.⁸ In August and September 1792, however, the overthrow of the monarchy and the September massacres led most of the former avocats au Parlement to withdraw from political activity.⁹ Furthermore, having overthrown the monarchy, the Commune was not about to allow that action to be possibly reversed by electing men who were "professionally concerned with legal proprieties" and might be inclined to restore the king to the throne.¹⁰ As a result, the victors in the elections to the Convention were those whose antecedents were in municipal politics; two-thirds of the deputies elected from Paris had been affiliated with the Commune. Consequently, the Parisian delegation included significantly fewer former members of the Order than either of the previous delegations. Moreover, the two former members of the Order who were elected, Jacques Nicolas Billaud-Varennes and Etienne Jean Panis, neither of whom had figured prominently in the Order under the Old Regime, had little identification with the profession, having abandoned it completely since the Revolution. Although a few former colleagues with views more harmonious with their own were elected from departments outside Paris, many of these men had had their ties to the profession attenuated by their absence from Paris or by their assumption of administrative, judicial, or political positions since 1790. For several reasons, then, most of the former Parisian barristers to the Parlement still in practice were from the beginning more estranged from the National Convention than from previous assemblies, and the Convention's subsequent actions only served to exacerbate the rift.

The mistrust exhibited toward the new regime was not confined to the former barristers to the Parlement who had continued to practice as hommes de loi. A considerable number of judges in the courts, many of whom were also former members of the Order, evinced a similar attitude. And the fact that every judge in France had accepted his commission from the king was a matter of some concern to the National Convention and was one of the first issues it treated after it convened. On September 22, 1792, after a delegation from Orléans announced the suspension of some municipal officers there, the Convention began a discussion on the reliability of the administrative personnel then in office throughout France. Georges Couthon, a deputy from the Puy-de-Dôme, proposed that new elections be held to renew the administrators, and his proposal gained support from other deputies. This led Pierre Philippeaux, a deputy from the Sarthe and formerly a judge in the district court of Le Mans, to suggest broadening the mandate to include the renewal of judicial personnel as well. In the course of the debate Philippeaux asserted that the administration and judiciary were "gangrenous, not with aristocracy, but with royalism." A prolonged and desultory discussion ensued before the Convention decreed that new elections would be held to renew administrative and judicial personnel, including the justices of the peace. Following this decision, a new issue emerged when the deputy Jean Lambert Tallien advocated making all citizens eligible for judgeships, rather than only those with legal training, as had been the case in 1790. Several deputies resisted Tallien's proposal, but a speech by Danton supporting the measure carried the day; the Convention decreed that the new judges could be chosen from among all citizens without regard for education or experience.[11] Thus, as one of its first acts, the Convention, by ordering the renewal of the judiciary, had not only breached the principle of the inviolability of judges, but had at the same time removed all professional qualifications from the position as well. Since the choice of judges in 1790 had been one of the factors reconciling many of the former barristers to the Parlement who had remained in practice to the new courts, these actions served further to alienate them from the Convention.

Joined to the disaffection produced by political events was the lingering discontent caused by the declining state of their profession. As the refusal of the commissaire du roi Ferrier to return to private practice suggests, by late 1792 the decline had reached serious proportions. The case of Louis Claude Raymond is particularly illustrative. Raymond was an homme de loi who had been arrested in November 1792 for suspected involvement in the theft at the Garde-meuble, the building in which various royal treasures were stored. Under questioning Raymond admitted that he had previously been imprisoned, on one occasion for indebtedness and on another as a suspect in a theft. While in prison awaiting indictment on the latter charge he had been set free by the crowd during the September massacres, only to be arrested again two months later as a suspect in the Garde-meuble theft. Additional information provided by Douligny, who was subsequently convicted of the crime and executed, absolved Raymond of any involvement in the theft at the Garde-meuble. But in the course of his interrogation Douligny did admit that while Raymond played no part in the theft at the Garde-meuble, he was "one of them" (referring to the gang of thieves) and that Raymond had as a sobriquet "casseur de portes."[12] To see their profession infiltrated by such men appalled the former avocats au Parlement, but they were powerless to act.[13] In a report to the Legislative Assembly in July 1792 the minister of justice had indicated that he might seek legislative action to deal with the situation. The instability of the Ministry of Justice, however, precluded any attempt to pursue such a course or to treat the problem in an effective manner; during the year 1792 there were six different ministers of justice, which meant that no minister occupied the office long enough to intervene forcefully to remedy the state of affairs in the courts.

The antipathy of many of the former avocats au Parlement for the National Convention and their loyalty to Louis XVI culminated at the time that the Convention began preparations for the monarch's trial. A large number of the former barristers to the Parlement assembled to plan a hypothetical defense for Louis, and their role appears to have been more significant than has generally been recognized.

The Convention initially vacillated on whether Louis should be permitted to have counsel, but on December 12 he was accorded the right to choose his defenders. His first choices were two former members of the Order, Guy Jean Baptiste Target and François Denis Tronchet. Tronchet accepted, but Target refused Louis's request, an action that many of his former colleagues considered unprofessional. Dismayed by Target's refusal, many of the former barristers to the Parlement who had continued to practice in the new courts met at the residence of one of their number, Guillaume Alexandre Tronson-Ducoudray, to discuss strategy in the event that the king chose one of them to replace

Target. Entirely unsolicited, they planned a defense strategy based upon the Convention's attribution of authority as both prosecutor and judge. Moreover, they agreed to form a defensive league among themselves: if any one of them was chosen, the remainder would assist him.[14] The monarchist sympathies of the bar were further demonstrated when other former members of the Order, apparently not affiliated with the group that had maintained itself and therefore unaware of its collective undertaking, volunteered individually to defend Louis in letters to the National Convention, an action that entailed some degree of risk.[15] All of these efforts were in vain, however, for Louis chose Malesherbes as his second counselor.

Not believing that they could adequately prepare the king's defense by the date set for his trial, Tronchet and Malesherbes wrote to the Convention on December 17 asking for a delay of Louis's trial and for the addition of a third counselor, Raymond de Sèze, another former member of the Order. The Convention denied the first request but acceded to the second, and de Sèze, who had withdrawn from practice when the new courts were implemented, emerged from retirement to assist in the king's defense. Due probably to the small amount of time available to him before the trial, de Sèze did not convene the league mentioned by Berryer. Nevertheless, the defense that he prepared and presented to the Convention on December 27 closely paralleled the strategy formulated by the group. Moreover, Garran de Coulon, the only other individual mentioned by Berryer who played a direct role in the trial, adopted precisely the same line of argument. Although Berryer's account cannot be corroborated, his memoirs are considered reliable, and they suggest a greater degree of involvement by the former barristers to the Parlement from Paris than has generally been recognized.[16] More important, the stance adopted by the former barristers to the Parlement put them completely at variance with the new political system represented by the Convention. Whether collectively or individually, virtually all of the remaining members of the Order in practice had arrayed themselves against the Convention in defense of the king. Therefore, when only a few days later loyalty to the new political order became a condition for practicing in the courts, most of the former barristers to the Parlement considered themselves compromised and ultimately withdrew from the courtrooms.

This criterion was imposed on January 26, 1793, when the Convention decreed that a *certificat de civisme* would be required of all avoués and hommes de loi in order to practice in the courts. The law specified that individuals currently exercising the duties of avoué or homme de loi had to provide themselves with a certificat de civisme within two weeks.[17] In Paris, however, the requirement was initially not carried out, and not until the spring of 1794 was it strictly and uniformly enforced. Shortly after the promulgation of the decree, the judges of Paris discussed its implications in their weekly conference. They saw a conflict between the statute and the right of a litigant or defendant to choose freely his counsel; thus, the judges did not believe that the law applied to défenseurs officieux. After considering the issue for several weeks without reaching a solution, the judges concluded that it would be left to each separate court in Paris to decide for itself which categories of individuals should be required to have a certificat de civisme.[18] As a result, enforcement of the provision varied widely. The Tribunal of the Fifth Arrondissement, for example, seems to have been more concerned with carrying out the law than any of the others. In contrast, the Tribunal of the Sixth Arrondissement seems scarcely to have occupied itself with the matter at all. The Tribunal of the Second Arrondissement granted several extensions in an attempt to expedite the administration of justice. As late as 15 nivôse year II (January 4, 1794) confusion still existed over whether a certificat de civisme was required in criminal courts.[19] The inconsistent execution of the law provided many of the former barristers to the Parlement with a respite that allowed them to remain in practice throughout much of 1793. But by late 1793, as enforcement of the provision became more strict, and when one's failure to receive the certificat after application for it could result in being placed on the list of suspects, the former barristers to the Parlement felt more threatened by the statute and retired.[20] Indeed, the Tribunal of the Second Arrondissement complained to the minister of justice that when it started enforcing the decree strictly in October 1793, its sessions were virtually brought to a halt because so few hommes de loi and avoués were able to meet the requirements.[21] Throughout 1793 and 1794 nearly all of the former barristers to the Parlement who had remained in practice, and who had formed the coalition that had sought to continue the memory and standards of the abolished Order, withdrew from the courtrooms altogether.[22]

Although the imposition of the certficat de civisme was the primary cause of the retirement from practice of most of the former avocats au Parlement, the results of the elections ordered by the Convention for the judiciary were doubtlessly a contributing factor as well. The elections began in January 1793 and concluded in April, with results that the former barristers to the Parlement could only have regarded as calamitous. In the elections of 1790 thirty-four of the fifty-four judges and substitute judges chosen in Paris had been former members of the Order, and most of the other men selected had been noted jurists who had seved as deputies in the National Assembly and had particularly distinguished themselves in the course of that body's existence. The presence of so many of their former colleagues on the bench, complemented by the choice of renowned jurists from the provinces who had been legislators, had served to reassure those former barristers to the Parlement who had remained in practice in the new Parisian courts.

In 1793, however, the amended rules for eligibility, by which one did not have to possess a law degree or any legal background, as well as the tension between the Commune and many of the deputies from the departments, served to produce a magistracy of an entirely different complexion. Only five of the fifty-four judges and substitute judges elected were former members of the Order, and the majority of them were not men with notable juristic reputations, but rather men who had become active in municipal politics.

If this was true for the former avocats au Parlement who were elected, it was even more true for most of the rest of the men chosen for the bench, for just as the elections to the Convention marked the triumph of the Commune in the political arena, the elections of 1793 represented its victory in the judicial sphere. There were no deputies from the legislature elected to judgeships. Moreover, the elimination of a background in law as a precondition for election meant that men could be chosen for reasons other than expertise in law, and this was precisely what occurred. The judgeships seem to have been treated as a reward for service to the Commune rather than as a recognition of one's abilities as a jurist. Thus, among those elected as judges in 1793 were Jacques Auvray, a gardener; André Toutin, a sculptor; Jacques François Dalloz, a gem cutter; Jacques François Alix, an engraver; Jean Jacques Lubin fils, a painter; Antoine Jean Jacques Carcenac, a messenger; and Etienne François Belliot, a rent collector. The substitute judges included Guillaume Seminé, a carpenter; Pierre Testard, a wood merchant; Jacques Mathurin Lelievre, a stone carver; Joseph Bodson jeune, a painter and engraver; and Jean Baptiste François Lefebvre, a former hairdresser.[23] A letter written by one of the men elected to a judgeship in the civil courts declining the position is indicative of not only the lack of judicial expertise that was common among the judges, but also the manner in which the judgeships were apparently viewed as spoils. The citizen Champeaux, whose occupation was not listed, wrote the electors to refuse the post, candidly admitting that he was not versed in civil law and did not regard himself qualified to be an effective civil court judge. In turning down the position, however, he hastened to add that he would readily accept a post in the criminal court since, he said, the laws in this area were recent and well known.[24]

Jacques François Dalloz, the gem cutter, is representative of many of the judges who assumed office in 1793. Born in Saint Charles (Jura), he was the son of a shoemaker, a trade that he took up himself at the age of nine. When he was fourteen his father gave him permission to learn the trade of gem cutter, and he continued in this occupation right up to the time he entered his post in the magistracy at the age of forty-six. He had excellent political credentials, claiming to have taken up arms on both July 13, 1789, and August 10, 1792. Shortly after the latter date, he was named commissaire of his section, and one can safely assume that it was his political antecedents that propelled him into judicial office in 1793.[25] To the former avocats au Parlement, who above all viewed themselves as jurists, the prospect of practicing their profession before such men as judges must have seemed totally repugnant, and clearly contributed to their withdrawal from the courts.

The establishment of the Revolutionary Tribunal in March 1793 was an additional, though somewhat less important, factor in the retreat of many of the former barristers to the Parlement from the courts. This was due not merely to its punitive dimension, which directly threatened the former avocats au Parlement in the carrying out of their duties, particularly since most did not possess a certificat de civisme, but also because of its purpose and procedure. The purpose of the Revolutionary Tribunal was to deal solely with political crimes, but these were defined so broadly and vaguely that the jurisdiction of the tribunal could extend over a wide variety of activities.[26] Moreover, its mandate dictated much of its procedure, which ensured that counselors would argue not points of law, but rather political motivation, arguments with which most of the former avocats au Parlement would have been unfamiliar and doubtlessly uncomfortable. It reduced significantly the role of the defense counsel in the proceeding, even before the law of 22 prairial, which will be discussed later in this chapter.[27] Throughout 1793 and 1794, as the Revolutionary Tribunal became the most important court in Paris, most of the former barristers to the Parlement elected not to plead before it. In all, only about six former members of the Order acted as counselors at the Revolutionary Tribunal, and by 1794 most of them were no longer in practice.[28] Since the Revolutionary Tribunal usurped much of the jurisdiction of the criminal court, and with the civil courts an unattractive alternative because of the requirement of a certificat de civisme and because of the results of the elections of 1793, the majority of former barristers to the Parlement saw retirement as essentially the only course open to them.

Above all else, however, the mandate of a certificat de civisme led most of the former avocats au Parlement to retire, and the manner in which the requirement was enforced virtually assured that a transformation would occur among the practitioners in the tribunals. It was applied only to the hommes de loi and the avoués — in short, those with some degree of legal training. It was not applied to the défenseurs officieux, those in whom a litigant or defendant had confidence and most of whom were devoid of any background in law. The rationale behind the policy was that an individual's right to choose his defender should not be abridged; by definition, the défenseur officieux had only his client's interests as his concern. Theoretically, acting as a défenseur officieux was not a vocation, but a generous act for which one could not demand to be paid. The abuses that had occurred since the implementation of the défenseurs officieux demonstrated that the ideal was illusory, but the official view still prevailed in the Revolutionary government of 1793. In contrast, because of their attachment to such vestiges of the Old Regime as their Order and the Parlement, those for whom the practice of law had been a profession were suspect — *mauvais citoyens* was the term used by the Tribunal of the Second Arrondissement to characterize them — and had to have their patriotism certified.[29] Thus, those individuals who possessed legal skills were compelled to retire, while those without any such background went unchallenged. Moreover, this diminution of professional skills was reinforced when the Convention abolished the avoués on 3 brumaire year II (October 24, 1793). Previously, the avoués had been the only practitioners for whom some legal training had been mandated so that procedural uniformity could be maintained in the new judiciary. In

1793, however, the Convention abolished the position of avoué and replaced it with that of *fondé de pouvoir*. Like the défenseur officieux, the fondé de pouvoir could be any individual in whom one had confidence, and, like the défenseur officieux, he could not demand compensation for his services.[30] Since the avoué had been granted the right to plead a case as well as handle its procedural aspects, this prerogative was also passed to the fondé de pouvoir.

While the coalition that had revived the corporate ethos of the profession was disintegrating through the withdrawal from the courts of most of the former avocats au Parlement who had remained in practice, the last tangible sign of the Order's anterior existence was dismantled as well. On July 12, 1793, the Convention ordered that the holdings of the library of the suppressed Order be transferred to the Committee of Legislation of the Convention.[31] Although the library had been impounded in 1791, no disposition had been made of its contents since that time, and just as the Order had been able to continue an unofficial existence from 1791 until 1793, so, too, its library had remained intact and undisturbed during this period. Thus, it was apt that the breakup of the library occurred at the same time that the last traces of the Order in the courtrooms were also disintegrating.

As the former barristers to the Parlement vacated the courtrooms they were replaced by a variety of practitioners, nearly all of whom were devoid of any training in law. Their presence in the tribunals became pervasive, affecting all jurisdictions—the civil and criminal courts as well as the Revolutionary Tribunal. A little known project sponsored by the Jacobin Club of Paris in 1793 is illustrative of the new type of personnel who took up practice at this time. As one of its charitable activities the club founded a "Comité des défenseurs officieux," which had as its purpose "to defend, as much as will be in its power, the interests of all oppressed citizens—fathers of families, widows, orphans, soldiers and in general all sans-culottes." The committee was composed of twenty-seven members who were named by the club, and they were to represent individuals whose cases were accepted by the committee. Ironically, the committee arrogated to itself powers remarkably similar to those of the suppressed Order, including censure and even a manner of disbarment, in the form of expulsion from the committee for failure to carry out one's duties. More important, however, since the Jacobin Club's membership in this era was composed largely of artisans and tradesmen, the existence of the committee served as a conduit to channel inexperienced or unskilled practitioners into the courts.[32]

Incompetence or lack of professional skills were only one dimension of the new situation. Another aspect was the misconduct of many of the new practitioners, a problem particularly acute in the criminal courts. Investigtions of défenseurs officieux by the Committee of Surveillance of the department of Paris in germinal year II (March–April 1794) indicate the problems apparently were widespread. In one case a wine merchant named Billardon had been arrested for adulterating wine, but under questioning the committee discovered that Billardon had had no involvement in preparing the written brief, filled with false statements, that had been filed on his behalf. As a result, the committee ordered that Billardon be set free and summoned the author of the mémoire, a défenseur officieux named Renaud, to explain himself on the matter. Renaud, however, defied the committee and refused to appear before it; moreover, he did not appear in court the next day to defend Billardon.[33] In another instance on 9 germinal year II (March 30, 1794) the committee wrote to the court used for appeals of minor criminal sentences to complain about the conduct in court of several défenseurs officieux. It particularly assailed the unprofessional tone of their pleadings, which it characterized as insulting and sarcastic.[34] On 11 germinal year II (April 1, 1794) the committee wrote to the General Council of the Commune to denounce the actions of a défenseur officieux named Sastuce, whom it accused of distorting facts in his mémoires, and it used the occasion to inveigh against the tone of the arguments of other défenseurs officieux as well.[35] Although the sources are incomplete and cannot be complemented by those of the Commune, it appears that complaints of misconduct became so great that the General Council of the Commune decided to devote a meeting to the censuring of défenseurs officieux from all of the various courts of Paris.[36]

The jurisdiction in which abuses were most rampant, however, was the Revolutionary Tribunal. The desperate plight of the defendants left them vulnerable to exploitation, and the tribunal attracted many unscrupulous individuals as counsel. One account of a trial, though perhaps exceptional, epitomizes the problems of neglect and malfeasance among defenders at the tribunal. On 21 pluviôse year II (February 9, 1794) the tribunal tried eight nuns for maintaining contact with refractory priests and sentenced them to deportation, although Robespierre was overthrown before the deportation could be carried out. Subsequently, one of the nuns, Angelique Françoise Vitasse, wrote a long letter recounting their experience. After they were arraigned, she said, the nuns were promised a defender, but instead they did not speak to anyone for eight days, and no counsel ever appeared. Transferred before the Revolutionary Tribunal for judgment, they were assigned by the judge a defender who happened to be present. According to the nun, not only was the defender unfamiliar with their case, he was also uninterested in it. After the judge questioned all of the nuns, their defense counsel was given permission to speak. He turned upon his clients and said that there was no law severe enough to deal with such individuals, and stated that if they were judged with all the severity of the law it would be an act of justice. Finally, the counsel asked for permission to preach a "republican sermon" to the women, which he did with great vehemence, and concluded by trying to induce them to take the oath and not to be refractory.[37]

Although this incident may have been somewhat atypical,[38] there can be little doubt that the problem of exploitation of prisoners awaiting trial reached grave proportions, for on 28 pluviôse year II (February 16, 1794), when the tribunal announced that the requirement of a certificat de civisme for all defenders would be strictly enforced, it also castigated the défenseurs officieux practicing at the tribunal. "The Tribunal, informed that extortions are being committed against defendants by individuals who, under the pretext of defending them, introduce themselves into the prisons, invites the defenders to supervise themselves, so that by their good renown they will correspond better to the confident expectations of the law, and that at the same time they will more effectively serve the interests of their clients."[39] In the courtrooms of Paris—civil, criminal, and at the Revolutionary Tribunal—such conditions appear to have prevailed in 1793 and 1794. Clearly, the judiciary was profoundly affected by the political turmoil of the period, and it led to a major change in the type of men practicing in the courts. Nearly all remaining members of the abolished Order departed and the courts became the preserve of unlearned and often unscrupulous practitioners.

The profession received yet another major setback when the Convention eliminated all existing law schools in voting to suppress the universities on September 15, 1793. At the Paris law school enrollments had declined steadily since the beginning of the Revolution, and by January 1793 only fifteen students were inscribed there. By April the total had fallen to thirteen, and by July it stood at the incredibly low figure of three.⁴⁰ Thus, in the case of Paris, and doubtlessly elsewhere as well, the closing of the university was essentially a formality, ratifying what was already an established fact. Nevertheless, it posed a long term threat to the profession because it meant that trained legal specialists would no longer be forthcoming.

When the former barristers to the Parlement initially vacated the tribunals, most simply retired to their offices and sought to oversee the interests of their clients. Subsequently, however, such idleness became dangerous, for at a meeting of the General Council of the Commune on 26 germinal year II (April 15, 1794) the national agent of the Commune denounced the défenseurs officieux who had abandoned the courts rather than apply for a certificat de civisme. He said that such individuals ought to be regarded as suspects and suggested that at a later point they should be arrested and interrogated on their conduct.⁴¹ Recognizing the danger of continued inactivity, but still fearful of applying for a certificat de civisme, many of the former barristers to the Parlement began to seek employment that would place them above suspicion and allow them to escape classification as suspects; most assumed positions in the governmental bureaucracy, particularly at the treasury, which did not come under the jurisdiction of the Committee of Public Safety.⁴² These positions gave the former avocats au Parlement a means to deflect suspicion and to appear loyal and patriotic, and Berryer, for one, sought to strengthen this impression by conspicuously attending meetings of his section as well. Moreover, with their government employment as a shield, some of the former barristers to the Parlement covertly attended to the interests of their clients from their offices during their nonworking hours.⁴³

The primacy of political criteria over matters of law had been the principle promulgated by the National Convention when it instituted the certificat de civisme and when it established the Revolutionary Tribunal; both actions had been inimical to the legal profession. In 1794 the doctrine was asserted even more forcefully in Paris, to the further detriment of the profession in the courts. On 17 nivôse year II (January 6, 1794) the Committee of Public Safety arrogated to itself the right to dismiss and appoint judges in all jurisdictions of the department of Paris. Political reliability rather than legal skill became the touchstone of one's tenure on the bench, and the inviolability of judges was once again breached. The precepts had been offensive to the former barristers when they had been enacted previously, and their expansion, affecting all the tribunals of Paris, confirmed the former avocats' belief in the wisdom of their withdrawal from the courts. Furthermore, the ordinance, which was used liberally, led to the displacement of most of the few remaining judges for whom the former barristers had professional regard, especially when Jacques Millet de Gravelle, the president of the Tribunal of the First Arrondissement, was removed along with several other men on 12 messidor year II (June 30, 1794). Millet de Gravelle, a respected former member of the Order, was the only judge elected in 1790 who had taken a seat on the bench after the elections of 1793; the reason given for his dismissal was that he had "always been regarded as a partisan of the monarchical constitution."[44] With few exceptions, it was an accusation that could have been made against the overwhelming majority of the former members of the Order in 1794.

Nowhere is the irreconcilable conflict between the professional values of the former barristers to the Parlement and the exigencies of Revolutionary politics more evident than in the law of 22 prairial year II (June 10, 1794), concerning the Revolutionary Tribunal.[45] After specifying the structure and personnel of the Revolutionary Tribunal, the law defined the tribunal's purpose. It said nothing about the court adjudicating the guilt or innocence of the accused; rather, it proclaimed the Revolutionary Tribunal existed in order to punish enemies of the people. On the question of evidence for conviction, the law accorded "moral" proof the same degree of validity as material proof, and death was the only penalty for those found guilty. It suppressed the preliminary hearing as "superfluous," and witnesses were to be heard only if they could help to expose accomplices. The law entirely forbade legal counsel for the accused, an action that implicitly embraced the belief that the defense of an accused counterrevolutionary was in itself a counterrevolutionary act, and rejected the notion of the barrister as the advocate of his client's point of view. In the final analysis the law denied altogether the legitimacy of the legal profession.

These laws, along with the law of 14 frimaire — often called the "constitution of the Terror" — highlight the evolution of the notion of law during the Terror. Law was no longer regarded as a collection of imprescriptible rights and formal rules to regulate the behavior of autonomous individuals seeking their own ends in society; instead, it was considered an expression of the general will, so that justice could be unhampered by the usual rules of law. In the Revolutionary government of the year II, legal rights were merely a subterfuge utilized by conspirators to contravene the general will, which is why no preliminary examination was necessary, and defense for the accused was explicitly prohibited. The Revolutionary Tribunal, then, was not to be a mediator of differences between the individual and society, but an agency of the general will, punishing those who transgressed it.

A corollary of this rejection of the earlier concept of law was the rejection of the notion of professionalism, for no specialized knowledge was needed to recognize the general will; thus, barristers were bound to be more adversely affected than any other group. Given this changing notion of law, which intensified the already sharp political and philosophical divergences between the Revolutionary government and the former barristers to the Parlement, it is not surprising that many of the former avocats au Parlement came under suspicion during the Terror; its impact on them was severe. In Paris nearly 10 percent of the men who had comprised the Order in 1789 were incarcerated, and proportionately the percentage of those arrested was even higher among those who had remained in practice. Moreover, several more were forced to go into hiding to escape imprisonment.

Many of the former barristers to the Parlement who were arrested were charged with offenses that reflected their attachment to the monarchy and their inability to accept the Revolution after the events of 1792. Similarly, in another manifestation of political dissension, one that revealed the provincial origins of many members of the abolished Order, others were apprehended for federalism.[46]

These accusations merely demonstrated the political disaffection of many of the former avocats au Parlement with the Revolution, and were charges that could have been made against any individual; the fact that those named happened to be former barristers to the Parlement was incidental. In several instances, however, the indictments lodged against former avocats au Parlement were a direct consequence of their profession, and they underscore the unique problems faced by the former barristers to the Parlement during the Terror. The sense of obligation felt by the barrister toward his clients, the blurring of the distinction between counsel and accused—such issues contributed to the antagonism between the former avocats au Parlement and the Revolution. It is in these matters, as well as the law of 22 prairial, that the clash between the professional values of the former barristers to the Parlement and the Convention is evident.

The obligation of the barrister to his client was a point of conflict, particularly where it concerned émigrés, for it is clear that several of the former avocats au Parlement felt a strong sense of responsibility toward their clients who were émigrés. Even at the height of the Terror, for example, Pierre Nicolas Berryer, who was a cautious man, gave shelter to a client who was an émigré. Moreover, underscoring the special problems confronting the former barristers to the Parlement during the Terror, Berryer's continued dealings with his clients in the evenings resulted in a denunciation against him at his post in the treasury. It was only through extraordinary efforts, utilizing the friendship of two members of the Convention whom he had known in his youth, that Berryer was able to have the denunciation retracted.[47] Other former barristers to the Parlement were not as fortunate. Jean Louis Sarradin, for example, was arrested in vendémiaire year II (October 1793) for being in possession of household effects, papers, and silver of the marquis de Chambrai, an émigré, items that Sarradin had apparently moved to his house for safekeeping. Jacques Serpaud moved into the residence of the duc de Montmorency, his client, after Montmorency emigrated. He was charged with and convicted of communicating with Montmorency after Montmorency's emigration, and was executed on 25 frimaire year II (December 15, 1793). Likewise, Julien François Boys, another former member of the Order who was executed on 15 floréal year II (May 4, 1794), also seems to have been convicted of correspondence with émigrés.[48]

Allowing for the fact that émigrés were avowed enemies of the Revolution, such actions or correspondence by the former avocats au Parlement could be regarded as treasonous, and therefore meriting arrest or punishment. Less understandable, and again illustrating the unique problems faced by the former barristers to the Parlement during the Terror, was the fact that simply having been at one time the barrister for a noble or a perceived counterrevolutionary institution could lead to one's arrest, even where no correspondence or communication was alleged. Thus, former avocats au Parlement were sometimes penalized not only by the nature of their profession, but also, on some occasions, for duties performed before the Revolution had even occurred. The basis of the indictment against Jean Godard, for example, centered on the fact that he was "homme de loi and chargé d'affaires for different former nobles."[49] There were no allegations that Godard had been in contact with any émigrés; his offense was simply having had a noble clientele. Similarly, one of the accusations made against François Gorguereau, a distinguished member of the Order under the Old Regime, was that he had been the counsel for the former chapter of Notre Dame; another complaint was that he had associated only with "aristocrats and hommes de loi," a charge that further points up the hostility between the former barristers and the Convention.[50] Alexis Jules Benoît de Bonnières, another noted member of the Order under the Old Regime, was arrested for having been the agent of the comte d'Artois, although again there were no claims that communication had occurred after the latter's emigration.[51]

A further problem was the blurring of the distinction between the barrister and his client. As early as August 29, 1792, Jean Baptiste Vulpian had had seals apposed on his residence because of his position as administrator of the royal estate at St. Cyr.[52] During the Terror the tendency to obscure the division between the barrister and his client became more pronounced. On 19 vendémiaire year II (October 11, 1793), the Committee of General Security ordered that Raymond de Sèze be arrested and seals placed on his papers so that they could be examined. As his wife pointed out in several petitions, the only justification offered for his arrest was as a measure of general security, yet he was not in violation of any of the provisions of the law of September 17, 1793 (the Law of Suspects). The inescapable conclusion was that he had been arrested solely because of his defense of Louis XVI.[53] The arrest order for Claude François Chauveau-Lagarde and Guillaume Alexandre Tronson-Ducoudray was more explicit. It stated that immediately after the judgment of Marie Antoinette, for whom they were the defenders, they were to be arrested, interrogated separately and provisionally imprisoned at the Luxembourg prison. The questioning of Chauveau-Lagarde shows that the Revolutionary authorities perceived an incompatibility between being a "citizen" and being a "défenseur officieux"; the clear assumption of the interrogators was that a defender was not the advocate of his client's position, but virtually a collaborator with the accused.[54.] Even after this episode, Chauveau-Lagarde continued to practice at the Revolutionary Tribunal following his release, much to the admiration of his former colleagues. In a letter written in germinal year II (April 1794) to the judges there, he complained about the imputation attached to individuals who practiced as defenders at the Revolutionary Tribunal. In a passage that once again reflects the obscuring of the distinction between counsel and accused, he deplored the fact that simply being a défenseur officieux at the Revolutionary Tribunal was sufficient to raise suspicion and anger in patriots. He asserted the demarcation between himself and his clients, and pointedly closed his letter by reminding them that "I perform, *as a citizen*, my duties of defender." But his protestations were in vain, for he was arrested again and released only after 9 thermidor.[55]

It was complications such as these, difficulties specific to the profession of barrister, as well as the degree of political involvement by members of the profession, that account for the severe impact of the Terror on the legal profession.[56] Ultimately, eleven former members of the Order, including Claude Nicolas Collet at Lyon, were executed during the course of the Terror. Nine were executed for counterrevolutionary acts, while two, both of whom had been active in municipal politics and had become judges in Paris in 1793, were condemned after 9 thermidor for being associates of Robespierre.[57] In addition to those arrested or executed, many other former avocats au Parlement went into hiding or withdrew from Paris.[58]

Other former members of the Order, unable to withstand the fear and tension produced by the Terror, elected to emigrate. The state of the sources, particularly the frequent absence of such corroborating evidence as addresses, first names, or vocations, makes it impossible to calculate the exact number of former members of the Order who emigrated. Also, the lists are not always reliable, so that inclusion on the list did not necessarily mean that the individual had emigrated; moreover, the reverse was true — many of those who emigrated were not included on the various lists.[59] It is with these provisos in mind that the following information must be considered. Probable émigrés from the Order were Joseph Simon Godineau de Villechenay, Jacques Parisot, and Claude Jacques Vautrin. Possible émigrés include François Joseph Maugue-Massis, Jean Pierre Siméon, Charles Boursault de Troncay, and Denis Foisy de Tremont.[60] In all likelihood, however, the extent of emigration was greater than these figures suggest. Although Greer's classification encompassisng barristers is extremely broad, his research indicates that professional men, especially lawyers and magistrates, comprised one of the largest categories of non-noble émigrés.[61] The factors that caused the arrest of many former avocats au Parlement, and led a considerable number of others to go into hiding, could also be expected to have induced others to emigrate, and since the number of individuals who emigrated greatly exceeded the number of persons who were executed, it is probable that the number of men from the abolished Order who emigrated would have been equal to, or even greater than, the number executed.

The Terror completely intimidated the former avocats au Parlement. Whether by compelling them to seek refuge in the bureaucracy, whether through imprisonment or execution, whether by inducing them to go into hiding or to emigrate, the effect of the Terror was to obliterate entirely the bonds and contacts that had been maintained after the aboliton of the Order. Few, if any, of the former avocats au Parlement remained in practice, so that by mid-1794 the Order, even in the unofficial coalition maintained after its statutory abolition in 1790, was extinct.

The overthrow of Robespierre brought some relief. Many of the former barristers to the Parlement who had been arrested were released in the weeks after thermidor, and those who had been in hiding slowly began to reemerge. Several of the judges who had been elected in 1793 were replaced by the Committee of Public Safety during this time.[62] On 23 thermidor year II (August 10, 1794), the Convention repealed the law of 22 prairial, thus restoring counsel to the accused. On 7 fructidor year II (August 24, 1794), the administration of justice in Paris was removed from the Committee of Public Safety and vested with the Committee of Legislation of the Convention. In addition, a decree of 7 vendémiaire year III (September 28, 1794) ordered that all courts would be renewed before 1 brumaire (October 22, 1794). And the law of 8 nivôse year III (December 28, 1794) reorganized the Revolutionary Tribunal and promulgated a strict legal procedure for it.[63]

These developments, which the former barristers to the Parlement could only have welcomed, seemed to indicate an amelioration of the conflict between the Convention and the legal profession that had characterized the Terror. The changes, however, were not sufficient to persuade most of the former avocats au Parlement to resume practice. The political climate remained uncertain. The maintenance of the Revoultionary Tribunal, "an institution for the achievement of the revolutionary purpose and not as a court for the administration of law and justice as ordinary social necessities,"[64] represented not only a lingering political threat to the former barristers to the Parlement, but also, despite the new procedures, an affront to their professional values. Moreover, the requirement of a certificat de civisme to practice in the courts remained. Such factors led the majority of the former avocats au Parlement to persist in their caution and to refrain from returning to the courts. The process of regroupment began, slowly and hesitantly, only in 1795.

5 / Regroupment: 1795–1799

> We observe, however, that it was impossible for us to put in the entry on the men of law the names of all those who wrote to us on this subject; the vast amount of names that reached us would have obliged us to create a volume on this entry alone. Finding ourselves in this difficulty, we examined the registers of the tribunals and have put in our list only those indicated to us as practicing in a publicly-known manner the duties of attorneys or of défenseurs officieux.
>
> *Almanach des Tribunaux pour l'an VI de la république*

The experience of the Terror had deeply shaken the former avocats au Parlement, and few were anxious to return to practice. Despite additional actions by the Convention that they could only have viewed favorably, most of the former barristers to the Parlement continued to avoid the courtrooms. Not until late 1795, after the Convention had disbanded, did they begin to regroup, and the process was slow and difficult. The profession was almost completely dominated by untrained practitioners. Just as they had done in 1791–92, the former avocats au Parlement revived the corporate configuration of the profession and associated only with individuals whom they respected on the basis of credentials, integrity, and ability. By 1799 the former barristers to the Parlement had largely recovered from the effects of the Terror and had once again succeeded in organizing themselves in an unofficial fashion.

One of the actions taken by the Convention in the weeks after thermidor had been a declaration that all judicial personnel would be renewed by 1 brumaire year III (October 22, 1794); the Convention failed to meet this deadline, however, and did not implement the measure in Paris until several months later. On 14 nivôse year III (January 3, 1795), the Committee of Legislation revamped the membership of the Paris judiciary. The new composition of the courts must have encouraged the former avocats au Parlement, for the appointments seemed not only to reaffirm juridic ability as a major criterion for holding office, but also signified a genuine change in the political climate. Among those removed from judgeships were Jacques Dalloz, a gem cutter; André Toutin, a sculptor; Jacques Auvray, a gardener; and most of the other men who had been elected in 1793. In their place the committee appointed many former barristers to the Parlement—in the civil courts fifteen of the thirty judges, eight of the twenty-four substitute judges, and four of the six commissaires nationaux selected were former members of the Order. In the criminal court three of the seven individuals appointed, including the president, one of the two vice-presidents, and the prosecutor were former barristers to the Parlement.[1] Not all of them accepted their nomination,[2] but most did, so that the former avocats au Parlement once again emerged as an important element in the judiciary. Moreover, several of the nominations indicated a tempering of the political climate. Target, for example, was named to a judgeship even though his name was mistakenly carried on the list of émigrés; shortly after his appointment he successfully petitioned the departmental authorities to have his name removed.[3] Similarly, some of the other former avocats au Parlement placed in judicial posts were individuals who had been arrested during the Terror.[4]

The dissolution of the Revolutionary Tribunal on 12 prairial year III (May 31, 1795) was another sign that important political changes were taking place, and was a measure that the former barristers to the Parlement could only have welcomed. From the beginning, the tribunal's purpose and values had been repugnant to the former avocats au Parlement. Its suppression indicated that justice would be dispensed through regular courts, and that, as a result, cases would be decided on points of law rather than on political considerations.

These developments, as substantial as they were, led only a very small number of former avocats au Parlement to return to the courtrooms; most chose not to resume practice. There were several reasons for this. The experience of the Terror was still vivid, and some events of the year III were reminiscent of episodes that had occurred in 1793 and 1794. The political jostling in the Convention that resulted in the arrest of numerous deputies, most notably Billaud-Varennes and Collot d'Herbois, doubtlessly evoked memories of the factionalism of the year II. For many of the former barristers, it may have seemed to presage further political instability and possibly even a revival of the Terror. Moreover, the establishment of a military commission to try suspects after the uprising of prairial recalled the creation of the Revolutionary

Tribunal, for it sharply deviated from past practice and almost certainly weakened the effect of the Revoutionary Tribunal's abolition only a few days later. Finally, there were severe problems with the nature of many of the practitioners in the courts. When the Convention at the end of the year III moved against suspected participants in the September massacres of 1792, for example, at least one of the individuals accused of active involvement in them was practicing as a défenseur officieux.[5]

Under such conditions, most of the former barristers to the Parlement still preferred to enter or to remain in the bureaucracy rather than face the uncertainties and difficulties of practicing in the courts, although many assumed or sought positions that would enable them to put to use their legal expertise. The agency that was best suited to this objective was the Committee of Legislation of the National Convention, which was working on the preparation of a new civil law code, and once again professional bonds from the abolished Order, through the assistance of a former member of the Order on the committee, Jean Philippe Garran-Coulon, helped them. After completing his law studies at the University of Orléans, Garran-Coulon had become a member of the Order in 1775. In 1789 he embarked upon what was already by 1792 a noteworthy political and judicial career. In 1789 he had been an elector and an alternate deputy fom Paris to the Estates-General, and in 1790 he had become a member of the General Council of the Commune. In December 1790 he had been elected by his native department, the Deux-Sèvres, to the Tribunal de cassation. In 1791 he had been selected as a deputy for Paris to the Legislative Assembly, and in 1792 the department of the Loiret elected him to the National Convention, in which he served on the Committee of Legislation. Unlike most of the former avocats au Parlement who took up political pursuits, however, Garran-Coulon seems to have maintained contact with his former colleagues who remained in the profession. In 1793, after the impeachment of Marat, he confined himself largely to matters concerning the Committee of Legislation and became quite influential there.[6] In a phenomenon that recalls Duport-Dutertre's actions at the Ministry of Justice in 1790–91, Garran-Coulon appears to have used his position to place former members of the Order on the staff of the committee. He was assisted in this endeavor by Jean Guillaume Locré, another former member of the Order, who became general secretary of the Committee of Legislation after thermidor, as well as by Claude

Antoine Guyot-Desherbiers, also a former member of the Order, who became general director of the administrative and judicial sections of the committee.[7] Overall, during the year III several former avocats au Parlement secured posts with the Committee of Legislation. Several other former members of the Order applied for positions with the committee in the year III; although they were unsuccessful, their effort further reflects the preference of most of the former barristers to the Parlement to use their skills elsewhere than in the courts.[8] Some of the former barristers to the Parlement who had taken refuge in the bureaucracy in 1793 were beginning to advance to more important places in their organizations and were content to remain there until the uncertainties of resuming practice in the courts were resolved.[9]

Only at the beginning of the year IV (September–October 1795), at the time of the disbanding of the Convention and the installation of the Directory, did the former avocats au Parlement begin to resume practice. One reason appears to have been the suppression, on 1 ventôse year III (February 19, 1795), of the revolutionary committees in Paris. In particular, the abolition of certificats de civisme on 18 thermidor year III (August 5, 1795) encouraged several of the former barristers to the Parlement to reappear in the courts. Furthermore, the Directory redefined the notion of law yet again, aligning it more closely with the concept held during the years 1789–1791. In the initial stages of the Revolution law had been the instrument for achieving equity and the unifying value of the common good; at the outset, the Directory attempted to revert to a similar principle. Where from 1789 to 1791 the ideal of law had been elevated in opposition to privilege, in 1795 it was asserted not merely against privilege, but especially against Jacobin arbitrariness. To deal with the recent legacy of disunion and discord, the Directory sought to implement the rule of law; law and ordinary judicial institutions, rather than extraordinary measures, would be utilized to redress grievances. Thus, the Directory initially accorded law and legality a primacy that may have lured some of the former avocats au Parlement back to the courtrooms.[10]

Those who initially reappeared were for the most part the younger barristers who had remained with the profession after its abolition in 1790—Bellart, Berryer, Bonnet, Chauveau-Lagarde, and others. In 1791 and 1792, before the dispersion caused by the Terror, the former barristers to the Parlement had sought to preserve the corporate framework of the abolished Order by observing its unwritten regulations and by associating only with individuals who would adhere to them, and they again took this as their touchstone in 1795 as they attempted to reestablish the spirit of the Order. In 1795 their task was much more difficult, however, because of the predominance of large numbers of untrained men in the profession; as they began to regroup, the former avocats au Parlement constituted only a small percentage of the practitioners in the courts. In the year V (1796–97), the first year after the Terror in which the *Almanach National* published a list of hommes de loi, only 19 of the 304 men listed as practicing in the courts of Paris had formerly been associated with the Order. Similarly, at the Tribunal de cassation, only 7 of the 113 hommes de loi whose names were published were former members of the Order. Not all of those who took up practice after 1791 were untrained or unethical, of course, but a large number of them were, and the desire to drive the unqualified and unethical practitioners out of their profession infused the former avocats au Parlement with a sense of purpose as they began the rebuilding process.[11]

Various developments reinforced the effort of the younger barristers to the Parlement to rejuvenate the Order once again on an unofficial basis. One was the gradual return to the profession of several senior and distinguished former avocats au Parlement who had been particularly prominent before 1790. Honoré Marie Nicolas Duveyrier, for example, returned to Paris from Copenhagen, where he had taken refuge during the Terror, and resumed the practice of law. Two especially important figures were Gaspard Gilbert Delamalle and François Placide Nicolas Ferey, both of whom had been particularly respected members of the Order under the Old Regime. Their rejoining of the profession during this era inspired the younger barristers and provided an additional impetus for the regeneration of the Order.[12] Most of the senior former avocats au Parlement limited themselves to consultations or other similar duties that did not require an appearance in the courtrooms, but their joining of the coalition of former barristers to the Parlement was critical in rallying members of the abolished Order.

A second factor was the dissolution of the Convention and the establishment of the Directory. In planning the transition from the Convention to the Directory, the Convention decreed that two-thirds of the deputies in the new legislative bodies had to be drawn from its membership. Of the one-third who were not elected or chosen by their former colleagues for a seat in the councils, several chose to practice law in Paris. In subsequent elections under the Directory other deputies who were not reelected followed the same of course of action. Many of them had been renowned barristers in their departments before they had undertaken their legislative duties, and the former avocats au Parlement in Paris, seeking to segregate themselves entirely from the unlearned or unsavory elements in their profession, gladly accepted them as associates.[13] For their part, many of the ex-deputies were appalled by the conditions that they found at the Paris bar, and they welcomed the opportunity to affiliate with the former members of the Order. The comments of Thibaudeau, who left the Council of Five Hundred when he was not reelected in the year VI and decided to remain in Paris to practice law, are illustrative. After speaking of the difficulty of resuming his legal career after a hiatus of eight years, he said:

> It was not only a matter of different times and different circumstances; but the bar, renowned for its great talents, noble courage and glorious memories, had fallen into a state of degradation. These companies of barristers, inviolable sanctuaries of learning, of integrity, of independence and honor, had been replaced by a mob of défenseurs officieux who, born in anarchy, without schooling and without degrees, took advantage of freedom to overrun access to the courts and to profane the sanctuary of justice. Beside Bonnet, Bellart or Berrier [sic] and a score of other worthy names, one saw a horde of unknown men who would argue over clients with disgusting greed; next to Cambacérès, Tronchet and Ferrey [sic], men who had no understanding of law had the audacity to establish themselves of their own accord and to give themselves the title of jurisconsultes. The profession of barrister was not confined, as it had been formerly, to consulting in one's office and pleading in the Palais; it greedily embraced anything that could produce money: removing names from the lists of émigrés, liquidations, the solicitation of jobs, pardons or favors. The défenseurs officieux, jurisconsultes or hommes de loi were agents and brokers; they pursued profit and scorned glory; they went through the streets at full speed in their cabs to go from the Directory to the home of ministers, from the Palais to the Bourse. Under the name Cabinet d'affaires they formed societies, they had offices, clerks, bookkeepers, cashiers; they exploited legal proceedings as if they were a branch of commerce, and it was not rare to hear it said: Monsieur such and such, jurisconsulte, has gone bankrupt.[14]

Although for most of these men the resumption of their legal career was a merely temporary phenomenon, they at least brought to it many of the same notions on the practice of the profession as the former avocats au Parlement.[15] The prospect of having such men as colleagues encouraged some former barristers to the Parlement to return to the courts, and thereby facilitated the informal reconstitution of the abolished Order. Moreover, the appearance of these individuals at the Paris bar provided the former barristers to the Parlement with contacts that would later be beneficial under the Empire, when many of the ex-deputies went back to public duties. Some of the men with whom the former avocats au Parlement came into association during this era were Cambacérès, Portalis, who became a member of the Council of State and minister of cults, Muraire, Regnault de Saint-Jean d' Angély, and Thibaudeau, all of whom became members of the Council of State.[16]

Another factor that contributed to the renovation of the remnants of the Order was the judicial reorganization implemented with the Constitution of the Year III, which established the Directory. In place of the district courts set up by the Constitution of 1791, the Constitution of the Year III created only one civil court per department. This particularly benefited the former avocats au Parlement at Paris, who had previously had to practice in six courts dispersed throughout Paris. The consolidation of civil and criminal courts into one location at the Palais de Justice allowed the former barristers to the Parlement to consort with one another more easily, thereby facilitating the process of regroupment.

The men who used the inauguration of the Directory to resume practice nevertheless represented only a small portion even of the former barristers to the Parlement who had remained in the profession ofter 1790. Several others, particularly those who held positions that allowed them to utilize their legal expertise, did not return to the courts. Many of those who had been with the Committee of Legislation, for example, transferred to the newly reestablished Ministry of Justice.[17] The men at the Ministry of Justice are especially significant, for they appear to have supplemented in another realm the regroupment of the former members of the Order. They worked closely with the minister of justice,[18] and seem to have used their influence to secure the appointment of former colleagues to judicial positions, thus sustaining the gains made by the former avocats au Parlement in the judiciary of Paris in early 1795. The law of 25 brumaire year IV (November 16, 1795) authorized the Directory to name individuals to administrative and judicial posts in departments where the electoral assembly had not completed the nominations within the period prescribed by the constitution. The appointment was valid until the next scheduled election, and the Directory used this power extensively. Although the evidence is not conclusive, it seems virtually certain that there was a deliberate effort made to name former members of the Order to judicial posts. Many of the men named to judgeships and ministerial positions in Paris by the Directory in frimaire year IV (November 1795) were former avocats au Parlement, and subsequent designations included several others as well. Even more indicative, however, is the fact that in outlying departments also, where their presence was far less pervasive, former members of the Order were often selected for judicial positions.[19]

The former barristers to the Parlement were desirable candidates for the Directory, not only because they were able jurists who could bring proficiency to the judiciary, but also because they could be expected to accord a primacy to law. The attempt by the Directory to reestablish competence in the judiciary complemented the efforts of the former avocats au Parlement to regenerate their profession. Just as the election of many colleagues to judgeships in 1790 had led several former avocats au Parlement in Paris to practice in the new courts, so, too, in 1795 the appearance of many former colleagues as judges could only have encouraged the former barristers to the Parlement who were regrouping. In addition, the general resurgence of right-wing opposition to the Directory also seems to have aided their revival, for there can be little doubt that the former barristers found the growing royalist and monarchist environment of the First Directory far more agreeable than the feverish political atmosphere of the Terror or the uncertainty of the Thermidorean era. Indeed, the impetus initially provided by the appointments of January and November 1795 was maintained in the elections of the year V, which were an overwhelming success for those opposed to the government, particularly in Paris. The elections, the first judicial elections in Paris since those of 1793 that had proven so calamitous to the former barristers to the Parlement, were propitious for them. Three of the five men elected to the criminal court, including the president and vice-president, were former barristers to the Parlement, and more than one-third of the judges chosen for the civil court had been members of the Order in 1789.[20] Although this proportion, particularly in the civil court, was not as favorable as that of 1790, it was a significant recovery from the debacle of 1793, and the elections enabled the reemergence of former barristers to the Parlement to proceed in the sphere of both the bench and the bar.

In addition to the civil and criminal courts, several former avocats au Parlement also received positions at the Tribunal de cassation. This court had been exempted from the renewal mandated for the judiciary in 1793 by the Convention, so that there had been far less disruption in it than in other jurisdictions. Gilles Boucher de la Richarderie, for instance, a former member of the Order who had been elected as a judge in 1791, remained in that post until the year VI, when he was not reelected.[21] Since the Tribunal de cassation had experienced less dislocation than many other courts, most men were willing to accept a position there, and under the Directory the Tribunal de cassation became a channel for some of the former avocats au Parlement to reestablish themselves in the field of law. The example of Laurent Jean Babille is representative. He had been judge in the Tribunal of the First Arrondissement in 1791 but had not been reelected in 1793. He subsequently assumed a position in the Ministry of the Interior, where he remained until he was elected to a judgeship in the Tribunal de cassation by the department of the Golo in the year IV. Its relative stability also made it attractive to many of the former barristers to the Parlement who returned to practice. Several resumed their career there exclusively and remained out of the civil and criminal courts of Paris.[22] Throughout the Directory, many former members of the Order maintained or received, either through election or appointment, places at the Tribunal de cassation. It became a focal point for the reintegration of numerous former avocats au Parlement into the realm of jurisprudence, both as judges and as practitioners.

Another channel through which a few of the former barristers to the Parlement sought to reestablish or maintain contact with their original profession was through the central schools (*écoles centrales*), which were institutions of secondary education. The Convention had authorized their establishment in the law of 7 ventôse year III (February 25, 1795), but the law of 3 brumaire year IV (October 25, 1795) — passed the day before the Convention disbanded — provided the real impetus for their implementation. The law provided for the founding of one école centrale in every department and prescribed its curriculum, which included a course in legislation.[23] The purpose of the course in legislation was never made clear, however, and as a result its content varied widely from school to school. Some professors defined it in terms of politics and legislation, with a focus on ordinary statutes or the Constitution of the Year III, while others viewed it as a forum for professional instruction in the absence of schools of law. During the Directory several former avocats au Parlement taught a course in legislation in schools both in Paris and in outlying departments.[24] The best example of the manner in which a post in a central school could serve as a passage back into the field of law is that of Pierre Paul Nicolas Henrion de Pansey. Henrion de Pansey, a specialist in feudal law, had been one of the most renowned members of the Order under the Old Regime. In 1790 he retired from practice, left Paris, and subsequently was elected procureur syndic of the district of Joinville (Haute-Marne). In hiding during most of the Terror, he was appointed president of the administration of the Haute-Marne by the Directory in the year IV. In the year V he returned tangentially to his initial profession when he became the instructor for the course of legislation in the central school of the Haute-Marne, almost certainly his first involvement with jurisprudence since his retirement. Later, under the Consulate, he was named to the Tribunal de cassation, where he enjoyed a distinguished career and reaffirmed his reputation as one of the most brilliant jurists in all of France.[25]

For various reasons the courses in legislation attracted few students. The vague nature of the course made it extremely unpopular. Some parents believed that the course was designed for political indoctrination and regarded it with suspicion. And it must be remembered that legal training was not necessary to practice law, so that in 1798 and 1799 there were several departments in which there were no students whatsoever enrolled in the course of legislation.[26] Nonetheless, throughout the Directory, the central schools were the sole institutions that offered any sort of legal education, even though it was only at a secondary level.

For those former barristers to the Parlement who returned to the profession by actually resuming practice in the courts, conditions were forbidding. The administration of justice was in complete disarray. The demands of ancillary duties, deaths, resignations, and purges by the Directory often left the tribunals in a state in which they could barely operate. In pluviôse year IV (February 1796), for example, only twenty-eight of the forty-eight judges in the civil court of Paris were available for duty, so that the dispensation of civil justice was seriously impaired. After several months the Directory was still unable to resolve the situation, and in fructidor year IV (September 1796) it simply advised the court to attempt to function with a truncated contingent of judges.[27] In the criminal sphere as well the administration of justice was seriously disrupted.[28] Moreover, even when the courts were able to hold session, the hearing could be quite disorganized. The *Gazette des Nouveaux Tribunaux* recounted with some amusement an episode that involved a former member of the Order, Pierre François Leprestre-Boisderville. In connection with a case with which he was charged, Leprestre-Boisderville, as was customary, exchanged dossiers with the homme de loi against whom he was pleading. On the day of the audience Leprestre-Boisderville mistakenly returned to his colleague his own client's dossier and kept that of his adversary's, and as a consequence argued the latter's case rather than his own. Following Leprestre-Boisderville's presentation, the opposing homme de loi simply stood and announced that he agreed with everything that had just been said. Confused, Leprestre-Boisderville asked his adversary what he meant by this, and was astonished to learn that he had pleaded the wrong case. He quickly recovered, however, and stated that he was now going to plead his own. He then began to argue his suit, and of course contradicted all of the arguments that he had just made. Ultimately, the court decided in favor of his client.[29] Besides the obvious humor of the situation, the incident had an additional significance. In an era of political instability the likelihood of maintaining a stable and dignified judicial system was remote, as the case demonstrates; also apparent is how far removed the proceedings of the new judicial system were from the dignified and stately ceremonies of the Parlement. Thus, it served to underscore for the former avocats au Parlement the reduced condition of their profession.

The Constitution of the Year III established a new system of appeal and presented the former barristers to the Parlement who returned to practice with another change. Although the new constitution consolidated the various district courts into one tribunal per department, it maintained the single degree of jurisdiction. Therefore, instead of the appeal court being one of the adjoining district courts in the department, or, in Paris, one of the district courts within the city, it was the tribunal of one of three neighboring departments that became the court of appeal. One never knew in advance, however, which court would be the court of appeal because of the process of selection. The appellant first rejected the court that he thought would be least sympathetic to his case, and the defendant in his turn did the same. Whichever court remained became the court of appeal. For Paris, the three tribunals designated as courts of appeal were those of the Seine-et-Oise at Versailles, the Seine-et-Marne at Melun, and the Eure-et-Loire at

Chartres. The necessity of often having to journey as far as Melun or Chartres was burdensome, and most of the former avocats au Parlement considered the system exacting, believing that the obligatory travel reduced the time that they could devote to preparing a case, and that the fatigue caused by the trips made them less effective in court.[30] In addition to such narrowly professional considerations there was an additional reason why many of the former barristers to the Parlement were so averse to this method of appeal: they viewed the system as an impediment to the possible reinstitution of the Order because the unpredictability of the appeals court meant that companies of barristers could not be established at fixed sites. For the entire period of the Directory, then, the former barristers to the Parlement resented the structure of the judiciary not only because of the trips it imposed upon them, but also because they considered it an obstacle to the reestablishment of their Order.[31]

The most widespread and refractory problem confronting the former avocats au Parlement who began to practice again was the character of many of the practitioners in the courts. Corruption and lack of competency were rampant among the défenseurs officieux and hommes de loi, and outrage at their actions was general and not confined merely to former members of the Order. Mercier, for example, who had not been a member of the Order of Barristers under the Old Regime, was thoroughly disgusted with their conduct.[32] Another observer, Jean Baptiste Pujoulx, also denounced the hommes de loi in the bitterest of terms: "They have replaced the attorneys and the barristers, but these were only schoolboys in the art of fleecing their clients. A suit today costs double what it cost formerly, and the cases drag out longer . . . One ought to leave to these vultures the long robe that enveloped them; since they no longer have it I see only their claws."[33] The former barristers to the Parlement found the presence of such unprincipled men exasperating, and they defined themselves in opposition to them. They derisively termed the unscrupulous practitioners *avocats de prison* because of their habit of soliciting cases in the prisons, and one of their constant aims was to expel such men from the profession. At the same time, as part of their attempt to rebuild the Order, they sought to assimilate men whom they believed would make worthy colleagues.[34] Jacques Quesnel exemplifies the men incorporated into the group of former avocats au Parlement during this era. After completing his education at the Collège d'Harcourt, he worked for several years as a clerk in the office of different procureurs and notaires in Paris. He subsequently enrolled in the law school and was taking courses there when the Revolution began, but the schools of law closed before he received his degree. He continued to study law independently and took up practice in the courts of Paris in the year VI when, at the age of twenty-seven, he affiliated himself with the coalition of former avocats au Parlement.[35] A retrospective reading of the tableau of 1811, however, shows that there were few such individuals among the practitioners under the Directory. Although there were hundreds of men in practice during this era, the former avocats au Parlement received only two men in 1795, one in 1796, four in 1797, six in 1798, and two in 1799 before the Directory was overthrown.[36] While not all non–former members of the Order were corrupt, it is nonetheless clear that untrained practitioners were predominant and that this predominance compounded the frustration resulting from the unreliability of the judicial system. Clearly, the political role of the minister of justice in persecuting the regime's opponents must be recognized as a factor, but it may also be a measure of indignation that police reports from Paris during the Directory mention the minister of justice as being the most hated minister of government in public opinion.[37]

The task of reforming the profession and of regaining public confidence was a formidable one, and one well beyond the abilities of the former avocats au Parlement alone, particularly since they were so heavily outnumbered by the unqualified men in practice. The problem was of such great dimensions that truly effective action could only come from the government. In fact, a Parisian justice of the peace, François Laurent, an homme de loi who had not been a member of the Order in 1789, appealed to the Council of Five Hundred to rectify the situation in the courts. He praised the judicial reforms of 1790 as well intentioned but asserted that they had led only to "chaos and disarray." Concerned that only a few members of the Council of Five Hundred were aware of the condition of the courts, he sought to apprise the legislators of it and appealed to them to correct it:

The learned man, the honest man has been mixed with the ignorant and the crooked; a mass of individuals without skills, scorned or always rejected at the bar, have dared to present themselves in order to undertake the defense of their fellow citizens; in short, this calling [état] of defender, formerly so respected, has fallen into disgrace, whether by incompetence or whether by the lack of integrity by the majority of those who have encroached upon it.

It is time for this abuse to stop, it is time that a citizen be able to claim his rights without running the risk of becoming the victim of greed and inexperience; it is up to you, citizen representatives, to put an end to this anarchy and to restore order into this vital part of judicial administration.[38]

The government was not entirely insensitive to the situation. As early as 22 frimaire year IV (December 14, 1795), it had ordered an investigation into the abuses of the practitioners in the courts. Its purpose had been to stem acts of extortion by the practitioners and to encourage victims to attempt to recover some of the sums that they had paid to them.[39] This endeavor does not appear to have come to fruition, however, and it did little to ameliorate the situation. Prosecution of the war effort and the matter of its own political survival were more urgent undertakings for the Directory, and it was not until the year VI, as part of a larger project on civil justice, that the Council of Five Hundred began to treat the problems of the hommes de loi. The debates merit a brief examination, both because they confirm the parlous state of the courts and because of the issue that was of greatest importance to the legislators.

Debate began on 21 vendémiaire year VI (October 12, 1797), with the presentation of a project to the Council of Five Hundred for the reestablishment of avoués.[40] Charles François Oudot introduced it by noting that there was widespread indignation against the activities of many of the men practicing law in the courtrooms. He argued that the establishment of only one tribunal per department meant that some litigants from more remote areas of a department had to travel a considerable distance for their case; as a result, they could not know the integrity of the various men in practice at the court and ran the risk of being defrauded or extorted. Oudot contended that it was the duty of the government to protect litigants against incompetence and greed.[41] His legislation therefore proposed that the local authorities designate a limited number of men of integrity and ability to manage litigation. In fact, the bill made the retention of an avoué mandatory for a case to be processed. It is clear from Oudot's presentation, and from the response to his project, that the avoués were to handle both the procedural and juristic aspects of a case, and that they were to be the sole practitioners in the courts. There would not be, as there had been in 1791, a distinction between avoués and hommes de loi.

Reaction to Oudot's proposal varied. On the one hand, some legislators were quite sympathetic to the plight of the former barristers. The deputy François Marie Joseph Riou, for example, maintained that it was important to encourage former avocats to return to the courts. He feared that the title *avoué* would discourage former barristers from resuming practice, however, because they would conceive the title in its narrower 1791 definition and therefore equate it with the Old Regime post of procureur. Accordingly, on 5 brumaire year VI (October 26, 1797) Riou introduced a project of his own which, among other things, substituted the term *légiste* for *avoué*.[42] Similarly, the deputy Bernard Laujac sought to define the position of avoué in a manner that tended to favor former avocats.[43]

On the other hand, the notion of regulating the profession aroused intense opposition in the council, although the deputies who took a stand against the proposed statute did not dispute the fact that there was a serious problem in the courtrooms. Alexis François Pison du Galand, for example, acknowledged that it was absolutely necessary "to purge the tribunals of the ignorant vampires who dishonor them," but he warned the council that in seeking to abolish one abuse it should not give rise to a greater one. The greater abuse to which Pison du Galand alluded — and the focal point of most of the resistance to the bill — was the specter of a privileged corporation once again arising. To Pison du Galand and others, limiting and designating who could practice in the courts, as well as making their retention mandatory, not only deprived a citizen of the right to defend his own case, but also amounted to the creation of a privileged corporation. Indeed, Pison du Galand stated flatly that the project offered by Oudot recalled the corporations of avocats and procureurs.[44] The proponents of the legislation realized that this was a critical issue and sought to minimize it, but with little success. Laujac, to give but one example, contended that the statute would not create a corporation because the avoués would not have any financial prestation.[45] Pison du Galand introduced his own bill in frimaire year VI (December 1797), and it was voted priority over that of Oudot, which was retired.[46] The new measure did not limit the number of individuals who could practice and mandated merely that a candidate be twenty-one years of age, that he pass an examination, and that the fees of the practitioners be set to prevent abuses. In addition, a citizen would be permitted to handle a case himself and would not be required to employ an avoué.

Even this revised and more limited legislation encountered resistance in the council. Joseph François Beytz, while admitting that Pison du Galand's plan required few formalities, claimed that it still allowed the existence of a potentially privileged corporation. Beytz asserted that avoués accredited through the examination process would be demarcated from the ordinary citizen, and would therefore have a distinct, corporate identity, and insisted that such a development must not be tolerated.[47]

Despite such objections, the Council of Five Hundred ultimately forwarded the bill to the Council of Ancients, where it came up for consideration in ventôse year VI (February–March 1798), with the deputy Claude Ambroise Regnier reporting it from committee.[48] Like the adversaries of the legislation in the Council of Five Hundred, Regnier acknowledged the desire of the public to see the situation in the courts corrected. Nonetheless, Regnier, in the name of the committee, recommended disapproval of the statute because it ratified the establishment of a privileged corporation. In fact, Regnier felt so strongly about the matter that even when the bill's defeat was clear, he published independently of the committee an additional pamphlet attacking the measure for this reason. Although a few other minor issues emerged, it was this one that was decisive. On 16 germinal year VI (April 5, 1798) the Council of Ancients, following the recommendation of its committee, rejected the project, thus dashing any prospect of significant reform.[49]

The debate on the project, as well as its ultimate rejection, reflect the critical significance that the legislators attached to the destruction of privileged corporatism as one of the fundamental achievements of the Revolution. Indeed, the Constitution of the Year III had, in articles 355 and 360, restated in a slightly different manner the proscription of corporations and associations proclaimed in the preamble to the Constitution of 1791. Clearly, members of both councils viewed the legacy of the total repudiation of privilege and corporations as so important that to compromise on it would be to betray altogether the Revolution.

The manner of dealing with the legal profession was again in contrast to the treatment of other professions such as the medical profession, where the legislators showed themselves more responsive to abuses, seeking to limit the practice of medicine by introducing requirements for practice. In the field of medicine, the deputies demonstrated a capacity to relent sufficiently in their hostility toward corporatism and privilege to seek "a closed domain" without reverting to the corporate structures of the Old Regime, but in law even a minimal closed domain was deemed unacceptable.[50] Once again, the reason lay in the primacy the regime accorded to law—in this instance, law as an equitable instrument for arbitration to deter arbitrary or extralegal behavior. As a result, the deputies believed that untrammeled access to the law was imperative.[51] However much they may have acquiesced in the illegality and manipulation that characterized the Second Directory, and however contradictory or hypocritical it may appear in hindsight, the deputies continued to adhere to a belief in law and did not want to restrict in any way the access of citizens to it in order to redress grievances. Thus, it was once again the centrality of law to the political system that led to the divergence of the experience of the legal profession from that of other professions in France during this era.

Given the preference of most of the former barristers to the Parlement for a constitutional monarchy, and given also the relative indifference of the Directory to the plight of the legal profession, it is not surprising that during this period many of the former barristers to the Parlement actively opposed the government. Whether in the intellectual or political domain, former Parisian avocats au Parlement were often conspicuous in their anatagonism toward both the Convention and the Directory.

In the intellectual sphere a few of the former barristers to the Parlement constituted an important element of a formidable intellectual opposition. In late 1794, Jacques Vincent Delacroix, a former member of the Order, published a work challenging the Convention to hold a plebiscite in which voters could choose between the Constitution of 1791 and the Constitution of 1793. The proposal posed a serious challenge to the Convention, since it appealed to the concept of popular sovereignty upon which the Convention justified its authority. After a reading of his work in the Convention, the Convention ordered Delacroix's arrest, and he was subsequently sent before the Revolutionary Tribunal on 2 ventôse year III (February 20, 1795), on the charge of advocating the reestablishment of the monarchy. He was defended by his former colleague Tronson-Ducoudray and won a unanimous acquittal, which doubtlessly brought greater attention to the work, and one study has claimed that Delacroix raised the issue that dominated all major political debate of the era. In addition, between 1795 and 1797 another lesser known former member of the Order, Jean Thomas Langlois, published several pamphlets and newspaper articles that disputed the political legitimacy of the Revolutionary government; his work has been characterized as "the most serious effort any of the French domestic counter-revolutionary writers made to refute the Revolution's fundamental claim" of political sovereignty.[52]

But the former avocats au Parlement did not limit their hostility merely to the realm of political theory; many of them assumed a more active role in opposing the government. Former members of the Order, for example, played a part in the two major right-wing insurrections against the Convention and the Directory. Several former barristers to the Parlement were implicated in the revolt of 13 vendémiaire against the Convention, an uprising precipitated largely by the promulgation of the Two-Thirds Decree.[53]

An additional, and even more telling, indication of the opposition of many of the former barristers to the Parlement to the government is their extensive participation in royalist activities in the year V. While their involvement in these efforts does not necessarily indicate that they were royalists (although many were constitutional monarchists), it does at least reflect their animosity toward the Directory. In the elections of the year V, which were an overwhelming success for those opposed to the government, particularly in Paris, royalist pamphlets urged electors to back such former barristers to the Parlement as Lacretelle, Chauveau-Lagarde, de Sèze, and de Bonnières, and the latter, who was a royalist, won election to the Council of Ancients.[54] Moreover, it was in the elections of the year V that former avocats au Parlement made an impressive showing in the judiciary.

The extent of the former barristers' involvement in antigovernment ventures is most clearly evident in the wake of the right-wing *coup de fructidor*. Four former members of the Order—de Bonnières, de la Metherie, Tronson-Ducoudray, and Brunet—either lost their seat in the legislature or had their election annulled.[55] Tronson-Ducoudray, who had played a key role in regrouping the former members of the Order after the Terror, was subsequently deported to Guyana, where he died in 1798, a loss felt heavily by his former colleagues.[56] In addition, many former avocats au Parlement who had been serving in judicial positions in Paris were removed from office in the aftermath of the coup.[57] This represented a setback in the consolidation of the former avocats au Parlement in the judiciary, but its effects were short-lived. One reason was that the Directory appointed in their place other former members of the Order. Moreover, some of the men removed were soon reappointed or otherwise found their way back into office.[58] The continued presence of former colleagues in the judiciary seems to have prevented any serious disruption in the regroupment of the former barristers to the Parlement. Nonetheless, the events of fructidor year V clearly showed the aversion of many of the former avocats au Parlement to the Directorial regime — an aversion that could only have intensified with the blatant illegalities that occurred during the following years of the Second Directory.[59]

Thus, when Bonaparte overthrew the Directory in 1799, few of the former members of the Order lamented its demise. Nevertheless, the period from 1795 through 1799 had been valuable for them because it had provided them with a reprieve from the frenzied political atmosphere of the Terror. Although the respite had been punctuated by some uncertainty, particularly in its initial stages, it ultimately enabled the former avocats au Parlement to recover from the extinction of their coalition between 1792 and 1794. By 1799, there were approximately thirty former members of the Order once again practicing in various courts in Paris. They, along with a few senior members of the Order practicing as consulting barristers (*jurisconsultes*) in their offices, succeeded in reviving their unofficial organization to such an extent that they even began to assimilate new members. With the reorganized nucleus of the former Order once again in place by 1799, the former avocats au Parlement began anew the attempt to meet the challenges that the Revolution had presented to their profession.

6 / The Promise of Reconstruction: 1800–1804

> The barristers formerly constituted a corporation bound by duties and a discipline that all of its members respected. The government believed it appropriate to reestablish this corporation, and Title V of the project provides for it by ordering the formation of the tableau of barristers.
>
> *Fourcroy to the Legislative Body*
> *16 ventôse year XII*

The regroupment of the Order, which had proceeded so tentatively during the Directory, greatly accelerated under the Consulate. In late 1800 and in early 1801 two private law schools were founded in Paris, the Académie de Législation and the Université de Jurisprudence. These establishments soon became critical focal points in the attempt of the former barristers to the Parlement to reorganize. The government looked favorably upon the institutions, and, in turn, most of the former avocats au Parlement viewed Bonaparte's accession to power positively. The law of 22 ventôse year XII, which reorganized the schools of law, attested to the compatibility between the former barristers to the Parlement and the government; the statute recognized the contribution made by the Académie de Législation and the Université de Jurisprudence and pledged a comprehensive reform of the legal profession, including the formation of a tableau des avocats and the reestablishment of the Order.

The attempt of the former barristers to the Parlement to rebuild their profession was already underway when Bonaparte seized power, but Bonaparte's effort to reestablish order and authority in France and to forge a strong centralized state aided their attempt. Most of the former avocats au Parlement had been hostile to the Directory and saw in the advent of Bonaparte a movement against anarchy. Moreover, Bonaparte's concern for an efficient judiciary as a vital component of the state paralleled in many respects the former barristers' own efforts to restore proficiency and integrity in their profession, so that in its first years of existence the Consulate enjoyed the support of most of the former avocats au Parlement.[1]

In December 1799, only weeks after taking power, Bonaparte promulgated the Constitution of the Year VIII.[2] It established a Council of State and a three-house legislature; and former members of the Order, almost all of them individuals who had embarked upon political careers in 1789 or afterward and who now formed part of "the Brumairian elite," belonged to all of these bodies.[3] Although nearly all of these men had taken up political careers, several of them had maintained contact with their former colleagues who had remained in practice.[4] In addition, Bonaparte chose as minister of justice André Joseph Abrial, a former member of the Order renowned for his integrity. The presence of so many former colleagues in the government, as well as such men as Cambacérès, whom the former barristers to the Parlement had known when he practiced law in Paris during a hiatus in his political career, and who was a strong and influential ally, facilitated acceptance of it by most of the former members of the Order in practice. For the most part, they welcomed the new regime and did not have the same sense of disaffection toward the government that they had had during the Convention and the Directory.

The Constitution of the Year VIII did not merely announce a new political regime in France; it decreed a new administrative and judicial structure as well. The latter was enacted principally on 27 ventôse year VIII (March 18, 1800), in a law that broke with several of the major innovations introduced by the Revolution.[5] In the judiciary established by Bonaparte, there was no longer only one civil court per department, as there had been under the Constitution of the Year III; rather, there was a court of first instance for each arrondissement (except for Paris, which had only a single court) that had jurisdiction over both civil and criminal matters. More important, the law created twenty-nine courts of appeal for civil cases, thus destroying the single degree of jurisdiction instituted by the Revolution. The criminal courts, which had also been set up at the proportion of one per department, were maintained at the same ratio. Although they continued to hear serious criminal cases in the first instance, they were transformed primarily into courts of appeal for criminal cases from the tribunals of first instance. Whereas their personnel had formerly been drawn from judges in the civil court serving on rotation, the criminal courts now received their own personnel, except for the president, who was drawn from the court of appeal.

Another major change enacted by Bonaparte involved the judges of the courts. Henceforth, only the justices of the peace, whose number was reduced considerably, as was the scope of their duties, were elected. Judges in the civil and criminal courts were appointed for life by the First Consul, while the members of the Tribunal de cassation, which consisted of forty-eight judges, were named for life by the Senate. The law reestablished avoués and gave them the right both to handle the procedural aspects of a case and to plead, although their use was not mandatory and parties could still handle their own case. The law specified, however, that avoués would be named by the First Consul after their presentation to him by the court at which they would practice. This provision implied not only that there would be a limited number of avoués, but even more important that there would be a screening process to reject many of those who were guilty of abuses.

These changes were warmly welcomed by the former avocats au Parlement. Whereas some of the more ardent Revolutionaries were disgruntled with the courts of appeal because they saw in them a return to the parlements of the Old Regime,[6] it was precisely this attribute that was most attractive to the former barristers. The attraction of the new courts of appeal did not lie solely in the greater stature given them by the law; the former barristers were particularly pleased that they no longer had to travel to neighboring departments to appeal a case. Also, the provisions relating to the avoués represented a commitment by the government to reform the situation with the practitioners in the courts, a commitment that the Directory had declined to make. Berryer asserted that the reforms of the year VIII restored a sense of dignity to the judiciary, and there can be little doubt that the measures played an important role in the former barristers' acceptance of the new regime.[7]

A subsequent aspect of the reforms that also led many of the former barristers to the Parlement to approve of the new government was the choice of judges. Although the power of appointment had been vested with the First Consul, he was unfamiliar with most of the judicial personnel and had to rely on the opinions of others, chiefly men of the Brumairian elite. Cambacérès and Abrial did much of the work, and they were thorough in their undertaking.[8] Their sense of loyalty to former colleagues from the abolished Order was apparent in many of their choices, for in both the Appeals Court and the Tribunal of First

Instance in Paris more than one-quarter of the judges were former members of the Order, while in the Criminal Court three of the ten judges and assistant judges named had been members of the Order in 1789.[9] Former barristers to the Parlement were chosen for the posts of government commissioner and assistant to the government commissioner at all three courts as well. In addition, after the initial designations, the former avocats au Parlement seem to have been accorded preference in advancement to the prestigious Appeals Court or in receiving appointments to vacancies between the years VIII and XII, particularly in Paris.[10] Similarly, in departments outside Paris, dozens of other former members of the Order gained judgeships. Moreover, as in Paris, others received nominations as government commissioners.[11]

A similar phenomenon occurred at the Tribunal de cassation, where ten of the forty-eight judges named by the Senate were men who had belonged to the Order in 1789, as had the man designated as the government commissioner.[12] With few exceptions, most of the former avocats au Parlement chosen for judicial positions at every level, from the Tribunal of First Instance up to the Tribunal de cassation, were able jurists respected by their former colleagues; their selection inspired confidence and won praise from members of the bar.[13]

As another element in his drive for centralization, Bonaparte in August 1800 appointed a commission of four men to draw up a project of a civil code for France. The development and significance of the Civil Code are beyond the purview of this study, but two of the four individuals named, Tronchet and Bigot de Préameneu, had been members of the Order in 1789.[14] Tronchet in particular played an especially important role in drafting the project, which was ultimately promulgated in 1804 and is generally viewed as one of Bonaparte's most enduring achievements.

After the law of 27 ventôse reestablished the avoués, that of 18 fructidor year VIII (September 5, 1800) specified their role. Although avoués retained the right to plead, their functions were defined largely in terms of the Ordinance of 1667. They were made mandatory for parties in a lawsuit, and they were primarily to guide their party in procedure. In short, their duties were analogous to those of the procureurs of the Old Regime. Thus, in contrast to the chaotic state of affairs under the Directory, the Consulate adopted standardized procedures in the courts that imparted greater organization to the legal process and thereby conferred greater dignity on the tribunals as a whole. It was a procedure with which the former avocats au Parlement were comfortable and familiar, since it was reminiscent of the code that had guided their professional roles in the Parlement. After the enactment of this law many défenseurs officieux became avoués and were thereby relegated largely to procedural tasks.[15]

This reform in particular revealed a new attitude toward law that would ultimately affect critically the status of the legal profession. In the various Revolutionary governments from 1789 to 1799, law had been inextricably connected to the political system's definition of itself, and successive regimes had believed that the access of citizens to the law should not be infringed in any way. Under the Consulate, however, law did not enjoy the same ascendancy that it had under the Revolutionary governments; the regime defined itself chiefly in terms of a systematized, well-regulated state in which law had no place as an organizing principle and would instead be subordinated to centralized control. The introduction of standardized procedures and the mandatory retention of avoués for recourse to the law signified the supplanting of citizens' access to the law by a greater concern for order and efficiency.

One consequence of the preeminence accorded to order was that professionalism and professional organizations were viewed much more favorably as components of a well-ordered state. The various reforms enacted for the judiciary met with the approval of the former barristers to the Parlement, and their own effort to rebuild their profession harmonized with the government's attempt to reinvigorate the judiciary. Indeed, the initial sense of common purpose between the former avocats au Parlement and the government is seen clearly in the operation of two private law schools in Paris during the Consulate. From their foundation until their eventual demise, the Académie de Législation and the Université de Jurisprudence were an important element in the effort of the former avocats au Parlement to reform their profession and to revive their Order, with the Académie de Législation in particular becoming in many respects a virtual surrogate for the Order during this era.

By 1800 the inadequacy of the law curriculum in the central schools was widely recognized. Since there were no obligatory courses in the central schools, there was no cohesive program of study. Most of the former barristers regarded the course as superficial and insufficient because it often examined only legislation rather than the philosophy or principles of law. In many departments, perhaps even in a majority of them, there were frequently no students whatsoever enrolled in the course of legislation. Paris was no exception — the course of legislation attracted only a few students.[16] By the time of the Consulate, many in the legal profession were openly contemptuous of the law studies in the central schools, and many of the former avocats au Parlement believed strongly that a return to an emphasis on Roman law was needed. In an effort to fill the lacuna in legal education, some former members of the Order offered private instruction in law on a tutorial basis, but such courses obviously could accommodate only a few individuals. There was a clear need for a larger program of educational reform.[17]

In the year IX two private law schools were established in Paris; one was the Lycée de Jurisprudence, which was organized on 5 vendémiaire year IX (September 27, 1800). When the government claimed the title *lycée* exclusively for its own educational establishments, the institution changed its name to the Université de Jurisprudence.[18] Its founder was Louis François Aubin Lefebvre, who was aided by several other men serving as editors and contributors to the *Annales de Législation et de Jurisprudence,* a publication of the institution. The director of the Université de Jurisprudence was de la Rivallière.[19]

The other institution, the Académie de Législation, was organized seven months later, on 9 floréal year IX (April 29, 1801). According to Berryer, its founders included Guy Jean Baptiste Target, François Denis Tronchet, Michel Louis Etienne Regnault de Saint-Jean d'Angély, and Jean Baptiste Mailhe, and, although he did not initially occupy the post, J. T. Bruguière was the director of the Académie de Législation for most of its existence.[20] The académie issued several publications — the *Bulletin de l'Académie de Législation, Mémoires de l'Académie de Législation, Etat des travaux de l'Académie de Législation,* and the *Journal de Jurisprudence.*

Both establishments emphasized their intention of teaching Roman law and openly presented themselves as alternatives to what they viewed as the deficient curriculum in the écoles centrales. The prospectus for the Académie de Législation openly spoke of the "vacuous lessons of legislation in the central schools" and implied that the académie would not only surpass the central schools, but would improve on the law schools from the Old Regime as well.[21] Above all, then, the Université de Jurisprudence and the Académie de Législation were educational establishments. Moreover, although both were located in

Paris, they sought to make themselves institutions of national scale. In order to attract students whose families did not reside in Paris, the Université de Jurisprudence set aside a portion of its building as a boarding area for students and also made provisions allowing the prefect of each department to designate one outstanding student to attend the université, free of tuition charges. In addition, it sought to publicize its activities in journals in departments outside of Paris.[22] Likewise, the Académie de Législation sought to form a boarding section for students from outside Paris, and it, too, authorized the prefect of each department to nominate one student, known as a *sujet d'élite*, who would be allowed to enroll for three years without having to pay any tuition costs. The académie also strove to organize a network of affiliated members in departments outside Paris.[23]

Although sharing similar educational functions, the Université de Jurisprudence and the Académie de Législation were differentiated by their respective ancillary objectives. A few men were members of both establishments, but, in the final analysis, the only bond between the two institutions was a mutual commitment to improving legal education. The schools were two separate entities, and they shall be examined as such.

The Université de Jurisprudence did not begin to offer classes until two years after its organization. At the initial meeting, the members elected as president Frédéric Ignace Mirbeck, a former avocat aux conseils,[24] but thereafter the institution stagnated, in all probability because the Université de Jurisprudence, unlike the Académie de Législation, was formed as a commercial venture. In many ways it was organized like a modern publicly held corporation, with six hundred shares in the institution offered at the price of one thousand francs each. The shares, registered with the université and allegedly guaranteed by patrimonial property worth twice the value of the offering, were of seven years duration and paid an annual interest rate of 5 percent. In addition, each shareholder received the right to send a pupil to the université free of charge.[25] One possible reason for the inactivity that followed its formation, then, could have been the difficulty of attracting investors.

A second problem appears to have been the ambitious agenda that the organizers attempted to undertake. The establishment of the Université de Jurisprudence was only one element of the venture, for the organizers of the université aspired to other activities and sought, in effect, to become a law firm of national scope. They proposed to form a bureau of consultations to process cases for litigants in any court in any location in France. Although the université pledged to offer free consultations to the poor, which it defined as those who could provide certification of indigence, it is clear that the bureau of consultations would not operate as a charitable activity similar to the Bureau de bienfaisance judiciaire that had been formed shortly before the Revolution. Rather, the bureau of consultations was intended to be a profitable enterprise that promised litigants skillful and expeditious handling of their cases. The organization was comprised of fifty members and a general regulating commission (commissaire général régulateur), and no one could be a member if he had not practiced law for at least ten years. A small council, which included four men who had been members of the Order in 1789, would sign consultations of the université and the bureau fixed the fee for routine cases at seventy-two francs. In its prospectus the bureau claimed that it would not collect a fee unless the case went in favor of the client, but it dropped this statement in other literature. It advanced a similar service for litigants at the Tribunal de cassation as well. In order to attract clients, particularly from outside Paris, the Université de Jurisprudence strove to establish a vast administrative network, with local representatives in each department, arrondissement, and canton in France. The representatives were urged not only to attempt to gain cases for the université, especially at the Tribunal de cassation, but also to try to sign up subscribers to the *Annales de Législation et de Jurisprudence*. Representatives of the institution at the department and arrondissement level were required to purchase a subscription. The scope of the project was enormous, and there is little evidence that it was at all successful. Furthermore, the attempt to implement the administrative structure may have been an additional cause of delay, until the directors realized the impracticality of the effort.[26]

Whatever the cause, the Université de Jurisprudence did not begin to hold classes or to publish its journal until ventôse year XI (February–March 1803). In a copy of its regulations published in the year XI the administrator of the Université de Jurisprudence claimed that there were 360 students enrolled, but this figure was probably an exaggeration, perhaps designed to reassure nervous investors.[27] Nevertheless, the université drew many students, and the student body was genuinely national in dimension, as the results of an awards ceremony at the end of its first year show. The winners and runners-up in various fields of competition came from the departments of Charente, Deux-Nethes, Puy-de-Dôme, Bas-Rhin, Haut-Rhin, Dordogne, Aveyron, Gers, Côtes du Nord, Creuse, Finistère, and Cantal. Indeed, as it began its second year, the Université de Jurisprudence lured students away from central schools outside Paris.[28]

In its first year the Université de Jurisprudence offered six courses. More important, it employed an innovative approach to the teaching of law that surpassed any of the instruction offered in the écoles centrales or in the law schools of the Old Regime. The program not only concentrated on academic instruction, but also devoted attention to the more practical aspects of the profession. The six courses comprised the "theoretical" aspect of the curriculum and imparted knowledge of general legislation, French and Roman law, criminal law, maritime and commercial law, and civil procedure. The course of study also tried to instill speaking ability in students; one of the six courses was a course in eloquence taught by Geoffri, a former professor of rhetoric in the Collège Mazarin of the University of Paris. Other instructors were François Morand for general legislation; Michel Agresti for Roman and French law; Scipion Jérôme Bexon, the vice-president of the Tribunal of First Instance of the Seine, for criminal law; Jacques Peuchet for maritime and commercial law; and Eustache Nicolas Pigeau for civil procedure. Virtually all of these men had established reputations as legal scholars, with treatises on the subjects that they taught at the université.[29]

In addition to the academic or theoretical element, the program of the Université de Jurisprudence had a practical dimension, a dimension that reflected many of the concerns of the avocats au Parlement under the Old Regime. During the Old Regime many members of the Order had believed that programs in the schools of law were not necessarily sufficient because of their concentration on the acquisition of knowledge, to the exclusion of instruction in technique. The probationary period required by the Order had provided an opportunity to acquire technique, and, as a result, the probationary period of the prospective avocat au Parlement was often partially devoted to working in the office of an established barrister in order to learn procedural details. Moreover, because many barristers to the Parlement had believed that the academic program of the universities was insufficient, the probationary barrister had been required to attend a series of conférences directed by a senior member of the Order in which points of law were discussed. The course of study at the Université de Jurisprudence addressed these concerns. Students received training in the preliminary proceedings of a case, studied the various types of legal actions available, and learned procedure. They were also required to attend conférences in which they read and discussed consultations written by noted jurisconsultes. The most novel part of the instruction, however, was a mock court that was designed to give students insight into courtroom practice.[30] The mock court in which the students practiced was comprised entirely of fellow students, and it was a high honor to be named as a judge in it. The students were given the facts of a case and had to plead it before the judges, and the best pleadings or arguments by the competing students were published in the *Annales de Législation et de Jurisprudence*. Through the simulated trials the pupils gained experience in trial advocacy and courtroom procedure. The Université de Jurisprudence took great pride in its plan of study; its literature often referred to the université as an "école théoretique et pratique de législation et d'éloquence."

But during the year XII, its second year, the Université de Jurisprudence experienced severe problems. Pigeau and Morand left to teach at the Académie de Législation, and Geoffri did not return to teach éloquence. As a result, the course offerings of the Université de Jurisprudence were reduced. The imminent promulgation of the Civil Code was the pretext utilized for not offering a course in civil procedure, the subject that had been taught by Pigeau.[31] It also did not offer a course in general legislation, the topic taught by Morand. The new instructor in eloquence was Dorfeuille, who appears to have been an actor. Although the choice at first seems unusual, it perhaps represented a reversion to a custom from antiquity, when prospective barristers were trained by actors.[32] A further hint of hardship for the Université de Jurisprudence was a brief notice in the *Moniteur* confirming that one of the courses it offered had, in fact, been held, which suggests that other courses may have been encountering problems.[33] Also, in what may have been an effort to increase its enrollement and to broaden its base, in its second year the Université de Jurisprudence offered a notarial course. The cessation of publication of the *Annales de Législation et de Jurisprudence* after the appearance of the fourth volume in the year XII is an additional indication of difficulties.[34] The journal had been heavily promoted, and its demise was a blow to the prestige of the institution and almost certainly could have resulted only from serious problems. Finally, in the year XII students began transferring from the Université de Jurisprudence to the Académie de Législation. The reasons for this are unclear, but the attrition continued during the following year as well—students who had attended the Université de Jurisprudence during the year XII enrolled in the Académie de Législation for the year XIII.[35] After the year XII the Université de Jurisprudence closed its doors, although other aspects of the venture of which it was a part seem to have continued.[36]

It is clear that the Université de Jurisprudence was less successful as an educational institution than the Académie de Législation.[37] After its first year it failed to attract either the number of students or the distinguished legal scholars that the Académie de Législation did, and its proprietary nature limited its utility largely to those who were willing to invest. Nevertheless, along with the Académie de Législation, the Université de Jurisprudence filled a void in legal education in France. Many students completed its curriculum and went on to enjoy illustrious careers, not only in law but in other fields as well.[38] Godwin Joseph de Stassart, one of the three winners in eloquence at the awards ceremony held at the end of the first year, is illustrative. His success at the université caught the attention of the government, and, after the completion of his studies, he was named as an auditor to the Council of State in 1804. From the Council of State he went on to various prefectoral assignments. His distinguished administrative career lasted until the end of the Empire, and included being decorated with the Cross of the Legion of Honor for averting civil disorder by his adept handling of a provisioning crisis while serving in Germany. After the Hundred Days, he returned to his native Belgium, where in 1821 he was elected to the second chamber of the Estates-General. In 1830 he played an important role in the formation of the Belgian monarchy, became governor of the province of Namur, and was named to the commission charged with drafting provincial and communal laws in Belgium. In the 1840s he became president of the Royal Academy of Belgium, where he sat until his death in 1854.[39] Several other students from the Université de Jurisprudence enjoyed notable careers in law as both judges and barristers.

The Académie de Législation, originally called the Institut de jurisprudence et d'économie politique, was organized seven months after the founding of the Université de Jurisprudence. The reasons for its establishment are not entirely apparent, although the proprietary nature of the Université de Jurisprudence, which seemed to limit its utility, may have played a role, for the Académie de Législation, unlike the Université de Jurisprudence, was not a commercial venture. Men could be affiliated with the académie without financially investing in it; as a result, its membership was ultimately much larger.

It is not altogether clear who founded the Académie de Législation. Its early literature and public announcements mention Lamouque, a jurisconsulte and former magistrate; Reynaud, a jurisconsulte, ex-president of the civil court of the Seine, and avoué at the Appeals Court; Carbonnel, a jurisconsulte and ex-judge in the civil court of the Seine; and Gisor, a former government official, as directors of the institution. Hayem, in his study, evidently inferred from this that they were the founders.[40] There are indications, however, that several noted former barristers who held important posts in the government established the Académie de Législation, a view strengthened by the fact that many prominent figures in the government affiliated with the académie (as will be discussed later in this chapter). The organizers of the Académie de Législation seem to have included the following: Target, vice-president of the Tribunal de cassation; Lanjuinais, a member of the Senate; Portalis, who sat on the Council of State; and Maleville, who was also a member of the Tribunal de cassation.[41] Target, Lanjuinais, and Portalis all held major administrative positions early in the académie's existence, again suggesting that they were instrumental in its founding. Under the Old Regime these men had all been distinguished avocats au Parlement in different parlementary towns of France—Target, a former member of the Order at Paris; Lanjuinais, an avocat au Parlement, as well as a professor of law, at Rennes; Portalis, an avocat au Parlement at Aix; and Maleville, one at Bordeaux. All had enjoyed reputations as learned barristers and evidently saw the Académie de Législation as a vehicle for rehabilitating their former profession.

The primary objective of the Académie de Législation was to improve the teaching of law and elevate it to a new standard, surpassing both the écoles centrales and the law schools of the Old Regime, although ultimately the founders of the Académie de Législation hoped to raise the quality of practitioners in the courts as well. The académie adopted the same innovative curriculum, stressing both the practical and academic aspects of the profession, that the Université de Jurisprudence used.[42] The académie was also unorthodox in its handling of gifted students. If a student showed great promise, he was not required to fulfill the entire three year course of study; rather, he could complete his studies in as little as one year and enter into practice. The student Jean Baptiste Teste, for example, completed his education in one year; in an awards ceremony held at the end of the year XII the académie announced that Teste had not been included in the competition because he had already completed his studies and made his debut at the bar.[43]

The Académie de Législation began instruction with seven courses in the year X (1801–2), one year earlier than the Université de Jurisprudence. They were political economy, taught by Perreau; Roman and French law, taught by Bernardi; practical jurisprudence, taught by Gallais; criminal law, taught by Morand; history of law / constitutional law and civil law, taught by Millon; and commercial and maritime law, taught by Peuchet. Perreau, Bernardi, and Peuchet were particularly well known as legal scholars and as authors of important treatises.[44] Despite such a distinguished faculty, the first year of instruction was characterized by interruption in some of the courses.[45]

In the year X, the first full year of its existence, the Académie de Législation had a total affiliation of 179 members in Paris. For the year XI this number increased to 225, and it drew 102 students for the year.[46] The académie attracted additional scholars as well, and expanded its course offering to ten, structuring a complete program of study for its students. In his first year the pupil studied natural and international law, logic, morality and eloquence, and positive French public law. In his second year he studied Roman law, private French law, French criminal law, and the history of law. In his final year he studied public economy, civil procedure and notarial matters, and commercial and maritime law.[47] An awards ceremony held at the end of the year XI shows that the Académie de Législation, like the Université de Jurisprudence, succeeded in attracting students from all over France. Winners and runners-up in the competition came from the departments of the Isère, Lot-et-Garonne, Ille-et-Vilaine, Deux-Sèvres, Haut-Rhin, Puy-de-Dôme, Gironde, Somme, and Morbihan.[48]

In contrast to the Université de Jurisprudence, however, the Académie de Législation continued to develop. In the year XII (1803–4), when enrollment at the Université de Jurisprudence declined, the Académie de Législation saw its total affiliated membership, both inside and outside Paris, rise to 612. Each affiliated member paid a fee of fifty-four francs, and the revenue thus produced was important in defraying the operating costs of the académie.⁴⁹ Moreover, it even began to expand beyond France, and had affiliated members in Göttingen and Moscow.⁵⁰ In the year XII the académie expanded its offerings to twelve courses, and its enrollment rose to over 200 students, including 40 sujets d'élite nominated by prefects of the departments. One additional indication of the vitality of the institution is that it moved into an area of law that had never before been seriously examined when it established a course on the use of medical expertise to illuminate legal issues *(questions medico-légales)*—for example, medical testimony on the cause of death, a course taught by a former avocat who had become a doctor.⁵¹

Both the Université de Jurisprudence and the Académie de Législation enjoyed the patronage of members of the government. Muraire, for example, the president of the Tribunal de cassation and a member of the Council of State, attended the awards ceremony held at the Université de Jurisprudence at the end of the year XI, and at the end of the ceremony agreed to accept the title of honorary president of the université.⁵² Although he doubtlessly looked favorably upon its purpose, his involvement (or that of any other member of the government) with the institution remained largely titular and of little consequence. The Académie de Législation, by contrast, had been founded by several prominent officials of the government, and they remained closely associated with it. The first president of the académie was Pierre Pérignon, an avocat aux conseils under the Old Regime who had affiliated with the coalition of former avocats au Parlement in 1795.⁵³ After his tenure, the remaining presidents—Lanjuinais, Portalis, Fourcroy, and Regnault de Saint-Jean d'Angély—were all noted men of state, although their official duties precluded them from taking a major role in the daily operations of the institution. The administrator Lamouque, for example, rather than the president, handled salary details with the instructor in commercial and maritime law.⁵⁴ In less routine matters, however, they lent their prestige and authority to the Académie de Législation and worked actively on its behalf. In the year XI, for example, Lanjuinais revamped the curriculum and drew up the plan of study to be followed by students of the académie. In the same vein it was Portalis who, using his title Councillor of State, promoted the awards ceremony held at the end of the year XI.⁵⁵ Lanjuinais, Portalis, Fourcroy, and Regnault de Saint-Jean d'Angély were only the most visible members of the government; many others were associated as well. In the year XII, when the académie was at its zenith, the affiliated members included Regnier, the minister of justice, eight members of the Council of State, eight members of the Senate, fourteen members of the Tribunate, and eighteen members of the Legislative Body.[56] Most of them were former barristers who, in the absence of any schools of law, supported the efforts of the Académie de Législation to restore the profession to their vision of respectability.

In addition to its educational purpose, the Académie de Législation had an ancillary objective — to separate trained barristers from unskilled or unscrupulous practitioners. In this respect, as well as in others, the académie acted as a virtual surrogate for the abolished Order.

In its prospectus the académie made it clear that its agenda went beyond improving the state of legal education in France; it was also concerned with the conditions under which trained barristers practiced.

The confusion, the harmful mingling that exists today between the former barristers and these wretched practitioners, devoid of any training and without any legal or recognized capacity, who, disowned by the courts and by society, of which they are the disgrace and the scourge, indiscriminately take for themselves the title of men of law, without any education except an obscure and almost always incorrect routine, artfully reinforcing bad faith and stirring up the most iniquitous cases: in short, the necessity of finding a point of contact and of assembly which simultaneously offers the guarantee of learning and probity in men destined for the honorable profession of the bar has been obvious.[57]

Under the Old Regime this had been one of the ways in which the Order had characterized itself, and the prospectus subsequently stated that the académie was, in fact, modeled after the abolished Order: " . . . they will find especially in the ethics of the Institute these ancient principles of scrupulousness, of disinterestedness, and of probity that formerly were so characteristic of the honorable Order of Barristers."[58] The Académie de Législation offered an institutional framework for the attempt of the former avocats au Parlement to regenerate their Order. Many of the former Parisian barristers to the Parlement who had struggled to preserve the corporate ethos of the Order in 1790, and who had associated during the Directory to rebuild it — Beilart, Berryer, Delacroix-Frainville, Blacque, Poirier, Bonnet, and others — affiliated with the Académie de Législation in its first year, and the leadership of the académie regularly included at least one former member of the Order who had remained in practice.⁵⁹ In addition to its educational mission, which itself was based largely on the experience of the avocats au Parlement from the Old Regime, the académie performed other functions that the Order had carried out before the Revolution. Under the Old Regime, for example, one of the ways in which the Order instilled in its stagiaires a sense of esteem for the profession was to have them present discourses on various aspects of the profession during their probationary period. Similarly, the académie, as an exercise separate from its academic curriculum, often had its students offer perorations on different aspects of the profession. Before the Revolution the Order of Barristers at Paris had utilized its probationary barristers to make legal services available to the poor; likewise, the Académie de Législation offered a similar service to indigents in which its students participated.⁶⁰ Like the Order, the académie often eulogized deceased members, and the eulogy for Louis René Chauveau, a former avocat au Parlement and a member of the académie, indicates the manner in which the académie regarded itself as the heir of the Order. Although Chauveau's legal career had been undistinguished, the eulogy offered at the académie praised him for appearing before the Committee of the Constitution in 1789 in an effort to prevent the abolition of the Order.⁶¹

One should be aware of but not overstate the role of the Académie de Législation as a surrogate for the Order, for not all of the former avocats au Parlement in practice joined the Académie de Législation; indeed, many of them during this era did not affiliate themselves with it at all.⁶² To the extent that it provided an organization around which trained barristers could assemble, and to the extent that it qualitatively evaluated aspirants to the profession, the Académie de Législation fulfilled a capacity similar to the abolished Order. The parallel between the académie and the Order can be seen in a letter written to the minister of justice in the year XIII. The author of the letter, Regnier, was teaching law privately in Paris and was seeking appointment as a substitute judge. Referring to the Académie de Législation, he did not allude to its educational functions; rather, he noted with pride that some of his students "have gained some repute and have even been judged worthy of sitting among the members of the Académie de Législation, and admitted into this society of senior jurisconsultes."⁶³

In the same vein, the Académie de Législation, and to a lesser extent the Université de Jurisprudence, gave the former avocats au Parlement a greater degree of control over their profession than they had had at any time since the abolition of the Order. Through the auspices of the académie, they were able to mold younger men in much the same fashion as had the probationary period of the Order under the Old Regime. Not only did the académie enable the former barristers to train young men professionally, it also gave them the opportunity to survey aspirants over an extended period of time.

For several years the remaining members of the Order had augmented themselves almost exclusively with older men who had come to Paris for various reasons. Joseph Elzéar Bernardi, for example, who had been a magistrate *(lieutenant général)* for the comte de Sault under the Old Regime, was forty-nine years of age when he associated with the former avocats au Parlement in 1800. Louis Isidore Parfait Daupeley, who before the Revolution had served as an *avocat fiscal* in various seignorial jurisdictions, and who during the Revolution had served as a justice of the peace in Rouen for several years before coming to Paris to practice law, was thirty-six years old when he allied with them in 1800. Similarly, Pierre Joseph Grappe, who had joined the Order of Barristers at Besançon in 1779, and who had been a professor of Roman law at the University of Besançon from 1790 to 1792, was forty-eight when he affiliated himself with the former avocats au Parlement in Paris in 1803.[64] While these individuals were welcomed as respected colleagues, the predominance of older men did not allow the coalition to renew itself to the extent that would be necessary to continue into the future, and before the founding of the Académie de Législation and the Université de Jurisprudence few younger men had been affiliated with the former avocats au Parlement. After the establishment of the académie and the université, the former avocats au Parlement were able to draw younger men into their coalition.[65] Several of the men who emerged, particularly from the Académie de Législation, became pivotal figures in the Order during the nineteenth century.

The attempt of the Académie de Législation and the Université de Jurisprudence to restore professionalism into the practice of law was far more extensive than similar, albeit less systematic, efforts in the field of medicine. In medicine, the impetus generally came not from among the practitioners themselves, but from municipal administrators or from members of medical schools that had been closed but had continued to function more or less clandestinely.[66] In law, however, the initiative came much more from within the profession itself, underscoring both the independent manner in which the profession had evolved and how well defined it had been before the Revolution. To be sure, the involvement of men of state in the operation of the Académie de Législation and the Université de Jurisprudence appears to conform to the norm of professions developing under the aegis of the state early in the nineteenth century, but in the final analysis even these men, along with their counterparts in private practice, were seeking to restore the profession to its Old Regime definition rather than have its regeneration take place in association with the state.

The Académie de Législation, then, was much more than an academic institution. Although its primary role was educational, to view the académie simply as analogous to the schools of law of the Old Regime understates the entire range of its activities. A more appropriate comparison would be to envision the académie as the amalgamation of the Order of Barristers and the schools of law of the Old Regime, for even the curriculum of the académie was based on the experience of the Order rather than that of the law schools. During this period and beyond, the académie had a critical place in the fortunes of the abolished Order.

The judicial reforms enacted by the government, as well as the greater degree of control over their profession provided by the Académie de Législation and the Université de Jurisprudence, ameliorated the situation of the former avocats au Parlement during this era. In the year VII there had been 131 men listed as practicing as hommes de loi at the Tribunal de cassation, and 337 as exercising in the tribunals of the department of the Seine, and in both jurisdictions former members of the Order had comprised only a very small portion of these totals. The same had been true in the consolidated list of hommes de loi that had been published in the year VIII; former avocats au Parlement had comprised only a small percentage of the 298 individuals recorded. The judicial reforms of the year VIII, however, drove many of the untrained practitioners out of the profession, and this development seems to have drawn many former avocats au Parlement back into practice. For the year IX, in the wake of the reforms, the list of hommes de loi dropped to 45 and former members of the Order were prevalent. By the year X, when the effects of the acts were becoming recognized, and following the establishment of the Université de Jurisprudence and the Académie de Législation, the number of hommes de loi increased to 84 and continued to rise thereafter, reaching 132 in the year XI and 154 in the year XII.[67]

Other measures taken by the government during this period also helped the former avocats au Parlement. Beginning in the year X, it became necessary for a prospective homme de loi in Paris to present himself either to the president or government commissioner of either the Appeals Court or the Tribunal of First Instance in order to secure an attestation before being listed in the *Almanach National*.[68] The policy favored the former avocats au Parlement, who had little difficulty meeting the requirement, as the case of Marc Guillaume Cathala demonstrates. Cathala had been a member of the Order at the time of its abolition. Apparently resuming practice in the year XII after a long hiatus, he was unaware of the requirement that he present himself to the court. He neglected to do so and, as a consequence, was omitted from the list of hommes de loi for the year XII. When Cathala produced a letter signed by ten former members of the Order certifying that he had belonged to the Order under the Old Regime and presented it to the vice-president and government commissioner of the Appeals Court, the *Almanach National* published his name in the year XIII.[69] The extent to which the process favored the former avocats au Parlement is illustrated by the fact that Agier, the vice-president of the Appeals Court who signed Cathala's attestation, was himself a former member of the Order. Indeed, once again the strength of the links of the abolished Order is apparent. During this era, when a former avocat au Parlement applied for a judgeship, his petition was frequently embellished with supporting remarks in the margin from former members of the Order occupying high judicial or political office. The request of Denis Alexis Bizet, for example, included among its declarations statements from former members of the Order sitting on the Tribunal de cassation, the Appeals Court, and the Tribunal of First Instance, as well as testimonials from several other former avocats au Parlement. The declaration of Babille, of the Tribunal de cassation, a supplement to a statement written by two of his colleagues praising Bizet's professional abilities, simply stated "I attest to the same facts as a former barrister to the Parlement of Paris."[70] Thus, the corporate loyalty that induced former avocats au Parlement occupying judgeships to support the candidacy of former colleagues also expedited their appearance before the courts and facilitated their inclusion in the published list of hommes de loi. Certainly, it was much more difficult for individuals not formerly associated with the Order to have their names published in the *Almanach National*.[71]

Moreover, beginning in the year X former members of the Order listed as practitioners in the *Almanach National* had the year of their inscription in the Order placed beside their name. Not only did this confer upon them a slight advantage in Paris over hommes de loi who had not previously belonged to the Order, it also amounted to a tacit recognition of their separate identity.

A more important step toward regaining their former standing was the promulgation of the law of 2 nivôse year XI (December 23, 1802), which reestablished the wool robe and white tie for *gens de loi* and avoués. Although the phrase *gens de loi* was ambiguous,[72] and almost certainly deliberately ambiguous in its avoidance of the term avocat, the restoration of the professional attire of the former barristers represented the first official reversal of any of the provisions of the law of September 2, 1790, which had abolished the Order.

Although these actions strengthened the position of the former avocats au Parlement, problems with the practitioners in the courts continued, and in the year X the government made a more substantive commitment to reforming the legal profession by decreeing that legal education would be reestablished in France. In a far-ranging report made in brumaire year IX, Jean Antoine Chaptal had declared that it was the responsibility of the government to reorganize the study of law as one means of combating the immorality and ignorance prevalent among many of the new practitioners in the courts.[73] Chaptal's plan called for the establishment of "Schools of Legislation" around each Appeals Court for the purpose of teaching law. Chaptal's plan was not accepted, but in ventôse year X (March 1802) a survey of education in France was made through questionnaires sent to the prefects. On the basis of the replies, Antoine François Fourcroy drafted a new project for French education that, among other measures, provided for the creation of ten law schools throughout France. Fourcroy's educational plan received approval on 11 floréal year X (May 1, 1802), but implementation of it occurred only at the secondary level; no action was taken on the schools of law.

In any case, a more comprehensive measure was necessary, for the reestablishment of the law schools addressed only one facet of the problem. It dealt with future entrants into the profession, but not with practitioners already in the courts, which was a more difficult issue. The debates held during the Directory had demonstrated that although recognition of the condition of the legal profession existed, there was much aversion to returning control of the profession to the former barristers by restoring its corporate structure. Moreover, Bonaparte, himself committed to many of the accomplishments of the Revolution, shared this hostility toward corporations, regarding them, like many of the Revolutionary legislators, as fiscal devices spawned by the monarchy to alleviate financial difficulties, and viewing them as a potential source of conflict. Bonaparte was above all a pragmatist, however, who desired to be in control of matters, and when the corporate paradigm could be employed to advance the well-regulated, well-ordered state, he was prepared to utilize it.[74] In the case of the former barristers, Bonaparte's desire to exercise direction over events overcame whatever aversion he may have felt for corporations, for in the current state of affairs the control of practitioners in the courts was beyond the reach of the government, frustrating its efforts to reform and rationalize the judiciary. Thus on 16 ventôse year XII (March 7, 1804) the government introduced a measure that dealt comprehensively with the condition of the legal profession in France.[75]

The Councillors of State Berlier, Fourcroy, Boullay, and Regnault de Saint-Jean d'Angély introduced the project to the Legislative Body. Although presented as a proposal implementing the law of 11 floréal year X concerning the schools of law, the project was actually far more extensive. The measure was divided into seven sections. The first part mandated the creation of the law schools and specified the subjects that would be taught — chiefly French civil law, French public law, criminal law, and civil and criminal procedure. The second determined the course of study, which would be three years in duration, or four for those wishing to take a doctorate. Students would take one exam in the first and second year and two in the third year. The third part of the bill related to those who were excused from having to fulfill all of the requirements; one of the clauses in this section provided that students from the Académie de Législation and the Université de Jurisprudence would receive full credit for any instruction pursued in those institutions before the opening of the schools of law. If they had completed their studies, their law degree would be recognized; if they had completed fewer than three years of course work, they would receive credit for the courses completed. The fourth part specified the date when possession of a law degree would be required to practice in the judiciary. An article in this section decreed that, beginning in vendémiaire year XVII (September 1808), a law degree would be required in order to practice as a barrister. The fifth concerned the formation of the Tableau des avocats at the courts. Like the clause that had abolished the Order in 1790, the article authorizing the reorganization of the Order of Barristers was implicit rather than explicit; article twenty-nine indicated simply that a tableau des avocats would be formed, so that the reorganization of the Order and restoration of the term avocat were implied rather than stated. The sixth part of the bill dealt with the supervision of the law schools by the inspectors and the selection procedure for the inspectors, while the seventh declared that more detailed legislation on several of the points, including the formation of the tableau and the discipline of the bar, would be forthcoming.

In a long review of the motives for the bill, Fourcroy echoed Chaptal in asserting to the Legislative Body that the government had an obligation to offer legal study, claiming, in fact, that this was even more true since the Civil Code was about to be promulgated. He emphasized that the schools of law to be established would not perpetrate any of the abuses that were common under the Old Regime. Furthermore, he admitted that the reorganization of the barristers established a corporation, although he understated the point. In concluding his presentation, Fourcroy argued that the bill was designed to revive a branch of learning that had been dormant for many years, and sought to rid the legal profession of men who had debased it. The Legislative Body forwarded the measure to the Tribunate the same day.[76]

The bill, reported by the tribune Claude Joseph Mallarmé, came up for discussion in the Tribunate on 19 ventôse, and his explication of it reveals the matters on which the government felt vulnerable to criticism.[77] Mallarmé commented at length, for example, on the article concerning the Académie de Législation and the Université de Jurisprudence. Referring to the écoles centrales, he asserted that the government had a moral obligation to recognize studies pursued in them since they had been state institutions, arguing that students had attended the central schools in good faith and that the government therefore had to accept the courses or otherwise betray the students it had invited to study there. Mallarmé acknowledged that such considerations did not apply to the Académie de Législation and the Université de Jurisprudence, since they had never enjoyed the official status accorded to the central schools. He contended, however, that they had been official institutions in virtually every other respect. Although they had not been authorized by law, they had been virtually recognized by the regime, because several of the officers of both institutions, as well as some of the professors of the Académie de Législation, belonged to the highest echelons of the government. Mallarmé declared that both institutions had national reputations and attracted students from all areas of France. He told the Tribunate, however, that the action should not be construed as an endorsement of the institutions themselves, but as a just recognition of the academic achievements of the students who had been educated there.

Another section of the bill about which the government was clearly sensitive was the portion relating to the formation of the Tableau des avocats. Mallarmé opened his discussion by admitting that this segment was only distantly related to the other parts of the legislation; like Fourcroy before the Legislative Body, he acknowledged that the proposal would once again allow barristers to form a corporation. In an effort to deflect anticipated criticism, he told the tribunes that the future legislation reestablishing the Order would not allow it to have control over its members comparable to that enjoyed under the Old Regime.[78]

Once discussion began, however, the issues on which the government felt vulnerable to criticism did not emerge as a focus for debate. In his comments on the project, for example, Mathurin Louis Etienne Sedillez warmly praised the Académie de Législation, and heartily welcomed the reestablishment of the name and the tableau of the avocats; his remarks focused on the curriculum that would be offered in the schools of law. Similarly, Michel Carret, the only other tribune who expressed an opinion on the project, limited his comments primarily to its educational aspects and did not allude either to the formation of the tableau or to the private law schools.[79] After these speeches, and under the eyes of a police spy, the Tribunate approved the measure by a margin of fifty votes and returned it to the Legislative Body. After a presentation by Jean Baptiste Perrin, which was thematically similar to the one made by Mallarmé, the Legislative Body overwhelmingly approved the measure on 22 ventôse year XII (March 13, 1804), by a vote of 240 in favor and only 7 opposed.[80]

The passage of the law of 22 ventôse year XII seemed to represent the culmination of the effort of the former barristers to the Parlement to rebuild their professional organization, for its provisions overturned all of the remaining measures enacted against the Order in 1790. Moreover, the law sharply delineated the duties of the avoué and the avocat, and specifically prohibited the avoué from pleading a case unless he possessed a law degree. Thus, the law of 22 ventôse year XII also reversed the legislation of March 1791, which had created the défenseurs officieux and had allowed avoués to plead a case if authorized by their party. Although not completely comparable, the profession was in many respects restored to its Old Regime structure, with avoués analogous to procureurs, and avocats assuming their former role. The law was national in scope, but the prospects of the former Parisian avocats au Parlement in particular were bright. The educational establishments with which they had been closely affiliated had won the respect and admiration of the government, and the restoration of their Order, for which they had striven throughout the Revolution, seemed imminent.

7 / A Hollow Victory: 1804–1815

> At last, on December 14, 1810, under the title of decree, the regulation on the practice of the profession of barrister and the discipline of the bar, announced by the law of ventôse year XII, appeared. This decree, whose articles are preceded by a grand preamble on the honor of the profession of barrister, restored the former appellation of Order of Barristers (art. 19), but reestablished the barristers only very imperfectly in the use of their former discipline. Consequently, this decree, from its beginning and ever since, has not ceased to be the object of protests by the Order, and of a constant emission of the desire to see it amended.
>
> *André Marie Jean Jacques Dupin*
> Profession d'avocat

Only a few weeks after passage of the law of 22 ventôse year XII, which appeared to reflect a sense of harmony and common purpose between barristers and the government, the trial of General Jean Victor Moreau began. Moreau's trial irreparably harmed the rapport between the government and the avocats that had been embodied in law of 22 ventôse and embittered relations between Bonaparte and the barristers. It led Bonaparte to delay the reorganization of the Order and also influenced the manner in which he ultimately reconstituted it. Bonaparte successfully resisted all attempts by the Council of State to grant the Order some degree of autonomy. As a result, the reorganization of the Order in 1811 represented a hollow victory for the barristers, because the law authorizing it vested control of the Order more with the government than with the members of the Order itself.

On February 15, 1804, Bonaparte ordered the arrest of General Jean Victor Moreau for plotting with royalists to overthrow the government. Moreau had long been a rival of Bonaparte's, and the antipathy between them had increased markedly since Bonaparte's assumption of power. From the time of Bonaparte's accession, Moreau had remained at his estate at Grosbois, refusing to go to the Napoleonic court and holding in contempt those who did. When Bonaparte established the Legion of Honor, Moreau allegedly conferred a collar of honor upon his dog. Bonaparte became so angered by Moreau's affronts that at one point he contemplated challenging him to a duel in the Bois de Boulougne.[1] They subsequently professed to have settled their differences, but Bonaparte continued to harbor a visceral dislike for Moreau.

The degree of Moreau's involvement in the plots against Bonaparte is unclear, but most scholars agree that Moreau, whose indecisiveness was well known, was not a royalist and did not wish to associate himself with Cadoudal. Most also believe, however, that he was aware that a conspiracy existed, and that he wanted to see Bonaparte overthrown. In any event there can be little doubt that Bonaparte saw in Moreau's apparent participation an opportunity to discredit a feared and hated rival.

Between the time of Moreau's arrest in February and the beginning of his trial in May, two events occurred that served to give the case far greater significance. The first, and most important, was the kidnapping and execution of the duc d'Enghien in March 1804; the brutality and blatant illegality of the act seriously undermined Bonaparte's moral standing and damaged his image,[2] and it was followed barely two weeks later by the death in prison of General Pichegru. His death was officially termed a suicide, but, coming so soon after the execution of the duc d'Enghien, many believed that Pichegru had been murdered. Consequently, by the time the trial was ready to begin, a substantial portion of public opinion openly favored Moreau, who was perceived as being sacrificed to Bonaparte's personal ambitions. One contemporary described well the acrimony provoked by the trial when he noted the contrast between the fate of two generals who had previously been illustrious rivals sharing equally the glories of war. One, he said, was ascending to the imperial throne, the other to the scaffold, and sympathy naturally gravitated toward the less fortunate of the two. The case reached such proportions, in fact, that one police official asserted the trial had become more threatening than the plot itself.[3]

Accordingly, the government, which had been cautious in its handling of the proceedings since Moreau's arrest, took extraordinary precautions when the trial opened, including extensive spying on the barristers involved in the case. Within days of Moreau's arrest police spies attempted to learn who would represent Moreau in court. They reported that many hommes de loi had offered to defend him, and that Moreau's family had chosen Gaspard Gilbert Delamalle. When the trial began, the police intensified their observation of the barristers.[4]

The barristers sympathized with Moreau, and most appear to have been genuinely convinced of his innocence.[5] Before the Revolution, Moreau had been a law student at Rennes, and this seems to have elicited additional support for him; the barristers tended to view him virtually as one of their own. The execution of the duc d'Enghien, whom more than a score of barristers had volunteered to defend, further strengthened the barristers' support for Moreau. By the time the trial began even the police spies—whose early estimation of the Moreau case, before the execution of the duc d'Enghien, was that the barristers saw in it only an opportunity to make money—admitted that his defense had been laboriously prepared.[6]

The decision to try Moreau was clearly a mistake, and the error was compounded by the skillful defense conducted by his barristers. Moreau's chief counsels were Bellart and Bonnet, and virtually all of the other major defendants were represented by barristers formerly associated with the Order. For the entire duration of the trial Bonaparte worried about its outcome.[7] Police reports concentrated especially on the barristers as ardent partisans of Moreau, and blamed them for much of the agitation resulting from the proceedings. A report of 15 prairial year XII, for example, claimed that Moreau's trial had become comparable to that of Louis XVI, and mentioned that Moreau seemed to have several coteries among those involved with the law. A report of 17 prairial was even more explicit, stating that the barristers were continuing their intrigues and that they were using their offices to speak in favor of Moreau to their clients. This report, and others, charged the barristers with starting rumors and fomenting discord.[8]

The Université de Jurisprudence, in particular, came under heavy criticism from the police. After mentioning that Bexon, the vice-president of the université, had resisted a plan for the members of the governing board of the institution to make an address to Bonaparte, the report of 15 prairial stated:

The spirit of this establishment is absolutely opposed to the present order of things; they do not occupy themselves with political matters during the meetings, but before and after they spill out into the hallways, and there each member chats to his liking with his friends and acquaintances. Moreau has a great number of friends in this assembly, which is directed by barristers, whose nature is always turbulent and insubordinate, although they are not yet a corporation as in the Old Regime. In general, this class of citizens, which calls itself independent, does not miss any opportunity to embitter minds against the government.[9]

On 19 prairial the police once again sharply attacked the université in a report that stated that officers of the université had said that the entire bar was revolted by the case and implied that directors of the université may have been in contact with some generals, who were in turn attempting to discuss the matter with Bonaparte. The report could only have enraged Bonaparte, for he was aware that the greatest threat to his power came from disaffected generals. Indeed, the degree of suspicion with which the police regarded the Université de Jurisprudence can be seen in an interrogation of Charles Jean Baptiste Papet, who was arrested a few weeks after the conclusion of Moreau's trial. Papet had a loose affiliation with the Université de Jurisprudence, and the first question put to him in his interrogation related not to his activities on the evening of his arrest, but instead to his ties to the université. Throughout the entire period of the trial and afterward, police reports continually linked the dissent in favor of Moreau with the barristers.[10]

The Senate had ruled earlier that cases involving attempts on the life of the consuls could be decided without juries. Consequently, Moreau and other defendants were tried before a panel of twelve judges with no jury, and the government placed extraordinary pressure on the judges to produce a guilty verdict.[11] Despite the pressure, the panel decided by a vote of eight to four that Moreau was "guilty with extenuating circumstances," and even this equivocal decision was reached only after difficult deliberations. The court sentenced Moreau to two years in prison, but Bonaparte subsequently allowed him to go into exile.

The verdict, clearly the moral equivalent of an acquittal, infuriated Bonaparte, who, most contemporaries believed, had wanted a death sentence imposed on Moreau so that he could pardon him.[12] Bonaparte had four of the judges appear before him at Saint-Cloud, where he bitterly upbraided them. He apparently also considered deporting three of the barristers who participated in the trial — Bellart and Bonnet, who had defended Moreau, and Billecocq, who had represented the marquis de Rivière — but Cambacérès and Dubois, the prefect of police, dissuaded him from this. Nevertheless, at Bonaparte's insistence, the barristers were summoned before the minister of justice, who reprimanded them for their conduct and warned them to be more circumspect in the future.[13] Beyond all of this, the Moreau proceedings had long-lasting ramifications. They left Bonaparte with a deep aversion for Paris; by one account, he even considered moving the seat of government elsewhere. In addition, he became extremely suspicious of barristers in private practice, especially the barristers of Paris. He was particularly apprehensive about the influence barristers had on public opinion through their pleadings, and seems to have increased surveillance of the courts to deal with avocats who spoke out against the government. Most significant, his bitterness against barristers was so great that, in the wake of the Moreau trial, Bonaparte decided to delay the reorganization of the Order of Barristers.[14]

The estrangement between Bonaparte and the barristers became apparent in the plebiscite on the establishment of the Empire, which was held just before the beginning of the trial of Moreau. In the register recording the preference of most of the Parisian barristers, only three barristers out of the more than two hundred who were associated with the coalition of former avocats au Parlement voted for the Empire.[15] The results reflected the distrust that many of the barristers felt for Bonaparte, largely because of the Moreau trial, which could only have increased Bonaparte's suspicion of barristers.

The mutual antipathy between Bonaparte and the barristers complicated the task of the Council of State as it began preparing to implement the law of 22 ventôse year XII. Although Bonaparte had vowed not to reestablish the Order of Barristers after the Moreau trial, he directed the Council of State to begin work on the regulation of the profession of avocat. The organization of the law schools and the reconstitution of the Order of Barristers were considered as a single project in the deliberations that began the following month, fructidor year XII. The proposal for the establishment of the schools of law met with few difficulties, and the Council of State completed work on it in four meetings over a period of less than three weeks, with Bonaparte quickly approving and promulgating it on the fourth complementary day of the year XII (September 21, 1804).[16]

But work on the formation of the Order of Barristers proceeded slowly because of disputes that sharply divided the Council of State, a stronghold of the Brumairian elite and a body sympathetic to the legal profession. As drafted by Regnault de Saint-Jean d'Angély, the plan for Paris provided that the first tableau would be drawn up by the *procureur général impérial* of the court.[17] After that the task of drafting the tableau would revert back to the "collège des avocats." The project empowered the collège des avocats to elect a *chef,* who would have to have been in practice for at least ten years, and a *chambre de censure* of twelve members. Aspirants to the collège would present their law degree and take the oath prescribed by article 31 of the law of 22 ventôse, which required the candidate to swear that in the performance of his duties he would not say or publish anything contrary to the law, regulations, good morals, public tranquility, or security of the state, and would never transgress the respect due to the tribunal and public authority. The chambre de censure would take and verify information on the candidates presenting themselves for admission to the collège, and then the *chef* would meet with the chambre de censure and report on them. The candidates were either admitted, in which case they would begin a three year probationary period under the scrutiny of the chambre de censure, or they were refused admission. In the event of the latter, the *chef* had to submit a written justification for the action to the procureur général impérial of the court, who, in turn, would make a report to the tribunal, which would then decide whether or not the candidate would be admitted. Either the collège des avocats or the candidate could appeal an unfavorable decision by the court to a higher body; decisions from a tribunal of first instance would be appealed to an appeals court; appeals from a criminal court or an appeals court would be forwarded to the Council of State.

Internal discipline of the bar was structured in a similar manner. Article 18 of the project declared that the rights of surveillance, reprimand, and correction belonged to the collège, but these were the least punitive forms of discipline. The chambre de censure was supposed to receive and investigate complaints lodged against avocats as a result of the exercise of their profession and to settle internal disputes among barristers of the collège. If some sort of reprimand was deemed appropriate for an offense, the *chef* exercised disciplinary powers in conjunction with the chambre de censure. In cases in which this body recommended suspension or disbarment as a penalty, it had to convoke the entire collège. If the collège upheld the suspension or disbarment, the reasons had to be stated in a written report and submitted to the appeals court, which would make the final pronouncement. Once again, however, either party could appeal an unfavorable decision to the Council of State.

Article 40 was a final noteworthy provision of the bill. It decreed that the collège des avocats could not interfere in, propose, or hold any discussion on any political case *(affaire politique)* without risking prosecution under the laws against illegal assemblies that disturbed the peace.[18]

These were the major features of the project, and they merit further comment. The most conspicuous characteristic of the project was its absolute avoidance of any Old Regime terminology, except that of *avocat* itself. *Collège* was used in place of *ordre*, *chef* in place of *bâtonnier*, and *chambre de censure* instead of *conseil* or *députation*. The government, still sensitive about reorganizing an Old Regime corporation, sought to disguise the restitution of the professional organization of barristers by utilizing terms other than those of 1789. Also obvious are the limits placed on the collège des avocats in comparison with the Old Regime. During the Old Regime the Order had possessed absolute and final authority on the admission of candidates, as well as on questions of suspension and disbarment. But under the plan considered by the Council of State, the collège ultimately had to defer to the judgment of an outside body, either the court or the Council of State, although the initiative for disciplinary action remained with the collège itself.

The clause prohibiting the collège from interfering in political cases was another important feature of the bill. Political cases were not defined, which left the barristers vulnerable to prosecution by the government. In addition, the distinction between a political case and a nonpolitical case was tenuous, as was the distinction between interfering in a case and offering a professional opinion to a colleague. The clause was almost certainly a result of the Moreau trial and reflected Bonaparte's apprehension about the ability of the barristers to influence public opinion through their briefs and pleadings. It potentially represented a situation somewhat analogous to that of 1793–94, when the barristers' professional role in defending counterrevolutionaries rendered them politically suspect. Once again the barristers were, in effect, caught in a conflict between their professional duties and the perceived political needs of the state.

Cambacérès rightly foresaw problems with the plan, and disagreements over the project arose immediately. On 8 fructidor year XII, after the first day of examination of the proposal, Cambacérès reported to Bonaparte that the question of the Order of Barristers presented great difficulties. One of the most divisive issues was the fact that control of the Order was ultimately vested with the Council of State, and it is apparent that several members saw the proposed legislation as too limiting.[19]

The reasons for the impasse were the result of differing attitudes and objectives between the Council of State and Bonaparte. It is clear that the council, without necessarily wanting to return to the self-rule of the Old Regime, nevertheless sought to grant barristers freedom in the exercise of their profession in order to prevent matters of law from becoming politicized, which is why they did not want ultimate control to reside with the Council of State. Members of the council regarded law as an autonomous set of principles to regulate the conduct of individuals within society, and believed that some of that autonomy should be extended to practitioners in order to guarantee the inviolability of the law.

Bonaparte, however, did not accord law such independent or allodial status, and was therefore certainly not prepared to grant any measure of independence to the legal profession. Instead, Bonaparte believed that law should be subordinated to centralized control and the needs of the state, which is the reason he insisted that control of the profession should be vested with the minister of justice or the Council of State.

The differences were deep, and it was this division of opinion that led to a separation of the plan for the law schools from that for the Order of Barristers.[20] Even after the promulgation of the law regarding the law schools, contentious discussions about the Order of Barristers continued. Hopelessly divided, the Council of State sent the project to Bonaparte for his opinion, apparently hoping that he would return to the council to contribute personally to the deliberations. Bonaparte's reaction to the bill was remarkable. He sent a scathing letter to Cambacérès that not only revealed his deep bitterness toward the legal profession, but also divulged his reason for seeking to reorganize the Order: "My cousin, I receive a proposed decree on the barristers. There is nothing in it that gives the minister of justice the means of controlling them. I would prefer to do nothing rather than deprive myself of the means of taking measures against this pack of chatterboxes, artisans of revolutions, almost all of whom are inspired only by crime and corruption. As long as I have my sword at my side I will never sign a decree as absurd [as this one]. I wish that one could cut out the tongue of a barrister who will serve against the government."[21] The reply doubtlessly stunned Cambacérès, who had envisaged completing work on the project by 15 brumaire year XIII, when the courts returned from vacation.[22] Cambacérès strongly recommended that Bonaparte return to the Council of State in order to participate personally in the discussion. Bonaparte took his advice and attended the session of 24 vendémiaire year XIII (October 16, 1804) dealing with the question of barristers.[23]

Bonaparte made clear his dissatisfaction with the project drawn up by the Council of State during his absence, and spoke at length on the need to curtail the independence of the profession, especially denouncing the influence of barristers on juries and public opinion. Bonaparte declared that he wanted barristers to be under the direct control of the minister of justice, with the minister having the power to dismiss or suspend barristers from practice, a statement that reveals how Bonaparte framed the reorganization of the Order within the scheme of centralized power developed by the regime. The response of the Council of State demonstrates the belief of several of its members in the autonomy of law and a measure of self-determination for those who practiced it; Cambacérès, who had close ties to the barristers of Paris, Treilhard, a member of the Order in Paris under the Old Regime, and Lebrun all argued for the independence of barristers. Berlier, while claiming that he did not fear misuse by the current government, saw a potential for the abuse of such strong power from a future government and proposed that the measure be put into effect for only ten years. Lebrun spoke again, stating that he was too much of a friend of freedom and property to concentrate so much power in a single hand.

Bonaparte, probably surprised and clearly annoyed by the opposition to his proposal, continued to disparage the profession, apparently at length, and it is obvious from an example he gave that the trial of Moreau was the precedent guiding him. The meeting ended in a deadlock, however, for the council reached no decision on the structure of the profession, and work on the project did not resume.

Although deliberations on the Order of Barristers came to a halt, the effort to establish the schools of law moved forward. In his letter acknowledging Bonaparte's approval of the plan, Cambacérès noted that is would be difficult to place all twelve law schools authorized in operation by the year XIII; he suggested that those in Paris and Toulouse be established first and placed in activity by that time, even if the others were not.[24] But this goal was not met, and the Académie de Législation and the Université de Jurisprudence remained the only functioning law faculties in France. Although no enrollment figures are available, the Académie de Législation continued to progress during the year XIII, whereas the Université de Jurisprudence, as has been noted, closed at the conclusion of the year XIII.[25]

The future of the Académie de Législation was uncertain, however, because of the imminent reorganization of state-operated schools of law. While the law of 22 ventôse year XII had provided that students from the Académie de Législation and the Université de Jurisprudence would receive full credit for studies pursued there until 1 vendémiaire year XV (September 1806), the law of the fourth complementary day year XII organizing the law schools made no mention of them whatsoever. The administrator of the académie, Bruguière, urged the government to declare the académie the school of law for Paris, an action that he claimed would save the government 150,000 francs, but his recommendation was ignored. Bruguière also forwarded to Bonaparte a proposal whereby the académie would have been recognized as a branch of the law school at Paris, but this, too, was rejected. Bruguière clearly regarded the organization of the law school as a threat to the existence of the académie, and he attempted to postpone the scheduled opening of the school of law at Paris from the year XIV to the year XV.[26] The effort was unsuccessful, however, and when the school of law at Paris opened in the year XIV, the académie was forced to reexamine its function.

Initially, the académie sought to compete with the Paris law school. In his letter arguing for the postponement of the law school at Paris, Bruguière reminded Fourcroy, the Director General of Public Instruction, that the académie had been authorized to offer classes until the year XV. He questioned whether the law school was prepared to assume its duties, and implied that the académie would offer its courses, a decision that it had recently decreed and publicized.[27] The académie held classes in the year XIV, even after the opening of the law school, and competition between the Académie de Législation and the school of law for students led to much resentment by the latter against the académie; a pamphlet war between them ensued. Moreover, students attending the académie were threatened by the administration of the law school with nonrecognition of studies performed at the académie during the year XIV. In the midst of such uncertainty, the year XIV was a difficult one for the académie, and the precipitous drop in both revenues and expenditures indicates the greatly reduced level of activity that year.[28]

By the fall of 1806, which corresponded to what would have been the year XV, the académie announced that while waiting for the government to clarify precisely what its role would be, it would again offer courses beginning November 20. The académie now sought to complement rather than compete with the school of law, not only by admitting exclusively students already registered at the school, but also by offering courses conforming to those taught there.[29] It also intended to supplement the curriculum at the school of law by holding exercises in pleading and public speaking.

Other steps taken by the académie to redefine itself underscored its sense of affinity with the abolished Order. It proclaimed that it would increase the number of conférences on questions of law, and specifically mentioned the conférences formerly held in the Bibliothèque des avocats as its model. It even went so far as to suggest that graduates of the law school could enroll at the académie for an initial probationary period.[30] In the fall of 1806, then, with its role as an educational institution diminished, the académie increasingly reverted to its function as a surrogate for the Order.

By late 1806, however, the financial condition of the académie was precarious, due primarily to a large accumulated debt. The government seems to have taken advantage of the situation to weaken the académie further by overruling a financial transaction favorable to it. In November 1806 the académie could not offer the courses that it had scheduled, and Bruguière wrote a desperate and unsuccessful letter to Fourcroy asking him to help save the institution. It is a measure of his desperation that Bruguière even wrote a long, obsequious poem to the Emperor in an attempt to save the académie but, predictably, this effort also failed; the académie apparently closed early in 1807.[31]

Despite its relatively brief existence, the Académie de Législation had helped to revive the legal profession in Paris, and in many other parts of France, at a critical time when it was suffering from abuses. As Bruguière proudly noted, with some exaggeration, "when neither the government nor private individuals offered any means for learning law, it brought back the study [of law] with honor" and "maintained it with glory." Moreover, several of its former students went on to achieve distinguished careers in various fields of French law in the nineteenth century. Indeed, for much of the nineteenth century, the Académie de Législation was renowned for the contributions it had made to the French legal profession.[32]

Beginning in 1806, then, the state offered all legal education in France under the auspices of the law schools. The manner in which they were established again reflects Bonaparte's distrust of the legal profession. The curriculum was rigidly structured and the subject matter narrowly prescribed, with the law even specifying the fashion in which the courses would be taught. Above all, Bonaparte sought to ensure that the teaching of law would not allude to the major economic, legislative, or social problems of the day.[33] In addition, Bonaparte was vested with the right to name all of the professors and substitutes. After their appointment, they had to take an oath at the Appeals Court that included a vow not merely to execute their duties faithfully, but also to swear obedience to the constitutions of the Empire and to promise loyalty to the Emperor. The professors were named for life, but those appointed in the initial organization would have their appointment validated only after three years of probation, and only if Bonaparte deemed it appropriate to confirm them. Bonaparte also chose the director and secretary of the school, with the former selected from among the professors. The director served a three-year term and could be reappointed.

Some of the individuals appointed as professors or substitutes had been members of the Order before 1789, but few of them had remained affiliated with the coalition formed after the Order's abolition. Claude Etienne Delvincourt had belonged to the Order under the Old Regime and had become a member of the faculty of the law school at Paris in 1790. After the suppression of the school in 1793, he worked in the Ministry of the Marine until the law schools were reorganized. At that time he applied for a position, and was selected to teach the course on the Civil Code. Eustache Nicolas Pigeau had become a member of the Order on December 22, 1774, but left it in 1786. During the Revolution he worked as a clerk in the publishing house Desaint, a noted publisher of works in law that had published Pigeau's own book. Subsequently, he offered private instruction in law until called to teach procedure at the school of law at the time of its reorganization. Only Henri François Caillau, who received the less important position of substitute, had continued in close association with the coalition formed by members of the Order after its abolition.[34]

The background of the occupants of the other chairs varied. Jean François Berthelot had been a member of the faculty of the law school at Paris under the Old Regime but had not belonged to the Order of

Barristers. After the creation of the central schools, he had taught the course of legislation at the central school of the Gard. With the reorganization of the law school at Paris, he received an appointment to teach Roman law. François Morand had studied law at the University of Toulouse and the University of Bourges under the Old Regime. He apparently came to Paris during the Revolution and taught the course of legislation at the central school of Quatre Nations in Paris. Subsequently, he taught at both the Université de Jurisprudence and the Académie de Législation before being called to the chair of French public law at the school of law. Finally, with his experience as a legislator in the Convention, the Council of Five Hundred, and the Tribunate, Louis François René Portiez (de l'Oise) would appear to have been a sound choice for the position of French civil law in relation to public administration. The reality, however, was quite different. Not only had Portiez never earned a law degree, but he was also well known for his lack of intelligence, and his tenure as a professor and as director of the law school was less than successful.[35] His appointment, and particularly his designation as director of the law school, revealed above all Bonaparte's contempt for the legal profession.

The reorganization of the law school at Paris produced a strong revival of interest in legal education. In 1806 the school had 667 students enrolled for the fall term, including 276 who were just beginning their studies, a surge of interest that surprised even the administrators of the school, and by the spring of 1808 the number of students had risen to 885.[36] At the same time, other law schools authorized by the government were coming into operation. Whatever other problems might confront it, the profession would never again be threatened by a potential shortage of trained aspirants, as it had been only a few years previously; the reopening of the law schools assured the renewal of the profession.

Although work on the project to reconstitute the Order of Barristers had stopped altogether, the Council of State did win approval for the implementation of other provisions of the law of 22 ventôse year XII designed to reintroduce competency into the profession of avocat. In accordance with article 24 of the law, on 6 vendémiaire year XIV (September 28, 1805) the Council of State passed a measure by which the procureurs généraux of the appeals courts had to verify law degrees earned under the Old Regime or to confirm that one had taken the oath of barrister. Bonaparte approved the plan, and promulgated a law on the matter on 10 brumaire year XIV (November 1, 1805). The act, which appears to have been strictly enforced, would have winnowed out untrained men who might still be in practice. A few weeks later, on January 11, 1806, the Council of State advised Bonaparte not to extend the interval provided in article 18 of the law for défenseurs officieux and hommes de loi to obtain a law degree; on January 23 Bonaparte agreed and terminated the delay that had been granted.[37] The action prevented those without law degrees who had not received a dispensation from the government under article 28 of the law from practicing. Thus, the impasse on the project for reestablishing the Order did not impede other measures for reforming the legal profession.

Discussion of the reorganization of the Order resumed in 1806 through an unusual circumstance. On March 10, 1806, François Denis Tronchet, the last president of the Order before its abolition, died. At the time of his death, Tronchet was a senator and a member of the Cour de cassation, but he had maintained close contact with his former colleagues from the Order, who decided to hold a memorial service in his honor. The coalition chose Gaspard Gilbert Delamalle, a prominent avocat au Parlement under the Old Regime who was closely involved in the effort of the former barristers to the Parlement to rebuild their Order, to deliver the eulogy. The eulogy posed a sensitive problem and caused Bonaparte some concern. Because he had been associated with Tronchet in the government, and because of his close ties to the barristers of Paris, Cambacérès was to be among those in attendance, which meant that the service for one of the defenders of Louis XVI would be held in the presence of one of the men who had voted for Louis's death. Delamalle, however, was quite prudent in his treatment of the matter and no incident ensued. In a communication that betrayed the apprehension he had felt, Bonaparte wrote Delamalle a kind note commending him for his civility. He alluded to the delicate situation and told Delamalle that a "mauvais esprit" could have used the occasion to give offense to many and to reopen old wounds, something that Bonaparte said would have been most contrary to his wishes. Delamalle's discretion may have reduced Bonaparte's suspicion of barristers, for shortly afterward he instructed the minister of justice, Regnier, to prepare a project on the practice of the profession of avocat and the discipline of the bar.[38]

Regnier submitted his plan to Bonaparte in June 1806. As it would have applied to Paris, the project called for the procureur général of the Appeals Court to convoke all those who had the right to practice as barristers. If there was a dispute concerning an individual's right to participate, the court would decide his eligibility. Under the presidency of the oldest member, the avocats would proceed to select a committee of discipline to draw up the tableau. There would be only one tableau in Paris, located at the Appeals Court. Those barristers inscribed at the Appeals Court could practice at any court within its jurisdiction, but to practice at a court beyond the jurisdiction of the Appeals Court would require authorization from the minister of justice.[39] In future years the committee of discipline itself would draft the tableau.

In the years after its initial organization, the collège des avocats would elect the committee of discipline, which in turn would select the president. Besides drawing up the tableau, the other duties of the committee were to maintain order and regulations among the barristers, to preserve the honor and reputation of the collège, to supervise the probationary barristers, and to punish infractions by barristers that were beyond the competence of the court. The possible penalties that could be inflicted were warning, censure, reprimand, suspensions for three or six months, and disbarment. The committee of discipline had the power to impose warning, censure, or reprimand after hearing the accused barrister; the reasons for its action had to be given at the next meeting of the collège. For a suspension, the committee had to hear the accused avocat at least twice, with a minimum interval of eight days between the hearings. The recommendation of the committee had to go to the minister of justice, along with any evidence that might have been presented, and the decision required the minister's approval. In cases of disbarment, the committee had to make its recommendation in writing. The president had to convene the entire collège within three days, and present to the assembly the opinion of the committee and all evidence in the case. The accused barrister had to be heard, and was entitled to request a delay of up to two weeks to prepare a defense. If the collège concurred in disbarment, its opinion had to be sent within three days to the minister of justice for confirmation; the minister could then either approve the action or order the avocat reinstated.

Other prominent aspects of the project included article 2, which decreed that barristers had to take the oath prescribed in article 31 of the law of 22 ventôse year XII annually. Article 21 stipulated that if a barrister in his pleading or in his writings attacked the constitutions of the Empire, the law, the government, or established authorities, the court could pronounce his suspension at once. Article 42 strictly forbade barristers from interfering in matters of state under the penalty of suspension or even of disbarment, which the government reserved for itself through the minister of justice.[40]

A cover letter that Regnier sent to Bonaparte with the project is of particular interest, for it shows the conflicting demands that had to be reconciled in the proposal. Regnier began by confessing that the plan contained few provisions that were new. He asserted that former laws and usage offered sensible rules and principles that, with some modifications, could be profitably emulated. This was clearly a tacit recognition of the desire of the barristers and some members of the Council of State to have the reestablished Order conform as much as possible to the structure and custom of the abolished Order and to confer upon it some autonomy.

Yet Regnier was also acutely aware of Bonaparte's mandates and priorities. Therefore, after telling Bonaparte that the project included many tendencies from the Old Regime, Regnier sought to assure him that the bill met his dictates. Regnier wrote: "I am proposing an important reform only in the part that concerns the police and discipline of the barristers because it seems to me necessary to place narrow limits on the complete independence that the barristers of several parlements, and particularly those at Paris, formerly appropriated."[41] Obviously, Bonaparte's resolution to control barristers—a view forcefully expressed several times in 1804—was not merely a temporary phenomenon brought on by his anger over the Moreau trial; rather, the trial had caused Bonaparte such great concern that his determination to wield restraint over barristers and to subordinate law to the needs of the state continued to be governing tenets for any discussion of the reorganization of the Order. In addition, Regnier's special mention of the barristers of Paris, toward whom Bonaparte was most antagonistic, indicates that while the plan was ostensibly designed to regulate the legal profession throughout France, it was, in fact, directed above all against the barristers of Paris.

The remainder of the letter gave details on the principles that had guided Regnier in his drafting of the project. In a sentence that most likely reflects another injunction that Bonaparte had given him, Regnier claimed that there was a need to regulate avocats because of "the influence that they naturally have on a multitude of individuals." He asserted that although the infractions or offenses that a barrister might commit in his duties were within the competence of the judiciary, it would be "against the nature of things" to have the courts responsible for purely disciplinary matters. At the same time, it was essential not to allow a barrister to be abandoned entirely to the impulses of some or all of his colleagues.

Regnier therefore proposed to allow the collège des avocats to regulate questions of honor and integrity in the exercise of the profession. The discretionary powers available exclusively to the collège would be the warning, the censure, and the reprimand. For more serious offenses, the collège would not be permitted to act on its own. It would have to defer to the authority of the government, which would be the ultimate arbiter.[42]

Regnier's proposal formed the basis for extensive discussions throughout the summer of 1806. His original project, dated June 27, 1806, went through five revisions dated July 3, July 11, July 29, August 4, and August 12. The main points of dispute concerned the formation of the first tableau, the oath to be taken by the avocats, and jurisdictions in which barristers were free to practice.

Regnier's bill had specified that the first tableau would be drawn up by an assembly of avocats which, under the presidency of its oldest member, would elect a council of discipline to draft the tableau. Beginning with the second revision on July 11, however, the initial tableau was not to be drawn up by the barristers themselves, but by the president, most senior member (doyen), and procureur général of the court, an action that clearly gave the government a far greater degree of control over the profession in the initial stage of reorganization. All those who were eligible by the law of 22 ventôse year XII would be included if they could substantiate their personal integrity *(bonne vie et moeurs)*, and there was no provision for settling disputes concerning the eligibility of an individual to belong to the Order.[43] Moreover, according to the next revision, that of July 29, the tableau had to be approved by the minister of justice. In addition, while the proposal of July 11 had given the council of discipline the right to regulate the tableau subsequently, the proposal of July 29 held that the tableau could be amended only with the concurrence of the procureur général.

In the revisions through the project of July 11 the barristers only had to swear the oath prescribed by article 31 of the law of 22 ventôse year XII annually. Article 13 of the project of July 29, however, prescribed a new oath that was quite vague, almost certainly to facilitate disciplinary action against avocats whose conduct was suspect.[44] Article 28 mandated that the Order meet annually as a body to swear it. In addition, article 29 of the project of July 29 also required the Order to convene two times per year to admonish members of the Order — barristers who had lost a large number of cases, or those who had accepted unworthy cases, were to be advised to be more discriminating in the cases that they accepted.

The proposal of July 29 also placed greater restrictions on the barristers' freedom to practice in courts within the jurisdiction where they were inscribed, although only one segment of the article affected the barristers at Paris. According to article 9 of the bill, a barrister's first appearance before a criminal court required prior introduction to the president and the procureur général of the court.[45]

The revised draft of July 29 was obviously far more restrictive and unfavorable to the barristers than the original project submitted by Regnier. It left the avocats with no real control over their tableau and attenuated even the limited discretionary powers available to the Order by requiring two meetings a year to admonish members. The ambiguity of the oath to be taken also left them vulnerable to disciplinary action by the government. The repressive provisions, doubtlessly inserted at the behest of Bonaparte, provoked another response by the Council of State, which continued to seek to accord barristers a measure of independence in the practice of law. The Council of State reacted in a revised bill dated August 4, which contained a preamble that had not been in any previous drafts.

The preamble began by pointedly noting that "when we reestablished the schools of law through the law of 22 ventôse year XII, we did so particularly with a view to restoring to the profession of barrister its former brilliance; we ordered, for this purpose, the formation of the tableau of barristers." The preamble asserted that the maintenance of the tableau had been shown by experience to be the most appropriate means for upholding the qualities desirable in barristers, and continued by recalling that formerly the barristers had "always made it a duty to maintain themselves a rigorous discipline among their colleagues and to admit to the tableau only those who were worthy of it." It concluded with a statement of purpose regarding its plan for reorganizing the Order of Barristers. In speaking of the profession of avocat, the concluding statement said "we wish to guarantee its freedom, its independence and its nobility, while placing limits that separate it from license, insubordination and corruption."[46]

The preamble was a clear riposte to Bonaparte's attempt to subvert the rationale for reestablishing the Order. In seeking to restore the Order, Bonaparte, in accord with his focus on order and discipline in the state, had given priority to state jurisdiction over the legal profession—all other considerations had been secondary to this objective. The Council of State, however, in recalling the purpose for reinstituting the tableau, emphasized that the aim of reorganizing the Order was the restoration of ethics and proficiency. Moreover, by reminding Bonaparte that the avocats had formerly maintained a rigorous discipline themselves, and by stating that it sought to guarantee the freedom, independence, and nobility of the profession, the Council of State served notice that the effort to dominate barristers had gone too far.

The revisions that were put forward in the August 4 proposal further underscore the attempt to reorient the deliberations. The initial tableau, for example, would still be drawn up by the president, the senior member, and the procureur général of the court, but a new clause stipulated that they were to work with and take the advice of "several senior jurisconsultes." The qualifications necessary for joining the Order were expanded, with the August 4 project decreeing that *capacité, probité, délicatesse,* and *bonne vie et moeurs* were required, rather than bonne vie et moeurs only, as in the July 29 plan, and changes in the tableau in succeeding years did not require the concurrence of the procureur général. It relaxed some of the provisions limiting the geographical area in which a barrister could practice. In matters of discipline, the suspension or disbarment of a barrister had to be approved only by the court rather than by the minister of justice, although the procureur général of the court had to apprise the minister of justice of the action when it was imposed.

The August 4 project did not rescind all of the restrictive provisions. Those that remained included the approval of the minister of justice for the tableau, the swearing of the annual oath, the wording of which remained unchanged, and the requirement of the Order to meet twice a year to admonish members. Nevertheless, the August 4 proposal restricted the professional organization of barristers less than that of July 29, thereby reversing the trend toward greater control over the Order that had developed in earlier projects.

On August 12, 1806, the Council of State adopted the August 4 plan substantially unchanged and sent it to Bonaparte for approval. But on August 21, 1806, Bonaparte disapproved the project, with a notation that it be sent to the archchancellor for his opinion as his only comment.[47] There can be little doubt that his disapproval resulted from a belief that the proposed legislation did not afford the state a sufficient amount of control over the profession, so that once again the effort to reorganize the Order had failed.

Indeed, during this interregnum the government did not accord the coalition of barristers any authority over their profession; in virtually all matters affecting it, it was the government alone that acted. In a case involving professional conduct, for example, in early 1807 the minister of justice investigated the comportment of Pierre Nicolas Berryer at a trial in Compiègne. Both the procureur impérial and the president of the Tribunal of First Instance wrote letters assailing Berryer's bearing in their courtroom. The president of the court, Poulletier, who said he had formerly been an avocat au Parlement at Paris, was particularly taken aback by Berryer's behavior. Poulletier stated that Berryer had set a poor example for the bar at Compiègne and declared that if any of its members had conducted themselves in a similar manner, he would not have allowed them to continue. He further said that he had not acted against Berryer because he had not wanted to humiliate him, out of "consideration for the bar of Paris," and also due to his "esteem for the former barristers to the Parlement of this capital, among whose number I had the honor of being included."[48] Under the Old Regime such an infraction would have been within the jurisdiction of the Order, and Poulletier's assertion that he did nothing out of "consideration for the bar of Paris" at least hints that the incident might have been a matter for the "bar of Paris" to resolve. All of the drafts of projects for the reorganization of the Order had given it the power of warning, censure, or reprimand, which is all that such an offense would have merited, without the approval of the court or the government. Thus, the government could have allowed the coalition to deliberate on the episode without having to reverse itself; instead, however, it was the Ministry of Justice that attended to the matter.

Another incident in late 1807 involving practitioners at the Criminal Court of Paris further illustrates the lack of authority by the barristers over their profession. In October 1807 the president of the Criminal Court of Paris, Hémart, wrote to the minister of justice to bring to his attention the scandalous activities of several barristers in the Criminal Court. He told the minister that many counselors were introducing themselves into the prisons, and were even forging close ties with prison guards in order to gain access to a greater number of prisoners. Hémart stated that in court these counselors often altered transcripts or evidence and calumniated opposing witnesses; he also cited other reprehensible practices, including soliciting money from clients in prison by telling them that it was necessary to bribe individuals who could be useful. Hémart went on to complain about two avocats in particular, Herici and Lauze de Perret, whose behavior he found especially objectionable. Reputable barristers abhorred the conduct of such men, he noted, and had often refused to represent individuals in criminal cases because of the risk of associating with these counselors. Hémart concluded by suggesting two measures to deal with the situation. The first was to allow only avocats and avoués listed in the *Almanach Impérial* to represent the accused, and the second was to give the court the right to interdict any counselor in whom the court had no confidence.[49]

The minister of justice wrote Bonaparte to advise him of the situation and to endorse the two proposals advocated by Hémart. Bonaparte, however, refused to approve the first measure, ordering instead that the procureur général and the president of the court compose a list of those guilty of abuses. They were then to forward the list to the police, who would keep the men from appearing in court.[50]

Bonaparte's action is revealing, for it once again highlights his intention to subordinate the Order of Barristers completely to the authority of the state. To have empowered the court to admit only avocats listed in the *Almanach Impérial* would have been tantamount to implicit recognition of an Order in Paris, a group that in turn could have asserted certain rights and established certain precedents before the Order was officially reestablished by the government. Bonaparte sought to avoid such a situation, and therefore could not approve Hémart's recommendation. He wanted to ensure that the reorganized Order's structure and authority were clearly delineated, and that they resulted solely from governmental decree rather than precedent; in the interim Bonaparte strove to deprive the barristers of any self-determination in their profession.

Although Bonaparte's response did not give Hémart all of the prerogatives he sought, it did result in action against unscrupulous practitioners, for several months later, in February 1808, Lauze de Perret, one of the barristers cited by Hémart, was arrested. The example of Lauze de Perret epitomizes the inability of the barristers to exercise very much influence over their profession. Pierre Joseph Lauze de Perret had been an inspector general of police in Turin, but had stolen sums of money intended for "secret expenses." After being removed from his position, he fled to Paris, where, in thermidor year XII (July 1804), he was accused of fraud and theft and imprisoned. He remained in prison until frimaire year XIII (December 1804), when he was sent to his place of birth, St. Etienne (Lozère), to be kept under surveillance. Subsequently, he returned to Paris and began to practice law. Despite his questionable past, Lauze de Perret succeeded in having himself included in the list of jurisconsultes published in the *Almanach Impérial* in 1806 and 1807, and even after Hémart wrote his letter to the minister of justice in October 1807, noting that he received complaints against Lauze de Perret daily, Lauze de Perret remained on the list in the *Almanach Impérial* for 1808. In February 1808 he was arrested for receiving jewelry, money, and other items from prisoners being transferred before the Criminal Court by claiming that they were necessary to bribe the procureur général and judges. Along with a substitute judge of the Criminal Court, Vinot, Lauze de Perret was tried before the Tribunal de police correctionelle, a lesser criminal court, for fraud and abuse of confidence. After attempting unsuccessfully to escape during the trial, he was found guilty of the charges against him, as was Vinot; both were fined fifty francs and sentenced to six months imprisonment.[51]

The fact that the former avocats au Parlement were forced to tolerate the presence of an individual such as Lauze de Perret in the profession, and particularly to see him receive virtually the same degree of professional accreditation as they in the *Almanach Impérial*, demonstrates how powerless they were in governing their profession. It was only after the government had brought charges against him, a development that itself came only after the president of the Criminal Court had taken up the matter with the highest authorities, that Lauze de Perret was removed from practice. Moreover, Lauze de Perret was by no means unique.[52] Despite the promise of the law of 22 ventôse year XII to reorganize the Order, the coalition could do no more than it had done since the abolition of the Order in 1790, which was merely to segregate itself from such men.

Other actions taken in 1808 concerning the judiciary affected the profession of barrister. In October 1807 the Senate voted to form a commission of ten senators to examine judges in France and the annexed departments. Its mandate was to replace judges who for various reasons — physical infirmities, venality, questionable conduct — were considered unfit to hold office. The commission completed its work in 1808, when over one hundred judges, including some former avocats au Parlement from Paris, were dismissed or compelled to retire.[53] The purge, and a subsequent one in 1811, coinciding with the reorganization of the appeals courts, led several of the magistrates affected to take up the profession of avocat.

Similarly, in 1808 the government suppressed 112 avoués in Paris and fixed the number of avoués at 150. Each remaining avoué was required to pay a sum of 14,933 francs, so that each of the 112 suppressed avoués received an indemnity of 20,000 francs. Nevertheless, the 112 avoués whose positions were eliminated were forced to find a new livelihood, and several, who were qualified by virtue of their possession of a law degree, became barristers. More than 25 percent of the new entrants into the profession in 1808, in fact, were avoués whose position had been annulled.[54] Like the magistrates who had been discharged, they entered the profession essentially involuntarily.

Despite its impotence, the coalition of avocats continued to operate throughout the period, and one of its functions provided the impetus for the resumption of discussion on the reestablishment of the Order. On July 5, 1807, François Alexis Nicolas Ferey died. Ferey had been one of the most respected and distinguished members of the Order under the Old Regime, and in 1790 he had figured prominently in forming the coalition that had sought to maintain the values and standards of the abolished Order. In his will, written in 1806, he left his law books to the "Ordre des avocats, under whatever name His Majesty the Emperor and King will see fit to reestablish it" for its library.[55] He also designated a sum of money to go to the Order to provide for the purchase of other law books deemed necessary.

On February 5, 1810, the coalition of barristers, all wearing their professional robes, held a memorial service for Ferey. Cambacérès, who remained in close association with the coalition, directed the service, and Nicolas François Bellart, one of the younger barristers in 1789 who had been active in the coalition since the abolition of the Order, delivered the eulogy. It is important to remember the presence of Cambacérès, for there can be little doubt that Bellart's highly emotional oration was above all directed at him. Bellart recalled how fervently Ferey had wished to see the Order and its library reestablished. He alluded obliquely to the delay in reorganizing the Order by noting that Bonaparte had "already reestablished discipline in a great number of diverse professions," and said that the time would come when he would take notice of theirs. Then, said Bellart, the prayers of Ferey, "to which we [the coalition] dare to join ours, " would be fulfilled.[56] Bellart's oblique appeal to Cambacérès evidently succeeded, for only a few weeks later, on March 19, 1810, the Council of State resumed work on the reestablishment of the Order after a hiatus of nearly four years.

On March 19, 1810, the plan of August 12, 1806, was reprinted and utilized as the basis for consideration. According to notes on one copy of the project, the question came up for consideration on June 5, 1810, and as a result of the resolutions reached in this discussion a new project was drawn up on June 29 by Jean Baptiste Treilhard, a former member of the Order in Paris.[57]

Treilhard made several changes. In the June 29 draft he tempered the preamble so that it would not be inflammatory to Bonaparte. It did not say that the formation of the tableau had been ordered to restore the profession of barrister to "its former brilliance." Rather, it stated that "a profession whose practice powerfully influences the distribution of justice has caught our attention," and that in order to help assure the courts the esteem that was due them, it had ordered the formation of the tableau. It omitted the references to the barristers' maintenance of a rigorous discipline by themselves, instead placing greater emphasis on the need of the magistracy to supervise a profession with which it had such close ties.

Most of the other changes centered on issues that had figured prominently in past discussions. The procedure for the formation of the first tableau is an example. Where the March 19 project had ordered that it be drafted by the president, the most senior member, and the procureur général of the Appeals Court in conjunction with the advice of "one or several senior jurisconsultes," the June 29 proposal was more precise. It said that the tableau would be drawn up by the president and the procureur général of the court (the doyen was not mentioned), in conjunction with six senior barristers in places where there were more than twenty barristers, or three where there were fewer than twenty.

The project of March 19 had not set any necessary qualifications for election to the council of the Order. The June 29 proposal, by contrast, stipulated that members of the council had to be taken from among the most senior two-thirds members of the Order. In both projects, however, the council named the bâtonnier.

The June 29 project deleted the clause mandating the Order to take an annual oath as a body. While it maintained the provision requiring the Order to meet twice a year to admonish members, its conditions were relaxed somewhat. It did not single out for reprimand, for example, barristers who had lost many cases or those who had handled "notoriously unworthy" ones. There were other minor differences between the projects, but these were the most significant alterations.[58]

The council met on July 31, 1810, to debate the proposed bill, with Bonaparte in attendance. The discussion once again demonstrates the belief of the Council of State in some measure of independence and self-determination for the legal profession, and its resistance to Bonaparte's efforts to circumscribe it. The debate opened with a long discussion on the incompatibility of the profession of barrister with certain occupations or positions. A tedious examination of the question followed and ended only when Treilhard, in apparent exasperation, asked Bonaparte to make his opinion known.

Next, a brief discussion ensued on the oath to be taken by avocats. In the oath prescribed by the March 19 project, barristers had to swear that they would not "say or publish anything as defender or counsel contrary to laws, to rulings, to morals, to the security of the State or to public tranquility." Joseph Jacques Defermon suggested to the council that the words "as defender or counsel" be deleted as superfluous, and the council adopted his amendment, apparently without dissent.

Bonaparte initiated the next topic of deliberation, which concerned the choice of the president of the Order. Bonaparte asked why article 19, amended in the June 29 project so that members of the council that elected the president could be drawn only from among the most senior two-thirds members of the Order, did not mandate that the president be chosen by the president or the procureur général of the court. Honoré Muraire, a member of the Cour de cassation who had been a barrister under the Old Regime, demonstrated the desire of the Council of State to grant some self-determination to the profession when he indicated that a precedent already existed in the regulations governing the avoués, who were allowed to elect their leaders. Bonaparte's response—that the choice of a bâtonnier in larger towns was not an unimportant matter—revealed the apprehension with which he regarded avocats. Treilhard sought to uphold the barristers by noting that the section that had drafted the bill had believed it its duty to sustain barristers in all prerogatives that set them apart in their own eyes, so that they would further respect themselves. The statement encapsulates the divergence of purpose between Bonaparte and the Council of State in reorganizing the profession. The Council of State sought to restore barristers to their former standing as much as possible, whereas Bonaparte strove to restrain them, and this divergence accounts for the time required for the Order to be reestablished. The council returned to the question of the bâtonnier later in the meeting and had to yield to Bonaparte on the issue.

After a discussion in which the Council of State decided not to include a section for *avocats honoraires* on the tableau, it began to consider article 33, which forbade barristers from interfering in matters of state in their deliberations under penalty of suspension or disbarment. Bonaparte again initiated the discussion, and began with a caustic observation evidently inspired by Treilhard's earlier statement of principle. He said he did not see why the profession of barrister should be more honored than any other profession, particularly since barristers already gave themselves too much importance. He then launched into a tirade that included a sarcastic reference to Cambacérès. In citing one of the potential problems with the article, he used as an example the avocats in Paris, which again seems to indicate that the bill was above all directed against them.

At first glance, the article would seem to be attractive to Bonaparte, but Bonaparte objected because it allowed barristers to convene as an Order as often as they wished, provided that they did not deliberate on matters of state. He argued that such a development was contrary to the regime of the Empire, asserting instead that the spirit of constitutions drives back popular assemblies, which were "sources of trouble and anarchy." Bonaparte adduced the example of the electoral colleges as instructive. They never met on their own initiative and all were assembled at the same time, the duration of their sessions was limited, their agenda was fixed, they could not under any circumstances deliberate on public affairs nor on anything outside of the elections, and the Emperor named their presidents, who had to answer for any infractions of the rules. Referring to the right of assembly, Bonaparte asked why barristers should have a privilege that delineated them from the rest of the population.

Once again Treilhard sought to defend the interests of the Order. He said that the regulations could limit the barristers to occupying themselves only with matters affecting the Order, of their interior discipline, and the judgment of their colleagues. If they permitted themselves to deliberate on other matters, the bâtonnier could be held responsible.

The rejoinder further annoyed Bonaparte. He answered that it would be quite easy for avocats to find pretexts to escape such limits, and he provided a hypothetical example. Bonaparte said he did not understand why a barrister could be judged only by the Order as a whole. He contended that a barrister could be judged by the fifteen members of the council who were chosen by the Order, and who therefore had its confidence. In yet another attempt to maintain the Order's former prerogatives, Treilhard responded that emotions could easily affect the deliberations of such a small number of individuals. Bonaparte, however, was not persuaded; he said that a barrister who felt he was unfairly punished could appeal to the court.

The council then proceeded with a brief consideration of the means of choosing the bâtonnier. After rejecting a suggestion from Michel Louis Etienne Regnault de Saint-Jean d'Angély that the bâtonnier be chosen by the president of the court from a list of three candidates presented by the Order, Bonaparte ordered that he be chosen from among the fifteen members of the council, later indicating that the choice would be made by the procureur général. Since the men comprising the council were elected, he claimed, in this way barristers would not be excluded from the process of determining their leader.

Bonaparte concluded the discussion by summarizing the essential principles to be followed. The barristers were to assemble only to elect the members of the council of discipline, and only on the convocation of the prefect. The president and the council were to be held responsible for any violation of regulations, and would be liable to penalties under the Criminal Code against agitators and abettors of unlawful assemblies. Barristers accused of infractions were to be tried by the council of discipline rather than the Order as a whole, and could appeal its decision to the court. The president was to be drawn from the members of the council and chosen by the procureur général.

Regnault de Saint-Jean d'Angély said he believed that the Order ought to be convoked by the court rather than the prefect. Once again, Bonaparte stood firm. He said that since the prefect had police powers, all convocations of assemblies or bodies naturally belonged to him. Bonaparte ordered the section to present a new draft of the project conforming to the principles he had just enunciated.[59]

The revised project incorporating Bonaparte's precepts was drawn up on September 4, 1810. The maxim that the Order should meet only to elect its council effectively deleted the article requiring it to meet twice a year to admonish members, an article that had been included in both the March 19 and June 29 drafts. Article 36 threatened barristers with criminal action for professional misconduct, a further reminder of the Order's loss of autonomy. Other minor changes were also introduced, but these were the most important. The Council of State approved a final draft of the bill on September 8, 1810, and forwarded it to Bonaparte.[60]

Even at this late juncture, when his views had been embodied in the proposed legislation, Bonaparte evidently had misgivings about the bill and hesitated to approve it. He gave it careful attention and made several changes. The draft approved by the Council of State had directed, in article 19, that the council of discipline be formed of those members receiving a majority, and that members could be taken from all barristers inscribed on the tableau. Bonaparte amended the article so that the Order would elect two sets of candidates for the council of discipline, with each candidate having to be taken from among the most senior two-thirds of the Order's members. The list would then be transmitted to the procureur général, who decided the composition of the council. This was a disingenuous measure that enabled the government to ensure that the Order would not be able to elect fifteen men who would aggressively represent the interests of the Order. The new procedure gave the procureur général a final determination lacking in earlier projects, and marked a further diminution of the Order's prerogatives.

Similarly, article 33 of the project of September 8 allowed the Order to convene for the election of members of the council of discipline or for the election of the president. Bonaparte excised the latter disposition providing for the election of the president and, in keeping with his change in article 19, replaced the words "members of the council" with "candidates for the council." He made some other less significant alterations as well, and in some instances changed his mind about other modifications he had made after it was presented to him. On December 14, 1810, more than three months after the bill had been submitted to him by the Council of State, Bonaparte approved it, thus enacting it into law.[61]

With the law, Bonaparte attained the goal he had established in 1804 — the subjection of barristers to the state. The law gave the government ascendancy over the Order, from the choice of its leaders to the ratification of most of the sanctions imposed on its members. Except to elect the candidates for the council of discipline, the Order could not meet without the consent of the procureur général, and in addition the government had the power to suspend or disbar a barrister independently of the Order. In subjecting barristers in this manner, Bonaparte had also subordinated law, for it could not truly achieve autonomy while its practitioners had to fear unilateral action by the state. The reorganized Order was clearly but a shadow of the former Order, and the reinstatement of the old terminology could not mask this new reality. Without question, its reestablishment was a hollow victory for them, and the barristers were bitter about the structure of the restored Order.[62]

The manner in which the Order was reestablished marked the culmination of the unparalleled evolution of the French legal profession. Whereas most professions in France in the early nineteenth century developed through some form of association with the state, such was not the case with the legal profession. Once again, the reason lies in the standing of law within the political system. The Bonapartist regime could grant much latitude to professions such as engineering or medicine because these branches of knowledge in and of themselves posed little threat to the regime and, in fact, could be used to strengthen the state. Law as a discipline, by contrast, possessed a stature and legitimacy that was potentially disruptive or subversive to the Bonapartist ideal of a well-ordered, disciplined state. As a consequence, those involved with it had to be much more closely regulated to circumscribe its role, which is why there was much more antagonism between the legal profession and the state than was the case with other professions in France during this era.

In accordance with the procedure specified for drawing up the initial tableau, the president and the procureur général of the Imperial Court worked in conjunction with six former members of the Order, although the extant correspondence indicates that it was the six barristers who did most of the work.[63] The six barristers who executed the formation of the tableau were Gaspard Gilbert Delamalle, Jacques Delavigne, Jean François Lesparat, Charles Pierre Marie Gicquel, Joseph Delacroix-Frainville, and Louis Auguste Popelin, all of whom had remained closely associated with the profession since 1790 and had figured importantly in the maintenance of the coalition formed after the abolition of the Order. The procureur général submitted the first tableau to the minister of justice on February 26, 1811, but the minister refused to approve it. In returning it, he asked that three points be explained: why those carried on the tableau were not listed according to the date of their title of barrister or their reception at a court, why the avocats at the Cour de cassation were not included, and whether they had taken enough information on candidates for the tableau.

The procureur général transmitted the questions to the barristers, who prepared a lengthy response. The document reveals in detail the precepts that guided the barristers as they drafted the tableau. The response of the avocats focused especially on the first question, which was clearly the most important to them.

The barristers declared that in drafting the tableau they had established various catagories of individuals to be considered. They had given the greatest preference to former avocats au Parlement listed on the old tableau who had not retired from practice since the abolition of the Order. Comprising the second category were those who had completed their probationary period in 1789-90 and would have been included in the tableau of 1790 if there had been one. They, too, had to have practiced without interruption since the abolition of the Order. The third group consisted of those who had begun their probationary period before the destruction of the Order and who had remained in practice without any cessation. It is not surprising that these three categories received priority, for the men of these groups had formed the nucleus of the coalition that had continued after the abolition of the Order. Whatever their standing in the Order in 1789-90, they had become the inheritors and guardians of its traditions and values, and with obvious self-interest they were now rewarding themselves for their effort. Indeed, although the letter did not mention it, the men in the latter two categories were further compensated by having their inscription date in the new tableau made retroactive to the date that they had begun their probation, an action that gave them an advantage over men who affiliated themselves with the coalition after the abolition of the Order by giving them seniority. Without question, a clear distinction existed between the men of the first three classifications and those of the other two categories.

The next classification included those who had begun practice after the abolition of the Order, and who possessed law degrees under the terms of the law of 22 ventôse year XII. They were ranked according to the date at which they had begun to practice in Paris. This group included older men who had taken up practice in Paris after the abolition of the Order, as well as younger men who had taken law degrees at the Académie de Législation or the Université de Jurisprudence and who had begun to practice in Paris. They were followed by those who since the reorganization of the law schools had obtained a law degree, taken the oath of barrister, and practiced law.

There was a general category for all other cases, and it demonstrates that the members of the coalition of former avocats au Parlement were determined to enforce their Old Regime standards upon the profession. If any barrister, including former members of the Order, had ceased practicing law and had assumed duties deemed incompatible with the profession, he could not receive his former rank but only a new one based on the date of his cessation of his *fonctions incompatibles*. The sole exception was for former members of the Order who had become judges, who were regarded as "having only suspended practice, without having derogated it." There were both historical and practical reasons for this stance. Traditionally, under the Old Regime, the Order had allowed its members to act as judges in various seignorial jurisdictions. Although the duties had generally been exercised concurrently with those of avocat, the principle put forward by the commission of barristers was at least partially rooted in former custom. In a pragmatic sense, too, it was a prudent decision, for it doubtlessly spared the Order a difficult fight with the government had it refused to accept former members who had been judges, particularly since Bonaparte's judicial reforms had led to the retirement of several former avocats au Parlement who now sought to join the reestablished Order. Also included in the general category were former avoués who qualified for membership in the Order; those accepted were listed from the date on which they had stopped practicing as avoués.

The barristers claimed that these classifications seemed fairest and most logical. They argued that the only individuals adversely affected were those who had practiced at another court for a considerable time before coming to Paris. Such men, of course, had been placed in the fourth classification established by the commission of barristers. They argued vehemently against the alternative possibility that was implicit in the minister's first question — that time spent in practice at another court be credited in Paris, so that such men could be moved ahead of men who had practiced there continuously.

They cited first the precedent of the tableau of avocats au Parlement at Paris under the Old Regime. Whenever a barrister had come to Paris from another parlementary town, he had not been accorded a place on the tableau conforming to that in his former town; rather, he had been given a date that reflected the beginning of his practice in Paris. They gave as examples Ferey, Bigot de Préameneu, and de Sèze, all of whom had lost many years of seniority when they arrived from Rouen, Rennes, and Bordeaux, respectively. They also provided hypothetical examples of possible situations that could develop under such a system and argued them at great length.[64]

The former barristers to the Parlement had good reason to be concerned about the policy of giving credit for time spent in practice at another court. It would have undercut their favored position, fragmented the coalition that would form the nucleus of the Order, and disrupted the continuity that they had sought to preserve. Despite the obvious self-serving nature of their arguments, they apparently convinced the procureur général, the president of the court, and the minister of justice, for on this matter the norms of the barristers were utilized.

The barristers answered the other two questions in briefer fashion. They responded to the second question by noting that the avocats at the Cour de cassation had originally been avoués and had to post a bond to practice, and reminded the minister that this group had only subsequently received the authorization to call themselves avocats. Then, in a statement that demonstrates how deep-seated the Old Regime concepts of état, corps, and ordre were among the former avocats au Parlement, they wrote, "it is, then, a simple title that they have received that has done nothing to change their état." They followed up this observation by asking that if the état of the avocats at the Cour de cassation differed from that of the avocats at the Imperial Court "would they be able to be an integral part [*faire corps*] of the latter, and live under their discipline?"[65] In this matter, also, the arguments of the commission of barristers were successful, for the reorganized Order did not include the avocats at the Cour de cassation.

On the third and final question the barristers responded that they had found the evaluation of candidates to be their most difficult endeavor. More than seven hundred applicants had presented themselves, including many about whom the former avocats au Parlement knew little or nothing. They declared that if inappropriate candidates had been included on the tableau, it was because the commission had been unable to find any credible information by which it could deny them admission. In what was perhaps an attempt to ingratiate the Order with the minister of justice, and in what may also have been an effort to temper any potential interference from the Ministry of Justice, they mentioned that they had included the secretary-general and the heads of various divisions within the ministry on the tableau. The commission stated that these men were considered as cooperating by their daily conferences on the administration of justice. While it had sought to include only *"principal chefs,"* the commission said that it was unfamiliar with the various bureaus, and therefore it was conceivable that it had erred in this area. It also asserted that in evaluating former avoués who had applied, they had gone to the chambre des avoués to gather information on them, which in many instances had led to the exclusion of the applicant.

On March 12, 1811, the procureur général sent the barristers' response to the minister of justice along with a new tableau. Apparently stung by the minister's rejection of the first tableau, the procureur général emphasized in his cover letter that some omissions from that tableau had been rectified. Almost certainly, then, the barristers were forced to accept men whom they did not desire as colleagues, a development that underscores how empty the sense of victory at having the Order reestablished was for them. The minister of justice approved the revised tableau on March 14, 1811, thereby conferring official recognition upon the Order.[66] The first president of the reorganized Order was Gaspard Gilbert Delamalle, but shortly afterward he was named to the Council of State, and his place was taken by Joseph Delacroix-Frainville, who remained president through 1815.

The new structure of the Order was not the only aspect that embittered the barristers; the reestablished Order reflected the vicissitudes of the Revolution in other ways as well. The reorganized Order had only 300 members, so that it was only about half as large as the abolished Order of 1789. Even this figure was artificially large, for it included many men who were employed at the Ministry of Justice, as well as several who taught full-time at the school of law. For most of these men, membership in the Order was largely *ex officio,* and not based on the direct bonds that were so important to the former avocats au Parlement. Although these men belonged to the Order, there could be little doubt that their loyalty resided primarily with the Ministry of

Justice or with the school of law. Indeed, only 86 of the 300 members of the reconstituted Order had belonged to the Order at the time of its abolition, and this figure was achieved only because several of them had returned to the Order after their recent retirement from the judiciary.[67] Furthermore, the 86 also embraced individuals who had been at various levels of probationary status in 1790. In all, only slightly more than 10 percent of the men who had been full members of the Order in 1789 rejoined it in 1811.

The Revolution had clearly vitiated the Order. Its abolition in 1790 had led hundreds of its members to leave Paris or to seek alternate careers, and the reorganization of the Order after a hiatus of more than twenty years held little, if any, significance for them. Many were well established in their new locale or their new career and were not inclined to return. Claude François Charles Ferey, for example, was a young avocat au Parlement who had gone back to his native Burgundy early in 1790, where he continued to practice law. He had achieved some local prominence in his arrondissement of Gray (Haute Saône), and the reversion to relative obscurity that a return to Paris would have entailed was an unattractive prospect. Similarly, Simon Pierre Moreau was another young avocat au Parlement who had left Paris and had begun a new career in 1790 as a justice of the peace in the canton of Chatillon-sur-Marne. By 1811 he was president of the Tribunal of First Instance at Reims, and the idea of returning to Paris to practice as a barrister was preposterous.[68] Ferey and Moreau, who had been inscribed in 1782 and 1784, respectively, were men whose careers under normal circumstances would have been realizing their full potential by 1811; it was their group that would have provided many of the leaders and models for the Order. While this was, to some extent, the case—Berryer, Bonnet, Bellart, Gairal, and others had become members in the 1780s—their number was considerably reduced. Of the 172 men who had been inscribed in the Order between 1780 and 1789, only 28 belonged to it in 1811.

Likewise, although the number of probationary barristers in 1789–90 is unknown, only 17, almost certainly a small minority, were affiliated with the Order in 1811. Ange Christophe Gabaille, to give one example, had begun his probationary period in 1790, shortly before the destruction of the Order. He continued to practice after the abolition of the Order, but ceased after the judicial elections of 1793. Like many of the former avocats au Parlement he took an administrative position and remained in it for several years. Under the Consulate, he returned to his original profession, but in 1808 he entered the judiciary, and when the Order was reorganized he was a judge at Etampes (Seine-et-Oise).[69] Like numerous other former aspirants, he would never rejoin the Order.

Moreover, the restored Order was disproportionately older than that of 1789, for the vast majority of new adherents who received accreditation to the Order between 1790 and 1806 were older men. The opening of the law school at Paris alleviated the problem, but initially only marginally. The inscription dates of many men from 1806 and afterward belies their age. Jean Marc Nau was forty-one years of age when he affiliated with the coalition in 1806. At the time they joined in 1808, Gregoire Omer Ratel was forty-seven years old, Louis Picasse was thirty-seven, and Jean Baptiste Augustin Morillon was fifty. Gilles Le Cointre, who also became a member in 1808, had originally been received as an avocat in 1779. Likewise, Léon Pupil Hardi de Juine, who was inscribed in 1810 after ceasing practice as an avoué, had originally been received as an avocat in 1776. Jean Jacques Aubert Dubourg, whose inscription date was 1810, was fifty-eight years old at the time of the reestablishment of the Order.[70] Although it would be excessive to speak of a "lost generation," there can be little doubt that the Revolution seriously retarded the reinvigoration of the Order.

In addition, the reconstituted Order was not as unified and homogeneous as the Order in 1789 had been. In 1789 every member of the Order had shared the common heritage of having been molded by the tutelage of the probationary period. In 1811, however, the Order was fused together from disparate categories of individuals and shared no such common legacy. While the commission of six barristers formed to draft the tableau might assert that the classifications it devised were simple administrative categories, they were also qualitative judgments, and the groupings that the commission developed reveal the fissures within the restored Order.

There were other cleavages that the letter did not expose. In 1789 all of the men who belonged to the Order were members as the result of a positive choice freely made, whereas in 1811 several men were members of the Order largely by default — displaced magistrates, suppressed avoués, and the like. Theodore Anne Bourrée de Corberon, to give one of the more extreme examples, had been a conseiller in the Parlement of Paris under the Old Regime. His pursuit of a career as a barrister was essentially a historical accident, a choice imposed on him by the Revolution.[71]

Similarly, the vicissitudes of the Revolution had left deep political divisions that the ideal of corporatism or the bonds of professional association could never fully transcend. The reorganized Order, in which Bourrée de Corberon, the former conseiller in the Parlement of Paris and a former émigré, had as a colleague a former Jacobin such as François Xavier Audouin, could never be as reconcilable and unified as its Old Regime analogue.

Finally, individuals had been forced upon the Order by the government at two different junctures. The first had been under article 28 of the law of 22 ventôse year XII, by which the government could dispense individuals who performed legislative, administrative, or judicial duties from having to earn a law degree; the government regarded their experience as an acceptable substitute. Some members of the reorganized Order had successfully petitioned under this clause to receive a release from the obligation of possessing a law degree to practice as a barrister. Doubtlessly the Order could accept without difficulty Antoine Coffinières, the author of a legal treatise who for three years had taken courses in law offered privately by Michel Jacques Carpentier, a former avocat au Parlement. Nicolas Eloi Le Maire, by contrast, had been a professor of rhetoric at the University of Paris before the Revolution. In 1794 he had become a judge in Paris and subsequently served as a commissaire du pouvoir exécutif. The government granted him a dispensation that enabled him to become a member of the Order, but it is doubtful that the members of the Order could fully accept a man completely devoid of any formal legal training as a colleague. Jean Joseph Derché, another successful petitioner who was bereft of any legal education, but who cited his work at the Ministry of Foreign Affairs, as a member of the commission of émigrés and his experience as a défenseur officieux at the Council of Prizes, would in all probability have also been viewed as an interloper.[72] Whether acceptable or not, such men were ubiquitous reminders of the way in which the Order's autonomy had been compromised; their accreditation as barristers had resulted solely from governmental fiat — the Order had never been consulted about their suitability as barristers, yet it had little choice but to accept them. The second juncture at which the government had forced members upon the Order had been during the formation of the tableau.[73] The identity of these individuals is unknown, but they, too, would have been living symbols of the restored Order's less homogeneous composition and loss of self-determination.

Although its outcome was a bitter disappointment to them, the year 1811 marked the end of the barristers' struggle to reestablish their Order. They were unhappy with it but did not seek to challenge or amend any of the provisions of the law reorganizing the Order. This may have been due in part to the fact that for the duration of the Empire the government did not attempt to invoke any of the powers accorded to it to suspend or disbar any barrister. Nevertheless, relations between Bonaparte and the barristers remained strained, particularly after an incident involving the mayor of Antwerp, which illustrated the subordination of law and justice to the needs of the state. The mayor and three other officials had been accused of embezzlement in the collection of customs dues, but after a trial in a criminal court they were acquitted by a jury. The verdict enraged Bonaparte, who, through the Council of State and the Senate, ordered that the officials once again be arrested and imprisoned. He sought to have the case retried at Douai without a jury. The men were transferred to a prison in Douai, but Bonaparte fell from power before the case could be retried. Bonaparte's action, which displayed total contempt for the jury system and due process of law, seems to have galvanized the Order even further against him.[74]

As the allied troops approached Paris in 1814, the General Council of the Seine adopted a proclamation written by Nicolas François Bellart, a member of the Order of Barristers who served on the General Council. It contained a bitter denunciation of the Napoleonic regime and concluded by declaring that "it formally renounces all obedience toward Napoleon Bonaparte [and] expresses the most ardent wish that monarchical government be reestablished in the person of Louis XVIII and his legitimate successors."[75] Bellart's views reflected those of most of the Order, which welcomed the return of the Bourbons, a fact further underscored in 1815, during the Hundred Days.[76] On March 15, 1815, two weeks after Bonaparte's arrival in France and five days before he reached Paris, the council of discipline of the Order hastened "to manifest its devotion to King Louis XVIII the Desired and to his august family." In April the council decreed that its membership would not be renewed and that the status quo would remain because of political events. In June the council suspended its meetings and resumed them only in July, after the reinstallation of the Bourbons. This royalism, which was almost certainly a direct outgrowth of the Revolution, was not simply a momentary reaction against Bonaparte. In 1820 the Order subscribed to the building of an "expiatory monument" to the spirit of the duc de Berri.[77]

Ironically, the greatest threat to the Order's integrity between 1811 and 1815 came not from any action of the imperial government, but from the heirs of a former member of the Order. In 1813 the heirs of Jean Antoine Trumeau, a former avocat au Parlement who left a sum of 20,000 francs to the Order, contested his will. One of the principal arguments they adduced was that the Order in existence at the time of Trumeau's death in 1812 was not the same Order to which he had willed the money in his testament of 1766, but the case was decided in favor of the Order.[78] The suit is in many ways, however, a metaphor for the Order's predicament. The verdict notwithstanding, the reorganized Order was not the same Order as the one that had existed in 1789. It was not simply that the reestablished Order did not have as large a membership, that it was not as unified, or that it had been deprived of the autonomy and self-determination that had characterized its Old Regime counterpart. Rather, it was the result of a far more profound societal change. Whereas the Order in 1789 had been an integral part of a body politic defined by corporate structures and governed by privilege, the restored Order was in many respects an anachronism that fit far less congruently. Its reorganization had been brought about primarily to subordinate the legal profession within the centralized administrative state that the Revolution and Bonaparte bequeathed to the nineteenth century, rather than out of professional concerns or as a reaffirmation of the corporative values of the Old Regime so esteemed and nurtured by the former barristers to the Parlement.

Indeed, by 1813, as French society sought to redefine itself in the wake of the Revolution, concepts such as état, corps, and ordre had given way to the more malleable category of *notable,* which obliterated Old Regime corporate identities. Little of this, however, was apparent to the former avocats au Parlement, who continued to be animated by ideals that the Revolution had rendered obsolete. Even with the reestablishment of their Order, the sense of loss felt by the former avocats au Parlement was deeply felt and immeasurable.

Their disaffection continued for many years afterward, but in many respects it was somewhat misplaced. The government of the Restoration, more secure in its legitimacy, based itself more genuinely on the rule of law than did the Empire, and allowed barristers greater autonomy in the practice of their profession — several provisions of the restrictive Bonapartist legislation governing the Order were, in fact, repealed in 1822. Indeed, although the Order would never recover the prestige it had enjoyed under the Old Regime, by the 1820s the legal profession was on the eve of one of its greatest eras.[79]

Conclusion

> Privileges form part of the body politic as much as individuals themselves. A nation is not an aggregation of individuals placed beside each other as much as a building is not an assemblage of stones placed one on top of the other. Privileges and distinctions are necessary to the constitution of a state, as much as mountains and valleys are necessary to the existence of the physical world.
>
> Taillandier, Lettres à mon fils *(1820)*

For more than a generation the study of the French Revolution, particularly with respect to propertied commoners, was conducted largely within the framework of the Marxist interpretation on the one hand, and the critique of it offered by Alfred Cobban, on the other.[1] Both sides enriched our understanding of the Revolution, but the debate between them became increasingly polemical, leaving interpretation of the Revolution, in the words of one participant in 1967, in a "painful void." Over the following decades scholars attempted to break this impasse by devoting greater attention to political or intellectual forces, usually without dismissing altogether its social dimensions, and often emphasizing the emergence of the propertied group known as the *notables*.[2]

It is clear that the experience of the Parisian avocats au Parlement corresponds neither to the Marxist nor Cobban explication of the Revolution, and that while a broader consideration of political and intellectual factors is crucial to understanding that experience, it does not altogether conform to the idea that propertied commoners moved readily into political power as *notables* either. The Marxist paradigm, for example, has traditionally explained the Revolution as the product of a conflict between a rising capitalist bourgeoisie and a dominant feudal nobility. The bourgeoisie, unable to achieve a political or social recognition commensurate with its economic importance, took advantage of the weakening of the political authority of the Crown to launch a class struggle against the nobility's preponderant position. The Revolution is interpreted primarily as the deliberate advancement of class interests by a united and self-conscious bourgeoisie.[3] The cleavage between the barristers to the Parlement in the National Assembly and those who remained in practice, however, calls into question the unity of the bourgeoisie as a whole. Furthermore, the abolition of the profession of avocat by a body in which avocats were ascendant considerably undermines the idea that the men in the National Assembly were pursuing narrow professional interests, and casts doubt as well on the notion that they were asserting their class interests in any but the most abstract or even incidental fashion. The National Assembly's assault on privilege and corporatism was not simply the assertion of a bourgeois ideology of open competition or individual liberty. Rather, it was a richer and more altruistic movement that envisioned the nation as the focus for the highest ideals and conduct of its members. Gripped by this ideal of the sublimity of the nation, the National Assembly rejected the inequity and divisiveness of traditional privileged corporatism and sought instead to make the nation a source of equity. Through the medium of laws common to all, the National Assembly dedicated itself to remaking the French nation in a more equitable manner and to establishing a community of citizens. Indeed, the principle of the sublimity of the nation and the sentiment for a community of citizens are quite apparent in the abolition of the Order of Barristers. The Order was abolished not in accordance with Physiocratic or capitalist doctrines of a free economy, but because the Assembly desired to eliminate all distinctions between the "men of law" and the public they were to serve in the law courts of the nation, which was henceforth to be the source of all justice.

If the experience of the barristers during the Revolution does not conform to the Marxist interpretation of the Revolution, neither does it accord with Cobban's critique. Cobban's assertion that lawyers were a major element of the revolutionary bourgeoisie rested on his examination of the backgrounds of the men in the National Assembly and the National Convention rather than on an investigation of the legal profession as a whole. Clearly, he believed that as an occupational group lawyers supported the Revolution. But the reaction of the Parisian barristers to the Parlement shows that the majority of them did not support the Revolution, and Berlanstein found the same situation among the barristers at Toulouse.[4] Although many members of the

National Assembly were barristers, the Assembly was caught in a dynamic of its own, so that the barristers in it were not necessarily representative of the profession as a whole. Far from welcoming the changes produced by the Revolution, most of the practicing members of the Parisian Order deplored them. Their political and social beliefs, molded by the corporate ethos of the Order, were diametrically opposed to the Assembly's fundamental goals — the annihilation of privilege and corporate exclusivity.

It is this last aspect — the enduring strength of the corporate ethos among the former barristers to the Parlement — that places their experience at variance, albeit somewhat less strongly, with the interpretation that stresses the formation of the *notables*. Although it is undeniable that the fusion of nobles and non-nobles into such a group took place, the former barristers to the Parlement did not adapt readily to it. Rather, they remained attached to the repudiated standard of privileged corporatism, the destruction of which had ultimately made possible the transformation out of which the *notables* emerged.

More recently, a new and by no means unified political explication, which sees the Revolution primarily as a redefinition of the state in which social or class considerations were secondary, has begun to evolve.[5] It is in such a context that the experience of the Parisian avocats au Parlement can best be understood.

Under the Old Regime the corporate idiom determined the definition and identity of individuals and groups.[6] As a result, the nation was splintered into corporate fragments, each of which had its own particular privileges, prerogatives, rights, and duties, a fact of which most contemporaries were fully aware. Once one appreciates this, the rationale for the Assembly's actions becomes clearer.

The convening of the Estates-General had been an extraordinary act occasioned by impending governmental bankruptcy. It was apparent to most contemporaries that the privileged character of French society, particularly the financial privileges enjoyed by the Church and nobility, had become a luxury that the state literally could no longer afford.

Despite a recognition by the nobility, at least, that it would have to give up its financial privileges,[7] when the Estates-General met, the clergy and nobility did not join with the Third Estate in a sense of common purpose and voluntarily renounce their financial privileges. Rather, they attempted to cling to another vestige of the now discredited principle of privilege by seeking to deliberate and vote by order.

The Third Estate's refusal to acquiesce in this assertion of privilege threw the Estates-General into a deadlock, which ended only with its transformation into the National Assembly.

Not surprisingly, however, the National Assembly, as a largely artificial creation, initially had little sense of identity or purpose. Its mandate was to draft a constitution, but the contours of the task were quite unclear. Indeed, only after one month marked by frustration and impatience was the Assembly able to receive even a preliminary report on the project. It was not until the night of August 4, in renouncing privilege, that the National Assembly finally achieved a sense of identity and purpose. Seized by an ideal of the sublimity of the nation diametrically opposed to the traditional privileged, corporate idiom that had bankrupted the state and paralyzed the Estates-General, the National Assembly committed itself to a complete regeneration and reorganization of the French nation.

The extirpation of privilege and the eradication of the corporate structure that had buttressed it ultimately became the governing precepts of this reorganization. Since the two most clearly defined corporate entities of the realm, the Church and the nobility, possessed the most privileges, many have interpreted the Assembly's actions as the promotion of class interests. In fact, the movement to abolish privilege was more far-reaching and not nearly as selective as such an interpretation would indicate, for the assault transcended social lines and was directed against privileges of every sort. The abolition of provincial and urban privileges in August 1789, for example, involved members of all social classes. The redefinition of French society directed by the National Assembly not only affected all social groups, but also transformed the government and geography of France as well, for the attack on privileges and corporations destroyed provinces, estates, parlements, and innumerable other bodies. The onslaught against corporatism and privilege ultimately became so comprehensive that it extended even into such areas as art, theater, and, somewhat later, science.[8] The Assembly sought to remove intermediary bodies of every sort between the individual and the state, making the state the focus for the citizen's loyalties, and the destruction of the Order of Barristers was but one of the numerous attacks on privileges and corporations in pursuit of this goal.

The cohesion it achieved in its renunciation of privilege, however, moved the National Assembly far ahead of the rest of France. The

Assembly had difficulty communicating its moral imperative to bodies outside itself, and even its appropriation of Enlightenment discourse to articulate its goals failed to bridge the gap.[9] The abolition of the Order of Barristers, an act perfectly consistent with the Assembly's vision of a regenerated France swept clean of privilege and corporate bodies, was incomprehensible to the members of the Order at Paris who had remained in practice. This fundamental misapprehension became the basis of their profound disillusionment with the Revolution.

Although the hypothesis needs further testing, this study suggests that the Revolution may be best understood not so much as the mobilization of social classes or groups in pursuit of various aims, but more as the reaction of groups and individuals to the imposition by the National Assembly of its new vision of France. Such an interpretation is in accord with much literature concerning significant developments of the Revolution. To cite but a few examples, the Assembly's reorganization of the Church, in the words of one eminent scholar of the subject, "marked the end of national unity and the beginning of civil war." Many of the nonreligious factors that produced counterrevolution — suppression of rural protest movements by the National Guard, disparities in land sales, the resolution of land tenure, the reorganization of municipalities, and others — had their roots in measures taken by the National Assembly. Deep resentment at the usurpation of Bordeaux's privileges and powers by Paris was an important underlying factor in the federalist revolt there, and a development that also had its origins in the National Assembly.[10]

Scholars generally agree that the repression known collectively as the Terror was not an instrument of class warfare but a reaction to the circumstances of war and counterrevolution. Perhaps the period 1789–1791, and even beyond, should be interpreted somewhat analogously — not as a mobilization of class interests but as a reaction to events in the National Assembly.

It is one measure of the achievement of the National Assembly that no successive Revolutionary regime consciously breached its proscription of privilege and corporations. Bonaparte alone transgressed it in the synthesis by which he reformulated the French state, and even then, at least in the case of the Orders of Barristers, he did so only to subordinate law and the legal profession to the state.[11]

Not only does the experience of the Parisian avocats au Parlement fail to conform to standard interpretations of the Revolution, it also runs counter to the norm for the development of professions in France. Whereas most professions evolved early in the nineteenth century under the aegis of the state, the legal profession took shape much earlier, and for the most part independently of the state. In fact, it was the state that "deprofessionalized" it in 1790, under the influence of the ethos of the sublimity of the nation, which gave preeminence to untrammeled access to the law by all citizens. Moreover, rather than reemerging in a confluent relationship with the state in the early nineteenth century, the profession once again acted independently of it to restore professionalism. There was considerable antagonism between the legal profession and the state, however, and ultimately the reorganization of the Order was brought about chiefly to subjugate the legal profession to the centralized administrative state that Bonaparte had constructed, rather than to achieve strictly professional goals.

In a broader sense the French Revolution represented the transition between the privileged corporate paradigm of the Old Regime and the parliamentary government of the post-Napoleonic period. Clearly, however, most of the former barristers to the Parlement preferred the corporate idiom that the Revolution had destroyed; the vast majority who remained in practice were, if anything, in flight from politics. Most often, they simply reacted timidly to events and yearned for an ideal that was irretrievably lost, viewing the Revolution as more of an end than a beginning. They were seeking the security that they had formerly known in the Order of Barristers, and the new opportunities for political participation made possible by the Revolution meant little to them. A pamphlet by Charles Claude Montigny illustrates the Old Regime temperament of many of the former avocats au Parlement. Stating that the maxim "everything for the people and nothing by the people" ought to be inculcated in all of the subjects of a monarchical state, in 1815 he advocated abolishing the legislature, which he regarded as fractious, and restoring the Parlement.[12] Five years later Louis Auguste Taillandier, a probationary member of the Order in 1789, also demonstrated a sympathy for the Old Regime corporate structure in denouncing parliamentary representation. But so thorough had the Revolution been in its work that the comparison he offered between the Old Regime and the present doubtlessly seemed quaint to many even when he wrote it in 1820.

The members of corporations, in entering, blended their individual being with that of the corporation; the privileges of the corporation became theirs; these privileges created a fixed and permanent point, according to which they could govern their actions; the esprit de corps then became a pervading spirit [*passion*] that exalted them to the highest degree; and, as the privileges of the corporations were the freedoms and liberties of the people, these freedoms and liberties were defended with all appropriate energy. Place beside that a deputy today; this man has no exactitude to defend; he has no foundation for his conduct, no deep ethical sense [*passion morale*]; no burning sentiment to sustain him against suggestions of personal interest; he enters an assembly to choose between systems; he is a traveler suddenly thrown into uncharted seas, without directions, without a compass and without a rudder.[13]

The France molded by the Revolution had little place for sentiments such as those expressed by Montigny and Taillandier. In the France of the *notables,* the values of état, corps, and ordre were an anomaly, and the restoration of their Order, unaccompanied by the rehabilitation of the corporative ideals that had underpinned it, did little to assuage the sense of loss felt by most of the former Parisian avocats au Parlement.

Appendixes

Notes

Bibliography

Index

Abbreviations

A.D. Seine   Archives de Paris et de l'Ancien Département de la Seine
A.N.   Archives Nationales, Paris
B.A.P.   Bibliothèque des Avocats, Paris
B.H.V.P.   Bibliothèque Historique de la Ville de Paris
B.N.   Bibliothèque Nationale, Paris
B.M.O.   Bibliothèque Municipale d'Orléans

Appendix A

Members of the Order of Barristers at Paris in 1789

Name	Accredited date of inscription
Abrial, André Joseph	February 29, 1776
Ader, Pierre	September 6, 1760
Agier, Pierre Jean	August 7, 1769
Alix, François Julien	September 5, 1765
Alix de Murjet, Pierre Jean Louis	April 1, 1770
Allard, François Adolphe	May 8, 1780
Allouard, François René	July 16, 1736
Ameil, Gilbert	May 8, 1769
Amy, Louis Thomas Antoine	May 3, 1785
Anfrye, Pierre François	December 20, 1780
Angelsme de Saint Sabin, Charles Pierre	November 20, 1742
Angot, Pierre	September 7, 1775
Archambault, François Laurent	December 5, 1774
Arsandaux, Jean André	February 20, 1769
Artaud, Claude François Marguerite	April 29, 1784
Asport, Louis Bon	July 12, 1768
Aubertot, Nicolas	December 22, 1777
Aubery-Desfontaines, Jacques	March 12, 1767
Aubin de la Forest, Dominique	September 7, 1754
Aublet de Maubuy, Jean Zorobabel	December 10, 1764
Aubriet, Etienne Xavier	September 7, 1780
Aujollet, Pierre	May 12, 1760
Auvray des Guiraudieres, René Auguste	August 7, 1784
Aved de Loizerolles, Jean Simon	November 26, 1754
Babille de Prénoy, Laurent Jean	August 28, 1775
Badoulleau, Louis Magloire	April 26, 1784
Barbier, Michel	March 16, 1778
Barbier de Pompancourt, Vincent de Paul	February 10, 1784
Barrais, Pierre	May 3, 1785
Barré de Boismean, Jean Etienne	August 1, 1768
Basseville, Jean Claude	June 21, 1780
Bastard, Louis Joseph	December 12, 1782

Name	Accredited date of inscription
Baude, Marc Louis	March 19, 1781
Baudot, Pierre Louis (at Dijon, July 29, 1779)	December 27, 1787
Baurlier de Ballimore, Ange François Nicolas Simon	September 7, 1779
Bayard, Jean Baptiste François	July 17, 1769
Beaucousin, Christophe Jean François	August 7, 1752
Beaurain, Antoine Jean	May 6, 1784
Belime de Maisonneuve, Anne Michel	August 28, 1749
Bellart, Nicolas François	January 15, 1785
Bellet, Jean	March 14, 1785
Belot, Marie Philippe Auguste	September 6, 1751
Benoist, Pierre Vincent	April 18, 1782
Bercher du Martray, Charles François	February 5, 1765
Bergeras, Pierre (at Pau, July 21, 1762)	April 24, 1768
Bernard, Pierre	February 23, 1783
Bernard de Brindelles, Charles François	April 8, 1782
Berryer, Pierre Nicolas	April 29, 1780
Berthot, Clement Charles Louis (at Dijon, July 21, 1780)	January 20, 1785
Bertolio, Antoine René Constance	March 9, 1775
Bidault, Charles François	July 12, 1779
Bidault de Montreal, Charles Nicolas	April 24, 1766
Bigot de Préameneu, Felix Julien Jean (at Rennes, November 16, 1767)	May 8, 1779
Billard, Jean Hilaire	August 5, 1765
Billaud de Varenne, Jacques Nicolas	April 18, 1785
Bitouze de Linières, Jean Charles (at Rouen, November 18, 1766)	January 2, 1778
Bizet, Denis Alexis	March 23, 1775
Blanchard de la Valette, Claude	April 20, 1758
Blanchet, Antoine Philippe	August 29, 1737
Blonde, André (at Dijon, March 8, 1768)	March 14, 1769
Blondel, Jean	November 12, 1760
Bogne, Pierre François	September 2, 1769
Boicervoise, André Alexandre	March 10, 1780
Bonami Tripier, Jean François	May 22, 1776
Bonhomme de Comeyras, Pierre Jacques	September 7, 1775
Bonnal, Jean	December 20, 1774
Bonnet, Louis Ferdinand	April 8, 1783
Borderel, Jean François	February 9, 1762
Bosquillon, Charles Pierre	April 1, 1776
Bouchard, Nicolas	March 24, 1777

Appendix A

Name	Accredited date of inscription
Boucher, Athanase Jean	March 16, 1784
Boucher d'Argis, Antoine Gaspard	July 3, 1727
Boucher de la Richarderie, Gilles	September 3, 1759
Boudeau, Louis Jacques	November 12, 1774
Boudequin de Varicourt, Charles Jacques	May 30, 1740
Boudet, Ambroise Guillaume Gérard	April 6, 1775
Boudin, Pierre	December 27, 1780
Boudot, Augustin Etienne	August 17, 1780
Bouju, Jean François	September 4, 1724
Boulanger, Jean Louis	March 16, 1778
Boullay, Antoine Jacques Claude Joseph (at Nancy, November 13, 1783)	January 6, 1787
Boullemer de la Martinière, Jean Baptiste	November 27, 1758
Boullyer, Joseph François	September 5, 1757
Bourdereau, Jean	April 1, 1784
Boureau de Beausejour, Daniel Antoine	November 29, 1748
Bourgoin, Charles Pierre	March 7, 1767
Boursault de Troncay, Charles Etienne	no date given, but between November 29 and December 16, 1784
Boussenot, Jean Baptiste	August 12, 1748
Bouteix, Antoine	July 26, 1729
Bouttevillain de la Ferté, Pierre Etienne	May 14, 1778
Boys, Julien François	February 29, 1747
Braquehais, Antoine Claude	June 27, 1769
Brasseux, Louis Antoine	September 6, 1769
Breton, Henri	November 26, 1754
Briquet de Mercy, Odot	November 29, 1746
Brisse, François	December 18, 1769
Brodon, Claude Michel	August 31, 1775
Brosselard, Emmanuel	April 16, 1782
Broüet, Charles Edme	May 9, 1775
Brouillet de l'Estang, Henri	July 26, 1756
Brousse, Armand Bernard Honoré	February 6, 1777
Broutin de Longuerue, Célestin Joseph	December 5, 1774
Broyart, Pierre Jean Baptiste	April 1, 1776
Bruhier de la Neuville, Pierre Bernard	April 19, 1751
Brunel de Livry, Antoine Florent	January 20, 1785
Brunet, Jacques François	September 5, 1769
Brunetière, Pierre Jacques	May 10, 1775
Bruslé, Louis Augustin	May 17, 1781
Buisson de Champbois, Marie Pierre	August 10, 1778

Name	Accredited date of inscription
Bureau du Colombier, Etienne Denis	November 29, 1774
Burgat, Jean François	December 14, 1775
Cadet de Saineville, Jean Baptiste Claude	August 4, 1749
Cahier de Gerville, Bon Claude	February 16, 1775
Cahouet de Neuvy, Charles	June 11, 1779
Caillat, Charles	December 28, 1784
Caillau, Pierre Henri	July 14, 1732
Caillau de Courcelles, Henri François	August 21, 1780
Caillière de l'Etang, Pierre Jean George	July 21, 1747
Cairol, Gabriel Felix	September 3, 1777
Calmelet, Louis François Denis	May 6, 1784
Camus, Armand Gaston	July 21, 1760
Canet de Selincourt, Jean Baptiste Nicolas	December 20, 1774
Canuel, Jacques Michel	July 5, 1762
Carle, Henri	May 18, 1778
Carouge, Marin	May 12, 1760
Carpentier, Michel Jacques	April 30, 1783
Carteron, Thomas Anne	September 7, 1754
Cassart de Villeneuve, Louis Pierre Etienne	March 29, 1776
Castillon, Emmanuel Louis Jacques André	January 8, 1784
Cathala, Marc Guillaume	July 21, 1777
Cauche, Louis Marie	September 4, 1775
Cellier, Vincent	April 27, 1780
Chanin de Déast, Charles Claude Maximilien	March 11, 1782
Chanlaire, Pierre Gilles	August 17, 1780
Charié, Charles Joachim	July 23, 1784
Charpentier de Beaumont, François	March 28, 1748
Châtelain de Lorgemont, Pierre Geoffrey	July 24, 1758
Chauchard, Jean Baptiste	March 13, 1780
Chauveau, Louis René	February 26, 1778
Chauveau-Delagarde, Claude François	May 5, 1783
Chevillard, Etienne	July 23, 1779
Choel des Ambrieres, François Jean	September 7, 1778
Chopin de Villy, Joseph Germain	May 8, 1780
Clemenceau de la Lande, René	June 5, 1780
Clement de Malleran, Louis Nicolas	September 5, 1737
Clergeon, François Gilles	July 18, 1782
Closier, François Antoine	August 5, 1786
Cohin, Denis François	March 16, 1775
Collet, Claude Nicolas	April 20, 1752
Collette de Baudicourt, Joseph Magdelaine	August 23, 1764
Collin de Vaurancher, Pierre	April 22, 1779
Colombeau, Jacques Mathurin	July 22, 1736

Appendix A

Name	Accredited date of inscription
Condé, Antoine Pierre	May 5, 1785
Coquebert, Alexis Pierre Nicolas	January 11, 1768
Coqueley de Chaussepierre, Claude Genevieve	June 11, 1736
Corbeil, René Aimé	August 3, 1762
Costard, Jacques	August 17, 1758
Cothereau, Antoine Etienne	September 6, 1734
Cournault, Henri	July 16, 1781
Courtin, Claude Christophe	June 18, 1759
Daix, Claude Jacques	May 4, 1785
Dalléas, Jean	January 9, 1775
Dameuve, Louis Claude Charles Denis	December 9, 1782
Dampol, René Gilbert	January 23, 1759
D'Arbricelle Chasseloup, Jacques François Robert	April 14, 1783
Darigrand, Jean Baptiste	March 16, 1775
Darrimajou, Jacques	January 29, 1784
Dartis de Marcillac, Jacques Joseph	March 9, 1768
Daudebert, Louis Thomas	July 10, 1731
Daugy, Charles Elisabeth Martin	April 5, 1785
Dauphinot, Charles Gérard	November 12, 1774
D'Auterive, Etienne Firmin	April 7, 1766
De Beauvoir, Louis Antoine Bernard	February 21, 1782
De Blois, Gérard Henri	November 12, 1769
De Bonnières, Alexandre Jules Benoît	September 4, 1769
De Bussac de S. Martin, Pierre Michel	December 22, 1778
De Calonne, Louis François	September 1, 1738
De Chaillou, François Hubert (at Metz, August 2, 1770)	February 8, 1787
De Courbeville, George Etienne	February 12, 1765
De Courtive, Pierre Adrien Jean Baptiste	January 22, 1784
De Ferriere *(sic)*, Claude Jean Clair	September 7, 1780
De Fontaine, Edouard	April 25, 1782
De Hansy, André Claude	September 6, 1746
Delacroix, Joseph *(sic)* Vincent	August 30, 1768
Delacroix de Frainville, Joseph	November 29, 1774
De la Fleutrie, Antoine Jacques	June 15, 1780
De la Fortelle, Henri Louis	December 7, 1752
De la Fourniere, Pierre Memmie Louis	December 5, 1757
De la Goutte, Guillaume François Philippe	July 12, 1736
De la Londe, Anne Joseph Gilles	December 29, 1774
Delamalle, Gaspard Gilbert	November 29, 1774
De la Métherie, Louis	August 11, 1777

Name	Accredited date of inscription
Delaporte, Jean Baptiste	May 8, 1779
Delapresle, François Alexandre	March 12, 1782
Delaribardiere, Jean Jacques	November 22, 1784
De la Riviere, Jean Baptiste Etienne	November 28, 1780
De la Rivoire, Louis Etienne	April 23, 1759
De la Salle, Joseph	April 20, 1780
Delaune, Antoine Louis	July 6, 1752
De Lavaux, François Dominique	November 12, 1774
Delavigne, Jacques	November 21, 1774
De Leymerie, Denis	December 12, 1774
Delon, Mathias Nicolas	May 9, 1785
Delpech, Denis Nicolas	July 10, 1731
Delvincourt, Claude Etienne	April 28, 1785
De Miaquere, Augustin Casimir Crépin	July 10, 1780
De Moustier, Charles Albert	April 1, 1782
Denys, Jean Michel	March 28, 1763
De Pugieu, Pierre Barbé	September 6, 1781
De Sèze, Raimond Romain (at Bordeaux, July 7, 1767)	May 7, 1784
Des Fontaines, Pierre François Jean	July 10, 1769
De Singly, Jean Charles	December 18, 1777
Desmoulins, Charles Pierre Didier	July 28, 1760
Desparviés, Pierre	July 6, 1739
Despres de la Roziere, Nicolas Philippe Louis Charles	February 19, 1789
De Villantroys, Robert Etienne	April 10, 1775
Devins, Armand François	April 21, 1785
D'Herbelot, Léon	February 5, 1778
Didier, Jean François	May 30, 1765
Dinet, Charles Simon	July 23, 1761
Doillot, Jacques Bernard Jean	August 30, 1781
Doillot, Jacques François Henri	December 13, 1745
Dommanget, Louis Abraham	May 3, 1783
Dorival, Jean Henri	February 23, 1750
Douet d'Arcq, Antoine Nicolas	July 6, 1777
Douet d'Arcq, Nicolas Antoine	January 17, 1746
Doulcet, Augustin Jean Louis	July 10, 1769
D'Outremont, Anselme Joseph	August 3, 1733
Drapier, Nicolas	May 14, 1778
Dubois, Pierre	November 12, 1774
Dubois de Moulignon, Antoine Pierre Marie	July 6, 1775
Dubois de Niermont, Jean François	January 12, 1778
Dubois Descorbieres, Antoine Julien Alexis (at Rennes, August 18, 1777)	May 3, 1783

Name	Accredited date of inscription
Ducarin, Pierre François	May 8, 1783
Duflos, Louis François	December 30, 1779
Dufour, Jean François	September 6, 1751
Dufour de St. Pathus, Julien Michel	July 20, 1777
Dufresne, Augustin Julien	April 30, 1783
Dufresnel, Claude André	January 15, 1784
Dujardin de Mainville, Jean Philippe	April 5, 1781
Dumouchet du Bac, Philippe	October 6, 1757
Duportail, Antoine Augustin Benoît	May 5, 1780
Duport du Tertre, Marguerite Louis François	March 20, 1777
Dupré de Montdorin, François	May 7, 1781
Durand, Jean Nicolas	July 23, 1764
Durand de Miremont, Jacques Charles	May 9, 1766
Durif, Gilbert	March 5, 1781
Durot, Alexis Jean Baptiste	May 9, 1765
Du Rouzeau, Denis	June 9, 1755
Du Verne, Jean Baptiste	July 10, 1730
Duvert de Boutemont, François Martin	July 12, 1734
Duveyrier, Honoré Marie Nicolas	April 19, 1779
Duvivier, Pierre Gilles	May 1, 1780
Epoigny, Sebastien	July 14, 1777
Fabre, Jean Joseph	August 7, 1775
Faré, Jean Baptiste	May 9, 1766
Fauconnier, Henri Catherine	May 8, 1786
Faure, Louis Joseph	May 4, 1781
Féart, Hyacinthe	December 20, 1774
Fera, Louis Charles	September 6, 1762
Féral, Jean Pierre Victor	January 13, 1777
Ferey, Claude François Charles	April 8, 1782
Ferey, François Alexis Nicolas (at Rouen, March 24, 1755)	May 8, 1770
Ferré, Jacques René	July 22, 1776
Feval, Louis François	May 5, 1777
Fincken d'Autemarche, Guillaume	December 1, 1749
Fleury, Alexandre Sulpice	July 31, 1769
Fleury d'Assigny, Jean Baptiste François Joseph	January 4, 1778
Fleury de Villiers, Jacques Edme	April 25, 1776
Foisy de Tremont, Denis	July 16, 1770
Follenfant de la Douve, Jean Baptiste Pierre	December 5, 1774
Fontaine de Creteil, Jean Baptiste Jacques	December 5, 1774
Forestier, Charles Pierre Michel	December 16, 1776
Forestier, Jean Baptiste (doyen)	January 7, 1721

Name	Accredited date of inscription
Forez, Philippe	December 19, 1769
Forget, François	March 23, 1779
Fossey, Pierre	December 11, 1758
Fournel, Jean François	January 8, 1771
Fournier, Pierre Charles Marin	July 23, 1770
Fournier de la Chenaye, Pierre	August 27, 1770
Frion de Méry, Nicolas François Daniel	April 19, 1785
Fromentin, François Samuel	March 3, 1777
Gaborit, Pierre	September 1, 1750
Gaignant, François Michel	August 22, 1763
Gaigne, Marc René	September 6, 1759
Gaillard, Joseph	May 29, 1769
Ganilh, Charles	April 11, 1785
Garran de Coulon, Jean Philippe	February 23, 1775
Gattrez, Ambroise Jean Baptiste Pierre Ignace (at Dijon, January 4, 1770)	November 12, 1782
Gaulme de la Velle, Jean Baptiste	June 18, 1742
Gaultier du Breil, René	December 29, 1760
Gazon, Pierre Raphael	December 20, 1774
Gerard, André	March 19, 1781
Gerivaux, Louis	April 28, 1784
Gicquel, Charles Paul Marie	July 14, 1777
Gigot, Melchiade Corentin	April 28, 1766
Gillet, Charles Léon Eustache	March 12, 1785
Giroust, Pierre François	June 25, 1765
Gissey de Fontenay, Pierre	March 7, 1747
Godard, Jacques	February 22, 1783
Godart de Sergy, Jean Louis	September 4, 1747
Godefroy de Montours, Jean Emmanuel	December 5, 1774
Godineau de Villechenay, Joseph Simon	February 17, 1789
Gorguereau, François	May 10, 1775
Goudard, Etienne Pierre Germain	March 6, 1752
Grapin, Pierre Léonard (at Dijon, July 4, 1763)	June 1, 1764
Grau, Claude	December 12, 1740
Grouvelle, Charles Denis	March 13, 1775
Gudin, Pierre Louis	August 21, 1783
Gudin, Pierre Richard François	September 5, 1757
Guenepin, Etienne François Edme	July 6, 1775
Guerin de la Bréharderie, Alexis Louis	March 10, 1750
Guerin de la Cour, Pierre Augustin	April 4, 1758
Gueudar de la Haye, Simon	December 4, 1783
Guichard du Mareil, Augustin Charles	December 16, 1782

Name	Accredited date of inscription
Guillemot d'Alby, Jean Charles Ambroise	January 21, 1765
Guillon d'Assas, Charles Nicolas	May 10, 1775
Guyet, Jean Baptiste François	September 7, 1754
Guyot de Sainte-Hélene, Etienne	July 21, 1768
Guyot des Herbier, Claude Antoine	December 30, 1782
Hemeri, Pierre Augustin	January 16, 1769
Hénault de Tourneville, Etienne	May 20, 1776
Henrion de Pansey, Pierre Paul Nicolas	March 10, 1763
Henry, Timothée Arnould (at Nancy, November 12, 1770)	July 7, 1776
Herbaut Despavaux, Nicolas Alexandre	September 3, 1759
Heron, Mathurin	November 29, 1774
Hervé, François (at Rennes, May 2, 1775)	May 7, 1777
Hiver de Popincourt, Jean Baptiste Joseph	July 22, 1784
Hochereau, Louis François	September 1, 1760
Hocquet, Michel François	November 12, 1774
Hom, Gilbert	August 12, 1779
Horry, Didier	December 31, 1731
Horry, Didier François	April 11, 1783
Houard, David (at Rouen, March 7, 1747)	May 3, 1785
Hua, Eustache Antoine	November 12, 1784
Hubert de Matigny, Hilaire Joseph	September 4, 1769
Huet, François	November 25, 1754
Hugot, Antoine Nicolas	December 18, 1775
Hulin, Mathurin	April 29, 1780
Hulot de Veroncelles, Germain	February 19, 1770
Hureau, Christophe	April 25, 1780
Hutteau, François Louis	June 19, 1758
Hutteau, Jean Baptiste Louis Philippe	July 29, 1784
Jabineau, Henri	December 19, 1768
Jahan, Jean Baptiste	April 18, 1782
Jaillant, Antoine Nicolas	November 12, 1763
Jannyot, Jean François	November 22, 1784
Jéhanne, Thomas Charles Alexandre	September 6, 1779
Jeudy Dumonteix (sic), Joseph	May 3, 1785
Jobert, Jean Oliver	January 7, 1784
Jodon de Valtire, Robert Thomas François	November 12, 1774
Jolly, Jean François	June 1, 1764
Jouhannin, Jacques Philippe	July 9, 1736
Jozeau, Mathurin Pierre	December 30, 1776
Justal, Jean Baptiste Raymond	May 6, 1784
La Caze, Joseph	April 5, 1765
Lacretelle, Louis (sic) (at Nancy, May 7, 1772)	July 7, 1776

Name	Accredited date of inscription
Laget-Bardelin, Marc Antoine	August 8, 1735
Lalane, Léon (at Toulouse, July 13, 1758)	July 20, 1780
Lallemant de Fontenoy, Antoine Louis	April 26, 1785
Lambert, Antoine Simon	June 27, 1775
Landry, Louis Joseph	July 29, 1776
Langlois, Jean Thomas	May 7, 1784
Larrieu, Martin Pierre	May 7, 1784
Lasaudade, Charles François	June 5, 1769
Lasseray, Cyprien Athanase	July 15, 1765
Laurens de Courville, Louis Antoine	March 21, 1776
Laurent, Joseph André	April 30, 1783
Lauvin de Montplaisir, Edme Marguerite	January 25, 1776
Lavoisier, Pierre Claude	November 23, 1779
Le Bégue, Achilles	July 30, 1731
Le Blan, Claude Saintin	December 22, 1749
Le Blanc de Kirby, Guillaume	July 21, 1738
Leboucher, Joseph Firmin	February 24, 1756
Lebruin, Jean Baptiste	May 7, 1782
Le Brun, Pierre Augustin Joseph	January 22, 1759
Le Camus d'Houlouve, Bertrand Louis	May 11, 1739
Le Clerc, Claude Nicolas	September 7, 1764
Le Conte, Pierre François	September 6, 1776
Le Conte de Rouju, Joseph Louis	August 27, 1767
Le Cousturier, Pierre	January 16, 1775
Le Faivre, Jean Baptiste Philippe	July 10, 1780
Le Febvre de Beauvray, Claude Rigobert	August 6, 1748
Leger, Jean Baptiste	August 7, 1777
Leger de Monthuon, Edme Guillaume Jean Baptiste Bernard	January 10, 1771
Legrand, Jean	August 7, 1780
Legrand de Laleu, Louis Auguste (at Douai, March 26, 1779)	December 16, 1779
Legrand de Saint-René, René	February 21, 1782
Legras de Vigny, Jean Baptiste	July 26, 1776
Le Laurain, Ponce	May 10, 1776
Lemoine des Prez, Jean Baptiste	November 28, 1775
Le Moyne de Grandpré, Pierre Claude	September 6, 1751
Lenoir Delaroche, Jean Jacques (at Grenoble, December 9, 1771)	April 24, 1787
Le Page, Jacques Claude Paschal	November 25, 1777
Le Paige, Charles Pierre	November 14, 1774
Le Paige, Louis Adrien	July 9, 1733
Le Poitevin, Alexandre François Laurent	August 3, 1767

Appendix A

Name	Accredited date of inscription
Le Porquier de Vaux, Jean Baptiste Laurent	November 29, 1774
Le Prestre de Boisderville, Pierre François	August 28, 1761
Le Prestre de la Motte, Claude Barthelemy	September 3, 1759
Le Prevost du Rivage, François Marin	March 23, 1752
Le Roi de Montécly, Louis François	June 15, 1767
Le Rouge, Charles Louis	July 24, 1777
Le Roy, Louis	December 3, 1754
Le Roy de S. Charles, Michel Nicolas	September 6, 1759
Le Sage, Jean Etienne	September 7, 1754
Lescalier de Reymond, Jean Pierre	April 30, 1783
Lesparat, Augustin	July 21, 1783
Lesparat, Jean François	November 28, 1752
Le Vacher de la Terriniere, Marin	March 4, 1778
Le Vasseur, Antoine François Nicolas	July 10, 1769
Le Vasseur, Jean François Pierre	February 20, 1770
Le Verdier, Nicolas	December 30, 1776
L'Heritier, Louis Etienne Robert	December 9, 1780
Lhomme, Charles Jacques	July 8, 1776
Limanton, Jean François	July 7, 1746
Lochard, Claude François (at Besançon, August 2, 1748)	December 17, 1754
Locré, Jean Guillaume	Feburary 26, 1787
Lohier, Pierre Auguste Marie (at Rennes, August 18, 1744)	April 11, 1758
Lorry, François	July 26, 1742
Lourmand, François César	April 16, 1784
Louvet de Villiers de Romaincourt, Louis Anne	May 8, 1782
Madoré, Jean Denis	April 1, 1784
Maignan de Champromain, André Etienne	September 7, 1768
Maignan de Saint Hermain, Claude François	April 11, 1783
Maignan de Savigny, François Anselme	July 12, 1735
Maillard de Montluy, Alexandre César	March 25, 1783
Maiziere, François	July 27, 1739
Mallet, Jacques Ambroise Sylvain	February 26, 1776
Manen, Jean Nicolas François Alexis	December 5, 1774
Mannet *(sic)*, Clément	May 4, 1784
Marchand du Chaume, François	February 17, 1777
Marcilly, Laurent	May 9, 1774
Marguet, François Antoine	November 29, 1774
Marnier, Annet	February 10, 1763
Marnier-Despeux *(sic)*, François	May 4, 1778
Marteau, Charles	August 4, 1777

Name	Accredited date of inscription
Martineau, Louis Simon	February 5, 1760
Mascou, Pierre Remi	May 4, 1785
Mascrey de la Haie (sic), Nicolas Denis	February 24, 1778
Massé, Jean	May 9, 1782
Masson, Joseph	July 12, 1725
Mathieu, Pierre Louis	May 8, 1780
Maucler, Jean Edilbert	July 1, 1747
Mauduison, Jean Baptiste Michel	August 30, 1751
Maugue Massis, François Joseph	November 28, 1778
Maultrot, Gabriel Nicolas	July 6, 1733
Mélin, Salomon Antoine	December 18, 1775
Mennessier, Jacques Hilaire	August 13, 1765
Merlet, Louis Magdelaine	May 9, 1777
Mestiviers, René	December 19, 1768
Metayer, Denis	April 3, 1767
Meunier, Alexandre Joseph	May 6, 1783
Mey, Claude	December 14, 1739
Michaut de Larquelais, Georges François Monique	March 1, 1749
Mignien du Planier, Jean Charles	March 3, 1768
Millard, Pierre Claude	April 22, 1785
Millet de Gravelle, Jacques Joseph	November 12, 1774
Millet de Marcilly, Antoine Louis Joseph Marie	December 11, 1783
Minier, Charles	August 22, 1768
Mitouflet de Beauvois, Louis Charles	August 28, 1780
Molé, Guillaume François Roger	July 1, 1765
Mollet, Innocent Lazare	May 3, 1770
Monniot, Louis Charles	November 29, 1774
Montagne, Jacques	February 12, 1742
Montigny, Charles Claude	July 26, 1768
Mordan de Launay, Jean Claude Michel	April 10, 1775
Moreau, Paul Augustin	February 27, 1787
Moreau, Simon Pierre	January 5, 1784
Moreau de Saint-Méry, Médéric Louis Elie	February 6, 1784
Morel, Etienne	July 30, 1778
Moriceau, Alexandre Remy	November 23, 1779
Morin, Louis Jean	December 11, 1783
Mortier du Parc, Jacques René	February 20, 1777
Motron, René	August 7, 1769
Mouricault, Thomas Laurent	August 18, 1763
Moynat de l'Isle, Alexandre Charles	September 4, 1780
Musnier, Pierre Maurice	March 9, 1784

Appendix A

Name	Accredited date of inscription
Nau, Pierre Cécile	December 18, 1775
Noyer, Charles	August 2, 1784
Oeillet de Saint-Victor, Victor Simon	January 16, 1766
Oudart, Nicolas	May 20, 1776
Oudet, Jean Baptiste	September 2, 1749
Oudet, Jean Baptiste (fils)	February 7, 1783
Palourd du Vergier, Henri Augustin	September 2, 1765
Panis, Etienne Jean	March 7, 1782
Papon, Silvestre Antoine	May 25, 1778
Paré, Jules François	April 11, 1782
Parent, André	June 30, 1766
Parisot, Jacques	January 7, 1775
Pauly, Jacques Nicolas	January 8, 1760
Pelart, Christophe Henry	August 22, 1740
Pelé, Bon Thomas	January 5, 1769
Pelletier, Pierre Claude Simon	July 3, 1760
Pelletier de Rilly, Jean Ange Maximin	September 6, 1756
Pelletier de Vallieres, Achilles Marie	April 11, 1783
Pellier des Forges, André Louis François	August 1, 1768
Perier, Jacques César	April 1, 1784
Perré, Jean François	December 12, 1776
Perron, Alexandre César Michel	November 26, 1754
Petit, Henri	April 1, 1788
Phelipeaux, Pierre Marie Elizabeth	August 18, 1763
Piales, Jean Jacques	December 4, 1747
Picard, Louis Claude	January 17, 1763
Pichois, Michel Germain	May 7, 1787
Pierret de Sancieres, Jean Baptiste	March 6, 1758
Pigeon, Marie Nicolas	August 28, 1760
Pinault, Pierre Olivier	June 8, 1736
Pineau, Mathurin	January 4, 1785
Pion de la Roche, Claude Philibert	August 9, 1756
Plaisant de la Houssaye, Jean	February 8, 1769
Pléney, Nicolas	June 2, 1738
Poirier, Jean Etienne	March 2, 1775
Polverel, Etienne (at Bordeaux, August 27, 1759)	May 6, 1780
Poncet de la Grave, Guillaume (at Toulouse, August 9, 1751)	December 18, 1752
Poncy, Bernard	January 21, 1779
Pons, Philippe Laurens	April 24, 1780
Ponsard, Jean Baptiste	February 20, 1783
Popelin, Louis Auguste	May 17, 1779

Name	Accredited date of inscription
Porcher, Paul	April 27, 1767
Poriquet, Jean Gabriel	July 27, 1769
Prevost de Saint-Lucien, Roch Henri	February 3, 1767
Procope-Couteaux, Alexandre Julien	September 1, 1744
Prousteau, Pierre Claude	January 15, 1781
Prunget des Boissieres, Sylvain	September 3, 1736
Pulleu, Pierre François	September 5, 1757
Quenard, Philippe	December 16, 1784
Rat de la Poiteviniere, Jean	November 26, 1765
Rathier, Nicolas	January 15, 1771
Recolene, Annet	March 17, 1755
Regnard, François Théodore	January 15, 1768
Regnault, Aglibert Jacques	November 22, 1784
Regnier, Etienne Guillaume	April 26, 1779
Remy de Mery, Jean Léonard	December 2, 1777
Renard, Pierre Joseph	May 21, 1764
Reynaud, Claude André	May 21, 1746
Riché, Nicolas Louis Gabriel François	November 12, 1774
Richer, François	July 20, 1744
Rigault, Charles Louis	July 11, 1782
Rimbert, Louis Claude	April 1, 1765
Riviere, Antoine	January 15, 1755
Robert, Louis Antoine	July 20, 1780
Robet, Louis	March 11, 1784
Robin, Léonard	September 4, 1770
Robin de Mozas, Louis (at Grenoble, December 19, 1771)	April 2, 1781
Rogier, Guillaume	December 22, 1784
Rouhette, François Théodore	January 24, 1743
Roussel, Pierre	February 6, 1738
Rousselot de Chambriant, Etienne	August 5, 1739
Royer, Claude	May 4, 1775
Rozet de la Saussaye, Jacques Claude	September 2, 1782
Rozier, Antoine Vincent	April 19, 1783
Sabarot, Pierre Fidel	May 8, 1779
Salivet, Louis Georges Isaac	February 19, 1781
Sanson, Claude Nicolas	January 4, 1745
Sarot, Charles Ponce	February 17, 1763
Sarradin, Jean Louis	July 28, 1777
Satens, Jean Mathias	December 11, 1769
Savet, Jean Jacques	August 23, 1752
Savy, Louis Michel	July 21, 1777

Name	Accredited date of inscription
Seran, Jean Jacques Guillaume	April 9, 1770
Serpaud, Jacques	February 17, 1763
Serson de Moitiers, Charles Henri	August 30, 1781
Siméon, Jean Pierre	August 23, 1756
Simon, Pierre Marie	September 6, 1769
Simonet de Maisonneuve, Alexandre Jacques	November 28, 1782
Sionnest, François Laurent Dominique	August 23, 1751
Soreau, Jean Baptiste Etienne Benoît	December 12, 1774
Target, Guy Jean Baptiste	July 6, 1752
Tenneson, Quentin Vincent	July 2, 1749
Tessier du Breil, Antoine	November 21, 1757
Texier, Jacques	September 7, 1754
Thetion, Jacques	July 29, 1769
Thetion, Jacques Louis	July 22, 1737
Thiercelin, Jean Nicolas	July 23, 1764
Thilorier, Jean Charles	July 31, 1777
Thirria de Valsene, Charles Dominique	April 2, 1778
Thuillier de Bonée, Claude Louis	September 4, 1747
Thuriot de la Rosiere, Jacques Alexis	July 9, 1778
Timbergue, Pierre Alexandre Charles	September 7, 1754
Tirrion, Jean Michel	August 27, 1733
Tournemine, Jean Etienne	August 10, 1778
Tournemine d'Hurbal, Louis	December 14, 1778
Treilhard, Jean Baptiste	July 12, 1761
Tronchet, François Denis (elected bâtonnier, May 8, 1789)	August 9, 1745
Tronson du Coudray, Guillaume Alexandre	July 30, 1778
Trumeau de Boissy, Jean Udislas François Frédéric J.	April 5, 1781
Turquet, Albert François Stanislas	January 16, 1775
Vallée Duchesne, Guillaume	April 9, 1779
Vallet de Senneville, Roch Alexandre	January 19, 1775
Vancquentin, André Jacques	June 16, 1739
Vasselin, Georges Victor	November 29, 1784
Vaubertrand, Jean Baptiste Claude	July 20, 1750
Vautrin, Claude Jacques	May 8, 1777
Vermeil, François Michel	January 12, 1756
Verrier, Louis Pierre	May 1, 1779
Viaud de Belair, Pierre Jacques Calixte	May 5, 1784
Viel, Etienne René	July 29, 1743
Villedieu, Jean Antoine	March 21, 1768
Villot de Fréville, Pierre	May 15, 1766

Name	Accredited date of inscription
Vincendon, Guillaume	July 6, 1775
Vivier de la Chausée, François Hyacinthe Benoît	August 21, 1775
Vivier de Launay, Nicolas Joseph	December 29, 1774
Voguet, Pierre Jean Baptiste	September 2, 1776
Vulpian, Jean Baptiste	December 2, 1754

Source: B.A.P., Tableau de 1789.

Appendix B

Parisian Barristers to the Parlement Who Assumed Positions in Civil Courts in Paris

Name	Date of election
Judges	
Guy Jean Baptiste Target	November 26, 1790
Jean Baptiste Treilhard	November 27, 1790
Pierre Jean Agier	November 28, 1790
François Denis Tronchet	November 30, 1790
Felix Julien Jean Bigot de Préameneu	December 1, 1790
Jean Philippe Garran de Coulon	December 2, 1790
Charles Minier	December 2, 1790
Annet Recolene	December 2, 1790
Nicolas Oudart	December 3, 1790
Jacques Delavigne	December 4, 1790
François Michel Vermeil	December 4, 1790
François Gorguereau	December 9, 1790
François Julien Alix	December 10, 1790
Thomas Laurent Mouricault	December 11, 1790
Jacques François Brunet	December 13, 1790
Laurent Marcilly	December 13, 1790
Substitute Judges	
Léonard Robin	December 14, 1790
Jacques Nicolas Millet de Gravelle	December 16, 1790
Louis Abraham Dommanget	December 18, 1790
Joseph Lacaze	December 19, 1790
Marin Carouge	December 20, 1790
Jean François Jolly	December 21, 1790
Antoine Riviere	December 22, 1790
Claude Antoine Guyot-Desherbiers	December 23, 1790
Pierre Augustin Hemery	December 23, 1790
François Laurent Archambault	December 24, 1790
Jacques Hilaire Menessier	December 26, 1790
Etienne Denis Bureau du Colombier	December 27, 1790

Name	Date of election
Philippe Laurent Pons de Verdun	December 29, 1790
Marc René Gaigne	December 29, 1790
Jean André Arsandaux	December 30, 1790
Nicolas Bouchard	December 30, 1790
Jean Baptiste Pierre Follenfant	January 19, 1791

Source: A.N., B^I 1.

Appendix C

Parisian Barristers to the Parlement Who Assumed Positions in District Courts outside Paris

Name	Location	Source
Judges		
Amy, Louis Thomas Antoine	Janville (Eure-et-Loire)	A.N., BB⁵ 173
Anfrye, Pierre François	Montfort (Ille-et-Vilaine)	A.N., BB⁵ 356
Bastard, Louis Joseph	Vendôme (Loir-et-Cher)	A.N., D^{III} 257/258
Baude, Marc Louis	Etampes (Seine-et-Oise)	A.N., BB⁵ 191
Belot, Marc Philippe Auguste	Corbeil (Seine-et-Oise)	A.N., BB⁵ 356
Bidault, Charles François	Melun (Seine-et-Marne)	A.N., F¹c III Seine-et-Marne 1
Boulanger, Jean Louis	Sezanne (Marne)	A.N., BB⁵ 356
Bruslé, Louis Augustin	Vervins (Aisne)	A.N., BB⁵ 3
Cahouet de Neuvy, Charles	Orléans (Loiret)	A.N., BB⁵ 356
Clemenceau, René Mathurin	Saint-Florent (Maine-et-Loire)	A.N., F¹c III Maine-et-Loire 1
Clergeon, François Gilles	Angoulême (Charente)	A.N., BB⁵ 31
D'Herbelot, Léon	Coulommiers (Seine-et-Marne)	A.N., BB⁵ 356
Dubois de Niermont, Jean François	Murat (Cantal)	A.N., F¹c III Cantal 2
Durand, Jean Nicolas	Grandvilliers (Oise)	A.N., F¹c III Oise 1
Faré, Jean Baptiste	Langeais (Indre-et-Loire)	A.N., F¹c III Indre-et-Loire 1
Hua, Eustache Antoine	Mantes (Seine-et-Oise)	A.N., BB⁵ 191
Hureau, Christophe	Joigny (Yonne)	A.N., BB⁵ 215
Jahan, Jean Baptiste	Chinon (Indre-et-Loire)	A.N., F¹c III Indre-et-Loire 1
Lavoisier, Pierre Claude	Crépy (Oise)	A.N., F¹c III Oise 1
Legras, Jean Baptiste	Saint-Germain-en-Laye (Seine-et-Oise)	A.N., BB⁵ 167

Name	Location	Source
Le Laurain, Ponce	Versailles (Seine-et-Oise)	A.N., AA 49, dossier 1391, document 58
Leprestre-Boisderville, P. F.	Montmorency (Seine-et-Oise)	A.N., BB^5 167
Maignan de Champromain, A. E.	Cosne (Nièvre)	A.N., W 382, no. 890
Marguet, François Ant.	Ste. Menehould (Marne)	A.N., W 466, no. 233
Mascrey, Nicolas Denis	Montmorency (Seine-et-Oise)	A.N., BB^1 46, dossier 2
Pulleu, Pierre François	Chaumont-en-Vexin (Oise)	A.N., F^{1}c III Oise 1
Thirria, Charles Dominique	Crépy (Oise)	A.N., F^{1}c III Oise 1
Thuriot, Jacques	Sezanne (Marne)	A.N., BB^5 169
Substitute Judges		
Alix de Murget, Jean	Orléans (Loiret)	A.N., F^{1}c III Loiret 1
Brouet, Charles Edme	Neuville (Loiret)	A.N., F^{1}c III Loiret 1
Cairol, Gabriel Felix	Versailles (Seine-et-Oise)	A.N., D^{III} 360
Lescalier, Jean	Gap (Hautes-Alpes)	A.N., D^{IV} 4, dossier 37
Pelé, Bon Thomas	Orléans (Loiret)	A.N., F^{1}c III Loiret 1
Poncy, Bernard	Nogent-sur-Seine (Aube)	A.N., F^{2}I 121^2

Appendix D

The Order of Barristers: Individual Portraits

The lives of the following men depict different experiences within the Order of Barristers in Paris. Their careers individually illustrate the larger forces of fragmentation and reconstruction at work between the abolition of the Order in 1790 and its reorganization in 1811.

François Denis Tronchet

François Denis Tronchet was born in Paris on March 23, 1726, the son of a procureur at the Parlement of Paris. He became a member of the Order of Barristers on August 9, 1745. During the Maupeou parlement he was among those who closed his office and refused to practice in it; resuming practice after the recall of the Parlement, he was conciliatory toward those who had appeared in the Maupeou court. He became a distinguished consulting barrister and was elected president of the Order on May 8, 1789, shortly before he was chosen as a deputy to the Estates-General for the Third Estate of Paris.

As a member of the National Assembly, he acquired a reputation for being cautious and non-innovative. Not surprisingly, he took a special interest in judicial matters; among other issues, the use of juries in civil cases was one in which he played an instrumental role, persuading the Assembly to reject such juries. Elected to a judgeship in the civil courts of Paris, he assumed the post after leaving the National Assembly, but with the renewal of the judiciary mandated in 1792, he retired to his estate at Palaiseau.

Called to assist as a *consultant* in the defense of Louis XVI, he conducted the case skillfully, earning the gratitude of Louis, who left him a bequest in his will. The Committee of General Security later sought to arrest him, but he succeeded in hiding until the fall of Robespierre, which of course ameliorated the situation. During much of the period of the Directory, he represented the department of the Seine-et-Oise in the Council of Ancients and also practiced intermittently as a jurisconsulte in Paris.

Under the Consulate he was named to the Cour de cassation and subsequently was designated for the Senate, with the text of the proclamation declaring him "le premier jurisconsulte de France." He played a major role in the drafting of the Code Napoléon and died in Paris on March 10, 1806, shortly before his eightieth birthday.

Tronchet is representative of those men from the Order who became deputies to the National Assembly—Treilhard, Camus, Target, and others. Assimilated into the political process, and ultimately co-opted by the spirit of the sublimity of the nation to which the night of August 4 gave birth, they abandoned their former corporate loyalties and acquiesced in the abolition of the Order of Barristers.

Pierre Nicolas Berryer

Pierre Nicolas Berryer was born in Sainte-Menehoulde (Marne), where his father was a glassware merchant, on March 17, 1757. He went to Paris in September 1774 and worked as a clerk in the office of a procureur while reading law. He became a member of the Order on April 29, 1780; through skill and an advantageous marriage to the daughter of a prominent procureur, he was able to build a successful practice by 1789.

Utterly dismayed by the abolition of the Order in 1790, Berryer nonetheless remained in practice and was one of the first former barristers to the Parlement to appear in the new tribunals in 1791. He was also one of those who played a significant role in attempting to provide direction to the unofficial coalition maintained after the abolition of the Order.

He remained in the courts until 1793, when he sought refuge from the Terror by taking a post in the treasury. He resumed practice only under the Directory and once again played a critical role in facilitating the regroupment of the former members of the Order.

Berryer initially welcomed the advent of Bonaparte, seeing him as a bulwark against Jacobinism. The execution of the duc d'Enghien and the trial of Moreau repelled him, however, and he became disaffected with Bonaparte's rule; in the plebiscite on the establishment of the Empire, he, along with many other former barristers to the Parlement, voted against it. During this era, Berryer also affiliated himself with the Académie de Législation and remained associated with it for the entire duration of its existence.

He welcomed the return of the Bourbons in 1814 and regretted Bonaparte's return from Elba. And the events of the Hundred Days gave rise to Berryer's most famous case—his brilliant but futile defense of Marshal Ney against charges of treason.

Berryer died in Paris on June 25, 1841. His son, Pierre Antoine Berryer, who joined the Order on December 26, 1811, became a noted Legitimist under the July Monarchy and the Second Empire.

Berryer's career epitomizes that of most of the men who remained in practice after the abolition of the Order—Bellart, Bonnet, Chauveau-Lagarde, Fournel, and others. These men provided the continuity between the abolished Order of 1790 and the reorganized Order of 1811.

Pierre Bergeras

Pierre Bergeras was born in Salies (Basses-Pyrénées) on February 28, 1737. He became a barrister to the Parlement at the parlement of Pau on July 21, 1762, before coming to Paris and joining the Order of Barristers on April 24, 1768.

Amid the uncertainty of 1789-90, Bergeras was among those who left Paris; he returned to Salies to practice law and was there in March 1790, when he was elected procureur général syndic of the department of the Basses-Pyrénées. In September 1791 he was elected as a deputy to the Legislative Assembly, after which he returned to his native department.

He became a judge in the Civil Tribunal of Pau in 1792, and became president of the tribunal in 1794. In the year VII he was elected to the Council of Ancients. One of the Brumairian elite favorable to the coup of brumaire, he was chosen by the Senate to represent the Basses-Pyrénées in the Legislative Body; he remained a member until the year XIII. He returned to Salies, where in 1814 the Duke of Wellington named him mayor of the town.

Bergeras is emblematic of many of the men who left the Order in 1789-90 to embark upon administrative, judicial, or political careers—Hua, Mouricault, Garran-Coulon, Duveyrier, among them. Although several clearly welcomed the Revolution of 1789, some were drawn to the new positions less out of "prorevolutionary" sentiment than as an alternative to an uncertain future in the legal profession as an homme de loi. Virtually all were political moderates, and their presence in the new Bonapartist regime helped to facilitate the acceptance of it by the former barristers to the Parlement.

Charles François Quequet

Charles François Quequet was born in Paris on May 29, 1768. He began his probationary period with the Order of Barristers on November 27, 1787, and was due to become a full member of the Order when it was abolished.

Staunchly opposed to the innovations introduced by the Revolution, he nevertheless remained in practice until 1793, when, like most of his colleagues, he sought refuge from the Terror in an administrative post—in this instance, the Bureau of Military Transport. He did not return to the legal profession until 1801.

He participated in various royalist activities and, on April 1, 1814, as allied troops approached Paris, Quequet and some associates prepared and sent a factum to the czar of Russia and the king of Prussia asking that Louis XVIII be placed on the throne, an action they believed was decisive in leading the allies to do so.

He served as a member of the Council of Discipline of the Order in 1814 and 1815, but in 1815 he was named avocat général at the Royal Court of Paris. In 1823 he was made president of the Royal Court, and the following year was elevated to the Cour de cassation, where he ended his career.

Quequet is representative of the men who were in their probationary period when the Order was abolished. With their clear ties to the abolished Order, they were an important element in its continuity; for this reason, they were accorded special treatment when it was reorganized by having their inscription date made retroactive to the beginning of their probationary period. Moreover, Quequet also typifies the political views of many of these men, several of whom—Billecocq, Taillandier, Piet (also known as Piet-Tardiveau), Falconnet, and others—were ardent royalists.

Louis Jean Baptiste Mathurin Couture

Louis Jean Baptiste Mathurin Couture was born in Amiens on March 5, 1769; his father was a procureur in the bailliage of Amiens and a judge *(bailli)* in several seignorial jurisdictions in the area around Amiens, and his mother was the daughter of a notary. After completing his education at the collège d'Amiens, he became a clerk in his father's office, during which time he also read law and aspired to a career as an avocat.

In 1793, however, he was conscripted to reinforce the republican armies in Flanders. He remained in the army until 1796, also serving in the Vendée. After an illness, he left the army to become a member of the departmental administration of the Somme, charged with supervising the sales of national lands.

In 1798, he began the practice of law in Amiens. Five years later, an avoué from Paris came to Amiens to handle a case with which he had been charged and asked Couture to act as the homme de loi. Pleased with Couture's effort, and pointing out to him that law was a free profession since the dissolution of the Order, the avoué encouraged him to take his practice to Paris. He left for Paris and affiliated himself with the coalition of former barristers to the Parlement. But his association with them was strictly professional and confined to the room they occupied at the Palais. In an action that perhaps stemmed from his lack of membership in the abolished Order of 1789, he did not belong to its interim surrogate, the Académie de Législation. He practiced law in Paris from 1804 to 1834, when an unspecified accident affected his ability to speak and forced him to retire. His most notable cases were in the field of criminal law and occurred under the Restoration.

After his retirement from practice he became an assistant judge in the Tribunal of the Seine. In 1844 he became a judge of the court at Douai. He retired in 1853 and died, in Douai, on August 18, 1859.

His career is emblematic of those men who had not been members of the Order in 1789, but who, after its abolition, came to Paris to practice law and were included in the Order when it was reestablished. With their diverse backgrounds, the members of this group were the most disparate of all, but they figured prominently in the reorganization of the Order.

André Marie Jean Jacques Dupin

André Marie Jean Jacques Dupin was born on February 1, 1783, at Varzy (Nièvre), where his father was an avocat. Only ten years old when the schools of law closed in 1793, Dupin came to Paris after his father was chosen for the Legislative Body in the year VIII, and briefly attended the central school of Quatre Nations. In the absence of the law schools, he also studied law in lessons with his father and worked as the head clerk in the office of an avoué.

When the Académie de Législation opened, Dupin attended as the scholarship student for the department of the Nièvre. He had a distinguished record and began to practice law in Paris. After the school of law reopened, he continued his studies, receiving a doctorate in law in 1806. In 1810 he unsuccessfully sought a chair in the law school at Paris; this failure led him to devote his energies entirely to the bar.

He went on to an eminent legal career under the Restoration; in 1817, he was placed on retainer by the duc d'Orléans. He assisted Berryer in the defense of Marshal Ney and pleaded in numerous important cases, although he refused to defend Louvel, the assassin of the duc de Berri, in 1820. After 1826 he also enjoyed a notable career as a deputy.

Dupin embodies many of the young men who were trained at the Académie de Législation or the Université de Jurisprudence and then entered practice in Paris or elsewhere, such as Hennequin, Teste, de Belleyme, and Bourguignon. Too young to have been members of the abolished Order, they nevertheless became an important element in its continuity, both through their tenure at the Académie de Législation and through their close association in the courts with the former barristers to the Parlement in the years before the Order of Barristers was reorganized. They were an important force for the progression of the unofficial coalition of former barristers to the Parlement—the "second generation" in the twenty-year hiatus between the abolition of the Order and its reestablishment.

Antoine Marie De Mante

Antoine Marie De Mante was born in Paris, where his father taught in the law school, on September 26, 1789. He himself studied at the reorganized Paris law school and in 1809 began to practice law at the Imperial Court of Paris. He became a member of the restored Order of Barristers, with an inscription date of August 26, 1809. He continued to practice law in Paris until 1821, when he received a post at the Paris law school to teach the Civil Code; he achieved a reputation as both an able scholar and a gifted teacher. In 1848 he was elected to the Constituent Assembly.

De Mante is emblematic of the young men who formed a large element in the restored Order of Barristers. With no direct ties to the abolished Order, nor any connection with the Académie de Législation or the Université de Jurisprudence, they were the "third generation" in the profession and the base for its continuation into the nineteenth century and beyond.

Notes

1. The Order of Barristers under the Old Regime

1. On the corporate nature of French society under the Old Regime, see Roland Mousnier, *Les institutions de la France sous la monarchie absolue 1598–1789*, 2 vols. (Paris: Presses Universitaires de France, 1974–1980); Emile Coornaert, *Les corporations en France avant 1789* (Paris: Gallimard, 1941); François Jean Marie Olivier-Martin, *L'organisation corporative de la France d'ancien régime* (Paris: Recueil Sirey, 1938); William H. Sewell, Jr., *Work and Revolution in France: The Language of Labor from the Old Regime to 1848* (Cambridge: Cambridge University Press, 1980); David D. Bien, "The *Secrétaires du Roi*: Absolutism, Corps and Privilege under the Ancien Régime," in Ernest Hinrichs, Eberhard Schmitt, and Rudolf Vierhaus, eds., *Vom Ancien Régime zur Französischen Revolution* (Göttingen: Vandenhoeck & Ruprecht, 1978), pp. 153–168; Dietrich Gerhard, *Old Europe: A Study of Continuity, 1000–1800* (New York; Academic Press, 1981).

2. William H. Sewell, Jr., "*Etat, Corps* and *Ordre*: Some Notes on the Social Vocabulary of the French Old Regime," in Hans Ulrich Wehler, ed., *Sozialgeschichte Heute: Festschrift für Hans Rosenberg zum 70, Geburstag* (Göttingen: Vandenhoeck & Ruprecht, 1974), pp. 48–68.

3. B.A.P., Tableau des Avocats au Parlement, mis au greffe de la Cour le 8 mai 1789; on Toulouse, see Lenard Berlanstein, *The Barristers of Toulouse in the Eighteenth Century, 1740–1793* (Baltimore: Johns Hopkins University Press, 1975), p. 11.

4. Antoine Gaspard Boucher d'Argis, *Règles pour former un avocat* (Paris: Durand, 1778), p. 212. Boucher d'Argis noted that in the confraternity "the barristers hold the foremost place and the attorneys the second."

5. Ibid., pp. 209–218.

6. B.N., MSS Joly de Fleury 2146, fols. 25–27, fols. 29–33. The barrister Pierre Nicolas Berryer once refused to perform certain duties that he felt were more proper to a procureur, even though a procureur was not available. Pierre Nicolas Berryer, *Souvenirs de M. Berryer*, 2 vols. (Paris: Ambroise Dupont, 1839), I, 80.

7. N. Lerasle, ed., *Encyclopédie méthodique: Jurisprudence*, 10 vols. (Paris: Panckoucke, 1782–1789), I, 627–628.

8. A. G. Camus, and J. B. F. Bayard, eds., *Collection de décisions nouvelles et de notions relatives à la jurisprudence, donnée par M. Denisart, mise dans un nouvel ordre, corigée et augmentée par MM. Camus et Bayard*, 8th ed., 14 vols. (Paris: Veuve Desaint, 1783–1807), II, 716.

9. Lerasle, ed., *Encyclopédie méthodique: Jurisprudence*, I, 623.

10. Boucher d'Argis, *Règles pour former un avocat*, p. 212. The fact that the profession of procureur was venal, while that of avocat was not, would also, of course, have contributed to their separate organization.

11. See Sewell, *Work and Revolution in France*, pp. 25–32.

12. Boucher d'Argis, *Règles pour former un avocat*, p. 211; Camus and Bayard, eds., *Collection de décisions nouvelles*, II, 716; Lerasle, ed., *Encyclopédie méthodique: Jurisprudence*, I, 625. See also Mousnier, *Les institutions de la France*, I, 344.

13. In Paris the Order's pretensions occasionally elicited scorn. See *Requeste presentée aux Avocats par les Décroteurs, pour demander la réunion des deux ordres* (n.p., n.d.), B.N., MSS Joly de Fleury 154, fol. 23.

14. The barristers' manifesto on their independence was Henri François D'Aguesseau, "Discours sur l'indépendance de l'avocat," which can be found in Jean Marie Pardessus, ed., *Oeuvres complètes du chancelier D'Aguesseau*, 16 vols. (Paris: Fantin, 1819), I, 1–13.

15. B.N., MSS Joly de Fleury 2133, fols. 108–119. See also Camus and Bayard, eds., *Collection de décisions nouvelles*, I, 717–718; Lerasle, ed., *Encyclopédie méthodique: Jurisprudence*, I, 626; VII, 172–177; Armand Gaston Camus, *Lettres sur la profession d'avocat* (Paris: Méquignon, 1777), pp. 16, 20.

16. B.M.O., MS. 1422, Mémoires de J. C. P. Lenoir — 1ere partie, Sciences, arts libéraux, Titre huitième. A large measure of the Order's autonomy doubtlessly resulted from the fact that the Palais de Justice, the seat of the Order, was part of the bailliage of the Palais, a separate jurisdiction beyond the reach of the police. See Alan Williams, *The Police of Paris, 1718–1789* (Baton Rouge: Louisiana State University Press, 1979), p. 169. Whatever the reason, the effect would have been to enhance the barristers' image of the independence of their Order.

17. B.M.O., MS. 1423, Extraits de divers rapports secrets faits à la police de Paris dans les années 1781 et suivantes, jusques et compris 1785.

18. Legal education in France in the eighteenth century was regulated by the edicts of April 1679, November 1690, and January 1700. See F. A. Isambert, ed. *Recueil général des anciennes lois françaises*, 29 vols. (Paris: Plon, 1821–1833), XIX, 195–202; XX, 111–113, 349–353.

19. Dispensations from this requirement were obtainable, however. See A.N., BB^{30} 512^A, dossier 2, Dispense d'âge pour le Sr Gautier d'Ecurolles. See also Christian Chêne, *L'enseignement du droit français en pays de droit écrit (1679–1793)* (Geneva: Librairie Droz, 1982), pp. 134–135.

20. A.N., MM 1088, MM 1089, Register of inscriptions in Law School, 1770–1777. Unfortunately, the registers for the years 1778–1789 are lost.

21. See Berryer, *Souvenirs*, I, 34, for a description of the regimen of the clerks.

22. Etienne Denis duc Pasquier, *A History of My Time: Memoirs of Chancellor Pasquier*, ed. duc d'Audiffret-Pasquier, 3 vols. (London: T. F. Unwin, 1893–1894), I, 16–17.

23. Richard L. Kagan, "Law Students and Legal Careers in Eighteenth-Century France," *Past and Present* 68 (August 1975): 41. See also A.N., D^{IV} 13 dossier 232, anonymous letter of January 20, 1790; Chêne, *L'enseignement du droit français*, pp. 96–99.

24. On Cahors, see Alfred de Curzon, *L'enseignement du droit français dans les universités de France aux XVIIe et XVIIIe siècles* (Paris: Sirey, 1920), p. 98; for Reims, A.N., D^IV 4, dossier 27, document 18, and on the sale of degrees, Chêne, *L'enseignement du droit français*, p. 315.

25. Lerasle, ed., *Encyclopédie méthodique: Jurisprudence*, I, 620–621.

26. Ibid., I, 621.

27. Boucher d'Argis, *Règles pour former un avocat*, p. 7.

28. Armand Gaston Camus and Henri François Caillau, for example, were both graduates of the University of Paris Law School. B.N., MSS Nouvelles acquisitions françaises 23067, fols. 63–64 (Camus); A.D. Seine, DE¹ 3, dossier 36 (Caillau); Louis Augustine Bruslé, Augustine Julien Dufresne, and Nicolas Alexandre Herbault-Despavaux, by contrast, had studied law while serving as clerks to procureurs. A.N., BB⁵ 3, letter of Bruslé to minister of Justice, 14 pluviôse an IX (Bruslé); A.N., D^III 257, letter of Dufresne, no date, messidor an III (Dufresne); A.N., F⁷ 4743, dossier Herbaut (*sic*) (Herbault-Despavaux).

29. Boucher d'Argis, *Règles pour former un avocat*, p. 7; Lerasle, ed., *Encyclopédie méthodique: Jurisprudence*, I, 620; Berryer, *Souvenirs*, I, 44. For a copy of the decree of May 5, 1751, see B.A.P., Tableau de 1789.

30. A.N., AD^II 46 contains an undated receipt for the fee paid by a probationary barrister. It shows that the total fee paid to begin the probationary period was 76.10 livres.

31. On the unwritten regulations that governed the Order, see B.N., MSS Joly de Fleury 2133, fol. 109; on the probationary period, Berryer, *Souvenirs*, I, 44–47. On the teaching of Roman law, Boucher d'Argis, *Règles pour former un avocat*, p.130. During their candidacy the probationary members were also referred to as *avocats écoutants*.

32. Berryer, *Souvenirs*, I, 47. Even under the Empire, a former probationary member of the Order mentioned in his application for a judgeship that he had followed the course of study at the Palais from 1788 until the suppression of the Parlement. Christophe Hureau in 1800 referred to himself as a student of Louis Simon Martineau, and Pierre François Anfrye described himself as a student of Gerbier, although neither Martineau nor Gerbier had ever held a position in any law school. Similarly, the barrister Godefroy-Montours said he was a student of Laget-Bardelin. A.N., BB⁵ 169, undated letter of Du Rouzeau to minister of justice; A.N., BB⁶ 2, Yonne (Hureau); A.N.,BB⁶ 2, Seine-et-Oise (Anfrye); A.N., BB⁵ 112, letter of Godefroy-Montours to minister of justice, 2nd complementary day, year XI. The barrister Philippe Dumouchet du Bac edited and published a collection of the proceedings of these discussions under the title *Traité sur les questions mixtes* (Paris: Herisant, 1787).

33. Berryer, *Souvenirs*, I, 47.

34. On the denial of admission, see Lerasle, ed., *Encyclopédie méthodique: Jurisprudence*, I, 626. It was precisely on this question that the Order drafted a consultation on the discipline of barristers in support of the barristers of Poitiers, who were the defendants in a case brought by a man to whom they had refused admission. As a supporting document in a case of importance to them, it offers a more concise

and candid insight into the ethos of the profession than that found in published works. B.N., MSS Joly de Fleury 2133, fols. 108–119.

35. B.N., MSS Joly de Fleury 2146, fol. 155.

36. See, for example, B.N., MSS Joly de Fleury 2146, fols. 29–33.

37. Lerasle, ed., *Encyclopédie méthodique: Jurisprudence*, I, 625; B.N., MSS Joly de Fleury 2133, fol. 111. To give but one example of the manifestation of trust, unlike the practice at many other courts, the members of the Order never requested or gave receipts to each other when they exchanged evidence or documents to be used in prepartion of a case. Boucher d'Argis, *Règles pour former un avocat*, p. 150.

38. Gerald L. Geison, ed., *Professions and the French State, 1700–1900* (Philadelphia: University of Pennsylvania Press, 1984); George Weisz, "Constructing the Medical Elite in France: The Creation of the Royal Academy of Medicine, 1814–1820," paper presented at the conference "Science, Medicine and Technology in the French Restoration," Paris, 1983; both stress the role of the state in the evolution of professions.

39. On the attributes generally associated with the concept of a profession, see Jan Goldstein, "Foucault among the Sociologists: The 'Disciplines' and the History of the Professions," *History and Theory* 23 (June 1984): 174–175.

40. Francis Delbeke, *Le barreau à la fin de l'ancien régime* (Brussels: Larcier, n.d.), p. 17; for the estimate of 500, Marcel Reinhard, *Nouvelle histoire de Paris: La Révolution, 1789–1799* (Paris: Hachette, 1971), p. 34.

41. On the hazard of trying to practice before the Parlement without being a member of the Order, see B.N., MSS Joly de Fleury 2146, fol. 232, Mémoire pour M. Morizot. Morizot, who held a law degree but was not a member of the Order, pleaded his own case at the Parlement involving a dispute with his sister over their father's will. Thorell, the barrister for Morizot's sister, upon learning from a greffier that Morizot was not a member of the Order, interrupted the latter's pleading by exclaiming, "I will not argue against this man: a clerk," a term, Morizot claimed, that he pronounced with "a disdainful air, added to the most indecent epithet." Years later, the memory of this incident inhibited another individual from pleading either at the Châtelet or the Parlement because he was not a member of the Order. See A.D. Seine, 1 AZ 4, Mémoire aux Etats-Généraux, pour M. Fardeau.

42. Berlanstein, *The Barristers of Toulouse*, pp. 17–19.

43. The barristers were exempt from all personal service, but not from obligations that were fiscal in nature. See Lerasle, ed., *Encyclopédie méthodique: Jurisprudence*, I, 624.

44. Jean Baptiste Denisart, *Collection de décisions nouvelles et de notions relatives à la jurisprudence actuelle*, 7th ed., 4 vols. (Paris: Veuve Desaint, 1771), I, 225.

45. Boucher d'Argis, *Règles pour former un avocat*, p. 6.

46. W. N. Hargreaves-Mawdsley, *A History of Legal Dress in Europe until the End of the Eighteenth Century* (Oxford: Oxford University Press, 1963), pp. 38–39.

47. Berryer, *Souvenirs*, I, 19, 49. A similar situation existed in Besançon and Toulouse. See Maurice Gresset, *Gens de Justice à Besançon: De la conquête par Louis*

XIV à la Révolution française, 1674–1789, 2 vols. (Paris: Bibliothèque Nationale, 1978), I, 94–97, 101; Berlanstein, *The Barristers of Toulouse*, p. 16.

48. John McManners, "France," in Albert Goodwin, ed., *The European Nobility in the Eighteenth Century* (London: Adam & Charles Black, 1953), p. 23; Lerasle, ed., *Encyclopédie méthodique: Jurisprudence*, VI, 134. See also Lenard Berlanstein, "Lawyers in Pre-Revolutionary France," in Wilfrid Prest, ed., *Lawyers in Early Modern Europe and America* (London: Croom Helm, 1981), p. 164.

49. Antoine Vincent Arnault, Antoine Jay, Etienne Jouy, Jacques Marquet Norvins, et. al., *Biographie nouvelle des contemporains*, 20 vols. (Paris: Librairie historique, 1820–1825), II, 237.

50. A.N., F^{17} 1310, dossier 10.

51. B.A.P., Tableau de 1789; *Almanach Royal 1789*, p. 507.

52. B.A.P., Tableau de 1789; on Bigot de Préameneu, see Auguste Nougarede de Fayet, *Notice sur la vie et les travaux de M. le Comte Bigot de Préameneu* (Paris: Claye et Taillefer, 1843), pp. 3–4; on Ferey, Nicolas F. Bellart, *Eloge de M. Ferey* (Paris: Demonville, 1810); on de Sèze, André Sevin, *Le Défenseur du Roi: Raymond de Sèze* (Paris: Gabriel Enault, 1936).

53. B.A.P., Tableau de 1789; on Polverel at Bordeaux, see William Doyle, *The Parlement of Bordeaux and the End of the Old Regime, 1771–1790* (London: Ernest Benn, 1974), p. 160.

54. Louis Petit de Bachaumont, *Mémoires secrets pour servir à l'histoire de la république des lettres en France, depuis MDCCCLXII jusqu'à nos jours; ou Journal d'un observateur . . .* , 36 vols. (London: J. Adamsohn, 1780–1789), XXV, 273.

55. To give only a few examples, Pierre Nicolas Berryer came to Paris from Ste. Menehould (Marne), Antoine Jacques Claude Joseph Boullay from Nancy, Louis Joseph Faure from Le Havre, and Nicolas Oudart from Eclaron (Haute Marne) to begin their careers. Berryer, *Souvenirs*, I, 41 (Berryer); *Biographie universelle (Michaud) ancienne et moderne*, new ed., 45 vols. (Paris: C. Desplaces, 1854–1865), V, 234 (Boullay); A.N., AA 48, dossier 1381, document 44 (Faure); B.H.V.P., MS. 776, document 136 (Oudart).

56. The claim is made in Francis Delbeke, *L'action politique et sociale des avocats au XVIIIe siècle* (Paris: Recueil Sirey, 1927), pp. 85–86, citing T. J. A. Cottereau, *Le droit Lodunois*, 3 vols. (Tours: F. Vauquer-Lambert, 1778–1788). On the strictness of the Order at Paris, B.N., MSS Joly de Fleury 2145, fol. 200; Camus and Bayard, eds., *Collection de décisions nouvelles*, II, 749.

57. Camus and Bayard, eds., *Collection de décisions nouvelles*, II, 748–749. Exceptions were made for those who purchased the office of *secrétaire du roi*, as long as one agreed not to fulfill the duties of sending letters, which would not have been a problem. See Bien, "The *Secrétaires du Roi*," pp. 153–154. Other exceptions were for *secrétaires de sceaux*, intendants of finance for Monsieur and for the comte d'Artois, and for the various seignorial judicial posts in the seignorial courts.

58. On the affinity that the barristers claimed with the magistracy, see Camus and Bayard, eds., *Collection de décisions nouvelles*, II, 708; Boucher d'Argis, *Règles pour former un avocat*, p. 189. As a few examples of barristers who served in seignorial courts: Jean Simon Aved de Loizerolles was lieutenant général in the bailliage de l'Arsenal, Marc Antoine Laget-Bardelin was bailli in the Abbaye

Royale de Saint-Germain des Près, Louis Adrien Le Paige was bailli général of the bailliage du Temple, and Louis Antoine Robert was *lieutenant* of the bailliage of the comte de Pontchartrain. A.D. Seine, 4 AZ 842 (Loizerolles); *Almanach Royal 1789,* p. 452 (Laget-Bardelin); Ibid., p. 451 (Le Paige); A.N., AA 41, dossier 4, document 9 (Robert). See also Pierre Lemercier, *Les justices seigneuriales de la région parisienne de 1580 à 1789* (Paris: Editions Domat-Montchrestien, 1933), p. 71.

59. A.N., BB^5 170, undated notice on Le Roy. A further word on sources is appropriate here. As anyone who has worked with it knows, the BB^5 series is a chaotic one. Often one will encounter two or even three dates on a document. One may be the date it was written, another might be when it arrived at the Ministry of Justice and another might be when it was processed by the bureau to which it was assigned. Quite often, however, the writers of documents did not date them and while dates of the last two categories just mentioned allowed archivists to classify the documents chronologically, unless the date appears in the same hand in which it was written, I have cited it, as in this instance, as undated.

60. The first bench was utilized by the entire Order for consultations with clients. The remaining eleven benches were divided as follows in 1781: banc 2, 38 members; banc 3, 60 members; banc 4, 39 members; banc 5, 147 members; banc 6, 9 members; banc 7, 55 members; banc 8, 7 members; banc 9, 47 members; banc 10, 92 members; banc 11, 59 members; banc 12, 10 members (source: B.A.P., Tableau de 1781). As reorganized in 1782, the Order was divided accordingly: column 1, 56 members; column 2, 55 members; column 3, 55 members; column 4, 55 members; column 5, 55 members; column 6, 56 members; column 7, 55 members; column 8, 55 members; column 9, 55 members; column 10, 54 members (source: B.A.P., Tableau de 1782). For an example of the column as the basic administrative unit of the Order, see A.N., D^{III} 257, note of Canuel to Vivier de Launay, January 7, 1789. The reorganization was also designed in part to restore a sense of cohesion and morale in the Order, which remained divided for several years after the recall of the Parlement in 1774. See *Lettre de M._____, Avocat au Parlement de Paris, à M._____, son Confrère, ce 27 avril 1782* (n.p., n.d.). B.N., Recueil Z Le Senne 17 (6).

61. Camus and Bayard, eds., *Collection de décisions nouvelles,* II, 718.

62. On Feval, see B.N., MSS Joly de Fleury 2147, fols. 8–13; on the rarity of complaints by clients against barristers, Delbeke, *L'action politique et sociale des avocats,* pp. 134–136.

63. Boucher d'Argis, *Règles pour former un avocat,* p. 111.

64. On Rimbert, see B.N., MSS Joly de Fleury 2432, fol. 127; for Dodin, Ibid., fols. 132–133.

65. *Mémoires d'un vieil avocat,* 3 vols. (Paris: Hippolyte Souverain, 1847), II, 6–11 (B.H.V.P. 4658); B.N., MSS Joly de Fleury 2432, fol. 129. His date of inscription had been June 8, 1733. B.A.P., Tableau de 1776.

66. B.N., MSS Joly de Fleury 2432, fols. 134–138.

67. Lerasle, ed., *Encylopédie méthodique: Jurisprudence,* VII, 176–177. On Dassy, see *Mémoires d'un vieil avocat,* II, 14.

68. *Mémoires d'un vieil avocat,* II, 47–49.

69. B.N., MSS Joly de Fleury 2133, fol. 111. Similarly, a member of the Order, Jacques Vincent Delacroix, in speaking of the Tableau des avocats, wrote that "the barrister who wishes to see his name maintained there ought to avoid whatever could jeopardize his integrity and his reputation: he cannot be too careful in the choice of his acquaintances and even his diversions." Lerasle, ed., *Encyclopédie méthodique: Jurisprudence,* VII, 177.

70. Camus, *Lettres sur la profession d'avocat,* pp. 16, 20; Lerasle, ed., *Encyclopédie méthodique: Jurisprudence,* I, 626; VII, 172–177.

71. B.N., MSS Joly de Fleury 2133, fol. 110; Lerasle, ed., *Encyclopédie méthodique: Jurisprudence,* I, 626.

72. Once again, the best exposition of these principles is found in B.N., MSS Joly de Fleury 2133, fols. 108–119, "Consultation sur la discipline des avocats."

73. Boucher d'Argis, *Règles pour former un avocat,* p. 189.

74. Ferdinand Dreyfus, "L'Association de bienfaisance judiciaire," *La Révolution Française* 46 (January–June 1904): 391.

75. For the list of members of the association, see *Recueil de pièces concernant l'Association de bienfaisance judiciaire, fondée en 1787* (Paris: Clousier, 1788), pp. 149–178; on the extent of its activities in 1788–89, Dreyfus, "L'Association de bienfaisance judiciaire," p. 395.

76. B.N., MSS Nouvelles acquisitions françaises 2499; B.N., MSS Joly de Fleury 2208.

77. Joachim Gaudry, *Histoire du barreau de Paris depuis son origine jusqu'à 1830,* 2 vols. (Paris: Auguste Durand, 1864), II, 67. Gaudry had access to records that were destroyed in 1871.

78. On the fee, see A.N., AD^{II} 46, which reveals that of 76.10 livres paid, nearly one-third, 25.00, went to support the library and chapel. On all of the sources of income, A.D. Seine, DQ^{10} 1434, dossier 2169.

79. Boucher d'Argis, *Règles pour former un avocat,* p. 130, for the 1778 figure; André Marie Jean Jacques Dupin, ed., *Profession d'avocat,* 2 vols. (Paris: Alex-Gobelet, 1832), I, 140, for the 1789 figure. On its status as a major Parisian library, *Almanach Royal 1789,* p. 500.

80. For a good description, see Berlanstein, *The Barristers of Toulouse,* pp. 7–8.

81. Eustache Antoine Hua, *Mémoires d'un avocat au Parlement de Paris* (Poitiers: Henri Oudin, 1871), pp. 13–14. In 1782, for example, a grand duke and duchess from Russia visited a session of the Parlement and were acknowledged by the barristers Martineau and Hardouin, who were pleading that day. Bachaumont, *Mémoires secrets,* XX, 318.

82. Boucher d'Argis, *Règles pour former un avocat,* p. 122.

83. Berryer, *Souvenirs,* I, 86. He noted proudly that he nonetheless won the case; Hua, *Mémoires d'un avocat au Parlement de Paris,* p. 24.

84. Some of the Parisian barristers noted for their pleading at the end of the Old Regime were Jean Baptiste Gerbier, Guy Jean Baptiste Target, Louis Simon Martineau, Jean Baptiste Treilhard, Armand Gaston Camus, Louis Eugene Hardouin, and Raymond de Sèze. Louis Ferdinand Bonnet, *Discours, plaidoyers et mémoires de M. L. Bonnet,* 2 vols. (Paris: B. Warée, 1839), II, 228.

85. Some of the more successful écrivains of this period were Pierre Aujollet,

Louis Auguste Popelin, Louis Claude Rimbert, Jean François Janniot, and Charles Simon Dinet. This is based on an analysis of A.N., X^{1b} 603–606.

Examples of *instructions* can be found in A.N., T 1112, dossier 6; A.N., T 45$^{1-2}$; A.N., T 1131$^{1-2}$. These are the papers of Vautrin, Lauvin, and Brisse respectively, all of whom were members of the Order.

86. Lerasle, ed., *Encyclopédie méthodique: Jurisprudence*, I, 620. For an example of such a consultation, see B.H.V.P., MS. 813, documents 168–171.

87. Hua, *Mémoires d'un avocat au Parlement de Paris*, p. 13.

88. Boucher d'Argis, *Règles pour former un avocat*, p. 175.

89. *Biographie universelle (Michaud) ancienne et moderne*, XIX, 214. Other prominent consulting barristers were François Denis Tronchet, the president of the Order in 1789; Anselme Joseph D'Outremont; Claude Nicolas Collet; Laurent Jean Babille; Marc Antoine Laget-Bardelin; François Alexis Nicolas Ferey; and Jean Etienne Poirier. Bonnet, *Discours, plaidoyers et mémoires*, II, 227.

90. See Berlanstein, *The Barristers of Toulouse*, pp. 20–22, and Olwen Hufton, *Bayeux in the Late Eighteenth Century* (Oxford: Clarendon Press, 1967), p. 62. D'Aguesseau also discussed this in his "Discours sur l'indépendance de l'avocat."

91. *Almanach Royal 1789*, pp. 580–581 (Treilhard and Blondel). The Royal General Farm in particular generated much litigation and had an extensive legal staff on retainer both to handle cases and to provide legal expertise to the provincial directors. See George T. Matthews, *The Royal General Farms in Eighteenth-Century France* (New York: Columbia Universty Press, 1958), p. 206. On Target, *Almanach Royal 1789*, pp. 140, 480–481. Other examples include Pierre Paul Nicolas Henrion de Pansey and François Alexis Nicolas Ferey, who were on retainer for the duc d'Orléans; Louis Le Roy, who was also on retainer for the duc d'Orléans, the house of Bourbon-Penthiviers, and several religious corporations; and Felix Julien Jean Bigot de Préameneu, who was counsel for the Estates of Provence. *Almanach Royal 1789*, pp. 147–148 (Henrion de Pansey and Ferey); A.N., BB^5 170, undated notice on Le Roy (Le Roy), and A.N., AF^{IV}1440, dossier 1, Département d'Ille et Vilaine, 3 messidor year XII (Bigot de Préameneu). For the names of other major figures, see Bonnet, *Discours, plaidoyers et mémoires*, II, 227–229 and *Almanach Royal 1789*, passim.

92. Berryer, *Souvenirs*, I, 95–96. Some other barristers who enjoyed comparable careers were Nicolas François Bellart, Louis Ferdinand Bonnet, Guillaume Alexandre Tronson-Ducoudray, Claude François Chauveau-Lagarde, and Joseph Delacroix-Frainville. Bonnet, *Discours, plaidoyers et mémoires*, II, 247–248.

93. On Paré and Billaud de Varennes, see Norman Hampson, *Danton* (London: Duckworth, 1978), p. 25; on Duport du Tertre, B.M.O., MS. 1423, Extraits de divers rapports.

94. Berlanstein, *The Barristers of Toulouse*, pp. 16–17.

95. Berryer, *Souvenirs*, I, 92.

96. Bonnet, *Discours, plaidoyers et mémoires*, II, 229. Bonnet mentions also that Target, who like Gerbier was then at the peak of his career, pleaded only rarely.

97. Lerasle, ed., *Encyclopédie méthodique: Jurisprudence*, I, 621.

98. See Berryer, *Souvenirs*, I, 53–54; Hua, *Mémoires d'un avocat au Parlement de Paris*, p. 14; and Bonnet, *Discours, plaidoyers et mémoires*, II, 240.

99. Camus, *Lettres sur la profession d'avocat*, p. 5. Jacques Pierre Brissot, *Un indépendant à l'ordre des avocats, sur la décadence du barreau française* (Berlin, 1781). Camus and Bayard, eds., *Collection de décisions nouvelles*, II, 719.

100. *Les injustices des parlements: Devoilées par un client ruiné* (n.p., Themis, 1790), pp. 80–81.

101. Brissot, *Un indépendant à l'ordre des avocats*, pp. 5, 48.

102. Hua, *Mémoires d'un avocat au Parlement de Paris*, pp. 24–25. Bien, "The Secrétaires du Roi," pp. 154–155, points out that church and state figured subsistence for a curé at 700 livres per year, and that professors at the Ecole Militaire in Paris, who were considered well paid, received 2,400 livres per year.

103. For a consideration of the issue in a different context, see Colin Kaiser, "The Deflation in the Volume of Litigation at Paris in the Eighteenth Century and the Waning of the Old Judicial Order," *European Studies Review* 10 (July 1980): 309–336.

104. For Rennes, see Henri Sée, *La France économique et sociale au XVIIIe siècle* (Paris: A. Colin, 1925), p. 160; for Toulouse, Berlanstein, *The Barristers of Toulouse*, pp. 67–72.

105. Berryer, *Souvenirs*, I, 88–90.

106. The barrister François Theodore Rouhette was a noble. A.N., F^7 4775^1, dossier Rouhette. In 1789 one of his sons became a magistrate in the Chambre des requêtes. *Almanach Royal 1790*, p. 303.

107. The father of Jules Paré, who was inscribed in 1782, was a carpenter; Claude François Chauveau-Lagarde, who became a member of the Order in 1783, was the son of a wigmaker; and Nicolas François Bellart, who was inscribed in 1785, was the son of a wagon maker in the Marais, and his origins were well known to the Order. *Biographie universelle (Michaud) ancienne et moderne*, XXXII, 128 (Paré); J. Balteau, M. Barroux, and M. Prevost, eds., *Dictionnaire de biographie française*, 14 vols. (Paris: Letouzey et Ané, 1933–), VIII, 899 (Chauveau-Lagarde); Jean Baptiste Billecocq, *Notice historique sur M. Bellart* (Paris: Pihan-Delaforest, 1826) (Bellart). On Brissot, see Eloise Ellery, *Brissot de Warville*, reprint ed. (New York: AMS Press, 1970), p. 18.

108. The figure for sons of artisans is from Kagan, "Law Students and Legal Careers in Eighteenth-Century France," p. 56. The two schools were Dijon and Pont-à-Mousson. On the incident at Besançon, see Delbeke, *L'action politique et sociale des avocats*, pp. 112–113.

109. The barrister Eustache Antoine Hua, for example, had to rely on money given to him by his father for several years before he earned enough from his practice so that he no longer needed such assistance. Hua, *Mémoires d'un avocat au Parlement de Paris*, pp. 24–25.

110. Lerasle, ed., *Encyclopédie méthodique: Jurisprudence*, I, 624; Boucher d'Argis, *Règles pour former un avocat*, p. 71; Gaudry, *Histoire du barreau de Paris*, I, 420. Clerical members of the Order in 1789 included Henri Jabineau, Antoine René Constance Bertholio, André Blonde, and Claude Mey. *Biographie universelle (Michaud) ancienne et moderne*, XX, 439–440 (Jabineau); A.N., D^{III} 384, dossier 504 (Bertholio); *Biographie universelle (Michaud) ancienne et moderne*, IV, 448–449 (Blonde); Ibid, XXVIII, 162 (Mey).

111. Jules Flammermont, *Le Chancelier Maupeou et les Parlements* (Paris: A. Picard, 1883), p. 244. Other studies include Jacques de Maupeou, *Le Chancelier Maupeou* (Paris: Editions de Champrosay, 1942), and Robert Villers, *L'organisation du Parlement de Paris et des conseils supérieurs d'après la réforme de Maupeou, 1771–1774* (Paris: Recueil Sirey,1937).

112. David Hudson, "In Defense of Reform: French Government Propaganda during the Maupeou Crisis," *French Historical Studies* 8 (Spring 1973): 64.

113. Much of what follows is drawn largely from Henri Carré, "Le barreau de Paris et la radiation de Linguet," *Bulletin de la Faculté des Lettres de Poitiers* (1892); Jean Cruppi, *Un avocat journaliste au XVIIIe siècle: Linguet* (Paris: Hachette, 1895), which is largely sympathetic to Linguet; and Gaudry, *Histoire du barreau de Paris*, II, 175–189, which is more favorably disposed toward the Order. A good recent biography of Linguet also examines his disbarment, but for the most part it, too, is somewhat sympathetic to Linguet: Darline Gay Levy, *The Ideas and Careers of Simon Nicolas Henri Linguet* (Urbana: University of Illinois Press, 1980), pp. 143–162.

114. Quoted in Cruppi, *Un avocat journaliste au XVIIIe siècle*, p. 380.

115. See *Lettre de M.* ———, *Avocat au Parlement de Paris, à M.* ———, *son Confrère, ce 27 avril 1782*. B.N., Recueil Z Le Senne 17 (6).

116. *Exposition abregée de la constitution de l'Ordre des avocats au Parlement de Paris* (Geneva, 1782) was the major response to it. Brissot claimed later, when it was reprinted, that an attempt had been made to suppress it, but this cannot be definitely ascertained. See J. P. Brissot, *Bibliothèque philosophique du législateur, du politique, du jurisconsulte*, 10 vols. (Paris: Desauges, 1782–1785), VI, 343.

117. These included *Réflexions d'un militaire sur la profession d'avocat* (n.p., 1781); *Idées d'un citoyen de Paris* (n.p., 1789); *Projets de création de charges d'avocats ou plutôt de destruction de l'ordre inquisitoriale et despotique des avocats au Parlement de Paris . . . par une société d'avocats non tablotants* (Berlin, 1789).

118. Camus and Bayard, eds., *Collection de décisions nouvelles*, VIII, " Avertissement de M. Bayard, éditeur" (no page number). During the strike Claude François Chauveau-Lagarde had to pawn his watch and table silver, and Raymond de Sèze claimed to have lost everything he had. Sevin, *Le défenseur du Roi*, p. 143.

119. On the reforms of Lamoignon, see Marcel Marion, *Le garde des sceaux Lamoignon et la réforme judiciaire de 1788* (Paris: Hachette, 1905); John F. Ramsey, "The Judicial Reform of 1788 and the French Revolution," in Frederick J. Cox, Richard M. Brace, Bernard C. Weber, and John F. Ramsey, eds., *Studies in Modern European History in Honor of Franklin Charles Palm* (New York: Bookman Associates, 1956), pp. 217–238.

120. Similarly, in his study of Besançon, Gresset found no evidence of social resentment or conflict between the barristers and the Parlement before 1789. Gresset argued, however, that such resentments most often remained "unformulated." Gresset, *Gens de Justice à Besançon*, II, 722–723.

121. Bonnet, *Discours, plaidoyers et mémoires*, II, 237.

122. William F. Church, "The Decline of French Jurists as Political Theorists, 1660–1789, " *French Historical Studies* 5 (Spring 1967): 35.

123. A.N., 163 AP, dossier 1. His effort apparently succeeded because the

work does not appear in the Catalogue of Printed Books of the Bibliothèque Nationale. The divergence of most of the Parisian avocats au Parlement from much of the Enlightenment may also serve to explain further one of Robert Darnton's findings concerning the sales pattern of the quarto edition of the *Encyclopédie*. In his case study of subscribers Darnton found that lawyers comprised one of the largest groups of subscribers, but his geographical analysis revealed that the work did not sell as well as expected in Paris market. Robert Darnton, *The Business of Enlightenment: A Publishing History of the Encyclopédie, 1775–1800* (Cambridge, Mass.: Harvard University Press, 1979), pp. 278–294. The Parisian barristers' aversion to the Enlightenment also contrasts with the situation at Toulouse. Berlanstein, *The Barristers of Toulouse*, chap. 4. Yet for professors of French law in southern France there was a divergence similar to Paris; in one study, in fact, none of them subscribed to the *Encyclopédie*. Chêne, *L'enseignement du droit français*, pp. 280, 322.

124. Church, "The Decline of French Jurists," pp. 27–28.

125. Louis Sebastien Mercier, *Tableau de Paris*, 10 vols. (Amsterdam, 1783–1788), I, 219.

126. François Michel Vermeil, *Essai sur les réformes à faire dans notre législation criminelle* (Paris: Savoye et Delalain le jeune, 1781).

127. Church, "The Decline of French Jurists," p. 28. Some examples are Gabriel Nicolas Maultrot, *Dissertation sur l'approbation des confesseurs* (n.p., 1784); Pierre Paul Nicolas Henrion de Pansey, *Dissertations féodales*, 2 vols. (Paris: T. Barrois, 1789); and François Hervé, *Théorie des matières féodales et censuelles*, 7 vols. (Paris: Knapen et fils, 1785–1788). Hervé's work continued up to the Revolution, for in 1790 he published *Théorie des dîmes* (Paris: Knapen et fils).

128. On Boucher d'Argis's contributions, see *Biographie universelle (Michaud) ancienne et moderne*, V, 169. Boucher d'Argis was a particularly active writer, but all of his work was strictly in the field of law. See also John Lough, *The Contributors to the Encyclopédie* (London: Grant & Cutler Ltd., 1973), pp. 10–11. On Diderot's rewriting of the entry on natural law, see René Hubert, *Rousseau et l'Encyclopédie* (Paris: Gambier, n.d.), pp. 27–29; Jacques Proust, *Diderot et l'Encyclopédie* (Paris: A. Colin, 1962), pp. 384–386. Arthur M. Wilson, *Diderot* (Oxford: Oxford University Press, 1972), pp. 233–234, acknowledges Diderot's authorship of the article on natural law but does not mention why he wrote it.

129. *Almanach Royal 1789*, pp. 494–495.

130. B.N., MSS Nouvelles acquisitions françaises 23068, fols. 258, 394–411; A.N., 163 AP, dossier 1.

131. On the ineffectiveness of censorship, see Robert Darnton, "Reading, Writing and Publishing in Eighteenth-Century France: A Case Study in the Sociology of Literature," *Daedalus* 100 (Winter 1971): 214–256.

132. J. P. Belin, *Le commerce des livres prohibés à Paris de 1750 à 1789*, reprint ed. (New York: Burt Franklin, n.d.), p. 21.

133. David T. Pottinger, *The French Book Trade in the Ancien Regime, 1500–1791* (Cambridge, Mass.: Harvard University Press, 1958), p. 65.

134. Daniel Mornet, "Les enseignements des bibliothèques privées (1750–1780)," *Revue d'Histoire Littéraire de la France* 17 (1910): 449–496. The criticism is found in Darnton, "Reading, Writing and Publishing," p. 215.

Although it is not sufficient evidence to make any generalizations, of course, it is nonetheless of interest that the one inventory of the library of an avocat au Parlement that I encountered supports Mornet's conclusions. The library of François Brisse was heavily weighted toward jurisprudence and almost entirely devoid of the work of the philosophes. It included only the works of Montesquieu and one work of Voltaire. See the list of books to be sold at chez Tabouret in Felletin, A.N., T 1131[1-2]. On the authors not included in the Bibliothèque des Avocats, see A.N., D[III] 390/391, Etat des livres à mettre dans la bibliothèque, à prendre ailleurs que dans la bibliothèque des avocats, où ils ne se trouvent pas.

135. Most of the barristers lived in specific areas near the Palais de Justice, especially in the Marais. Reinhard, *Nouvelle histoire de Paris,* p. 34. The same was true in provincial parlementary towns as well. See Berlanstein, "Lawyers in Pre-Revolutionary France," p. 171.

2. The Onset of Revolution

1. Jean François Fournel, *Histoire du barreau de Paris dans le cours de la Révolution* (Paris: Chez Maradan, 1816), pp. 17–19.

2. Armand Brette, ed., *Recueil de documents relatifs à la convocation des Etats-Généraux de 1789,* 4 vols. (Paris: Imprimerie Nationale, 1894–1915), I, 77, 114.

3. See Charles Louis Chassin, ed., *Les élections et les cahiers de Paris en 1789,* 4 vols. (Paris: Jouaust et Sigaux, 1888–1889), I, 402. Brette does not give the full text of the relevant decree.

4. For the overall figure, see Jacques Godechot, *The Taking of the Bastille* (New York: Scribner's, 1970), p. 135; for the district of Saint Victor, Chassin, *Les élections et les cahiers de Paris,* II, 317.

5. In order to appreciate how disproportionate this was, some comparisons are useful. If one assumes that every member of the Order was eligible as an elector in 1789 and uses Godechot's figure of approximately 150,000 eligible electors, the avocats au Parlement comprised only about .4 of 1 percent of those eligible. Nor does the light turnout explain the situation. Even on the assumption that every member of the Order participated in the assemblies, which is highly unlikely, the entire Order still amounted only to approximately 5 percent of those who participated.

6. Honoré Marie Nicolas Duveyrier and Jean Sylvain Bailly, eds., *Procès-verbal des séances et déliberations de l'Assemblée générale des électeurs de Paris, réunis à l'Hôtel de Ville le 14 juillet 1789,* 3 vols. (Paris: Baudouin, 1790), I, 4–6, 15–16.

7. *Les idées d'un citoyen de Paris sur le danger qu'il y aurait que la noblesse choisit les députés dans la tiers état et sur la choix qui a été fait des électeurs* (n.p., 1789), p. 6.

8. *Suite des idées d'un citoyen de Paris* (n.p., n.d.).

9. Berlanstein found a similar situation at Toulouse. Berlanstein, *The Barristers of Toulouse,* p. 149.

10. Fournel, *Histoire du barreau de Paris dans le cours de la Révolution,* pp. 17–19.

11. *Réponse d'un avocat à l'écrit intitulé Les idées d'un citoyen de Paris, etc.* (n.p., n.d.).

12. *Réplique d'un citoyen de Paris à la réponse d'un avocat* (n.p., n.d.), pp. 6–7.

13. The ascendancy of the barristers to the Parlement is further demonstrated by the fact that the sessions for the drafting of the general cahier for Paris were held in the Bibliothèque des avocats. Duveyrier and Bailly, eds., *Procès-verbal des séances et déliberations de l'Assemblée générale des électeurs*, I, 25. For a general discussion of the ambiguous position of avocats during this period, see Colin Lucas, "Nobles, Bourgeois and the Origins of the French Revolution," *Past and Present* 60 (August 1973): 84–126.

14. Armand Brette, *Les constituants* (Paris: Société de l'histoire de la Révolution française, 1897), pp. 8–10.

15. Ibid., pp. 5–7. The men chosen as deputies were Armand Gaston Camus, François Denis Tronchet, Louis Simon Martineau, Jean Baptiste Treilhard, and François Louis Hutteau.

16. Jean Paul Rabaut de Saint-Etienne, *Précis de l'histoire de la Révolution française* (Paris: Servier, 1827), p. 156.

17. It is perhaps a reflection of the transformation that although most of the men chosen as deputies from Paris were among the most successful and established, none of them ever permanently resumed their careers as barristers.

18. Sigismond Lacroix, ed., *Actes de la commune de Paris pendant la Révolution*, 1st. ser., 7 vols. (Paris: Noblet, 1894–1898), I, 2–8.

19. Ibid., I, 95–96.

20. Norman Hampson, *A Social History of the French Revolution* (Toronto: University of Toronto Press, 1963), p. 81.

21. For lack of an existing term, I have utilized "sublimity of the nation" in preference to the concept of "civic humanism" put forward by J. G. A. Pocock, *The Machiavellian Moment: Florentine Political Thought and the Atlantic Republican Tradition* (Princeton: Princeton University Press, 1975). Although there are obvious parallels, particularly the emphasis on the primacy of citizenship and on working for the common good, in the final analysis, civic humanism does not correctly capture the ideal that gripped the National Assembly on the evening of August 4 and thereafter guided it. Civic humanism derived from a Renaissance context that was republican, urban — even corporatist — in character, and certainly not democratic in impulse. The spirit of the sublimity of the nation, by contrast, was above all national in scope, anticorporatist in nature, and fundamentally democratic in outlook, however imperfectly this last ideal may subsequently have been implemented. Finally, in naming Louis XVI "the restorer of French liberties" at the conclusion of the session, the National Assembly deliberately sought to make the Crown an integral part of the new ideal of the sublimity of the nation, rather than posing it as an alternative program. In short, what emerged on the night of August 4 was specific and unique to the National Assembly, and however attractive civic humanism may be as a current and recognizable term, it is also somewhat anachronistic and inexact in this instance.

Patrice Higonnet, however, has successfully appropriated the concept of civic humanism for eighteenth-century France, although I disagree with his emphasis on it as a phenomenon before the Revolution; I see it much more as a product of August 4. Also, it is apparent that I would ascribe greater importance to civic humanism than does Higonnet, who sees it primarily as part of a synthesis he calls "bourgeois universalism," whereas I would prefer to give it more weight in its own right. Overall, I believe the differences between us are more differences of emphasis than of interpretation. Patrice Higonnet, *Class, Ideology and the Rights of Nobles during the French Revolution* (Oxford: Clarendon Press, 1981).

Finally, for a consideration in a different context of the regeneration of France and the ideal of the sublimity of the nation (although she does not use the term), see Lynn Hunt, *Politics, Culture, and Class in the French Revolution* (Berkeley: University of California Press, 1984), passim, but esp. pp. 12, 27, 123–124, 179.

22. The Breton separatist movement, for example, traces its origins back to August 4, 1789, and the "betrayal" of the Breton people by its own representatives generated disdain even nearly two centuries later. See Jack E. Reece, *The Bretons against France* (Chapel Hill: University of North Carolina Press, 1977), pp. 18–19. The issue illustrates how the National Assembly acquired a dynamic of its own. For other examples of the sense of renewal, Rabaut de Saint-Etienne, *Précis de l'histoire de la Révolution française*, pp. 201–202; Jean Sylvain Bailly, *Mémoires de Bailly*, 3 vols. (Paris: Baudouin Frères, 1821–1822), II, 211–219; Charles Elie Ferrières, *Correspondance inédite (1789, 1790, 1791), publiée et annotée par Henri Carré* (Paris: A. Colin, 1932), pp. 113–117.

23. J. Mavidal and E. Laurent, eds., *Archives parlementaires de 1787 à 1860*, 1st ser. (1787–1799), 82 vols. (Paris: Librairie administrative de P. Dupont, 1862–1913), VIII, 346, 349; *Procès-verbal de l'Assemblée nationale*, 75 vols. (Paris: Baudouin, 1789–1791), no. 40 bis, (August 4, 1789), pp. 18, 36.

24. On Ferrières's original recalcitrance, see A.N., AD^{XVIIIc} 135, *Compte rendu par M. le marquis de Ferrières à Messieurs les gentilhommes de la sénéchaussée de Saumur*, p. 72; for the letter of August 7, Ferrières, *Correspondance inédite*, p. 115.

25. Mavidal and Laurent, eds., *Archives parlementaires*, VIII, 395. The *Procès-verbal* for August 11 mentions only that venality of offices was discussed but does not give details. *Procès-verbal*, no. 47 (August 11, 1789), pp. 3–4.

26. Mavidal and Laurent, eds., *Archives parlementaires*, VIII, 395–396.

27. *Rapport du comité de Constitution sur l'organisation du pouvoir judiciaire, presenté à l'Assemblée nationale par M. Bergasse* (Paris: Baudouin, 1789), pp. 46–47.

28. Mavidal and Laurent, eds., *Archives parlementaires*, VIII, 449.

29. Beatrice Fry Hyslop, *French Nationalism in 1789 according to the General Cahiers* (New York: Columbia University Press, 1934), p. 141.

30. Raoul Aubin, *L'organisation judiciaire d'après les cahiers de 1789* (Paris: Jouve, 1928), pp. 166–169.

31. For example, in a matter as vital to them as the revision of feudal *terriers*, villagers in Burgundy contesting some of their *seigneur's* claims hired procureurs rather than avocats to represent them. Contact with barristers seems to have been rare. Robert Forster, *The House of Saulx-Tavanes: Versailles and Burgundy, 1700–1830* (Baltimore: Johns Hopkins University Press, 1971), pp. 95–98.

32. Philippe Sagnac, *La législation civile de la Révolution française (1789–1804)* (Paris: Hachette, 1898), pp. 1–35.

33. Mavidal and Laurent, eds., *Archives parlementaries*, VIII, 504; *Procès-verbal*, no. 62 (August 29, 1789), pp. 1–2. On Mounier, see Jean Egret, *La révolution des notables: Mounier et les monarchiens, 1789* (Paris: A. Colin, 1950).

34. Mavidal and Laurent, eds., *Archives parlementaires*, VIII, 641; *Procès-verbal*, no. 72 (September 15, 1789), p. 1.

35. *Projet de l'organisation du pouvoir judiciaire proposé à l'Assemblée Nationale par le Comité de Constitution, dont l'annexe a été ordonné au Procès-verbal du 21 décembre 1789* (Paris: Baudouin, n.d.).

36. Mavidal and Laurent, eds., *Archives parlementaires*, X, 718; *Procès-verbal*, no. 157 (December 22, 1789), pp. 18–19.

37. Mavidal and Laurent, eds., *Archives parlementaires*, XII, 344; *Procès-verbal*, no. 239 (March 24, 1790), p. 9.

38. Mavidal and Laurent, eds., *Archives parlementaires*, XII, 349; *Procès-verbal*, no. 239 (March 24, 1790), p. 10.

39. Mavidal and Laurent, eds., *Archives parlementaires*, XII, 408; *Procès-verbal*, no. 244 (March 29, 1790), p. 8; the pamphlet critical of the project is Jean Louis Viefville des Essarts, *Observations sur le projet de l'organisation judiciaire* (n.p., 1790).

40. Mavidal and Laurent, eds., *Archives parlementaires*, XII, 443–444; *Procès-verbal*, no. 245 (March 30, 1790), p. 11.

41. Mavidal and Laurent, eds., *Archives parlementaires*, XII, 450.

42. The barrister Eustache Antoine Hua considered Chabroud's ideas particularly influential. Hua, *Mémoires d'un avocat au Parlement de Paris*, pp. 28–31, 181.

43. Mavidal and Laurent, eds., *Archives parlementaires*, XII, 487; *Procès-verbal*, no. 246 (March 31, 1790), p. 3.

44. Mavidal and Laurent, eds., *Archives parlementaires*, XII, 489; *Procès-verbal*, no. 246 (March 31, 1790), pp. 3–4. Moreover, there are no archival sources that relate to this point either, so one must rely on the debates to discern the Assembly's motives.

45. Mavidal and Laurent, eds., *Archives parlementaires*, XVI, 702; *Procès-verbal*, no. 340 (July 5, 1790), pp. 11–12.

46. Mavidal and Laurent, eds., *Archives parlementaires*, XVI, 704; *Procès-verbal*, no. 340 (July 5, 1790), pp. 15–16.

47. This is noted only in the *Procès-verbal*; it is not indicated in the *Archives parlementaires*. See *Procès-verbal*, no. 340 (July 5, 1790), p. 15.

48. Mavidal and Laurent, eds., *Archives parlementaires*, XVI, 705; *Procès-verbal*, no. 340 (July 5, 1790), p. 16.

49. Mavidal and Laurent, eds., *Archives parlementaires*, XVIII, 261.

50. Antoine Omer Talon, *Idées sur l'organisation du pouvoir judiciaire dans Paris; presentés au comité de constitution avant le décret du 25 août* (Paris: Cailleau, 1790), pp. 6–7.

51. Mavidal and Laurent, eds., *Archives parlementaires*, XVIII, 262; *Procès-verbal*, no. 391 (August 25, 1790), p. 10.

52. Mavidal and Laurent, eds., *Archives parlementaires*, XVIII, 262.

53. Ibid., XVIII, 263; *Procès-verbal*, no. 391 (August 25, 1790), p. 11.

54. *Procès-verbal*, no. 399 (September 2, 1790), pp. 11–12; *Le Point du Jour*, no. 418 (September 4, 1790). The *Archives parlementaires* do not mention this development. See also, A.N., C 44, dossier 404, document 3.

55. Mavidal and Laurent, eds., *Archives parlementaires*, XVIII, 493; *Procès-verbal*, no. 399 (September 2, 1790). pp. 11–12.

56. Jean-François Fournel, *Histoire des avocats au Parlement de Paris*, 2 vols. (Paris: Chez Maradan, 1813) II, 541–542.

57. Ibid., II, 540.

58. This was his *Histoire du barreau de Paris dans le cours de la Révolution*, published in 1816.

59. For an example of the fact that the abolition of the Order was popularly understood in such a context by contemporaries, see P. N. Gautier, *Dictionnaire de la Constitution et du gouvernement française* (Paris: Guillaume, 1791), pp. 39–40.

60. For evidence that it was the corporate dimension of the Order against which the National Assembly acted, see Urbain René Pilastre de la Brardière and J. B. Leclerc, *Correspondance de MM. les députés des communes de la province d'Anjou avec leur commettants relativement aux Etats-Généraux . . . en 1789*, 10 vols. (Angers: Pavie, 1789–1791), VI, 325–326. This anticorporate thrust was recognized by contemporaries. See A.N., D^{IV} 50, dossier 1437, document 20.

61. See Michel Foucault, *The Birth of the Clinic: An Archaeology of Medical Perception*, trans. A. M. Sheridan Smith (New York: Pantheon Books, 1973), chap. 3, esp. pp. 44–46.

62. Vivian Gruder, "No Taxation Without Representation: The Assembly of Notables of 1787 and Political Ideology in France," *Legislative Studies Quarterly* 7 (1982): 263–279; "Paths to Political Consciousness: The Assembly of Notables of 1787 and the 'Pre-Revolution' in France," *French Historical Studies* 13 (Spring 1984): 323–355; and "A Mutation in Elite Political Culture: The French Notables and the Defense of Property and Participation, 1787," *Journal of Modern History* 56 (December 1984): 598–634, with the last two amending somewhat the judgments of the first, presents a different interpretation, one with which I obviously do not agree. Albert Goodwin, "Calonne, the Assembly of French Notables of 1787 and the Origins of the *Révolte Nobiliaire*," *English Historical Review* 61 (1946): 202–234, 329–377, remains more credible.

63. Rabaut de Saint-Etienne complained that those who had not observed this scene did not understand it. Rabaut de Saint-Etienne, *Précis de l'histoire de la Révolution française*, p. 201. Refer again also to the comments of de Ferrières in de Ferrières, *Correspondance inédite*, pp. 113–116.

64. See John McManners, *The French Revolution and the Church* (New York: Harper & Row, 1969), pp. 28–29; and Sewell, *Work and Revolution in France*, chap. 4, which traces similar developments affecting the artisanal classes. See also Grace M. Jaffé, *Le mouvement ouvrier à Paris pendant la Révolution française, 1789–1791* (Paris: F. Alcan, 1924).

65. George V. Taylor, "Revolutionary and Nonrevolutionary Content in the *Cahiers* of 1789: An Interim Report," *French Historical Studies* 7 (Fall 1972): 479–502.

66. For an illustration of the National Assembly's altruism manifesting itself in another sphere, see Alan Forrest, *The French Revolution and the Poor* (New York: St. Martin's Press, 1981), esp. pp. 30–31. See also William Doyle, "The Price of Offices in Pre-Revolutionary France," *The Historical Journal* 27 (December 1984): 859–860.

67. Bonnet, *Discours, plaidoyers et mémoires*, II, 247. Included in this group were such figures as Bonnet, Bellart, Berryer, Chauveau-Lagarde, Charles Dela-

croix-Frainville, and Charles Paul Marie Gicquel, most of whom had been inscribed only within the last decade.

68. Men such as Jean Baptiste Billecocq, Edme Jean Blacque, and Jean André Gairal were representative of this group.

69. Berryer, *Souvenirs*, I, 107.

70. Lacroix, ed., *Actes de la commune de Paris*, II, 677–691.

71. Ibid., II, 294–295, 304, 410, for the men chosen as procureur syndics; for the other posts, ibid., II, 691. Bureau du Colombier was one of the members of the Department for Subsistence and Provisioning, Duport-Dutertre was head of the police, and Etienne de la Rivière served on the Department of Public Works.

72. During the period from 1789 to 1791, Gilles Boucher de la Richarderie left to reside at Melun, Antoine Jacques Claude Joseph Boullay returned to Nancy, Jean Baptiste Nicolas Canet de Selincourt went back to Amiens, Claude François Charles Ferey returned to his native Burgundy, Pierre Bergeras went back to Salies (Basses-Pyrénées), Jean Baptiste Laurent Le Porquier de Vaux went to Chaumont (Oise), Clement Louis Charles Berthot departed for Langres (Haute Marne), Clement Manet retired to Rueil, and Jean Baptiste Joseph Hiver de Popincourt went to Péronne (Somme). *Biographie universelle (Michaud) ancienne et moderne*, V, 170 (Boucher de la Richarderie); ibid., V, 236 (Boullay); A.N., BB^5 198, letter of Canet de Selincourt to minister of justice, July 19, 1811 (Canet de Selincourt); A.N., F^{1}c III Haute Saône 1, Procès-verbal de l'Assemblée électorale pour la formation du département, May 10, 1790 (Ferey); A.N., F^{1}c III Basses-Pyrénées 1, Copie des procès-verbaux de l'Assemblée électorale du département des Basses-Pyrénées, September 26, 1790 (Bergeras); A.N., F^{1}c III Oise 2, Elections de l'an XI, Liste des candidats présentés pour le Corps Législatif (Le Porquier de Vaux); A.N., AF^{IV} 1425, Elections de l'an 1806, Liste des candidats présentés pour le Corps Législatif (Berthot); A.N., F^{1}c III Seine 2, Elections de l'an XI, Liste des 120 membres qui composent le collège électoral de l'arrondissement communal de Saint-Denis (Manet); A.N., F^{1}c III Somme 2, Liste des personnes les plus marquantes de département . . . , August 18, 1810 (Hiver de Popincourt). Similarly, Robert Etienne de Villantroys clearly considered leaving Paris during this period and checked with his former colleague Target about his options if he did so. A.N., D^{IV} 6, dossier 88, document 14.

73. Louis René Chauveau, *Sur l'organisation du pouvoir judiciaire* (Paris: Cloutier, 1789). A eulogy held for Chauveau mentioned his appearance before the committee, suggesting that his example was unique. *Bulletin de l'Académie de Législation, Mémoires XII* (Paris: Patris, n.d.), pp. 546–547.

74. A.N., D^{III} 257, letter of Rimbert to Vivier de Launey, March 20, 1790.

75. Le Maître (pseud.), *Reveil du bon homme Le Maître, à Messieurs les Avocats de Paris députés à l'Assemblée Nationale* (n.p., n.d.).

76. Le Maître (pseud.), *Discours de M. Le Maître, doyen de la Communauté des Avocats et Procureurs au Parlement de Paris* (n.p., n.d.); *Les adieux du bon homme Le Maître, à Messieurs les avocats de Paris, députés à l'Assemblée, dite Nationale* (n.p., n.d.). The attack on the barristers in the Assembly is found in the latter, pp. 3, 8.

77. Berryer, *Souvenirs*, I, 114–115. Berryer was mistaken in his assertion that Bigot de Préameneu was a member of the Constituent Assembly; he was, in fact, a

member of the Legislative Assembly. In Paris the proscription of the term *avocat* was quickly and strictly enforced. See A.D. Seine, 1 AZ 146, document 8F.

78. Fournel, *Histoire des avocats au Parlement de Paris*, II, 538; *Histoire du barreau de Paris*, pp. 82–83.

79. To underscore the different views resulting from these separate dynamics, contrast the judgments of Fournel with those of Target in Paul Boulloche, ed., *Un avocat du XVIIIe siècle* (Paris: Calmann Levy, 1893), pp. 59–61. For a remarkable example of how deeply the avocats au Parlement adhered to the corporate values of the Old Regime, see Auguste Louis Taillandier, *Lettres à mon fils sur les causes, la marche et les effets de la Révolution française* (Paris: Demonville, 1820). Taillandier was a probationary member of the Order at the time of its abolition.

3. A New Era

1. Fournel, *Histoire du barreau de Paris*, p. 52. His comment refers to the placement of two of the six district courts in Paris.

2. Bonnet, *Discours, plaidoyers et mémoires*, II, 246–247; Fournel, *Histoire du barreau de Paris*, pp. 176–177.

3. Richard M. Andrews, "The Justices of the Peace of Revolutionary Paris, September 1792–November 1794 (Frimaire an III)," *Past and Present* 52 (August 1971): 60. Moreover, if conciliation proved unsuccessful, the use of an arbitrator was recommended before recourse to a tribunal.

4. On the composition of the bureau, see Jacques Godechot, *Les institutions de la France sous la Révolution et l'Empire*, 2nd ed. (Paris: Presses Universitaires de France, 1968), p. 148; on the success of the institution in Montpellier, Albert Grivel, *La justice civile dans le district de Montpellier en 1790–1791* (Montpellier: L'Abeille, 1928), pp. 67–68.

5. See J. Q. C. Mackrell, *The Attack on Feudalism in Eighteenth-Century France* (London: Routledge and Kegan Paul, 1973), pp. 174–175; McManners, *The French Revolution and the Church*, chap. 4. According to one contemporary, feudal issues and ecclesiastical matters were two of the most important sources of litigation. Berryer, *Souvenirs*, I, 17.

6. Fournel, *Histoire du barreau de Paris*, p. 176.

7. Berryer, *Souvenirs*, I, 117–118. Berryer's statement is echoed less tactfully in the derisive comments on the new courts by another barrister who remained in practice, Fournel. See Fournel, *Histoire du barreau de Paris*, pp. 52, 176.

8. A.N., MM 1088, 1089, covering the years 1770–1778; on the figures for 1790, A.N., MM 1090.

9. Kagan, "Law Students and Legal Careers in Eighteenth-Century France," p. 72.

10. A.N., F^{17} 1310, dossier 10; A.N., D^{IV} 16, dossier 287, document 19; A.N., D^{IV} 23, dossier 505, document 1; A.N., D^{IV} 50, dossier 1432, document 11; A.N., D^{IV} 68, dossier 2051, document 1.

11. Clement Louis Charles Berthot was elected as a member of the directory of the department of the Haute-Marne in 1790 and became a procureur syndic in 1791. Jean Baptiste Le Porquier de Vaux was chosen president of the district of

Chaumont (Oise), Sebastien Epoigny became a procureur syndic in his district in the Yonne, while Pierre Bergeras was selected as procureur général syndic for the department of the Basses-Pyrénées. At a municipal level, Antoine Guillaume Gerard Boudet was elected to a municipal office in Riom (Puy-de-Dôme). A.N., AF^{IV} 1425, Elections de l'an 1806, Liste des candidats présentés pour le Corps Législatif (Berthot); A.N., F^{1}c III Oise 2, Elections de l'an XII, Liste des candidats présentés pour le Corps Législatif (Le Porquier de Vaux); A.N., F^{1}c III Yonne 2, Elections de l'an XII, arrondissement de Joigny, collèges électoraux d'arrondissement (Epoigny); A.N., F^{1}c III Basses-Pyrénées 1, Copie des Procès-verbaux de l'assemblée du Département des Basses-Pyrénées, September 26, 1790 (Bergeras); A.N., BB^5 146, letter of president and government commissioners of appeals court at Riom to minister of justice, 26 messidor year IX (Boudet).

12. Thus, as had been the case during the provisional Commune, most of the senior municipal officials below the mayor were barristers to the Parlement. Jean Baptiste Boullemer de la Martinière was elected procureur, the second ranking municipal post, and two others barristers, Bon Claude Cahier de Gerville and Marguerite Louis François Duport-Dutertre, were elected substituts de procureur. Paul Robiquet, *Le personnel municipal de Paris pendant la Révolution* (Paris: Noblet, 1890), pp. 342–346.

13. The functions of the procureur, for example, ranged from representing the king's views in council meetings of the Commune to acting as a public prosecutor on certain occasions, and his salary was 15,000 livres, while that of the two substituts was 6,000 livres. On the duties of the procureur, Godechot, *Les institutions de la France*, pp. 109–110; on the salaries of the positions, Robiquet, *Le personnel municipal de Paris*, p. 387.

14. Sigismond Lacroix, ed., *Actes de la Commune de Paris pendant la Révolution*, 2nd ser., 8 vols. (Paris: L. Cerf, 1900–1909), I, 16–23. The total of 14 includes Garran de Coulon, who replaced Danton after the latter was rejected; Robiquet, *Le personnel municipal de Paris*, pp. 433–434.

15. A.N., B^I 1, Procès-verbaux des élections . . . , November 24–December 13, 1790; Procès-verbaux des élections . . . , December 14, 1790–January 19, 1791. Much, though not all, of this series was published by Etienne Charavay, ed., *Assemblée électorale de Paris*, 3 vols. (Paris: L. Cerf, 1890–1905). For a list of judges and substitute judges elected in Paris, see Appendix B. For the election of Thouret and Gaultier de Biauzat, A.N., B^I 1, Procès-verbaux des élections . . . , November 26, 1790 (Thouret); December 10, 1790 (Gaultier de Biauzat).

16. Hua, *Mémoires d'un avocat au Parlement de Paris*, p. 29.

17. For a list of these men, see Appendix C.

18. One of the exceptions was Etienne Guillaume Regnier, who refused the post of substitute judge at Sens (Yonne) in order to remain at Paris. Similarly, the former barrister Augustin Jean Louis Doulcet did not accept a substitute judgeship in Paris. A.N., F^{1}c III Yonne 1, letter of Regnier, October 22, 1790 (Regnier); A.N., B^I 1, Procès-verbaux de élections . . . , January 19, 1791 (Doulcet).

19. Berryer, *Souvenirs*, I, 116.

20. Pascal Durand-Barthez, *Histoire des structures du ministère de la Justice* (Paris: Presses Universitaires de France, 1973), p. 15.

21. B.N., MSS Joly de Fleury 1105. Of several requests for consideration for the post, only one (fol. 14) is from an avocat au Parlement.

22. A.N., BB¹ 45, dossier 2, letter of Le Porquier to minister of justice, November 11, 1791; underlined emphasis in original.

23. *Almanach des tribunaux du Département de Paris . . . pour l'année 1791* (Paris: Chez Vacquez, n.d.); A.N., BB⁵ 356.

24. When Charles François Lasaudade went to the Tribunal de cassation in 1791 as commissaire du roi, his replacement as commissaire du roi in the Second Provisional Criminal Court was Louis Pierre Verrier, also a former member of the Order. Likewise, when Louis Joseph Faure resigned from the Third Provisional Criminal Court early in 1792, his replacement was Louis François Le Roy de Montécly, who had also belonged to the abolished Order. A.N., BB⁵ 356, mémoire to Louis XVI, December 18, 1791 (Lasaudade); A.N., BB⁵ 356, mémoire to Louis XVI, February 17, 1792 (Le Roy de Montécly).

Examples of those named to the position in their native district include Jean Etienne Barré de Boismean, who was named commissaire du roi to the district court at Chateaudun (Eure-et-Loire); Antoine Simon Lambert, who was appointed to that at Attigny (Ardennes); Robert Etienne De Villantroys, chosen for the tribunal at Vierron (Cher); Alexandre César Maillard, who was named to the tribunal at Montdidier (Somme); and Louis Robin de Mozas, who was appointed to the tribunal in Bourgoin (Isère). A.N., BB⁵ 58, letter of Barré de Boismean, 14 pluviose year IX (Barré de Boismean); A.N., BB⁶ 1, Ardennes (Lambert); A.N., BB¹ 56 (De Villantroys); A.N., BB¹ 56 (Maillard); A.N., BB¹ 43, dossier 7 (Robin de Mozas).

25. Berryer, *Souvenirs*, I, 116. The main sources for the totals on commissaires du roi are A.N., BB¹ 46, dossier 1; BB¹ 56; BB⁵ 356; and BB³⁰ 524, dossier 1.

26. Honoré Marie Nicolas Duveyrier was named secretary-general, a post from which he oversaw all details of administration, at a salary of 18,000 livres per year. A *Conseil judiciaire*, charged with examining questions on civil, criminal, and administrative law and ensuring that material sent to the council concerning these matters was forwarded to the proper agency, was composed of four hommes de loi, all of whom were former members of the Order. Pierre Jean Baptiste Broyard, a former member of the Order, became head of the Bureau d'envoi des lois, which printed and distributed new laws to all of the courts of France as well as to other ministries. Other posts in the ministry assumed by former barristers to the Parlement included Charles Louis Le Rouge serving as a substitute for the secretary-general and as first secretary for the Bureau de rédaction et correspondance, which also had two other former members of the Order, Augustin Lesparat and Georges Victor Vasselin, as personnel. Its task was to correspond with various royal officials in the courts. Finally, Pierre Jean Voguet became secretary to the Conseil judiciaire. A.N., BB⁴ 7, Département de la Justice, Etat des bureaux . . . , June 30, 1792.

27. For Paris, *Almanach Royal 1791*, pp. 559–594, and *Almanach des tribunaux du Département de Paris*. Examples of those elected in outlying areas or in their native area include Vincent de Paul Barbier, who was elected justice of the peace at Versailles; Henri Breton, who was elected at Charenton; and Claude

Nicolas Leclerc, who was elected in his native Villedieu (Loir-et-Cher). A.N., BB⁵ 177, letter of Barbier to minister of justice, June 18, 1810 (Barbier); A.N., BB⁵ 171, undated letter of Breton to minister of justice (Breton); Arnault, Jay, Jouy, and Norvins, eds., *Biographie nouvelle des contemporains*, XI, 204 (Le Clerc).

28. Berlanstein, *The Barristers of Toulouse*, pp. 165–170.

29. Figures from Augustin Challamel, *Les clubs contre-révolutionnaires* (Paris: L. Cerf, 1895), and François Victor Alphonse Aulard, ed., *La société des Jacobins*, 6 vols. (Paris: Librairie Jouaust, 1889–1897), I, xxxiv–lxxvi.

30. To give but one example, the justice of the peace Etienne de la Rivière was a noted monarchist. See Andrews, "The Justices of the Peace of Revolutionary Paris," pp. 64–65, 68 n. 19. Other similar examples abound.

31. Mavidal and Laurent, eds., *Archives parlementaires*, XVIII, 417. Salaries were based on the size of the town where one served so that men in outlying departments earned somewhat less; Andrews, "The Justices of the Peace of Revolutionary Paris," p. 59.

32. Some of the men who took this action were François Antoine Clozier, Jacques Vincent Delacroix, Mathurin Jean Baptiste Le Bruin, Louis de la Metherie, François Hyacinthe Benoît Vivier de la Chausée, Henri Carle, Charles Pierre Le Paige, François Marnier-Desreux, Pierre Claude Simon Pelletier, Raymond de Sèze, Pierre Angot, and Jacques Thetion. A.N., BB⁵ 170, undated letter of Clozier, no addressee (Clozier); A.N., BB⁶ 2, Seine-et-Oise (Delacroix); A.N., BB⁵ 177, undated letter of Le Bruin to minister of justice (Le Bruin); A.N., BB⁵ 176, letter of de la Metherie to minister of justice, April 10, 1810, (de la Metherie); A.N., BB⁶ 1, Cher (Vivier de la Chausée); A.N., BB⁶ 1, Rhône (Carle); A.N., F⁷ 4774¹⁸, dossier Le Paige (Le Paige); A.N., BB⁵ 6, Liste des candidats . . . pour remplir les fonctions de juge de paix . . . , October 9, 1807 (Marnier-Desreux); A.N., F⁷ 4774⁶⁶, dossier Pelletier (Pelletier); Sevin, *Le défenseur du Roi* (de Sèze); A.N., BB⁵ 179, undated letter of Angot to minister of justice (Angot); A.N., F⁷ 4775²⁷, dossier Thetion (Thetion).

33. Berryer, *Souvenirs*, I, 116.

34. Berlanstein, *The Barristers of Toulouse*, p. 169.

35. Berryer, *Souvenirs*, I, 117–118. See also Fournel, *Histoire du barreau de Paris*, p. 51.

36. A.N., AA 49, dossier 1396, document 72.

37. *Procès-verbal*, no. 500 (December 13, 1790), p. 10; J. S. Dinocheau, *Rapport fait au nom des Comités de constitution et de judicature: Liquidation des offices ministèriels* (Paris: Imprimerie Nationale, 1790).

38. *Procès-verbal*, no. 502 (December 15, 1790), pp. 6–7; Mavidal and Laurent, eds., *Archives parlementaires*, XXI, 487.

39. *Procès-verbal*, no. 503 (December 16, 1790), pp. 10–11; Mavidal and Laurent, eds., *Archives parlementaires*, XXI, 512–513; J. B. Duvergier, ed., *Collection complète des lois, décrets, ordonnances, règlemens, avis du conseil d'état* . . . , 108 vols. (Paris: Recueil Sirey, 1788/1790–1908), II, 184–185.

40. In Paris the few former avocats au Parlement who became avoués were generally men such as François Brisse who had been less successful in the profession. See A.N., T 1131¹⁻², patent of avoué, December 7, 1791. It was, in fact, the view of the Committee of the Constitution that the avoués were successors to the

procureurs. A.N., D^{IV} 7, dossier 113, document 38. Most avoués were former procureurs.

41. Foucault, *The Birth of the Clinic*, p. 46.

42. Berryer, *Souvenirs*, I, 117–119.

43. Fournel, *Histoire du barreau de Paris*, p. 51. Other former barristers who remained in practice also seem to have had their misgivings about the new judicial system eased by the choice of judges in Paris. See Bonnet, *Discours, plaidoyers et mémoires*, II, 247; Berryer, *Souvenirs*, I, 116, 120.

44. *Le Moniteur Universel*, February 13, 1791.

45. For the backlog of cases, B.H.V.P., MS. 763, document 58; A.N., BB^5 356, undated letter of public prosecutor of Tribunal of Second Arrondissement,"Observations sur l'administration de la justice criminelle dans le Département de Paris"; the provisional criminal courts have been studied by Antoinette Wills, *Crime and Punishment in Revolutionary Paris* (Westport, Conn.: Greenwood Press, 1981).

46. A.N., BB^5 355, Assemblée électorale du départment de Seine-et-Marne . . . , March 12, 1791 (Boucher de la Richarderie); *Le tribunal et la cour de cassation: Notices sur le personnel* (Paris: Imprimerie Nationale, 1879), p. 3; Ibid., p. 452 (Hom).

47. J. H. Shennan, *The Parlement of Paris* (Ithaca: Cornell University Press, 1968), pp. 45–46.

48. In Paris, Felix Julien Jean Bigot de Préameneu was elected assistant judge, but declined the position. Louis Joseph Faure became assistant to the prosecutor, while Thomas Charles Alexandre Jéhanne was appointed commissaire du roi. A.N., B^I 5, Assemblée électorale . . . Département de Paris, Procès-verbal, June 9, 14, 1791 (Bigot de Préameneu); Ibid., June 15, 1791 (Faure); A.N., BB^4 9, Etat des emplois du Département de la Justice . . . , October 23, 1791 (Jéhanne).

In departments outside of Paris, Hyacinthe Féart was elected president of the criminal court of the Ardennes, Jean Baptiste Faré was chosen president for the criminal court of the Indre-et-Loire, and Claude Blanchard de la Valette was appointed commissaire du roi in the criminal court of the Allier. A.N., BB^5 352, Procès-verbal de l'Assemblée électorale du Département d'Ardennes . . . , March 21, 1791 (Féart); A.N., BB^5 353, Procès-verbal . . . Département d'Indre-et-Loire . . . , September 3, 1791 (Faré); A.N., BB^5 6, undated letter of Blanchard de la Valette, no addressee (Blanchard de la Valette).

49. There had been uncertainty present almost from the moment the terms were introduced. See A.N., D^{IV} 7, dossier 113, documents 20–21; A.N., D^{IV} 15, dossier 268, document 17; A.N., D^{IV} 20, dossier 393, document 10; A.N., D^{IV} 50, dossier 1432, document 11. Much correspondence of the Committee of the Constitution dealt with the clarification of such terms, but confusion persisted. See "Qu'est-ce qu'un Homme de Loi? Qu'est-ce qu'un Défenseur officieux?" *Gazette des Nouveaux Tribunaux*, 16 vols. (Paris: Desaint, 1791–year VII) V, 91.

50. A.N., BB^{29} 1; A.N., BB^{29} 2. In addition, the Committee of the Constitution answered thousands of questions during this period.

51. See, for example, A.N., BB^{30} 156, letter of Mitouflet to minister of justice, March 21, 1791.

52. Aristide Douarche, ed., *Les tribunaux civils de Paris pendant la Révolution*,

1791–1800, 2 vols. (Paris: L. Cerf, 1905–1907). See also *Journal des Tribunaux*, 5 vols. (Paris: Gueffier, 1791–1792), and *Gazette des Nouveaux Tribunaux*, vols. 1–4 covering through 1792.

53. *Gazette des Nouveaux Tribunaux*, II, 23–24; *Journal des Tribunaux*, II, 8.

54. A.N., BB^5 356, Adresse des membres composant les six Tribunaux criminels établis à Paris par la loi du 14 mars 1791, à l'Assemblée Nationale, pp. 4–5.

55. Wills, *Crime and Punishment in Revolutionary Paris*, pp. 53–54; see also, A.N., BB^{29} 1, no. 566.

56. A.N., BB^{29} 1, no. 215.

57. A.N., BB^5 356, letter of commissaire du roi of First Provisional Criminal Court to minister of justice, November 5, 1791.

58. A.N., M 797, no. 18. On its impoundment, A.N., F^{17} 1167, letter of directory of department of Paris to Committees of Ecclesiastical Administration and National Lands, April 6, 1791.

59. Auguste Kuscinski, *Les députés à l'Assemblée législatif* (Paris: Société de l'histoire de la Révolution française, 1900), pp. 83–85.

60. Ibid., passim.

61. A.N., F^{1}c III Seine 27, letter of Roland, interim minister of justice to minister of interior, March 29, 1792; letter of administrators of department of Paris to minister of interior, April 27, 1792.

62. On the significance of the justices of the peace, see Andrews, "The Justices of the Peace of Revolutionary Paris," and Lenard R. Berlanstein, "The Other Side of Justice: Legal Disputes Among the Parisian Populace in the Eighteenth Century," *Proceedings of the Fourth Annual Meeting of the Western Society for French History* (Santa Barbara, 1977). pp. 182–191.

63. A.N., F^{1}c III Seine 27, letter of minister of justice to minister of interior, January 17, 1792; Ibid., letter of administrators of department of Paris to minister of interior, January 21, 1792. See also, A.N., D^{IV} 1, dossier 1bis, document 35.

64. A.N., F^{1}c III Seine 27, letter of minister of justice to minister of interior, May 24, 1792.

65. Mavidal and Laurent, eds. *Archives parlementaires*, XXXVIII, 328.

66. In Paris, A.N., F^2 I 121$^{6-7}$, letter of Millet de Gravelle to minister of interior, January 31, 1792. Similarly, in the Ardennes, for example, Antoine Simon Lambert, the commissaire du roi, was not paid at all throughout 1792. A.N., F^2 I 121^3, letters of Lambert, August 1, 14, and 27, 1793.

67. Jacques Aubery Desfontaines and Jean Baptiste Soreau were chosen for the Tribunal of the First Arrondissement, and Jean Baptiste François Bayard and Jacques Nicolas Billaud de Varennes were elected as substitutes in the tribunals of the second and fourth arrondissements respectively. Pierre François Pulleu was elected to that of the fifth arrondissement. A.N., B^1 12, Procès-verbal de l'Assemblée électorale . . . , February 17, 1792 (Soreau); February 18, 1792 (Aubery Desfontaines); February 23, 1792 (Bayard); March 6, 1792 (Billaud de Varennes); March 8, 1792 (Pulleu). In addition, Charles Minier, a former member of the Order, was elected substitute at the Criminal Court of Paris. Ibid., February 16, 1792. Outside Paris, François Brisse was elected substitute judge in the district of Felletin (Creuse) in March 1792 and left Paris to assume the post. A.N., T 1131$^{1-2}$,

Extrait du Procès-verbal de l'Assemblée électorale du district de Felletin . . . , March 25–26, 1792.

68. *Gazette des Nouveaux Tribunaux,* IV, 289–290; Edmond Seligman, *La justice en France pendant la Révolution,* 2 vols. (Paris: Plon-Nourrit, 1901–1913), I, 461–462.

69. A.N., Z³ 89.

70. Jean Bouchary, *Les faux-monnayers sous la Révolution française* (Paris: Marcel Rivière et Cie, 1946), pp. 83–84.

71. A.N., BB² 1ᴮ, conference of April 12, 1792. This interpretation of the law also underscores that contemporaries recognized the primacy the National Assembly had given to unrestricted access to the law by all citizens.

72. Berryer, *Souvenirs,* I, 313.

73. A.N., BB² 1ᴮ, conference of February 16, 1792; Ibid., conference of July 8, 1792.

74. A.N., AD^{II} 44, *Compte-rendu à l'Assemblée nationale, le 9 juillet 1792, sur l'état actuel des Tribunaux* . . . (Paris: Imprimerie Royale, 1792), p. 12.

75. A.N., MM 1092.

76. Berryer, *Souvenirs,* I, 312–314.

77. *Gazette des Nouveaux Tribunaux,* IV, 158–159.

4. The Impact of the Terror

1. Berryer, *Souvenirs,* I, 135. Cyprien Athanase Lasseray, who was a subcommandant of a batallion, attempted to prevent the passage of a batallion of Lombards that was marching on the Tuileries. Jacques Parisot was seriously wounded while defending the Tuileries against the insurgents. Nicolas François Bellart, who considered protection of the king to be one of the guard's main functions, quit the guard on August 10. A.N., F⁷ 4767, dossier Lasseray (Lasseray); *Biographie universelle (Michaud) ancienne et moderne,* XXXII, 147 (Parisot); J. B. Billecocq, "Notice historique sur M. Bellart," in *Oeuvres de N. F. Bellart,* 6 vols. (Paris: J. L. J. Brière, 1827–1828), VI, 19 (Bellart). See also A.N., F⁷ 4774⁶⁰, dossier Oudet.

2. Berryer, *Souvenirs,* I, 135.

3. Mavidal and Laurent, eds., *Archives parlementaires,* XLVIII, 129, 335–336.

4. A.N., C 161, no. 357, letter of Ferrier to president of Legislative Assembly, August 19, 1792; A.N., BB⁵ 168, undated letter of Ferrier to Consul Cambacérès.

5. Berryer, *Souvenirs,* I, 136; Bellart, "Pièces justificatives no. 1," in *Oeuvres,* VI, 109; Christophe Lavaux, *Les campagnes d'un avocat* (Paris: Panckoucke, 1815), pp. 16–17.

6. Charles Pierre Bosquillon, a monarchist and the justice of the peace for the section Observatoire, and Alexandre César Michel Perron, an administrator in the police department, were both killed in Paris. Jean Baptiste Etienne de la Rivière, another monarchist and the justice of the peace for the section Henri IV, who had been awaiting trial at the Haute Cour Nationale at Orléans, was murdered at Versailles. Pierre Caron, *Les massacres de septembre* (Paris: Maison du livre français, 1935), pp. 482, 498 (Bosquillon and Perron); A.N., AA 47, dossier 1372, document 18; *Le Moniteur Universel,* September 14, 1792 (Etienne de la Rivière). Hon-

oré Marie Nicolas Duveyrier, formerly a high official in the Ministry of Justice, barely avoided execution, and this appears to have been the case also with Antoine Auguste Benoît Duportail, the justice of the peace for the section Quatre Nations, who took flight and was later apprehended outside Paris. Honoré Marie Nicolas Duveyrier, *Anecdotes historiques* (Paris: A. Picard, 1907), p. 166; Caron, *Les massacres de septembre*, p. 488 (Duveyrier); A.N., D^{III} 254, document 5; Mavidal and Laurent, eds., *Archives parlementaires*, XLIX, 498 (Duportail). He seems to have fled to avoid execution.

7. Berryer, for example, had a case pending in the district court at Blois, and he used it as a pretext to leave Paris with his family, not returning until October. Jean Emmanuel Godefroy de Montours left Paris in 1792, almost certainly as a result of the massacres, and returned permanently to his native Sablé in the Sarthe. Berryer, *Souvenirs*, I, 136, 143; A.N., BB^5 112, letter of Godefroy-Montours to minister of justice, 2nd complementary day, year XI.

8. In fact, it produced a new professional activity for some of the former barristers to the Parlement as they acted on behalf of certain groups in the assemblies. Chauveau-Lagarde, for example, represented the Jews of Alsace before the Legislative Assembly on one occasion. A.N., AA 40, dossier 1300, document 49. Similarly, Jacques Godard represented the Jews of Paris before the National Assembly and the Commune. Arthur Hertzberg, *The French Enlightenment and the Jews* (New York: Columbia University Press, 1968), pp. 347, 361.

9. An examination of the lists of electors demonstrates this. In 1789, when enthusiasm for the Revolution was strong, sixty-five members of the Order were electors. In 1790, with the choice of electors made before the abolition of the Order, fifty-nine members of the Order were selected as electors (sixty, if one includes a probationary member who was due admission in 1790). By 1791, however, the first occasion after the abolition of the Order in which electors were chosen, only thirty-five men (thirty-seven with probationary members who had been due admission) from the abolished Order acted as electors. Moreover, Louis's flight to Varennes occurred during the balloting, and this may also have contributed to the precipitous decline in the number of former barristers to the Parlement who were electors. The disillusionment of the former avocats au Parlement in 1792, after the overthrow of the king, is reflected in the fact that only nine former members of the Order were electors, and nearly all of them were men who had become involved in municipal or national politics. "Liste générale des électeurs de Paris réunis à l'Hôtel de Ville le 14 juillet 1789," in Robiquet, *Le personnel municipal de Paris*, pp. 43–85; *Etat général des électeurs du tiers-état, nommés par le LX districts de la ville et faubourgs de Paris et par l'Université* (n.p., n.d.); *Liste des électeurs de département de Paris* (Paris: Cailleau, 1790); *Noms de MM. les électeurs du département de Paris, par ordre alphabétique* (Paris: Frault, 1791); *Liste des électeurs du département de Paris, de 1792* (Paris: Galletti, 1792).

10. Alison Patrick, *The Men of the First French Republic* (Baltimore: Johns Hopkins University Press, 1972), p. 222.

11. Mavidal and Laurent, eds., *Archives parlementaires*, LII, 83–87.

12. A.N., W 247, no. 1.

13. Berryer, *Souvenirs*, I, 313.

14. Ibid., I, 146–147, 301. A great number of them were present — Delacroix-Frainville, Berryer, Bellart, Bonnet, Chauveau-Lagarde, Roy, Blacque, Bitouze de Linières, Douet d'Arcq, Rimbert, Cailleau, Doucet, Gicquel, Archambault, Thilorier, Lourmand, Picart, Desfontaines, and (according to Berryer) de Sèze. A smaller number of other former members of the Order who had assumed judicial, administrative, or political positions were also in attendance — Bureau du Colombier, de la Fleutrie, Duveyrier, Moynat, and, astonishingly, since he was a member of the Convention, Garran de Coulon.

15. These included Mathurin Etienne Hulin and Pierre François Giroust. A.N., C 243, no. 304–305, letter of Hulin to president of the Convention, December 14, 1792; A.N., AA 53, dossier 3, document 48 (Giroust). Another published a pamphlet in favor of the king. Michel Germain Pichois, *Défense de Louis XVI*, 2 vols. (Paris: Dufresne, 1792–1793).

16. Jean Philippe Garran de Coulon, *J. Ph. Garran, député du Loiret à la Convention Nationale, sur le jugement de Louis XVI* (Paris: Imprimerie du Cercle Social, 1793), pp. 3–6. On Berryer's memoirs, see Jean Tulard, *Bibliographie critique des mémoires sur le Consulat et l'Empire écrits ou traduits en français* (Paris: Librairie Droz, 1971), p. 16. The details of the trial of Louis XVI are beyond the scope of this study. Additional information can be found in Patrick, *The Men of the First French Republic*; Seligman, *La justice en France pendant la Révolution*; Michael Walzer, ed., *Regicide and Revolution: Speeches at the Trial of Louis XVI* (Cambridge: Cambridge University Press, 1974); Albert Soboul, ed., *Le procès de Louis XVI* (Paris: Julliard, 1966); David P. Jordan, *The King's Trial* (Berkeley: University of California Press, 1979); John M. S. Allison, *Lamoignon de Malesherbes* (New Haven: Yale University Press, 1938); and Sevin, *Le défenseur du Roi*.

17. Duvergier, *Collection complète des lois*, V, 127–128.

18. A.N., BB^2 1^B, Conferences of January 31, 1793, February 7, 1793, and March 14, 1793.

19. On the Tribunal of the Fifth Arrondissement, see Douarche, ed., *Les tribunaux civils de Paris*, I, 434–435. Whereas most of the other tribunals granted extensions or otherwise sought to delay the imposition of the requirement, this court apparently did not. Douarche, who seems to have recorded all of the material relating to this matter, does not list the Tribunal of the Sixth Arrondissement as having enforced the provision. For the Tribunal of the Second Arrondissement, A.N., D^{III} 258/259, copy of letter from president of the Tribunal of the Second Arrondissement to minister of justice, October 2, 1793. See also Douarche, ed., *Les tribunaux civils de Paris*, I, 578–579, 597–598, 604–605, 615. On the Criminal Court, A.N., D^{III} 322/323, letter of minister of justice to president of Committee of Legislation, 15 nivôse year II.

20. A.N., BB^{30} 158, Observations sur l'arrêté du conseil général . . . sur les certificats de civisme, 20 frimaire year II, for the increased enforcement of the law; on the withdrawal of the former barristers, Bellart, *Oeuvres*, VI, 109; Bonnet, *Discours, plaidoyers et mémoires*, II, 248; Berryer, *Souvenirs*, I, 159–160.

21. A.N., D^{III} 258/259, copy of letter from president of the Tribunal of the Second Arrondissement to minister of justice, October 2, 1793.

22. A similar phenomenon took place at Nancy. The former barristers to the

Parlement there, aided by the president of the Criminal Court, remained organized informally for a period after the abolition of the Order, but under the Terror their coalition also could not be maintained. Hubert Thomas, *Le tribunal criminel de la Meurthe sous la Révolution, 1792–1799* (Nancy: Georges Thomas, 1937), pp. 141–144.

23. A.N., B^I 13.

24. Ibid., 2nd convocation, 86th meeting, March 7, 1793.

25. A.N., AA 44, dossier 1328, document 69.

26. James L. Godfrey, *Revolutionary Justice* (Chapel Hill: University of North Carolina Press, 1951), p. 7.

27. Ibid., p. 130.

28. Roblot is incorrect in his statement that most of the counselors pleading before the court were former members of the Order. Four of the six individuals whom he cites were not former barristers to the Parlement—Lavaux, for example, was a former *avocat aux conseils*. Moreover, Tronson-Ducoudray did not remain in practice after the trial of Marie Antoinette. René Roblot, *La justice criminelle en France sous la Terreur* (Paris: Librairie générale de droit et de jurisprudence, 1938), p. 168. Based on samplings of the W series of the Archives Nationales, the former members of the Order who practiced there with some regularity were Chauveau-Lagarde, Gattrez, and de la Fleutrie.

29. For the original definition of the postion, which was not amended in the course of the debates, Dinocheau, *Rapport . . . des comités de constitution et de judicature*, pp. 14–16, 25–26; A.N., D^{III} 258/259, copy of letter from president of the Tribunal of the Second Arrondissement to minister of justice, October 2, 1793, for the characterization of the former members of the legal profession. He asserted that some défenseurs officieux also fell in this category.

30. There were apparently some limits, however. In the year II the minister of justice wrote to the president of the Committee of Legislation asking if women were to be allowed to practice as fondés de pouvoir. I was unable to find a reply, but it was almost certainly negative. A.N., D^{III} 322/323, letter of minister of justice to president of Committee of Legislation, 24 pluviôse year II.

31. Duvergier, *Collection complète des lois*, VI, 14.

32. *Projet de règlement du comité des défenseurs officieux des amis de la liberté et de l'égalité, séant aux Jacobins* (n.p., n.d.), pp. 2, 6. Aulard makes only passing reference to this committee. On the composition of the club, Crane Brinton, *The Jacobins: An Essay in the New History*, reprint ed. (New York: Russell & Russell, 1961), p. 68.

A police report from April 1793 gives one of the most compelling examples of the nadir reached by the profession at this time. The procureur syndic of the Commune received a complaint against an individual who called himself "zealous patriot" and whose activities included the operation of "a barrister's office." When the police were sent to investigate, the agent found a nearly infirm old man in a booth adjoining some stables on the Rue St. Honoré who supported himself by writing verse and doing oral pleadings in the courts. A.N., AF^{IV} 1470, Feuille des rapports . . . le 17 avril, l'an II de la république, entry no. 8.

33. A.N., BB^3 81^3, Registre des délibérations & procès-verbaux du comité de

surveillance du Département de Paris, séance du matin, 8 germinal; A.N., BB³ 81⁴, Séance du 22 germinal.

A.N., BB³ 81³, Séance du 9 germinal. This was the Tribunal d'appel de la police.

35. Ibid., Séance du matin, 11 germinal.

36. A.N., BB³ 81⁴, Séance du 22 germinal.

37. A.N., W 175, document 33, pp. 26–28. Potentially biased, this source is nonetheless useful for its detail, and the account is largely in accord with the official record of the trial. A.N., W 321, no. 491.

38. There is some evidence to suggest that the incident may not have been atypical, for other instances of such malfeasance occurred. See J. B. Buchez and P. C. Roux, *Histoire parlementaire de la Révolution francaise, ou Journal des Assemblées nationales, depuis 1789 jusqu'en 1815,* 40 vols. (Paris: Paulin, 1834–1838), XXXIV, 425. See also Lavaux, *Les campagnes d'un avocat,* pp. 22–23.

39. A.N., W 502, letter of Herman, 28 pluviôse year II.

40. A.N., MM 1092.

41. *Le Moniteur Universel,* 28 germinal year II.

42. Pierre Nicolas Berryer, for example, used his contacts to secure a postion in one of its bureaus. Other former barristers to the Parlement who assumed posts in various divisions of the treasury included Jean Claude Basseville, Charles Marteau, and Charles Pierre Michel Forestier. The Committee of Finances also escaped direct subordination to the Committee of Public Safety, and Jean Baptiste Fontaine and Georges Victor Vasselin took posts there. Louis Ferdinand Bonnet and Denis Charles Prosper Le Page went to work for the Bureau of the National Domain. Nicolas François Bellart worked at the Commission for Arms, Powders, and the Exploitation of Mines, as did Pierre François Ducarin. Charles Pierre Marie Gicquel and Charles François Quequet assumed posts with the Commission for Military Transport. Claude Jean Ferrier (or variously, Ferrière) assumed a position in the Conservation général des hypothèques, while Mathurin Heron took one with the Commission des secours publics. Berryer, *Souvenirs,* I, 161 (Berryer); A.N., F⁷ 4588, dossier Basseville (Basseville); A.N., F⁷ 4774³⁶, dossier Marteau (Marteau); A.N., BB⁵ 175, letter of Defermon to Grand Juge, duc de Massa, July 12, 1810 (Forestier); A.N., F⁷ 4709, dossier Fontaine (Fontaine); A.N., F⁷ 4775⁴⁰, dossier Vasselin (Vasselin); Berryer, *Souvenirs,* I, 161 (Bonnet); A.N., F⁷ 4774¹⁸, dossier Le Page (Le Page); Bellart, *Oeuvres,* VI, 111–115 (Bellart); A.N., D^{III} 253, Section de Guillaume Tell, noms de citoyens . . . pour être assesseur du juge de paix (Ducarin); A.N., F⁷ 4725, dossier Gicquel (Gicquel); *Le Tribunal et la cour de cassation* (Quequet); A.N., BB⁵ 168, undated letter of Ferrière to Consul Cambacérès (Ferrière); A.N., BB⁵ 169, undated notice for Heron (Heron).

43. Berryer, *Souvenirs,* I, 162; A.N., BB⁵ 169, undated notice for Heron. The former barristers would consult or do other work that did not involve appearing in court.

44. A.N., F⁷ 4774⁴⁶, dossier Millet de Gravelle.

45. For the complete text of this law, see Duvergier, *Collection complète des lois,* VII, 190–192. See also the report introducing the law, given by Couthon. Georges Couthon, *Rapport sur le Tribunal révolutionnaire, fait au nom du Comité de*

salut public . . . *dans la séance du 22 prairial l'an II* (Paris: Imprimerie Nationale, n.d.), which includes the assertion that "to defend the side of the tyrants is to conspire against the Republic. One makes precisely the same mistake when one gives défenseurs officieux to the abettors of the tyrant, namely to all conspirators."

46. The recalcitrant behavior of Jean Baptiste Oudet père on August 10, for example, was one of the facts mentioned in his arrest warrant. Similarly, François Antoine Marguet was arrested and subsequently executed for "being a partisan of the Old Regime and an enemy of the Revolution" because he had written a letter in 1792 praising Louis XVI's behavior during the invasion of the Tuileries on June 20. Although the conduct cited occurred before August 1792, the same factors were apparent with Marguerite Louis François Duport-Dutertre, who was executed for having protected the royal family during his tenure as minister of justice. Other examples of arrests resulting from political disaffection include Nicolas Alexandre Herbault, Alexandre Charles Moynat, Cyprien Athanase Lasseray, Jean André Gairal, Léonard Robin, and Louis Antoine Brasseux, all of whom were arrested because their behavior in sectional assemblies in 1793 did not evince ardent support for the Revolution. In the same vein Jacques Thetion, who allegedly expressed satisfaction at the assassination of Marat, Charles Ganilh, and Jean Plaisant de la Houssaye were accused of *incivisme*. Alexandre Julien Procope-Couteaux was incarcerated when an anonymous denunciation claimed that a poem filled with counterrevolutionary sentiments had been read in his home. A.N., F^7 4774^{60}, dossier Oudet (Oudet); A.N., W 466, no. 233 (Marguet); A.N., W 298, no. 285 (Duport-Dutertre); A.N., F^7 4743, dossier Herbaut (*sic*; Herbault); A.N., F^7 4774^{55}, dossier Moynat (Moynat); A.N., F^7 4767, dossier Lasseray (Lasseray); A.N., F^7 4714, dossier Gairal (Gairal); A.N., F^7 4774^{95}, dossier Robin (Robin); A.N., F^7 4615, dossier Brasseux (Brasseux); A.N., F^7 4775^{27} dossier Thetion (Thetion); A.N., F^7 4715, dossier Ganilh (Ganilh); A.N., F^7 4774^{77}, dossier Plaisant de la Houssaye (Plaisant de la Houssaye); A.N.,F^7 4774^{83}, dossier Procope-Couteaux (Procope-Couteaux). For two additional examples of former members of the Order who came under suspicion, but were not indicted for their alleged sentiments toward the National Convention, see A.N., W 6, dossier 272 (Prevost de Saint-Lucien) and W 10, dossier 413 (Blondel).

Mathurin Pierre Jozeau was executed for allegedly attempting to incite his section to join the federalist insurrection, and Claude Nicolas Collet, a respected member of the Order under the Old Regime, was executed after the federalist revolt at Lyon. A.N., W 432, no. 971 (Jozeau); on Collet, A.N., T 1611; Fournel, *Histoire des avocats au Parlement*, I, xiii. These men were executed, but other former members of the Order were arrested or investigated for alleged federalist sympathies. See, for example, the interrogation of Jean Baptiste Jahan on charges of federalism. A.N., W 34, dossier 2091.

47. Berryer, *Souvenirs*, I, 164–167.

48. A.N., AF II* 289, 21 vendémiaire year II, A.N., F^7 4775^{13}, dossier Sarradin; A.N., W 302, no. 329 (Serpaud); A.N., W 358, no. 753 (Boys).

49. A.N., F^7 4727, dossier Godard. He had been the barrister for the comte de Tavanes. See Forster, *The House of Saulx-Tavanes*, p. 61.

50. A.N., F^7 4729, dossier Gorguereau. In a slightly different vein, the barris-

ter Jean Baptiste Billecocq burned his law degrees, which were made of parchment, because he feared that they would be mistaken for letters of nobility by members of a Revolutionary committee. Nicole Felkay and Hervé Favier, eds., *En prison sous la terreur: Souvenirs de J. B. Billecocq* (Paris: Société des Etudes Robespierristes, 1981), p. 19.

51. A.N., F^7 4664, dossier Bonnières. De Bonnières subsequently was involved in royalist intrigues, but the indictment in 1794 did not allege this.

52. B.N., MSS Nouvelles acquisitions françaises 2707, fol. 56.

53. A.N., AF II* 289, 19 vendémiaire year II; A.N., F^7 4672, dossier de Sèze. The Committee of General Security also sought to arrest Tronchet, but he successfully evaded arrest until the fall of Robespierre. *Biographie universelle (Michaud) ancienne et moderne*, XLII, 199. The defense of Louis XVI was the major charge adduced against Malesherbes at his trial. See Allison, *Lamoignon de Malesherbes*, p. 165.

54. A.N., AF II* 289, 23 vendémiaire year II; A.N., F^7 4775^{34}, dossier Tronson-Ducoudray. See, for example, the following comment in Chauveau-Lagarde's interrogation: "We remarked to the citizen Chauveau that after having performed his duties of defender at the tribunal, he ought not to be ignorant of the fact that as a citizen he owes to his *patrie* and to the constituted authorities the frank and candid statement of all of the schemes that sought to overthrow the state." Lavaux also alluded to the problem in his memoirs. Lavaux, *Les campagnes d'un avocat*, p. 22.

55. A.N., AA 40, dossier 1300, document 48 (emphasis in original); on his subsequent arrest, A.N., W 42, dossier 2835; A.N., F^7 4644, dossier Chauveau-Lagarde.

56. See Donald Greer, *The Incidence of the Terror during the French Revolution*, reprint ed. (Gloucester, Mass.: Peter Smith, 1966), p. 154.

57. The two men executed for being associates of Robespierre, Nicolas Joseph Vivier de Launey and Edme Marguerite Lauvin de Montplaisir, along with other former members of the Order such as Jacques Nicolas Billaud-Varennes and Etienne Jean Panis, are representative of a much smaller group of men who were closely involved in radical republican politics. It is clear that they placed political ideals above identification with their profession or the interests of the Order. Since this study is concerned with those individuals who remained in the profession, however, these men fall beyond its limits. This is not to dismiss them; but as an examination of the list of members of the Order shows, they were a very small and unrepresentative minority, comprising no more than approximately ten to twelve men. Nonetheless, they deserve mention, if only in passing, because they illustrate the variety of reactions to the Revolution from members of the Order.

58. Eustache Antoine Hua left Paris in December 1792 and spent the next three years in the village of Nogent hiding from Revolutionary authorities. François Louis Hutteau and his son, Jean Baptiste Louis Hutteau, both of whom were former members of the Order, retired to Malesherbes in the Loiret, where a popular assembly protected the elder Hutteau from seizure when Santerre came to Malesherbes to apprehend him. Honoré Marie Nicolas Duveyrier, with the help of his friend Garat, the minister of justice and the interim minister of the interior,

contrived to have himself sent to Copenhagen on a mission to avoid being taken into custody. Jacques Aubery, a former member of the Order who had been elected to a judgeship in 1791, retired to Melun in 1793 when he was not reelected. Likewise, Etienne Denis Bureau du Colombier, also a former member of the Order who had been a judge in Paris, retired to Orléans in 1793 and resumed the practice of law there. Guy Jean Baptiste Target went into hiding and was so successful at concealing his whereabouts that his name was placed on the list of émigrés, even though he did not emigrate. René Legrand de Saint-René eluded Revolutionary authorities by taking refuge in a cavalry regiment commanded by his brother in the Army of the Rhine. Hua, *Mémoires d'un avocat au Parlement de Paris*, pp. 175–176 (Hua); on the elder Hutteau, *Biographie universelle (Michaud) ancienne et moderne*, XX, 210; for his son, A.N., BB^6 2, Seine-et-Marne, undated letter of Jean Baptiste Louis Hutteau to minister of justice; Duveyrier, *Anecdotes historiques*, p. 165 (Duveyrier); A.N., BB^5 171, letter of Aubery to minister of justice, 16 prairial year XIII (Aubery); A.N., BB^5 175, letter of Bureau du Colombier to minister of justice, September 19, 1809 (Bureau du Colombier); A.N., F^{7*} 2549 (Target); A.N., BB^5 171, undated letter of Legrand de Saint-René in the name of his brother.

59. Donald Greer, *The Incidence of the Emigration during the French Revolution*, reprint ed. (Gloucester, Mass.: Peter Smith, 1966), pp. 8–10, 12–13.

60. A.N., BB^1 63; A.N., F^{7*} 2534; A.N., AD^{XII} 9 (Godineau de Villechenay); A.N., AD^{XII} 10; Arnault, Jay, Jouy, Norvins, eds., *Biographie nouvelle des contemporains*, XVI, 31 (Parisot); A.N., T 1112, dossier 6; *Liste par ordre alphabétique des émigrés du département de Paris* (Paris: Ballard, year II) (Vautrin); A.N., AD^{XII} 10; A.N., F^{7*} 2535 (Maugue-Massis); A.N., AD^{XII} 10; A.N., F^{7*} 2535; A.N., BB^1 63 (Siméon); A.N., AD^{XII} 8 (Boursault de Troncay); A.N., AD^{XII} 9 (Foisy de Tremont).

61. Greer, *The Incidence of the Emigration*, p. 133.

62. See F. A. Aulard, ed., *Recueil des actes du comité de salut public*, 27 vols. (Paris: Imprimerie Nationale, 1889–1951), XV, 634; XVI, 66.

63. Georges Lefebvre, *The French Revolution*, 2 vols. (New York: Columbia University Press, 1962–1964), II, 138; Duvergier, *Collection complète des lois*, VII, 288, 357–361.

64. Godfrey, *Revolutionary Justice*, p. 150.

5. Regroupment

1. A.N., D^{III} 257, Committee of Legislation, decree of 14 nivôse year III, with emendations in D^{III} 260/261, Changements a operée sur la liste concernant la nouvelle composition des tribunaux de Paris (undated). The totals given reflect only those who accepted the posts and omit those who declined.

2. See, for example, the letter of Bitouze-Linières, a former member of the Order, declining the post to which he had been named. A.N., AA 49, dossier 1402, document 84.

3. A.D. Seine, DE^1, carton 18, dossier 220; his name was removed on 30 brumaire year III. A.N., F^{7*} 2538.

4. These included Millet de Gravelle, Brosselard, and Faure. A.N., F⁷ 4774⁴⁶, dossier Millet de Gravelle; A.N., F⁷ 4619, dossier Brosselard; A.N., F⁷ 4703, dossier Faure.

5. A.N., AA 6, dossier 319; it was Pierre Louis Mayeur.

6. On Garran-Coulon, see Auguste Kuscinski, *Dictionnaire des conventionnels,* (Paris: F. Rieder, 1916), p. 282; *Le Tribunal et la cour de cassation,* p. 3; on the tendency of former barristers who were deputies to lose contact with their former colleagues, Hua, *Mémoires d'un avocat au Parlement de Paris,* p. 173; for evidence that Garran-Coulon remained in contact with his former colleagues, see Berryer, *Souvenirs,* I, 301.

7. A.N., BB³⁰ 248, Etat de service de M. le Baron Locré, December 9, 1828; A.N., BB⁵ 171, letter of Guyot-Desherbiers to First Consul, 27 germinal year XIII.

8. These included Louis Marie Cauche, who subsequently left to take a judgeship in Paris, François Gorguereau, Pierre Fidel Sabarot, and François Laurent Archambault. On Cauche, A.N., D^{III} 260/261, Changements a operée . . . tribunaux de Paris, 5ᵉ arrondissement; for the members of the committee, A.N., D^{III} 360, and A.N., C 364, dossier 4, Etat général des appointements . . . vendémiaire an III.

Unsuccessful applicants included Louis Bon Asport, Gabriel Felix Cairol, Edme Jean Blacque, Timothée Arnould Henry, Martin Pierre Larrieu, and François Marin Le Prevost. A.N., D^{III} 360. Another former barrister to the Parlement, Louis Michel Savy, demonstrated the same predilection in a slightly different manner by drafting a new forestry code for the Committee of Agriculture in the year III. A.N., BB⁵ 169, undated letter of Savy to minister of justice.

9. Louis Ferdinand Bonnet, for example, was promoted to director of one of the divisions of the Bureau du domaine nationale, and Charles Pierre Michel Forestier became head of one of the bureaus in the Direction générale de la liquidation de la dette publique. *Almanach National an IV,* p. 377 (Bonnet); Ibid., p. 127 (Forestier).

10. Berryer, *Souvenirs,* I, 248, on the certificats de civisme; Colin Lucas, "The First Directory and the Rule of Law," *French Historical Studies* 10 (Fall 1977): 231–260.

11. *Almanach National an V,* pp. 187–190, 361–369. For the entire period during which the Order was dissolved, it was only through the *Almanach* that a practitioner could make known the fact that he was in practice. See A. C. Thibaudeau, *Mémoires sur la Convention et la Directoire,* 2 vols. (Paris: Baudouin Frères, 1824), II, 354. On the sense of purpose that inspired the former barristers to the Parlement, Berryer, *Souvenirs,* I, 314.

12. Berryer, *Souvenirs,* I, 314–317; Duveyrier, *Anecdotes historiques,* p. xvii. According to Berryer, Raymond de Sèze, Guillaume Alexandre Tronson-Ducoudray, Antoine Roy, and Charles Pierre Marie Gicquel were others of note who reunited themselves with their former colleagues at this time.

13. Berryer, *Souvenirs,* I, 317.

14. Thibaudeau, *Mémoires sur la Convention et le Directoire,* II, 355–356.

15. Ibid., II, 357.

16. Berryer, *Souvenirs,* I, 317–318.

17. A.N., BB³⁰ 512ᴬ, decree of 16 brumaire year IV.
18. See B.H.V.P., MS. 776, document 106.
19. For Paris, see A.N., AF III* 283, Département de la Seine; A.N., AF III* 158, no. 52, 21 frimaire year IV.

To give but a few examples in outlying departments, Louis Augustine Bruslé was appointed as a judge in the civil court of the Aisne, Pierre François Pulleu was named a substitute judge in the civil court of the Oise, and Hyacinthe Féart was designated as president of the criminal court of the Ardennes, a post to which he was reelected in the year VI. A.N., AF III* 283, Département de l'Aisne (Bruslé); Ibid., Département de l'Oise (Pulleu); A.N., F¹c III Ardennes 1, Assemblée électorale an VI (Féart).

20. A.N., B¹ 17, Nominations fait par l'assemblée électorale . . . germinal an V.

21. *Le Tribunal et la cour de cassation*, pp. 1–2. Similarly, Charles François Lasaudade and Jean Baptiste Bayard, who had been named as assistants to the government commissioner in 1791 and 1792 respectively, stayed in their post until 1797. Ibid., p. 374.

22. On Babille, ibid., p. 47; on the former barristers to the Parlement practicing there, *Almanach National an V*, pp. 187–190, 361–369. See also Thibaudeau, *Mémoires sur la Convention et le Directoire*, II, 356.

23. Paris was slated to receive five schools, but only three were actually established.

24. In Paris Jean Jacques Lenoir-Laroche taught in the central school at the Pantheon. After failing to win election to a judgeship in the year V, Joseph Jeudy-Dumouteix, apparently still reluctant to practice law in Paris, went to the department of the Puy-de-Dôme and taught the course of legislation in the école centrale at Clermont. Similarly, after being named to the criminal court of Paris by the Committee of Legislation in the year III, Louis Auguste Legrand de Laleu was elected to the presidency of the criminal court of the Aisne in the year IV, a post that he accepted. While occupying the office he also taught the course of legislation in the central school of the Aisne at Soissons. A.D. Seine, 3 AZ 148, document 4, and B.H.V.P., MS. 771, document 49 (Lenoir-Laroche); A.N., B¹ 17, Procès-verbal de la séance électorale du Département de la Seine, 23 germinal year V, and A.N., BB⁵ 146, letter of Dugour to minister of justice, 12 floréal year IX (Jeudy-Dumouteix); A.N., BB⁵ 172, letter of Legrand de Laleu to minister of justice, April 1, 1806, and A.N., BB⁶ 1, Aisne (Legrand de Laleu).

On the varied content of the courses of legislation, Ernest Allain, *L'oeuvre scolaire de la Révolution, 1789–1802* (Paris: Firmin-Didot, 1891; reprint ed., New York: Burt Franklin, 1969), pp. 126–127; H. C. Barnard, *Education and the French Revolution* (Cambridge: Cambridge University Press, 1969), p. 194.

25. A.N., AF^IV 1424, Elections de l'an 1811, Listes des candidats présentés pour le Sénat-Conservateur par les collèges électoraux . . . Haute Marne; *Le Tribunal et la cour de cassation*, p. 143; *Biographie universelle (Michaud) ancienne et moderne*, XIX, 214–217.

26. Allain, *L'oeuvre scolaire de la Révolution*, p. 127; R. R. Palmer, "The Central Schools of the First French Republic: A Statistical Survey," in Donald N.

Baker and Patrick J. Harrigan, eds., *The Making of Frenchmen: Current Directions in the History of Education in France, 1679–1979* (Waterloo, Ontario: Historical Reflections Press, 1980), pp. 243–246.

27. A.N., AA 35, letter of Mouricault to minister of justice, 14 pluviôse year IV; A.N., AF III* 159, no. 442, 16 fructidor year IV.

28. A.N., AF III* 163, no. 1331, 15 floréal year VI.

29. *Gazette des Nouveaux Tribunaux*, XIII, 128.

30. Berryer, *Souvenirs*, I, 329–330; Bonnet, *Discours, plaidoyers et mémoires*, II, 246 n. 1.

31. Berryer, *Souvenirs*, I, 323.

32. Louis Sebastien Mercier, *Le nouveau Paris*, 6 vols. (Paris: Fuchs, year VII), II, 78.

33. Jean Baptiste Pujoulx, *Paris à la fin du XVIIIe siècle* (Paris: B. Mathé, 1801), pp. 69–72.

34. Berryer, *Souvenirs*, I, 313, 318.

35. A.N., BB^5 179, letter of Quesnel to minister of justice, December 31, 1810; A.N., BB^5 175, copy of attestation of April 20, 1808, of Bellart, Bonnet, Berryer, Billecocq, Blacque, Chauveau-Lagarde; copy of attestation of president and procureur impérial of Civil Tribunal of Paris, 17 prairial year XIII, copies dated August 3, 1810.

36. B.A.P., Tableau de 1811. The method is not all inclusive because it fails to take into account ex-legislators who affiliated with the former barristers to the Parlement during the Directory and then went on to political careers under the Empire. Moreover, there were a few men accepted into the group of former avocats au Parlement who did not live until 1811 to be listed on the tableau of the reestablished Order. A brief account of some of these individuals can be found in Berryer, *Souvenirs*, I, 318–321. Even allowing for these deficiencies, which omit only a few persons, the magnitude of the problem is clear from the tableau.

37. A.D. Seine, VD* 366, report of 11 prairial year V, A.D. Seine, VD* 386, report of 1 thermidor year V, A.D., Seine VD* 388, report of 3 thermidor year V. In particular, some of the hostility toward the minister of justice at this time may have been occasioned by the Babeuf trial.

38. François Laurent, *Aux Citoyens Représentans du Peuple, au Conseil des Cinq Cents, sur l'organisation des hommes de loi* (Paris: Fauvelle et Sagnier, n.d.), p. 3. The apparent surprise of Thibaudeau at the conditions he encountered when he resumed the practice of law lends credence to Laurent's suspicion.

39. *Le Moniteur Universel*, 5 nivôse year IV.

40. Charles François Oudot, *Projet de resolution sur les avoués, présenté par Oudot au nom de la Commission de la classification des lois* (Paris: Imprimerie Nationale, year VI).

41. *Le Moniteur Universel*, 23 vendémiaire year VI.

42. Ibid., 7 brumaire year VI; François Marie Joseph Riou, *Opinion de Riou sur le rétablissement des avoués* (Paris: Imprimerie Nationale, year VI). Riou's project was sent back to committee, and Riou was appointed to the commission.

43. *Le Moniteur Universel*, 25 brumaire year VI.

44. Ibid., 16 frimaire year VI.

45. Ibid., 25 brumaire year VI.

46. Ibid., 27 frimaire year VI; for Pison du Galand's project, see Alexis François Pison du Galand, *Opinion de Pison du Galand sur le projet d'établissement d'avoués* (Paris: Imprimerie Nationale, year VI).

47. *Le Moniteur Universel,* 10 nivôse year VI.

48. In its final form the bill can be found as Alexis François Pison du Galand, *Rapport fait par Pison du Galand, sur la première formation du tableau des hommes de loi & les dépens ou frais judiciaires* (Paris: Imprimerie Nationale, year VI); *Le Moniteur Universel,* 2 germinal year VI; Claude Ambroise Regnier, *Rapport fait par Regnier sur la résolution concernant la défense des parties devant les tribunaux* (Paris: Imprimerie Nationale, year VI).

49. Claude Ambroise Regnier, *Observations faites par Regnier, sur une opinion relative à la résolution concernant la défense des parties devant les tribunaux* (Paris: Imprimerie Nationale, year VI); *Le Moniteur Universel,* 26 germinal year VI.

50. Foucault, *The Birth of the Clinic,* pp. 72–78.

51. Again, on the centrality of law to the regime, see Lucas, "The First Directory and the Rule of Law." Although these debates took place under the Second Directory, I would argue that the conception of law underwent little or no change even if the political behavior of the regimes did.

52. Jacques Vincent Delacroix, *Le spectateur françois pendant le gouvernement révolutionnaire* (Paris: Buisson, year III); A.N., W 496, no. 516. The dossier gives a complete account of Delacroix's trail. On Delacroix and Langlois, Jeremy D. Popkin, *The Right Wing Press in France, 1792–1800* (Chapel Hill: University of North Carolina Press, 1980), p. 127.

53. Charles Denis Grouvelle, who does not seem to have remained with the profession after 1790, was sentenced to four months imprisonment and a fine for his involvement in the uprising. Louis Abraham Dommanget was charged with being "one of the authors and principal instigators of the revolt" and was arrested. He was freed several months later and rejoined the profession at that time. François Laurent Archambault, who had been a pivotal figure in rallying the Order after the Terror, received a judgment of death from the military commission but managed to evade the sentence. Similarly, Louis Auguste Popelin, who also remained closely associated with the profession, was inculpated in the revolt but was later amnestied. A.N., F^7 4734, dossier Grouvel (*sic*), Mémoire pour le citoyen Charles Denis Grouvelle; A.N., AA 6, dossier 320 (Grouvelle); A.N., T 1621 (Dommanget); A.N., AA 6, dossier 320, Arnault, Jay, Jouy, and Norvins, eds., *Biographie nouvelle des contemporains,* I, 230 (Archambault); J. R. Suratteau, "Les élections de l'an V," *Annales Historique de la Révolution Française* 30 (December 1958): 47 n. 123 (Popelin).

54. Harvey Mitchell, *The Underground War against Revolutionary France* (London: Oxford University Press, 1965), p. 149; W. R. Fryer, *Republic or Restoration in France? 1794–1797* (Manchester: Manchester University Press, 1965), p. 195. On the elections of the year V, see Suratteau, "Les élections de l'an V." Another interpretation of them can be found in M. J. Sydenham, *The First French Republic* (Berkeley: University of California Press, 1973), pp. 123–127.

55. Adolphe Robert, Edgar Bourloton, and Gaston Cougny, eds., *Dictionnaire*

des parlementaires françaises, 5 vols. (Paris: Bourloton, 1891), 2, 281 (de Bonnières); 2, 307 (de la Metherie); 5, 451 (Tronson-Ducoudray). On Brunet, whose expulsion is not mentioned in the *Dictionnaire des parlementaires françaises,* see Auguste Kuscinski, *Les députés au Corps législatif, Conseil des Cinq-Cents, Conseil des Anciens de l'an IV à l'an VII* (Paris: Société de l'histoire de la Révolution française, 1905), p. 202.

56. Berryer, *Souvenirs,* I, 314–315; Fournel, *Histoire des avocats au Parlement et du barreau de Paris,* I, xxix.

57. François Antoine Clozier, Jacques Bernard Jean Doillot, Louis Claude Denis Dameuve, Henri Caillau, Laurent Jean Babille, Jean Baptiste François Bayard, Jean Baptiste Le Bruin, Marin Carouge, Charles Minier, Pierre Augustin Hemery, Léon D'Herbelot, Charles François LaSaudade, Jean Antoine Villedieu, Pierre Claude Simon Pelletier, and Joseph LaCaze were all former members of the Order who were displaced from their positions. A.N., BB⁵ 170, undated letter of Clozier, no addressee (Clozier); A.N., BB⁵ 168, letter of Doillot to minister of justice, 25 thermidor year X (Doillot); A.N., BB⁵ 169, undated letter of Dameuve to Consul Cambacérès (Dameuve); A.N., BB⁵ 168, letter of Caillau to minister of justice, 6 pluviôse year IX (Caillau); *Le Tribunal et la cour de cassation,* p. 47 (Babille); Balteau, Barroux, and Prevost, eds., *Dictionnaire de biographie française,* V, 991 (Bayard); A.N., BB⁵ 170, undated letter of LeBruin to minister of justice (Le Bruin); all others Douarche, ed., *Les tribunaux civils de Paris pendant la Révolution,* II, appendix II, passim. Douarche's work is useful but marred by occasional errors or uncertainty on personnel; thus, whenever possible, I tried to use other sources.

58. Jean Baptiste Le Gras, Nicolas Bouchard, Louis Marie Cauche, and Louis Joseph Faure, for example, were all appointed to judicial positions after 20 fructidor. A.N., BB⁵ 404, decree of 20 fructidor. Others appointed include Etienne Guyot de Saint-Hèlene, Guy Jean Baptiste Target, and Louis Joseph Landry. Likewise, on 23 fructidor Laurent Marcilly, Marie Philippe Auguste Bélot, and Louis Joseph Bastard, all former members of the Order, were among those appointed to the civil court of the department of the Seine. A.N., AF III* 162, no. 1071, 23 fructidor year V.

Examples of those removed who soon resumed positions include D'Herbelot, who was reinstated only a few days afterward. Similarly, Bayard was restored to the Tribunal de cassation only a month later. Minier, La Caze, and Hemery were all elected to judicial positions in the year VII. A.N., BB⁵ 404, decree of 20 fructidor (D'Herbelot); Balteau, Barroux, and Prevost, eds., *Dictionnaire de biographie française,* V, 991, (Bayard); A.N., B¹ 17, elections for the year VII (Minier, La Caze, and Hemery). Doillot and Caillau returned to practice as hommes de loi after the coup, and in this sense the coup may have indirectly aided the former barristers to the Parlement in their regroupment.

59. For the personal perspective of one former member of the Order on the coup, see Felkay and Favier, eds., *En prison sous la Terreur: Souvenirs de J. B. Billecocq,* pp. 91–106.

6. The Promise of Reconstruction

1. Berryer, *Souvenirs,* I, 333–335. They were doubtlessly reassured especially

by the presence of the men around Bonaparte, several of whom were former colleagues who had embarked upon political careers in 1789 or later. One study has emphasized the background in law of many of the men who entered with Bonaparte and has noted that, like the former barristers to the Parlement themselves, most had been profoundly shaken by the Terror. Werner Giesselmann, *Die brumairianische Elite: Kontinuität und Wandel der französischen Führungsschicht zwischen Ancien Régime und Julimonarchie* (Stuttgart: Ernst Klett Verlag, 1977).

2. On the Constitution of the Year VIII, see Jean Bourdon, *La Constitution de l'an VIII* (Rodez: Carrère, 1942).

3. Antoine Jacques Claude Boullay and Médéric Elie Moreau de Saint Méry were members of the Council of State. Jean Philippe Garran-Coulon and Jean Jacques Lenoir-Laroche belonged to the Senate. Jean Charles Bitouze-Linières, Honoré Marie Nicolas Duveyrier, Louis Joseph Faure, Charles Ganilh, and Thomas Laurent Mouricault were all members of the Tribunate. Pierre Bergeras and Claude Antoine Guyot-Desherbiers entered the Legislative Body. *Almanach National an IX*, pp. 65–66, 73–85. For an examination of the individuals involved, see Giesselmann, *Die brumairianische Elite*; for a consideration of the institutions, Amédée Edmond-Blanc, *Napoléon Ier: Ses institutions civiles et administratives* (Paris: Plon, 1880); Godechot, *Les institutions de la France sous la Révolution et l'Empire*; Robert Holtman, *The Napoleonic Revolution* (Philadelphia: Lippincott, 1967), and Irene Collins, *Napoleon and His Parliaments* (London: Edward and Arnold, 1979).

4. Garran-Coulon and Guyot-Desherbiers had been critical figures at the Committee of Legislation when it had employed several former barristers to the Parlement and had placed many others in judicial positions in the year III. Duveyrier, during a hiatus in his political career after he returned from Copenhagen, had resumed the practice of law in Paris for a period and had reestablished contact with his former colleagues at that time. Similarly, under the Directory, Bitouze-Linières had played an important role in rallying the former members of the Order in practice before his election to the Council of Five Hundred in the year VI. In addition, Thibaudeau, who had not belonged to the Order in 1789 but had formed a close association with the former avocats au Parlement when he resumed the practice of law under the Directory, was named to the Council of State. Likewise, Cambacérès, who had also taken up the practice of law in Paris after his departure from the Council of Five Hundred in the year VI and therefore also had strong ties with many members of the abolished Order, became Second Consul.

5. For a detailed examination of the changes enacted, consult Jean Tulard, ed., *Atlas administratif de l'Empire français* . . . (Geneva: Librairie Droz, 1973); Felix Ponteil, *Napoléon Ier et l'organisation autoritaire de la France* (Paris: Armand Colin, 1965); the definitive work on the judiciary is Jean Bourdon, *La réforme judiciaire de l'an VIII*, 2 vols. (Rodez: Carrère, 1941).

6. A.N., F^7 3830, report of 10 fructidor year X.

7. Berryer, *Souvenirs*, I, 334; Dupin, *Profession d'avocat*, I, 129.

8. Georges Lefebvre, *Napoleon*, 2 vols. (New York: Columbia University Press, 1969), I, 87–88. A.N., BB^6 1 and BB^6 2 consist entirely of information gathered on magistrates in the year VIII.

9. *Almanach National an IX*, pp. 451–453, 463–464. Nine out of thirty-three in the Tribunal d'appel and seven out of twenty-four in the Tribunal de première

instance were former barristers to the Parlement; on the Criminal Court, ibid., p. 461.

10. As one example, Marin Carouge went from the Tribunal of First Instance to the Appeals Court. A.N., BB⁵ 171, letter of Carouge to minister of justice, 18 brumaire year XII, and letter of president of Appeals Court to minister of justice, 2 nivôse year XII.

11. To give but a few examples, Louis de la Metherie became the senior judge of the Appeals Court at Bourges, and Simon Pierre Moreau was named to the presidency of the Tribunal of First Instance at Reims, and Jean François Dufour was selected as the president of the Criminal Court of the Seine-et-Marne. Jacques Aubery was appointed to the Tribunal of First Instance at Melun, and Vincent de Paul Barbier was named as one of the judges in the Criminal Court of the Seine-et-Oise. A.N., BB⁵ 176, letter of de la Metherie to minister of justice, April 10, 1810 (de la Metherie); A.N., F¹c III Marne 1, Elections de l'an XI, Liste des membres qui composent le collège électoral de l'arrondissement communal de Reims (Moreau); A.N., BB⁵ 174, Etat des services du Sr Dufour et de ses deux fils, undated (Dufour); A.N., BB⁵ 171, letter of Aubery to minister of justice, 16 prairial year XIII (Aubery); A.N., BB⁵ 177, letter of Barbier to minister of justice, June 18, 1810 (Barbier). Once again, ties to the Order seem to have been fortuitous. In A.N., BB⁶ 2, each individual who is correctly identified as a former barrister to the Parlement at Paris received a judicial appointment. See especially the departments of the Seine-et-Oise and the Seine-et-Marne.

Examples of men appointed as government commissioners include Joseph Louis Lecomte-Roujou, who was designated as the government commissioner at the Tribunal of First Instance at Blois, while Antoine Jacques de la Fleutrie obtained the same post at the Tribunal of First Instance at Fontainebleau in the year IX. A.N., BB⁵ 93, letter of Debeine to minister of justice, 23 vendémiaire year XII (Lecomte-Roujou); A.N., BB⁵ 175, letter of de la Fleutrie to minister of justice, June 6, 1810 (de la Fleutrie).

12. The men named as judges were Pierre Paul Nicolas Henrion de Pansey, Laurent Jean Babille, Jean Baptiste François Bayard, Charles Minier, Nicolas Oudart, Jean Gabriel Poriquet, Guy Jean Baptiste Target, François Denis Tronchet, Charles François Lasaudade, and François Michel Vermeil. *Le Tribunal et la cour de cassation*, pp. 101–123. This work incorrectly lists Fleurent Jean Baptiste Oudart as a judge, but an examination of archival evidence shows that it was, in fact, Nicolas Oudart, a former member of the Order, who occupied the post. See A.N., F¹c III Haute Marne 1, Elections de l'an IX, Tableau dressé par le préfet du Département de la Haute Marne, en exécution des articles 51 et 52 de la loi du 13 ventôse an IX . . . , A.N., BB²⁹ 273, entry no. 107. Douarche in his work duplicates the error even while cautioning against confusing the two.

The man named as government commissioner was Felix Julien Jean Bigot de Préameneu. *Le Tribunal et la cour de cassation*, p. 371.

13. Dupin, *Profession d'avocat*, I, 129. One possible exception would be Louis Legrand de Sainte-René, who appears to have owed his appointment more to the solicitations of his brother, a prominent general in the army, than to his own juridical abilities. A.N., BB⁵ 171, letter of Legrand de Sainte-René to Bonaparte, 20 fructidor year XII.

14. On the Civil Code, see Bernard Schwartz, ed., *The Code Napoleon and the Common Law World* (New York: New York University Press, 1956).

15. Godechot, *Les institutions de la France*, pp. 622–623.

16. Palmer, "The Central Schools of the First French Republic," pp. 243–246; Felix Ponteil, *Histoire de l'enseignement en France* (Paris: Sirey, 1966), p. 83.

17. Dupin, *Profession d'avocat*, I, 130; Michel Jacques Carpentier, Eustache Nicolas Pigeau, and Georges Victor Vasselin all offered private instruction. A.N., BB¹ 59, dossier Coffinières (Carpentier); *Biographie universelle (Michaud) ancienne et moderne*, XXXIII, 307–308 (Pigeau); *Le Moniteur Universel*, 5 vendémiaire year X (Vasselin). On the belief that a return to an emphasis on Roman law was needed, see the review by Guillon d'Assas, a former member of the Order, in *Le Moniteur Universel*, 23 vendémiaire year IX.

The need for educational reform was tacitly admitted by the minister of justice when he sought, unsuccessfully, to establish "Schools of Legislation" in towns in which there was an appeals court. A.N., AF IV* 215, no. 810. See also A.N., AA 16, dossier 809, Mémoire sur l'établissement des Ecoles destinées à l'enseignement de la jurisprudence by Gouillard (undated).

18. A.N., F¹⁷ 1984, Observation essentielle (letter of Lefebvre, undated); *Le Moniteur Universel*, 7 vendémiaire year IX; A.N., T 1019, Université de Jurisprudence et Bureau de consultation.

19. A.N., T 1019, Université de Jurisprudence et Bureau de consultation; A.N., F¹⁷ 1984, letter of Lefebvre to comte de Fontanes, July 12, 1814; A.N., T 1019, Analyse des travaux de l'Université de Jurisprudence. The other men included François Dominique Reynaud de Montlozier, Pierre Louis Lacretelle (a former member of the Order), Jacques Peuchet, Xavier Agresty, Scipion Jérôme Bexon, and Michel Agresty; A.N., T 1019, Université de Jurisprudence—Instruction pour les directeurs; B.H.V.P., MS. 771, document 83; Berryer, *Souvenirs*, I, 326.

20. A.N., BB⁵ 170, diploma of Courtin, 22 prairial year X; Berryer, *Souvenirs*, I, 325.

21. *Bulletin de l'Institut de jurisprudence et d'économie politique* (Paris: Patris, n.d.), p. 3.

22. A.N., T 1019, Règlement; B.H.V.P., MS C.P. 3846, dossier 60, document 11; A.N., AA 44, dossier 1331, document 10.

23. *Etat des travaux de l'Académie de Législation* (n.p., n.d.), pp. 17–19; A.N., AA 44, dossier 1327, document 130; A.N., AA 63, dossier 5, document 133.

24. *Le Moniteur Universel*, 7 vendémiaire year IX.

25. A.N., T 1019, Université de Jurisprudence et bureau de consultation.

26. A.N., T 1019, Université de Jurisprudence—Instruction pour les directeurs; A.N., T 1019, Analyse des travaux de l'Université de Jurisprudence. In subsequently trying to explain the long delay between its organization and its opening, the institution claimed that several factors had impeded its progress, including construction delays on a new building. A close reading indicates, however, that financial problems were also a factor. See *Lycée de Jurisprudence, et bureau de consultation, conciliation et de défense général près le tribunal de cassation et les tribunaux civils, criminels et de commerce de la république* . . . (Paris: Imprimerie du Lycée de Jurisprudence, n.d.), pp. 4–5.

27. A.N., T 1019, Règlement.

28. *Le Moniteur Universel,* 7 vendémiaire year XII, for the awards ceremony. On students who transferred to the université, see A.N., AJ[16] 1787, entry of June 12, 1806 (Gandin-Desroches); entry of July 10, 1806 (Monier). Gandin-Desroches came from the department of the Charente, and Monier came from the Rhône.

29. A.N., T 1019, Analyse des travaux de l'Université de Jurisprudence; Eustache Nicolas Pigeau, *Le procedure civile du Châtelet de Paris et de toutes les jurisdictions ordinaires du royaume, demontrée par principes et mise en action par des formules* (Paris: Veuve Desaint, 1779). A revised edition was issued in 1807 and went through several printings. Jacques Peuchet, *Bibliothèque commerciale,* 3 vols. (Paris: F. Buisson, year X); Scipion Jérôme Bexon, *Developpement de la théorie des lois criminelles par la comparison de plusiers législations . . . suivi de l'application de cette théorie dans un projet de code criminel, correctionnel et de police,* 2 vols. (Paris: Garnery, 1802).

30. A.N., T 1019, Analyse des travaux de l'Université de Jurisprudence; A.N., T 1019, Règlement.

31. *Le Moniteur Universel,* 3 frimaire year XII.

32. Henri Hayem, "La renaissance de études juridiques en France sous le Consulat," *Nouvelle Revue Historique de Droit Français et Etranger* 29 (July 1905): 386.

33. *Le Moniteur Universel,* 6 frimaire year XII.

34. See *Annales de législation et de jurisprudence,* 4 vols. (Paris: Imprimerie de l'Université de Jurisprudence, years XI–XII).

35. A.N., AJ[16] 1787, entries for Lamare, 21 frimaire year XIV; Guissibert, January 2, 1806; Delafreye, 16 brumaire year XIV; Percaud, 30 brumaire year XIV; De Corné, 30 brumaire year XIV; Collibeaux, January 16, 1806, and others.

36. The Bureau de consultations dimension of the Université de Jurisprudence continued under the title of Conseil de Jurisprudence. See Louis François Aubin Lefebvre de Fabrimenil, *Mémorial du Conseil de Jurisprudence,* 3 vols. (Paris: Au Conseil de Jurisprudence, 1811). The Bibliothèque Nationale apparently does not possess the third volume, which may be found in B.H.V.P., 606298 (15). See also A.N., AA 44, dossier 1331, document 11; Jean Charles Lefebvre, *Almanach judiciaire pour l'année 1810* (Paris: J. C. Lefebvre, 1810), pp. 37–38; Conseil de Jurisprudence . . . , September 15, 1809, Baudry des Lozières Papers, Manuscripts Department, Perkins Library, Duke University.

37. A.N., AJ[16] 1787 indicates that the Académie de Législation drew many more students than did the Université de Jurisprudence. Moreover, the académie seems to have had a greater number of more notable alumni than the université.

38. The founder of the université subsequently claimed that 450 students had been trained there, but this cannot be verified. Lefebvre de Fabrimenil, *Mémorial du Conseil de Jurisprudence,* I, iii.

39. *Biographie nationale de Belgique,* 29 vols. (Brussels: H. Thiry–Van Buggenhoudt, 1866–1944), XXIII, 684–692.

40. *Le Moniteur Universel,* 11 ventôse year X; *Institut de Jurisprudence et d'économie politique: Observations* (Paris: Imprimerie de l'Institut de Jurisprudence et d'économie politique, n.d.), p. 11; Hayem, "La renaissance des études juridiques," p. 213.

41. See Dupin, *Profession d'avocat*, I, 130, where he asserts that men of state founded the académie, where Dupin was a student. See also *Biographie universelle (Michaud) ancienne et moderne*, XXIII, 203–208; *Oeuvres de J. D. Lanjuinais*, 4 vols. (Paris: Dondley-Dupré, 1832), I, 61–62. Berryer's claim that men of state founded the académie also accords with this view, although he does not list all of the same individuals. At the Université de Jurisprudence the founder had been Lefebvre, but the administrator had been La Rivallière, so the fact that men were administrators does not necessarily mean they were founders. Moreover, the resignation of all five administrators in favor of Bruguière in the year XI is inconsistent with the sense of attachment one would expect from founders of an institution. *Le Moniteur Universel*, 14 germinal year XI. Lanjuinais, Target, and other men, by contrast, remained closely associated with the académie throughout its existence.

42. *Bulletin de l'Institut de Jurisprudence et d'économie politique*, pp. 11–12; also, *Le Moniteur Universel*, 12 messidor year X. *Institut de Jurisprudence et d'économie politique: Observations*, p. 9.

43. *Le Moniteur Universel*, 24 fructidor year XI. See also the biography of Teste in M. O. Pinard, *Le barreau au XIXe siècle*, 2 vols. (Paris: Pagnerre, 1864), II, 204–237.

44. *Institut de Jurisprudence et d'économie politique: Observations*; *Le Moniteur Universel*, 11 vendémiaire year X. The course in commercial and maritime law was added later in the first year. See B.H.V.P., MS. 771, document 82. There was much privateering during the wars of the Directory and the Napoleonic period, and as a consequence maritime law was one of the major areas of practice during this era. Jean André Perreau, *Elémens de législation naturelle* . . . (Paris: Baudouin, year IX); Joseph Elzéar Dominique Bernardi, *Institutions du droit français civil et criminel, ou Tableau raisonné de l'état actuel de la jurisprudence français* (Paris: H. J. Jansen, year VIII) and *Nouvelle théorie des lois civiles* (Paris: Garnery, year X); Jacques Peuchet, *Bibliothèque commerciale* . . . , 3 vols. (Paris: F. Buisson, year X).

45. See the report of Bruguière in *Le Moniteur Universel*, 4 messidor year XI, in which he states that classes for the second year proceeded without interruption.

46. *Etat des travaux de l'Académie de Législation* . . . *an X*, pp. 17–31, "Membres de l'Académie de Législation résidants à Paris." *Etat des travaux de l'Académie de Législation* . . . *an XI*, pp. 3, 22–30, "Membres de l'Académie de Législation résidants à Paris."

47. *Le Moniteur Universel*, 15 brumaire year XI; *Etat des travaux de l'Académie de Législation* . . . *an XI*, pp. 3–4.

48. *Le Moniteur Universel*, 24 fructidor year XI.

49. *Etat des travaux de l'Académie de Législation pendant le dernier semestre de l'an XI et le premier de l'an XII* . . . , pp. 30–48, "Liste des membres résidans et non-résidans, composant l'Académie de Législation." On the financing of the académie, A.N., AA 44, dossier 1327, document 130. See also *Institut de Jurisprudence et d'économie politique: Observations*, pp. 7, 12. The académie appears to have aimed to expand its affiliated membership outside Paris significantly. See A.N., AA 63, dossier 5, document 133. A record of the financial state of the académie for several years can be found in J. T. Bruguière, *Compte rendu et rapport à la Commission, dans sa séance du 27 janvier 1806, sur la situation financière et morale de l'Académie* (Paris: Imprimerie des Sciences et Arts, n.d.), pp. 3–4.

50. *Etat des travaux . . . pendant le dernier semestre de l'an XI et le premier de l'an XII*, pp. 39, 48. See also, *Le Moniteur Universel*, 6 pluviôse year XII.

51. *Etat des travaux de l'Académie de Législation . . . an XII*, pp. 9–10.

52. *Le Moniteur Universel*, 7 vendémiaire year XII.

53. *Institut de Jurisprudence et d'économie politique: Observations; Etat des travaux de l'Académie de Législation . . . an X*, p. 31; *Pérignon* (Paris: Bureau centrale de la revue générale biographique et litteraire, 1841); inscription date from B.A.P., Tableau de 1811.

54. B.H.V.P., MS. 771, document 82. This transaction occurred before any of the men of state became president, but it nonetheless indicates the division of authority.

55. On Lanjuinais, *Oeuvres de Lanjuinais*, I, 61; *Bulletin de l'Académie de Législation—Mémoires*, V, 182–196; Eugene Mourier, *Eloge prononcé le 26 novembre 1838, à l'ouverture des conférences de l'ordre des avocats* (Paris: A. Guyot, n.d.); for the action by Portalis, B.H.V.P., MS. 772, document 137.

56. *Etat des travaux de l'Académie de Législation . . . an XII*, pp. 30–48.

57. *Bulletin de l'Institut de jurisprudence et d'économie politique*, p. 3.

58. Ibid., pp. 13–14. A subsequent and analogous effort was also undertaken in the field of medicine. In September 1804 a group of regent-doctors from the abolished Faculty of Medicine founded the Académie de Médecine de Paris, with the purpose of bringing doctors together in order to raise the status of medical practice. Just as the Académie de Législation sought to emulate the Order of Barristers, the Académie de Médecine de Paris stated that it sought to revive the former Faculty of Medicine, and much of its activity was apparently devoted to restoring the corporate structure and privileges of the abolished faculty. Weisz, "Constructing the Medical Elite in France."

59. This includes both the Bureau de conseil général and the Commission du conseil général, which appear to have been the main governing bodies.

60. On the Old Regime, see, for example, Louis Ferdinand Bonnet, *Discours prononcé à la Bibliothèque des Avocats . . . 1785* (Paris: Méquignon le jeune, 1787), or Pierre Florent Louvet, *Discours prononcé par M. Louvet . . . le 1er décembre 1787, à l'ouverture de la Conférence des avocats . . . sur les causes de la considération accordée par le public à la profession d'avocat* (Paris: Méquignon, 1787). On the Académie de Législation, see *Le Moniteur Universel*, 29 fructidor year XII, which mentions a discourse by the student Charié on the moral dignity of the avocat and the influence of the profession on society. The Université de Jurisprudence also had its students present such talks. See Dominique Boutard, *Discours sur la profession d'avocat* (n.p., year XII). On the matter of the académie's academic program being influenced by the experience of the Order, *Institut de Jurisprudence et d'économie politique: Observations*, p. 9. *Le Moniteur Universel*, 15 brumaire year XI, for the service to indigents offered by the Académie de Législation.

61. *Bulletin de l'Académie de Législation—Mémoires*, XII, 544–547. For more on eulogies, see *Le Moniteur Universel*, 12 messidor year X.

62. The seat of the coalition seems to have been a room at the Palais de Justice. This was the major location and was utilized as an informal meeting place for the former barristers at the site of their professional activity. See Louis Jean Baptiste Couture, *Mon portefeuille* (Paris: Edouard Proux, 1840), p. 81. The académie was

an adjunct endeavor, fulfilling many other tasks not directly related to the practice of law that had been performed by the Order under the Old Regime.

63. A.N., BB⁵ 171, undated letter of Regnier to minister of justice. For more on the criteria for membership in the académie, see *Etat des travaux de l'Académie de Législation . . . an XII*, p. 17.

64. *Biographie universelle (Michaud) ancienne et moderne*, IV, 71–73 (Bernardi); A.N., BB⁵ 175, notice on Daupeley, no date, December 1810 (Daupeley); *Biographie universelle (Michaud) ancienne et moderne*, XVII, 368–369; A.N., F¹⁷ 1982, dossier Grappe (Grappe). All inscription dates are from B.A.P., Tableau de 1811.

65. In 1802 Paul Porcher fils, the son of a prominent former member of the Order, came to the coalition from the Université de Jurisprudence, and André Marie Jean Jacques Dupin, Jean Baptiste Teste, and Ambroise Modeste Marie Rendu arrived from the Académie de Législation; others, particularly from the Académie de Législation, subsequently affiliated themselves; Berryer, *Souvenirs*, I, 325–329; on Rendu, A.N., BB⁵ 178, letter of duc de Plaissance to duc de Massa, June 17, 1811.

66. Foucault, *The Birth of the Clinic*, pp. 67–68; Weisz, "Constructing the Medical Elite in France."

67. *Almanach National an VII*, pp. 216–220, 413–421; *Almanach National an VIII*, pp. 430–437; *Almanach National an IX*, pp. 373–375; *Almanach National an X*, pp. 595–597; *Almanach National an XI*, pp. 627–630; *Almanach National an XII*, pp. 625–629.

68. A.N., BB⁵ 170, unsigned letter of 23 thermidor year X to presidents of Appeals Court and Tribunal of First Instance. The letter, however, is almost certainly from the minister of justice. The president and government commissioner of these two courts apparently drafted the list that appeared in the *Almanach National*.

69. A.N., BB⁵ 171, attestation of former barristers, 15 thermidor year XII, and attestation of Agier and Mourre, 23 thermidor year XII. See also the case of Vautrin, another former member of the Order, who was also successful in placing his name in the *Almanach* after it was omitted. A.N., BB⁵ 170, letter of Vautrin to minister of justice, 25 thermidor year X.

70. A.N., BB⁵ 169, undated letter of Bizet to minister of justice. See also A.N., BB⁵ 168, letter of Caillau to minister of justice, 6 pluviôse year IX, A.N., BB⁵ 168, undated letter of Charié to minister of justice. For subtler examples of the bond of the Order being invoked, see A.N., BB⁵ 168, letter of Pons de Verdun to minister of justice, 25 nivôse year IX; A.N., BB⁵ 168, letter of Forestier, 6 nivôse year X.

71. A.N., BB⁵ 170, letter of Bourbon-Busset to minister of justice, 5 frimaire year XI. He had not been a member of the Order and was not successful in his attempt to have his name placed in the *Almanach*.

72. See A.N., BB⁵ 141, letter of government commissioner to minister of justice, 7 messidor year XI, in which he asks plaintively "qu'entend-on par le mot gens de loi?"

73. A.N., BB³⁰ 1156, circular of minister of justice, 1 brumaire year X, on the continuing problem with practitioners in the courts; Jean Antoine Chaptal, *Rap-*

port et projet de loi sur l'instuction publique (Paris: Imprimerie de la République, year IX).

74. Jean Antoine Chaptal, *Mes souvenirs sur Napoléon* (Paris: Plon, 1893), p. 289, for his hostility toward corporations. On his desire to control events, see ibid., p. 261, and Jean Pelet de la Lozère, *Opinions de Napoléon sur divers sujets de politique et d'administration* (Paris: Firmin-Didot, 1822), pp. 182–183. For another example of Bonaparte's readiness to use the corporate paradigm to strengthen the state, *Correspondance de Napoléon Ier*, 32 vols. (Paris: Imprimerie Impériale, 1858–1870), X, 8328; since there are different editions of this work, only the volume and the number of the letter will be cited.

75. A.N., C 652/653; Mavidal and Laurent, eds., *Archives parlementaires de 1787 à 1860*, 2nd ser. (1800–1860), 127 vols. (Paris: Librairie administrative de P. Dupont, 1862–1913), VI, 1.

76. Antoine François Fourcroy, *Exposé des motifs de la loi concernant les écoles de droit* (Paris: Fain, n.d.); B.N., MSS Nouvelles acquisitions françaises 5900, fol. 321; Mavidal and Laurent, eds., *Archives parlementaires*, 2nd ser., VI, 5.

77. Claude Joseph Mallarmé, *Rapport fait par le citoyen Mallarmé au nom de la section de l'Intérieur sur le projet de loi relatif aux écoles de droit: Séance du 19 ventôse an XII* (Paris: Imprimerie Nationale, year XII). See also Mavidal and Laurent, eds., *Archives parlementaires*, 2nd ser., VI, 51–58. It would be incorrect to assert that bills were debated, for the speeches that were given were long prepared texts that made no reference to the arguments of the previous speakers. One was rarely allowed to interrupt the speaker to ask a question. Moreover, a bill could only be rejected or accepted; it could not be amended. Collins, *Napoleon and His Parliaments*, pp. 18–27.

78. Mallarmé, *Rapport fait par le citoyen Mallarmé*, pp. 22–23.

79. Mathurin Louis Etienne Sedillez, *Considérations sur l'organisation des écoles de droit, suivies d'un tableau de l'enseignement du droit, présentées au Tribunat par M. L. E. Sedillez: Séance du 21 ventôse an XII* (Paris: Imprimerie Nationale, year XII); Michel Carret, *Discours prononcé par Carret (du Rhône), sur le projet concernant les écoles du droit: Séance du 21 ventôse an XII* (Paris: Imprimerie Nationale, year XII). See also Mavidal and Laurent, eds. *Archives parlementaires*, 2nd ser., VI, 77–85.

80. On the observation of the proceedings by a police spy, A.N., F^7 3832, report of 21 ventôse year XII; on the proceedings themselves, A.N., C 652/653; Mavidal and Laurent, eds. *Archives parlementaires*, 2nd ser., VI, 85, 92. The proceedings of the Legislative Body were also observed by a police spy. A.N., F^7 3832, report of 22 ventôse year XII.

7. A Hollow Victory

1. Pierre Marie Desmarets, *Témoignages historiques ou quinze ans de haute police sous le Consulat et l'Empire* (Paris: Levasseur, 1833), pp. 79–80.

2. Pasquier, *Memoirs*, I, 215.

3. André François Miot de Melito, *Mémoires du comte Miot de Melito, ancien*

ministre, ambassadeur, conseiller d'Etat et membre de l'Institut, 1788–1815, 3 vols. (Paris: Michel Levy, 1873), II, 192; Desmarets, *Témoignages historiques,* p. 115.

4. A.N., F⁷ 3832, report of 1 ventôse year XII. The report of the choice of Delamalle was erroneous, for he was not involved in Moreau's defense; ibid., report of 14 prairial year XII is one example of the intensified observation of the barristers.

5. Ibid., report of 3 prairial year XII.

6. Dupin, *Profession d'avocat,* I, 134; André Marie Jean Jacques Dupin, *Mémoires de M. Dupin,* 4 vols. (Paris: Plon, 1855–1861), I, 12; A.N., F⁷ 3832, reports of 6 ventôse year XII and 7 prairial year XII.

7. Pasquier, *Memoirs,* I, 184, 216; Lefebvre, *Napoleon,* I, 182. There is much material in memoirs about the Moreau trial. For examples, see Pelet de la Lozère, *Opinions de Napoléon sur divers sujets,* p. 73; Madame de Staël, *Ten Years of Exile* (New York: Saturday Review Press, 1972), pp. 84–87; Madame Récamier, *Souvenirs et correspondance,* 2 vols. (Paris: Calmann-Levy, 1887), I, 103–107.

8. A.N., F⁷ 3832, report of 15 prairial year XII, of 17 prairial year XII, and of 18 prairial year XII; report of 19 prairial year XII.

9. Ibid., report of 15 prairial year XII.

10. Ibid., report of 19 prairial year XII; interrogation of Papet, 16 messidor year XII; report of 25 prairial year XII; report of 13 messidor year XII.

11. Jacques François Lecourbe, *Opinion sur la conspiration de Moreau, Pichegru et autres . . .* (Paris: G. Warrée, 1814), pp. 65–75. The judges were told, for example, that failure to convict Moreau could prevent foreign powers from recognizing the Emperor and that acquittal could touch off civil war.

12. See, for example, Pasquier, *Memoirs,* I, 216; Chaptal, *Mes souvenirs sur Napoléon,* p. 263.

13. Chaptal, *Mes souvenirs sur Napoléon,* pp. 262–263; M. Billecocq,"Notice sur N. F. Bellart," in Bellart, *Oeuvres,* VI, 35; Bonnet, *Discours, plaidoyers et mémoires,* II, 252. Billecocq claims that it was Regnault de Saint-Jean d'Angély who interceded against deportation. An avoué named Pepin was banished from Paris, however, for drafting a petition in favor of Moreau. A.N., AF^IV 1492, bulletin of 17 pluviôse year XIII.

14. Miot de Melito, *Mémoires,* II, 194; Pelet de la Lozère, *Opinions de Napoléon sur divers sujets,* pp. 75–76, 187–189, for his apprehension about the potential influence of barristers on public opinion and his decision to delay reorganizing the Orders of Barristers; on the increased surveillance of the courts, see, for example, A.N., AF^IV 1042, letter of Regnier to Bonaparte, 28 messidor year XIII; A.N., F⁷ 3833, report of 28 germinal year XIII; A.N., F⁷ 3758, 3rd arrondissement, report of January 13, 1808.

15. Berryer, *Souvenirs,* I, 337. In an examination of A.N., B^II 815–822, I was unable to corroborate this. Tulard, however, accepts Berryer's account as reliable, and there is little reason to doubt it, particularly in view of the feelings aroused by the execution of the duc d'Enghien and by the Moreau trial. Tulard, *Bibliographie critique des mémoires,* p. 16.

16. *Correspondance de Napoléon Ier,* IX, 7887; Jean Tulard, ed., *Cambacérès: Lettres inédites à Napoléon, 1802–1814,* 2 vols. (Paris: Klincksieck, 1973), I, 137,

no. 120; I, 138, no 121; Bibliothèque du Sénat, Collection Regnault de Saint-Jean d'Angély, Projet 1996—this collection contains the successive drafts. For a text of the law, see Duvergier, *Collection complète des lois*, XV, 86–90.

17. The provisions of the project differed according to the size of the town; for towns in which there were fewer than twenty barristers practicing, the rules were different. Regnault de Saint-Jean d'Angély's plan for Paris called for a separate tableau at each court, i.e., there would be one at the Appeals Court, one at the Tribunal of First Instance, and one at the Criminal Court.

18. Bibliothèque du Sénat, Collection Regnault de Saint-Jean d'Angély, Projet 1996, undated draft, but c. 2–4 fructidor year XII.

19. Tulard, ed., *Cambacérès: Lettres inédites*, I, 138, no. 121; I, 166, no. 149; I, 194–195, no. 197.

20. Ibid., I, 191, no. 191.

21. *Correspondance de Napoléon Ier*, X, 8094.

22. Tulard, ed., *Cambacérès: Lettres inédites*, I, 194–195, no. 197.

23. The account of this session is based on Alfred Marquiset, *Napoléon stenographié au Conseil d'Etat* (Paris: Champion, 1913), pp. 50–52.

24. Tulard, ed., *Cambacérès: Lettres inédites*, I, 189, no. 187.

25. J. T. Bruguière, *Compte rendu*, p. 4. It was in the year XIII that both the revenues and expenditures of the académie reached their highest level, suggesting that the institution was thriving.

26. J. T. Bruguière, *Académie de Législation: Considérations morales et politiques en faveur de cette institution* (n.p., n.d.), p. 13; A.N., BB^{29} 174, entry of 8 brumaire year XIV; A.N., F^{17} 1982, undated observations under heading "Ecoles de droit" attached to letter of Bruguière to Fourcroy, 28 vendémiaire year XIV.

27. A.N., F^{17} 1982, undated observations under heading "Ecoles de droit" attached to letter of Bruguière to Fourcroy, 28 vendémiaire year XIV. On the decision to offer courses, see *Le Moniteur Universel*, 20 thermidor year XIII and 27 vendémiaire year XIV.

28. Dulaton, *Réponse d'un licencié en droit, à deux écrits de M. Bruguière* (Paris: Fain et Compagnie, n.d.); J. T. Bruguière, *Observations de M. Bruguière sur un libelle diffamatoire publié contre l'Académie et contre lui adressés à MM. les professeurs de l'école de droit de Paris* (Paris: Imprimerie des sciences et des arts, 1807); A.N., F^{17} 1958, undated letter of Fourcroy to minister of justice; Bruguière, *Compte rendu*, p. 4. In the year XIII the receipts and expenditures for the académie were 62,698 francs and 75,173 francs, respectively. In the year XIV the comparable figures were 2,588 francs and 4,424 francs, respectively.

29. *Le Moniteur Universel*, November 9, 1806. The académie succeeded in attracting students from the school of law to follow its course as well. See A.N., BB^{1} 148, dossier Loiret, letter of Gaultier de Rontonnay to minister of justice.

30. *Le Moniteur Universel*, November 9, 1806; 20 thermidor year XIII; 27 vendémiaire year XIV.

31. A.N., F^{17} 1982, letter of Bruguière to Fourcroy, November 25, 1806; Bruguière, *Compte rendu*; Bruguière, *Considérations morales et politiques*, p. 13. For the poem, J. T. Bruguière, *Supplique respecteuse à Sa Majesté l'empereur et roi* (Fontainebleau: Imprimerie de Lequatre, n.d.). As to the closing of the Académie de

Législation, there is no formal record of its demise, but the last indication of its existence is a pamphlet published in 1807. Bruguière, *Observations . . . sur un libelle diffamatoire*.

32. A.N., F^{17} 1982, letter of Brugière to Fourcroy, November 25, 1806. André Marie Jean Jacques Dupin, for example, became a prominent member of the Order and was not only elected president in 1829, but went on to a significant parliamentary career as well. Similarly, Antoine Louis Marie Hennequin also enjoyed a notable legal and parliamentary career. Some of the highlights of the career of Jean Baptiste Teste, another alumnus of the académie, include his election as bâtonnier for 1837–38, his appointment as minister of justice in 1839, and his designation as president of the civil chamber of the Cour de cassation in 1843. Louis Marie de Bellèyme, another product of the académie, concluded his judicial career as a conseiller on the Cour de cassation as well. See J. Balteau, M. Barroux, and M. Prévost, eds., *Dictionnaire de biographie française*, XII, 355–357; Pinard, *Le barreau au XIXe siècle*, I, 316–390 (Dupin); Pinard, *Le barreau au XIXe siècle*, I, 189–247 (Hennequin); *Le Tribunal et la cour de cassation*, pp. 157–158; Pinard, *Le barreau au XIXe siècle*, II, 204–237 (Teste); *Le Tribunal et la cour de cassation*, pp. 287–288; A.N., AJ^{16} 1787, entry of 14 frimaire year XIV; C. A. Sapey, *Notice sur L. M. de Bellèyme* (Paris: Dupont, 1863) (Bellèyme). Pinard, *Le barreau au XIXe siècle*, II, 208, for the assessment of the contribution made to the legal profession by the académie.

33. See Duvergier, *Collection complète des lois*, XV, 86–90, articles 69 and 70; Holtman, *The Napoleonic Revolution*, p. 149. Holtman is incorrect, however, in his assertion that the law schools organized were "merely existing law schools with a new name and organization."

34. B.A.P., Tableau de 1789; *Biographie universelle (Michaud) ancienne et moderne*, X, 355–358; A.N., BB^{29} 174, entry of 8 brumaire year XIV; B.H.V.P., MS. 771, documents 105–106 (Delvincourt); B.A.P., Tableau de 1785; *Biographie universelle (Michaud) ancienne et moderne*, XXXIII, 307–308; A.N., BB^{29} 174, entry of 3 brumaire year XIV; B.H.V.P., MS. 771, documents 105–106 (Pigeau). Pigeau is not listed in the tableau of 1786. A.N., BB^{29} 174, entry of 3 brumaire year XIV; B.H.V.P., MS. 771, documents 105–106 (Caillau).

35. *Biographie universelle (Michaud) ancienne et moderne*, IV, 128; B.H.V.P., MS. 771, documents 105–106 (Berthelot); A.N., BB^5 170, letter of Morand to minister of justice, 28 brumaire year XI; B.H.V.P., MS. 771, documents 105–106 (Morand); *Biographie universelle (Michaud) ancienne et moderne*, XXXIV, 151–152; Collins, *Napoleon and His Parliaments*, p. 35 (Portiez de l'Oise).

36. On the figures for 1806, A.N., F^{17} 1982, letter of Portalis to Fourcroy, November 20, 1806; on those for 1808, A.N., F^{17} 1982, attestation of Reboul, April 18, 1808.

37. Duvergier, *Collection complète des lois*, XV, 273. For an example of how strictly it was enforced, see A.D. Seine, DE^1 carton 3, dossier 36. The law degree of Caillau, a well known barrister and a substitute at the school of law, was certified on October 25, 1808. A.N., BB^1 203, Ministry of Justice, decree of January 23, 1806; A.N., AF^{IV*} 217, no. 1848, for the measures of January 1806.

38. Gaspard Gilbert Delamalle, *Eloge de M. Tronchet . . .* (Paris: Imprimerie de Delance, n.d.); *Correspondance de Napoléon Ier*, XII, 10173; A.N., BB^{30} 524,

dossier 3, letter of Regnier, June 1806 (no date). The letter begins "In execution of Your Majesty's orders . . . " Also, A.N., AF^{IV*} 218, no. 1263.

39. A similar measure was already in force. See A.N., AA 4, letter of Berryer to minister of justice, 21 ventôse year XIII, and letter of Maret to minister of justice, 5 germinal year XIII.

40. A.N., BB^{30} 524, dossier 3, undated draft for an imperial decree; Bibliothèque du Sénat, Collection de Regnault de Saint-Jean d'Angély, Projet 1996, of June 27, 1806.

41. A.N., BB^{30} 524, dossier 3, letter of Regnier, June 1806 (no date).

42. Ibid.

43. In the July 11 draft the term *ordre* replaced *collège*.

44. The oath in article 31 of the law of 22 ventôse year XII centered on their professional conduct inside the courtroom. In the July 29 draft the oath required them to swear obedience to the constitutions of the Empire and fidelity to the Emperor and to accept only worthy cases. Thibaudeau said that the oath was yet another manifestation of Bonaparte's antipathy for barristers. A. C. Thibaudeau, *Le Consulat et l'empire,* 10 vols. (Paris: Jules Renouard, 1834–1835), III, 487–488.

45. More significant in the July 29 project was the control over those inscribed at a Tribunal of First Instance. They could plead only in the town of their residence. Bibliothèque du Sénat, Collection Regnault de Saint-Jean d'Angély, Projet 1996, of July 29, 1806.

46. Bibliothèque du Sénat, Collection Regnault de Saint-Jean d'Angély, Projet 1996, of August 4, 1806.

47. A.N., AF^{IV} 507, dossier 3920.

48. A.N., AA 4, Plaintes portées contre le Sr. Berryer père . . . , letter of procureur impérial of Tribunal of First Instance of Compiègne to minister of justice, March 2, 1807; letter of president of Tribunal of First Instance at Compiègne to minister of justice, March 8, 1807.

49. A.N., AA 2, dossier 6, document 35.

50. Ibid., documents 36–39.

51. A.N., F^7 3759, bulletins of April 26 and April 28, 1808; A.N., F^7 6604, dossier 4333.

52. See, for example, A.N., AF^{IV} 1501, bulletin of November 15–16, 1807, concerning Lepy, who was involved in a scheme to defraud veterans of military pensions.

53. Gabriel Vauthier,"L'épuration de la magistrature en 1808," *Revue des Etudes Napoléoniennes* 15 (1919): 218–223. The article, however, is too uncritical of the purge, ignoring, for example, Bonaparte's use of it to rid himself of political enemies. On the 1807 purge, see A.N., CC 50–58; A.N., AF^{IV} 1231.

54. A.N., AF^{IV} 1287, dossier 2, no. 3, Report on the indemnity owed to suppressed avoués, June 28, 1808. The figure for 1808 is based on a retrospective reading of the tableau of 1811. B.A.P., Tableau de 1811.

55. Dupin, *Profession d'avocat,* I, 140–142.

56. Ibid.; Bellart, *Eloge de M. Ferey.* The calculated nature of the appeal can be seen in the fact that Cambacérès became deeply religious under the Empire. See Pasquier, *Memoirs,* I, 254.

57. Bibliothèque du Sénat, Collection Regnault de Saint-Jean d'Angély, Pro-

jet 1996, of March 19, 1810. See Bibliothèque de l'Assemblée Nationale, Collection Locré, Projet 1996, of March 19, 1810, for the indication that discussion occurred on June 5, 1810.

58. Bibliothèque du Sénat, Collection Regnault de Saint-Jean d'Angély, Projet 1996, of June 29, 1810.

59. Jean Bourdon, ed., *Napoléon au Conseil d'Etat* (Paris: Berger-Levrault, 1963), pp. 97–103.

60. Bibliothèque du Sénat, Collection Regnault de Saint-Jean d'Angély, Projet 1996, of September 4, 1810; A.N., AF^{IV} 507, dossier 3920. The provision threatening criminal action became article 37 when the law was promulgated.

61. Ibid. Since Bonaparte had already stated that the president would be chosen rather than elected, the clause presumably sought to elect a bâtonnier if the incumbent died in office. A complete text of the final decree is in Duvergier, *Collection complète des lois*, XVII, 236–240.

62. Dupin, *Profession d'avocat*, I, 132–133, 620–677; Berryer, *Souvenirs*, I, 338, 340–341.

63. A.N., AA 2, dossier 1, documents 42–49, on which the following account is based.

64. Ibid., document 46. Since virtually all of the barristers had stopped practicing during the Terror, this was evidently not considered as an interruption of practice.

65. Ibid.

66. Ibid., documents 47–49.

67. B.A.P., Tableau de 1811. Those at the Ministry of Justice included Emmanuel Brosselard, Jean Baptiste Dalmassy, Pardoux Bordas, Louis André Rieff, Jean Baptiste Charles Collenel, François Edme Champion, Pierre Jean Baptiste Broyart, Benoît Michel Decomberousse, Jean Marie Emmanuel, François Le Graverend, Bernard Jean Maurice Duport, Joseph Elzéar Bernardi, and Nicolas Joseph Romer. A.N., BB^{29} 273; A.N., BB^{30} 516, dossier 1, documents 57 and 76; *Almanach Impérial 1811*, pp. 191–194.

The men at the school of law were Claude Etienne Delvincourt, Thomas Pascal Boulage, Jean François Berthelot, François Morand, Louis Barnabe Joseph Cotelle, Jean Marie Pardessus, and Eustache Nicolas Pigeau. *Almanach Impérial 1811*, pp. 836–837.

Those who had retired from the judiciary included Jean François Dufour, who became the doyen of the Order, Pierre Augustin Hemery, Louis Joseph Landry, Pierre Fidèle Sabarot, and Charles François Bidault.

68. A.N., F^{1}c III Haute Saône 1, Procès-verbal de l'Assemblée électorale pour la formation du département, May 10, 1790; A.N., F^{1}c III Haute Saône 2, Elections de l'an XII, justices de paix; A.N., AF^{IV} 1437, Département de la Haute Saône, nouvelle liste des six cent plus imposés, December 20, 1810 (Ferey); A.N., F^{1}c III Marne 1, Elections de l'an XI, Liste des membres qui composent le collège électoral de l'arrondissement communal de Reims; *Almanach Impérial 1811*, p. 526.

69. The figure of seventeen is known only because Fournel provides it along with the names of the individuals. Fournel, *Histoire des avocats au Parlement*, I, xxxviii. Even this number is deceptive, however, for not all of the seventeen were

young probationary members of the Order in 1789. Some — Bourrée de Corberon, Falconnet, Roi, and Pigeau, for example — were older men who had formerly been associated with the Order or the Parlement. They were placed in the category of probationary barristers to give them an advantage over men not formerly associated with the Order who subsequently came to Paris to practice. On Gabaille, see A.N., BB⁵ 168, undated letter of Gabaille to minister of justice; *Almanach Impérial 1811*, p. 527. For other examples, A.N., BB⁵ 166, letter of president of Criminal Court of the Sarthe to minister of justice, November 30, 1809, concerning Cothereau; A.N., BB⁵ 169, undated letter of Du Rouzeau to minister of justice.

70. A.N., BB⁵ 173, letter of Nau to minister of justice, December 30, 1807 (Nau); A.N., BB⁵ 173, letter of Ratel to minister of justice, August 26, 1808 (Ratel); A.N., BB⁵ 173, letter of Picasse to minister of justice, July 27, 1808 (Picasse); A.N., BB⁵ 173, letter of Morillon to minister of justice, August 6, 1808 (Morillon); A.N., BB⁵ 176, letter of Le Cointre to minister of justice, October 5, 1810 (Le Cointre); A.N., BB⁵ 177, letter of Hardi de Juine to minister of justice, September 15, 1810 (Hardi de Juine); A.N., D^III 360, dossier Aubert-Dubourg (Aubert Dubourg).

71. A.N., BB⁵ 177, letter of Bourrée de Corberon to minister of justice, July 12, 1810.

72. A.N., BB¹ 159, dossier Coffinières. The basis for his petition centered on the fact that Carpentier did not have the authority to grant degrees. It was necessary to petition to have private study recognized. See also A.N., BB²⁹ 174, entry of 3 brumaire year XIV (Coffinières); A.N., BB¹ 179, dossier Le Maire (Le Maire); A.N., BB¹ 164, dossier Derché; A.N., BB²⁹ 174, entry of June 9, 1806 (Derché). The Council of Prizes had been one of the jurisdictions in which major abuses had been perpetrated by counselors.

73. A.N., AA 2, dossier 1, document 47.

74. Pasquier, *Memoirs*, II, 100–101, and Berryer, *Souvenirs*, I, 349–354, offer different perspectives on the matter, but both condemn it.

75. B.H.V.P., MS. 517, document 14; also Bellart, *Oeuvres*, IV, 319–325, where it is reprinted. See also Pasquier, *Memoirs*, II, 287–288. During the Hundred Days Bellart was excluded from the amnesty Bonaparte offered to officials serving Louis XVIII. Jean Tulard, *Nouvelle histoire de Paris: Le Consulat et l'Empire* (Paris: Hachette, 1970), p. 388. Similarly, on April 1, 1814, as the allied armies approached Paris, another member of the Order, Charles François Quequet, composed and sent to the czar of Russia and the king of Prussia a factum urging them to place Louis XVIII on the throne. *Biographie universelle (Michaud) ancienne et moderne*, XXXIV, 622–623.

76. Dupin, *Profession d'avocat*, I, 134; Berryer, *Souvenirs*, I, 360–361; *Le Moniteur Universel*, May 19, 1814. On the views of members of the Order about the monarchy, see also Joseph Bernardi, *Observations sur l'ancienne constitution française et sur les lois et les codes du gouvernement révolutionnaire, par un ancien jurisconsulte* (Paris: Michaud frères, 1814); Ambroise Falconnet, *Le doigt de Dieu* (Paris: Gueffier, 1815); Charles Montigny, *De la bonté de la maison de Bourbon, et de ses effets* (Paris: Patris, 1815); Charles Guibert, *Observations sur la charte constitutionelle, donnée par S. M. Louis XVIII, le 4 juin 1814* (Paris: Testu, 1815); Ambroise Rendu,

Un garde national à ses concitoyens (Paris: Fain, 1815); Jean Baptiste Louis Billecocq, *Quelques considérations sur les tyrannies diverses qui ont précédé la Restauration, sur le gouvernement royal, et sur la dernière tyrannie impériale* (Paris: Nicolle, 1815); Alexandre Emmanuel François Janson de Sailly, *Le retour du roi* (n.p., n.d.). To the extent that they bothered to participate, barristers and men with legal training comprised a substantial bloc of the negative vote in Paris in the plebiscite held during the Hundred Days. Frédéric Bluche, *Le plébiscite des cent-jours* (Geneva: Librairie Droz, 1974), pp. 91–93. I disagree, however, with his assertion that the negative vote was largely a technical vote against the constitution more than a vote against the Emperor, particularly after the incident involving the mayor of Antwerp.

77. Berryer, *Souvenirs*, I, 362, 364–366. Whether it was for the same reasons or not, royalism was a feature of barristers in other former parlementary towns as well. See Alan Forrest, *Society and Politics in Revolutionary Bordeaux* (Oxford: Clarendon Press, 1975), pp. 251–252; David Higgs, *Ultraroyalism in Toulouse from its Origins to 1830* (Baltimore: Johns Hopkins University Press, 1973), pp. 163–165. As late as 1886 the Chamber of Deputies gave serious consideration to abolishing the Order of Barristers because of the royalist sympathies of many of its members. See A.N., BB^{30} 1470, dossier 140.

78. A.N., F^{15} 1868, Seine, Legs de 20,000^s fait à l'Ordre des Avocats par M. Trumeau; A.N., F^{15} 1940, letter of De Mailly, Podensan, and others to minister of justice, August 7, 1813.

79. Donald R. Kelley, *Historians and the Law in Postrevolutionary France* (Princeton: Princeton University Press, 1984).

Conclusion

1. The following list, necessarily selective, is illustrative. George V. Taylor, "Types of Capitalism in Eighteenth-Century France," *English Historical Review* 79 (July 1964): 478–497, and "Noncapitalist Wealth and the Origins of the French Revolution," *American Historical Review* 72 (January 1967): 469–496; Lucas, "Nobles, Bourgeois and the Origins of the French Revolution"; François Furet, "Le catéchisme révolutionnaire," *Annales: Economies, Sociétés, Civilisations* 26 (March–April 1971): 255–289; Elizabeth L. Eisenstein, "Who Intervened in 1788? A Commentary on *The Coming of the French Revolution*," *American Historical Review* 71 (October 1965): 77–103; Jeffry Kaplow, "On 'Who Intervened in 1788,'" *American Historical Review* 72 (January 1967): 497–502; Gerald J. Cavanaugh, "The Present State of Revolutionary Historiography: Alfred Cobban and Beyond," *French Historical Studies* 7 (Fall 1972): 587–606; Albert Soboul, *The French Revolution 1787–1799*, trans. Alan Forrest and Colin Jones (New York: Random House, 1974); Claude Mazauriac, *Sur la Révolution française: Contributions à l'histoire de la Révolution bourgeoise* (Paris: Editions Sociale, 1970); J. F. Bosher, *French Finances, 1770–1795: From Business to Bureaucracy* (Cambridge: Cambridge University Press, 1970).

2. Taylor, "Noncapitalist Wealth and the Origins of the French Revolution,"

p. 490, for the characterization of the debate. Some examples of works that explored political and intellectual currents include Denis Richet, "Autour des origines idéologiques lointaines de la Révolution française: Elites et despotisme," *Annales: Economies, Sociétés, Civilisations* 24 (January–February 1969): 1–23, and Richet, *La France moderne: L'esprit des institutions* (Paris: Flammarion, 1973); Guy Chaussinand-Nogaret, *La noblesse au XVIIIe siècle: De la féodalité aux lumières* (Paris: Hachette, 1976); Chaussinand-Nogaret, *Une histoire des Elites, 1700–1848* (Paris: Mouton, 1975); Norman Hampson, *The French Revolution: A Concise History* (London: Thames and Hudson, 1975); William Doyle, *Origins of the French Revolution* (Oxford: Oxford University Press, 1980); and François Furet, *Interpreting the French Revolution* (Cambridge: Cambridge University Press, 1981), which contains material not included in the original *Penser la Révolution française* (Paris: Gallimard, 1978).

3. For one of the more recent and explicit restatements of this thesis, see Albert Soboul, *A Short History of the French Revolution, 1789–1799*, trans. Geoffrey Symcox (Berkeley: University of California Press, 1977).

4. Berlanstein, *The Barristers of Toulouse*, pp. 166–170.

5. Theda Skocpol, *States and Social Revolutions: A Comparative Analysis of France, Russia and China* (Cambridge: Cambridge University Press, 1979); Sewell, *Work and Revolution in France;* Higonnet, *Class, Ideology, and the Rights of Nobles during the French Revolution;* and Hunt, *Politics, Culture, and Class in the French Revolution*. For an indication of how unsettled this interpretation is, however, see William H. Sewell, Jr., "Ideologies and Social Revolutions: Reflections on the French Case," *Journal of Modern History* 57 (March 1985): 57–85, and Theda Skocpol, "Cultural Idioms and Political Ideologies in the Revolutionary Reconstruction of State Power: A Rejoinder to Sewell," *Journal of Modern History* 57 (March 1985): 86–96, as well as the criticism of Skocpol in Hunt, *Politics, Culture, and Class in the French Revolution*, pp. 209–211.

6. Hubert Méthivier, *L'Ancien régime*, 8th ed. (Paris: Presses Universitaires de France, 1983), p. 4.

7. *Procès-verbal des séances de la chambre de l'ordre de la noblesse aux Etats-Généraux, tenues à Versailles en mil sept cent quatre-vingt neuf* (Paris: Imprimerie Nationale, 1792), p. 68. See also, Beatrice F. Hyslop, *French Nationalism in 1789 according to the General Cahiers*, reprint ed. (New York: Octagon Books, 1968), pp. 84–86. Despite Hyslop's assertion, the clergy was not prepared to yield its financial privileges until late June. See M. Vallet, *Récit des principaux faits qui se sont passés dans la Salle de l'Ordre du Clergé, depuis le commencement des Etats-Généraux, le 4 mai 1789, jusqu'à la réunion des trois Ordres dans la Salle commune de l'Assemblée Nationale* (Paris: Imprimerie Nationale, 1790), p. 113.

8. On art, see the complete text of the decree of August 21, 1791, concerning the exposition of 1791 at the Louvre in *Collection générale des décrets rendus par l'Assemblée nationale*, 22 vols. (Paris: Baudouin, 1789–1791), XVII, 322–323; for theater, Marvin Carlson, *The Theater of the French Revolution* (Ithaca: Cornell University Press, 1966), pp. 74–76; on science, Roger Hahn, *The Anatomy of a Scientific Institution: The Paris Academy of Sciences, 1666–1803* (Berkeley: University of California Press, 1971), pp. 237–240.

9. Taylor, "Revolutionary and Nonrevolutionary Content in the *Cahiers* of 1789: An Interim Report," pp. 501–502.

10. On religious factors, McManners, *The French Revolution and the Church*, p. 38. Nevertheless, the vote of February 23, 1790, designating *curés* as the agents for the dissemination of new laws and decrees, illustrates the way in which the National Assembly, under the impulse of the sublimity of the nation, aspired to make the Church an integral part of the state. Timothy Tackett, *Priest and Parish in Eighteenth-Century France: A Social and Political Study of the Curés in a Diocese of Dauphiné, 1750–1791* (Princeton: Princeton University Press, 1977), p. 277; on the nonreligious factors, see Paul Bois, *Paysans de l'Ouest* (Le Mans: Mouton, 1960); Marcel Faucheux, *L'insurrection vendéene de 1793: Aspects économiques et sociaux* (Paris: Imprimerie Nationale, 1964); Charles Tilly, *The Vendée* (Cambridge, Mass.: Harvard University Press, 1964); T. J. A. Le Goff and D. M. G. Sutherland, "The Revolution and the Rural Community in Eighteenth-Century Brittany," *Past and Present* 62 (February 1974): 96–119; T. J. A. Le Goff, *Vannes and Its Region: A Study of Town and Country in Eighteenth-Century France* (Oxford: Clarendon Press, 1981); Donald Sutherland, *The Chouans: The Social Origins of Popular Counter-Revolution in Upper Brittany, 1770–1796* (Oxford: Clarendon Press, 1982); on the factors that contributed to the revolt in Bordeaux, Forrest, *Politics and Society in Revolutionary Bordeaux*, p. 260.

11. A point addressed by Sydenham, *The First French Republic*, pp. 299–300. He does not stress strongly enough, however, that all of the new corporate bodies owed their existence to Bonaparte. In contrast to the system under the Old Regime, they supplemented his power—this was the reason for their existence—and it is this aspect that is more important than their conservatism.

12. Montigny, *De la bonté de la maison de Bourbon, et de ses effets.*

13. Taillandier, *Lettres à mon fils*, p. 251.

Bibliography

Primary Sources, Unpublished

(1) Archives Nationales

Series B: Elections et votes.
Series C: Assemblées Nationales.
Series D: Missions des réprésentants du peuple et Comités des assemblées.
Series F: Versements des ministères et des administrations qui en dépendent.
    F^1: Ministère de l'Intérieur. Administration générale.
        F^1a: Objets généraux.
        F^1b: Personnel administratif.
        F^1c III: Esprit public et élections.
        F^7: Police générale.
        F^{15}: Hospices et secours.
        F^{17}: Instruction publique.
Series M: Ordres militaires et hospitaliers, Universités et collèges, Titres nobiliaires. Mélanges.
Series T: Papiers privés tombés dans le domaine public.
Series W: Juridictions extraordinaires.
Series X: Parlement de Paris.
Series Z: Juridictions spéciales et ordinaires.
Series AA: Collections de lettres et pièces diverses.
Series AD: Archives imprimées.
Series AF: Archives du pouvoir exécutif 1789–1815.
Series AJ: Fonds divers remis aux Archives Nationales.
Series AP: Papiers privées.
Series BB: Versements du ministère de la Justice.
    BB^1: Personnel.
    BB^2: Justice. Affaires civiles.
    BB^4: Justice. Comptabilité.
    BB^5: Organisation judiciaire.
    BB^6: Cours et tribunaux.
    BB^{29}: Enregistrement de la correspondance du ministère de la Justice.
    BB^{30}: Versements de 1904, 1905, 1908, 1929, 1933, 1936, 1941, 1943–1944.
Series CC: Sénat, Chambre et Cour des Pairs.
Series MM: Registres et rouleaux: Archives de la Faculté de Droit de Paris.

(2) Archives de Paris et de l'Ancien Département de la Seine

1 AZ 4: Parlement de Paris.
1 AZ 146: Commune provisoire.
3 AZ 247: Papiers Godard.
4 AZ 842: Papiers Loizerolles.
DE^1 3, dossier 36: Papiers Caillau.
DE^1 18, dossier 220: Papiers Target.
DQ^{10} 1434: Domaines. (Bibliothèque des avocats.)

(3) Bibliothèque des Avocats à la Cour d'Appel (Paris)

Tableau des avocats au Parlement mis au greffe de la Cour, par Me Claude-Nicolas Sanson, ancien avocat, bâtonnier en 1786, et 1787, et encore bâtonnier en 1788 et 1789, à cause du décès de Me Jean-Baptiste Gerbier de la Massilaye, le 8 mai 1789.

Tableau des avocats à la Cour impériale de Paris, arrêté par Monsieur le Procureur-Général, assistés de Mes Lesparat, Delavigne, Delacroix-Frainville, Delamalle, Gicquel et Popelin, Avocats, conformément au décret de Sa Majesté, du 14 décembre 1810: Approuvé par S. Ex. le Grand-Juge Ministre de la Justice, le 14 mars 1811.

(4) Bibliothèque du Sénat

Conseil d'Etat. Collection Regnault de Saint-Jean d'Angély. Projets de décrets, de lois, de rapports, etc. de l'an X à 1815.
Projet 1996.

(5) Bibliothèque Historique de la Ville de Paris; Manuscripts, Revolution and Empire

763: Justice, tribunaux, prisons.
771: Instruction publique.
772: Arts. Lettres. Sciences. Presse. Clubs.
774–777: Biographie.
812–814: Députés de Paris à l'Assemblée nationale et l'Assemblée législative.

(6) Bibliothèque Municipale d'Orléans; Manuscripts

1421–1423: Mémoires de Jean Charles Pierre Le Noir, lieutenant-général de police de la ville de Paris sous le regne de Louis XVI, écrits dans les années 1790 et suivantes.

(7) Bibliothèque Nationale; Manuscripts

Fonds Joly de Fleury
   1105–1106: Affaires de l'année 1790.
   2133: Avocats.
   2145–2147: Avocats; pièces concernant les avocats de Paris au XVIIIe siècle.
   2432: Tableau des avocats à Paris et en province.
Fonds Manuscrits français
   10955–10957: Recueil des conférences tenues en 1712 et 1713 par M^{rs} les avocats au Parlement de Paris.

Fonds Nouvelles acquisitions françaises
1778: Journal de l'Assemblée nationale, 1 juillet-31 décembre 1790.
2476-2477: Registre des conférences de doctrine tenues en la bibliothèque de M^rs les avocats au Parlement, 1710-1719.
2499: Conférences sur différentes matières de droit tenues dans la Bibliothèque des avocats du Parlement de Paris, 25 février 1711-15 décembre 1714.
2707: Section du Théâtre-François.
4918-4944: Recueil de consultations juridiques relatives à l'histoire ecclesiastique de différentes provinces de France, données par A. G. Camus, avocat du clergé, 1767-1786.
5898-5900: Procès-verbaux des séances du Tribunat, 1803-1804.
6622-6626: Extraits des minutes du greffe du Tribunal criminel de Paris (1800-1801).
22099-22100: Papiers de Antoine Louis Marie Hennequin.
23067-23068: Papiers personnels et correspondance du conventionnel A. G. Camus.

Primary Sources, Published

(1) Published Collections of Documents, Laws

Aulard, Alphonse, ed. *La société des Jacobins*. 6 vols. Paris: Librairie Jouaust, 1889-1897.
Bourdon, Jean, ed. *Napoléon au Conseil d'Etat*. Paris: Berger-Levrault, 1963.
Brette, Armand, ed. *Recueil de documents rélatifs à la convocation des Etats-Généraux de 1789*. 4 vols. Paris: Imprimerie Nationale, 1894-1915.
Charavay, Etienne, ed. *L'assemblée électorale de Paris*. 3 vols. Paris: Jouaust et Noblet, 1890-1905.
Chassin, Charles Louis, ed. *Les élections et les cahiers de Paris en 1789*. 4 vols. Paris: Jouaust et Sigaux, 1888-1889.
Correspondance de Napoléon Ier. 32 vols. Paris: Imprimerie Impériale, 1858-1870.
Douarche, Aristide, ed. *Les tribunaux civils de Paris pendant la Révolution*. 2 vols. Paris: Plon, 1821-1833.
Duvergier, J. B., ed. *Collection complète des lois, décrets, ordonnances, règlemens, avis du conseil d'état . . .* 108 vols. Paris: Recueil Sirey, 1788/1790-1908.
Isambert, F. A., ed. *Recueil général des anciennes lois françaises*. 29 vols. Paris: Plon, 1821-1833.
Lacroix, Sigismond, ed. *Actes de la commune de Paris pendant la Révolution*. 1st ser. 7 vols. Paris: L. Cerf, 1894-1898.
——— *Actes de la commune de Paris pendant la Révolution*. 2nd ser. 8 vols. Paris: L. Cerf, 1900-1909.
Marquiset, Alfred. *Napoléon stenographié au Conseil d'Etat*. Paris: Champion, 1913.
Mavidal, Jérôme, and Emile Laurent, eds. *Archives parlementaires de 1787 à 1860: Recueil complet des débats législatifs et politiques chambres françaises*. 1st ser. (1787-1799). 82 vols. 2nd ser. (1800-1860). 127 vols. Paris: Librairie administrative de Paul Dupont, 1862-1913.
Procès-verbal de l'Assemblée nationale. Paris: Baudouin, 1789-1791.
Tulard, Jean, ed. *Cambacérès: Lettres inédites à Napoléon, 1802-1814*. 2 vols. Paris: Klincksieck, 1973.

(2) Memoirs or Collected Works (asterisk denotes a member of the Order, either 1789 or 1811)

Bachaumont, Louis Petit de. *Mémoires secrets pour servir à l'histoire de la république des lettres en France, depuis MDCCLXII jusqu'à nos jours; ou, journal d'un observateur* . . . 36 vols. London: J. Adamsohn, 1780–1789.
Bailly, Jean Sylvain. *Mémoires de Bailly.* 3 vols. Paris: Baudouin frères, 1821–1822.
*Bellart, Nicolas François. *Oeuvres de N. F. Bellart.* 6 vols. Paris: Brière, 1827.
*Berryer, Pierre Nicolas. *Souvenirs de M. Berryer.* 2 vols. Paris: Ambroise Dupont, 1839.
*Billecocq, Jean Baptiste. *En prison sous la terreur: Souvenirs de J. B. Billecocq.* Introduction, with commentary and annotations, by Nicole Felkay and Hervé Favier. Paris: Société des Etudes Robespierrists, 1981.
Bonnet, Jules. *Mes souvenirs au barreau depuis 1804.* Paris: A. Durand, 1864.
*Bonnet, Louis Ferdinand. *Discours, plaidoyers et mémoires de M. L. F. Bonnet.* 2 vols. Paris: B. Warée, 1839.
Chaptal, Jean Antoine. *Mes souvenirs sur Napoléon, par le comte Chaptal, publiés par son arrière petit-fils.* Paris: Plon, 1893.
*Couture, Louis Jean Baptiste Mathurin. *Mon portefeuille.* Paris: E. Proux, 1840.
——— *Quelques-uns de mes souvenirs.* Saint Omer: Fleury-Lemaire, 1857.
*Delamalle, Gaspard Gilbert. *Plaidoyers choisis et oeuvres diverses de M. Delamalle.* 4 vols. Paris: J. Renouard, 1827.
Desmarest, Pierre Marie. *Témoignages historiques.* Paris: Alphonse Levavasseur, 1833.
*Dupin, André Marie Jean Jacques. *Profession d'avocat.* 2 vols. Paris: Alex-Gobelet, 1832.
———*Mémoires de M. Dupin.* 4 vols. Paris: Plon, 1855–1861.
———*Discours et rapports.* Paris: Plon, 1862.
*Duveyrier, Honoré Marie Nicolas. *Anecdotes historiques.* Paris: A. Picard, 1907.
*Fournel, Jean François. *Histoire des avocats au Parlement et du barreau de Paris depuis S. Louis jusqu'au 15 octobre 1790.* 2 vols. Paris: Chez Maradan, 1813.
———*Histoire du barreau de Paris dans le cours de la Révolution.* Paris: Chez Maradan, 1816.
*Hua, Eustache Antoine. *Mémoires d'un avocat au Parlement de Paris.* Poitiers: Henri Oudin, 1871.
Lanjuinais, Jean Denis. *Oeuvres de J. D. Lanjuinais.* 4 vols. Paris: Dondey-Dupré, 1832.
Lavaux, Christophe. *Les campagnes d'un avocat, ou anecdotes pour servir à l'histoire de la Révolution.* Paris: Panckoucke, 1815.
Lecourbe, Jacques François. *Opinion sur la conspiration de Moreau, Pichegru et autres* . . . Paris: G. Warrée, 1814.
Mémoires d'un vieil avocat. Paris: Hippolyte Souverain, 1847.
Miot de Melito, André François. *Mémoires du comte Miot de Melito, ancien ministre, ambassadeur, conseiller d'état et membre de l'Institut* . . . 3 vols. Paris: M. Levy, 1873–1874.
Pasquier, Etienne Denis. *A History of My Time.* 3 vols. New York: C. Scribner's Sons, 1893–1894.
Pelet de la Lozère, Privat Joseph Claramond. *Opinions de Napoléon sur divers sujets de politque et d'administration* . . . Paris: Firmin-Didot, 1833.

Roederer, Pierre Louis. *Autour de Bonaparte: Journal du comte P. L. Roederer, ministre et conseiller d'état.* Paris: Daragon, 1909.
Staël-Holstein, Anne Louise Germain Necker. *Ten Years of Exile.* New York: Saturday Review Press, 1972.
*Taillandier, Louis Auguste. *Lettres à mon fils sur les causes, la marche et les effets de la Révolution française.* Paris: Demonville, 1820.
Thibaudeau, Antoine Claire. *Mémoires sur la Convention et le Directoire.* 2 vols. Paris: Baudouin frères, 1824.
———*Le Consulat et l'empire.* 10 vols. Paris: Jules Renouard, 1834–1835.

(3) Other Contemporary Sources

Almanach des Tribunaux du Département de Paris . . . Paris: Vacques, n.d.
Almanach Royal (1774–1791); *Almanach National de France* (1792–1804); *Almanach Impérial* (1805–1813).
Annales de Législation et de Jurisprudence. 4 vols. Paris: Imprimerie de l'Université de Jurisprudence, years XI–XII.
*Bernardi, Joseph. *Observations sur l'ancienne constitution française et sur les lois et les codes du gouvernement révolutionnaire, par un ancien jurisconsulte.* Paris: Michaud frères, 1814.
*Billecocq, Jean Baptiste Louis. *Quelques considérations sur les tyrannies diverses qui ont précédé la Restauration, sur le gouvernement royal, et sur la dernière tyrannie impériale.* Paris: H. Nicolle, 1815.
*Boucher d'Argis, Gaspard Antoine. *Règles pour former un avocat.* Paris: Durand, 1778.
Bulletin de l'Académie de Législation. Paris: Patris, n.d.
*Camus, Armand Gaston. *Lettres sur la profession d'avocat* . . . Paris: J. Hérissant, 1772.
*Camus, Armand Gaston, and Jean Baptiste Bayard, eds. *Collection de décisions nouvelles, et de notions relatives à la jurisprudence, donnée par M. Denisart, mise dans un nouvel ordre . . . et augmentée par MM. Camus et Bayard.* 8th ed. 14 vols. Paris: Desaint, 1783–1807.
*Chauveau, Louis René. *Sur l'organisation du pouvoir judiciaire.* Paris: Clousier, 1789.
*Delacroix, Jacques Vincent. *Le spectateur français pendant le gouvernement révolutionnaire.* Paris: Buisson, year III.
Denisart, J. B. *Collection de décisions nouvelles et des notions relatives à la jurisprudence actuelle.* 4 vols. Paris: Desaint, 1771.
Duveyrier, Honoré Marie Nicolas, and Jean Sylvain Bailly, eds. *Procès-verbal des séances et délibérations de l'Assembleé générale des électeurs de Paris, réunis à l'Hôtel de Ville le 14 juillet 1789.* 3 vols. Paris: Baudouin, 1790.
Etat des travaux de l'Académie de Législation. N.p., n.d.
Exposé abrégé de la constitution de l'ordre des avocats au Parlement de Paris. Geneva, 1782.
Ferrières, Charles Elie, marquis de. *Correspondance inédite (1789, 1790, 1791) publiée et annotée par Henri Carré.* Paris: A. Colin, 1932.
*Garran de Coulon, Jean Philippe. *J. Ph. Garran, député du Loiret à la Convention Nationale, sur le jugement de Louis XVI.* Paris: Imprimerie du Cercle Sociale, 1793.
Gautier, P. N. *Dictionnaire de la Constitution et du gouvernement français.* Paris: Guillaume, 1791.

Gazette des Nouveaux Tribunaux. 16 vols. Paris: Desaint, 1791 – year VII.
Gazette Nationale, ou le Moniteur Universel. 1789 – 1815.
Idées d'un citoyen de Paris. N.p., 1789.
Institut de Jurisprudence et d'Économie Politique. N.p., n.d.
Journal de Jurisprudence. 11 vols. Paris: Patris, n.d.
Journal des Tribunaux. 5 vols. Paris: Gueffier, 1791 – 1792.
Lefebvre de Fabrimenil, Louis François Aubin. *Mémorial du Conseil de Jurisprudence.* 3 vols. Paris: Au Conseil de Jurisprudence, 1811.
Le Maître (pseudonym). *Discours de M. Lemaître, doyen des avocats et procureurs au Parlement de Paris, et doyen de tous les officiers en charge du Royaume.* N.p., n.d.
——— *Les adieux du bon homme Le Maître, à Messieurs les avocats de Paris, députés à l'Assemblée, dite Nationale.* N.p., n.d.
——— *Reveil du bon homme Le Maître à Messieurs les Avocats de Paris, députés à l'Assemblée Nationale.* N.p., n.d.
Lerasle, N., ed. *Encyclopédie méthodique: Jurisprudence.* 10 vols. Paris: Panckoucke, 1782 – 1789.
Lycée de Jurisprudence, et bureau de consultation, conciliation et de défense générale près le tribunal de cassation et les tribunaux civils, criminels et de commerce de la république . . . Paris: Imprimerie du Lycée de Jurisprudence, n.d.
Mercier, Louis Sébastien. *Le nouveau Paris.* 6 vols. Paris: Fuchs, year VII.
——— *Tableau de Paris.* 12 vols. Amsterdam, 1783 – 1788.
*Montigny, Charles Claude. *De la bonté de la maison de Bourbon, et de ses effets.* Paris: Patris, 1815.
*Pichois, Michel Germain. *Défense de Louis XVI.* 2 vols. Paris: Dufresne, 1792 – 1793.
Le Point du Jour, ou Résultat de ce qui s'est passé la veille à l'Assemblée Nationale (1789 – 1791).
Projet de règlement du comité des défenseurs officieux des amis de la liberté et de l'égalité, séant aux Jacobins. Paris: Imprimerie des 86 départements, n.d.
Pujoulx, Jean Baptiste. *Paris à la fin du XVIIIe siècle.* Paris: Brigite Mathé, 1801.
Rabaut de Saint-Etienne, Jean Paul. *Précis de l'histoire de la Révolution française.* Paris: Servier, 1827.
Recueil de pièces concernant l'Association de bienfaisance judiciaire fondée en 1787. Paris: Clousier, 1789.
Réplique d'un citoyen de Paris à la réponse d'un avocat. N.p., n.d.
Réponse d'un avocat à l'écrit intitulé les Idées d'un citoyen de Paris. N.p., n.d.
Suite des idées d'un citoyen de Paris. N.p., n.d.
Talon, Antoine Omer. *Idées sur l'organisation du pouvoir judiciaire dans Paris.* Paris: Cailleau, 1790.

Secondary Sources

Allain, Ernest. *L'oeuvre scolaire de la Révolution, 1789 – 1802.* Paris: Firmin-Didot, 1891.
Allison, John M. S. *Lamoignon de Malesherbes: Defender and Reformer of the French Monarchy.* New Haven: Yale University Press, 1938.
Andrews, Richard. "The Justices of the Peace of Revolutionary Paris, September

1792 – November 1794 (Frimaire an III)." *Past and Present* 52 (August 1971): 56 – 105.
Aubin, Raoul. *L'organisation judiciaire d'après les cahiers de 1789*. Paris: Jouve, 1928.
Bar, Carl Ludwig. *A History of Continental Criminal Law*. Boston: Little, Brown and Co., 1916.
Barnard, H. C. *Education and the French Revolution*. Cambridge: Cambridge University Press, 1969.
Beck, Thomas D. *French Legislators, 1800 – 1834: A Study in Quantitative History*. Berkeley: University of California Press, 1974.
Behrens, C.B.A. "Nobles, Privileges and Taxes at the End of the Ancien Régime." *Economic History Review*. 2nd ser., no. 3, 15 (1963): 451 – 475.
——— *The Ancien Régime*. London: Thames and Hudson, 1967.
Belin, Jean Paul. *Le commerce des livres prohibés à Paris de 1750 à 1789*. Paris: Belin frères, 1913.
Bergeron, Louis. *L'épisode napoléonien: Aspects intérieures 1799 – 1815*. Paris: Editions du Seuil, 1972.
Berlanstein, Lenard. *The Barristers of Toulouse in the Eighteenth Century, 1740 – 1793*. Baltimore: Johns Hopkins University Press, 1975.
———"Lawyers in Pre-Revolutionary France." In *Lawyers in Early Modern Europe and America*, ed. Wilfrid Prest. London: Croom Helm, 1981.
Bien, David D. "The *Secrétaires du Roi*: Absolutism, Corps and Privilege under the Ancien Regime." In *Vom Ancien régime zur Französischen Revolution: Forschungen und Perspektiven*, ed. Ernst Hinrichs, Eberhard Schmitt, and Rudolph Vierhaus, pp. 153 – 168. Göttingen: Vandenhoeck & Ruprecht, 1978.
Bluche, Frédéric. *Le plebiscite des cent-jours (avril – mai 1815)*. Geneva: Librairie Droz, 1974.
Bosher, J. F. *French Finances 1770 – 1795: From Business to Bureaucracy*. Cambridge: Cambridge University Press, 1970.
Boulloche, Paul, ed. *Target, avocat au Parlement de Paris*. Paris: Alcan-Levy, 1893.
Bourdon, Jean. *La réforme judiciaire de l'an VIII*. 2 vols. Rodez: Imprimerie Carrère, 1942.
———"Le sénatus consulte de 1807: L'épuration de la magistrature en 1807 – 1808 et ses conséquences." *Revue d'Histoire Moderne et Contemporaine* 17 (1970): 829 – 836.
Bourne, Henry E. "Improvising a Government in Paris, July 1789." *American Historical Review* 10 (1904 – 5): 280 – 308.
———"Municipal Politics in Paris in 1789." *American Historical Review* 11 (1905 – 6): 263 – 286.
Boyer Chammard, Georges. *Les avocats*. Paris: Presses Universitaires de France, 1976.
Braesch, Frédéric. *La commune de dix août 1792*. Paris: Hachette, 1911.
Brinton, Clarence Crane. *The Jacobins: An Essay in the New History*. Reprint ed. New York: Russell & Russell, 1961.
Brissaud, Jean. *A History of French Public Law*. Boston: Little, Brown and Co., 1915.
Buteau, Henry. *L'ordre des avocats, ses rapports avec la Magistrature, histoire, législation, jurisprudence*. Paris, 1895.
Carlson, Marvin. *The Theater of the French Revolution*. Ithaca: Cornell University Press, 1966.
Caron, Pierre. *Les massacres de septembre*. Paris: La Maison du livre français, 1935.
Carré, Henri. "Le barreau de Paris et la radiation de Linguet." *Bulletin de la Faculté des Lettres de Poitiers* (1892).

———*La fin des parlements.* Paris: Hachette, 1912.
Casenave, Antoine Mathurin. *Etude sur les tribunaux de Paris de 1789 à 1800.* Paris: Firmin-Didot frères, 1873.
Censer, Jack Richard. *Prelude to Power: The Parisian Radical Press 1789–1791.* Baltimore: Johns Hopkins University Press, 1976.
Challamel, Augustin. *Les clubs contre-révolutionnaires.* Paris: Noblet, 1895.
Chêne, Christian. *L'ensegnement du droit français en pays de droit écrit (1679–1793).* Geneva: Librairie Droz, 1982.
Church, William F. "The Decline of French Jurists as Political Theorists." *French Historical Studies* 5 (1967): 1–40.
Claisse, Michel. *Le barreau lorrain sous la Révolution.* Nancy: G. Thomas, 1958.
Cobban, Alfred. *The Social Interpretation of the French Revolution.* Cambridge: Cambridge Uinversity Press, 1964.
———*Aspects of the French Revolution.* New York: George Braziller, 1968.
Collins, Irene. *Napoleon and His Parliaments.* London: Edward Arnold, 1979.
Coornaert, Emile. *Les corporations en France avant 1789.* Paris: Gallimard. 1941.
Curzon, Alfred de. *L'enseignement du droit français dans les Universités de France aux XVIIe et XVIIIe siècles.* Paris: Sirey, 1920.
Darnton, Robert. "Reading, Writing and Publishing in Eighteenth-Century France." *Daedalus* 100 (1971): 214–256.
———*The Business of Enlightenment: A Publishing History of the Encyclopédie, 1775–1800.* Cambridge, Mass.: Harvard University Press, 1979.
Dawson, Philip. "The *Bourgeoisie de Robe* in 1789." *French Historical Studies* 4 (1965): 1–21.
———*Provincial Magistrates and Revolutionary Politics in France, 1789–1795.* Cambridge, Mass.: Harvard University Press, 1972.
Debauve, Jean. *La justice révolutionnaire dans le Morbihan (1790–1795).* Paris: Chez l'auteur, 1965.
Delbeke, Francis. *L'action politique et sociale des avocats au XVIIIe siècle.* Louvain: Librairie Universitaire, 1927.
Delom de Mézerac, Joseph. *Le barreau pendant la Révolution.* Paris: Alcan-Levy, 1886.
———"Le barreau libre pendant la Révolution." *Revue des deux mondes* 118 (August 1, 1893): 572–590.
Desjardins, Albert. *Les cahiers des Etats-Généraux et la législation criminelle.* Paris: G. Pedone-Lauriel, 1883.
Doyle, William. *The Parlement of Bordeaux and the End of the Old Regime, 1771–1790.* London: Benn, 1974.
———"The Price of Offices in Pre-Revolutionary France." *The Historical Journal* 27 (December 1984): 831–860.
Dreyfus, Ferdinand. "L'association de bienfaisance judiciaire, 1787–1791." *La Révolution Française* 46 (1904): 385–411.
Durand, Charles. *Etudes sur le Conseil d'Etat napoléonien.* Paris: Presses Universitaires de France, 1949.
Durand-Barthez, Pascal. *Histoire des structures du ministère de la Justice, 1789–1945.* Paris: Presses Universitaires de France, 1973.
Egret, Jean. *La révolution des notables: Mounier et les monarchiens 1789.* Paris: A. Colin, 1950.
———*La Pre-Révolution française.* Paris: Presses Universitaires de France, 1962.
Esmein, Adhémar. *Précis elementaire de l'histoire du droit français de 1789 à 1814.* Paris: L. Larose et L. Tenin, 1908.

Fabre, Jules. *Le barreau de Paris (1810–1870).* Paris: Delamotte, 1895.
Flammermont, Jules. *Le chancelier Maupeou et les Parlements.* Paris: A. Picard, 1883.
Foiret, F. *Une corporation parisienne pendant la Révolution: Les notaires.* Paris: H. Champion, 1912.
Ford, Franklin. *Robe and Sword: The Regrouping of the French Aristocracy after Louis XIV.* Cambridge, Mass.: Harvard University Press, 1953.
Forrest, Alan. *Society and Politics in Revolutionary Bordeaux.* Oxford: Clarendon Press, 1975.
———*The French Revolution and the Poor.* New York: St. Martin's Press, 1981.
Forster, Robert. *The House of Saulx-Tavanes: Versailles and Burgundy, 1700–1830.* Baltimore: Johns Hopkins University Press, 1971.
Furet, François, and Denis Richet. *The French Revolution.* New York: Macmillan, 1970.
———*Interpreting the French Revolution.* Cambridge: Cambridge University Press, 1981.
Garaud, Marcel. *Histoire générale du droit privé français de 1789 à 1804.* 2 vols. Paris: Sirey, 1953–1958.
Gaudry, Joachim Antoine Joseph. *Histoire du barreau de Paris depuis son origine jusqu'à 1830.* 2 vols. Paris: Auguste Durand, 1864.
Geison, Gerald, ed. *Professions and the French State, 1700–1900.* Philadelphia: University of Pennsylvania Press, 1984.
Gerhard, Dietrich. *Old Europe: A Study of Continuity, 1000–1800.* New York: Academic Press, 1981.
Giesselman, Werner. *Die brumairianische Elite: Kontinuität und Wandel der französischen Führungsschicht zwischen Ancien Régime und Julimonarchie.* Stuttgart: Ernst Klett Verlag, 1977.
Giraud, Emile. *L'oeuvre d'organisation judiciaire de l'Assemblée nationale constituante.* Paris: M. Giard, 1921.
Godechot, Jacques. *Les constitutions de la France depuis 1789.* Paris: Garnier-Flammarion, 1970.
———*The Taking of the Bastille.* New York: Charles Scribner's Sons, 1970.
Godfrey, James L. *Revolutionary Justice: A Study of the Organization, Personnel and Procedures of the Paris Tribunal, 1793–1795.* Chapel Hill: University of North Carolina Press, 1951.
Goldstein, Jan. "Foucault among the Sociologists: The 'Disciplines' and the History of the Professions." *History and Theory* 23 (1984): 170–192.
Goodwin, Albert. "Calonne, the Assembly of French Notables of 1787 and the Origins of the "*Révolte Nobiliaire.*" *English Historical Review* 61 (1946): 202–234, 329–377.
———*The French Revolution.* New York: Harper & Row, 1962.
———, ed. *The European Nobility in the Eighteenth Century.* London: Adam & Charles Black, 1953.
Greer, Donald. *The Incidence of the Emigration during the French Revolution.* Reprint ed. Gloucester, Mass.: Peter Smith, 1966.
———*The Incidence of the Terror during the French Revolution: A Statistical Interpretation.* Reprint ed. Gloucester, Mass.: Peter Smith, 1966.
Gresset, Maurice. *Gens de Justice à Besançon: De la conquête par Louis XIV à la Révolution française.* 2 vols. Paris: Bibliothèque Nationale, 1978.
Grivel, Albert. *La justice civile dans le district de Montpellier en 1790–1791.* Montpellier: L'Abeille, 1928.

Gruder, Vivian. "No Taxation without Representation: The Assembly of Notables and Political Ideology in France." *Legislative Studies Quarterly* 7 (1982): 263–279.

——— "A Mutation in Elite Political Culture: The French Notables and the Defense of Property and Participation, 1787." *Journal of Modern History* 56 (1984): 598–634.

——— "Paths to Political Consciousness: The Assembly of Notables of 1787 and the 'Pre-Revolution' in France." *French Historical Studies* 13 (1984): 323–355.

Hampson, Norman. *A Social History of the French Revolution*. Toronto: University of Toronto Press, 1963.

Hargreaves-Mawdsley, W. N. *A History of Legal Dress in Europe until the End of the Eighteenth Century*. Oxford: Clarendon Press, 1963.

Hayem, Henri. "La renaissance des études juridiques en France sous le Consulat." *Nouvelle Revue Historique du Droit Français et Étranger* 29 (1905): 96–122, 213–251, 378–413.

Hermann-Mascard, Nicole. *La censure des livres à Paris à la fin de l'Ancien Régime*. Paris: Presses Universitaires de France, 1968.

Higgs, David. *Ultraroyalism in Toulouse from its Origins to the Revolution of 1830*. Baltimore: Johns Hopkins University Press, 1973.

Higonnet, Patrice. *Class, Ideology, and the Rights of Nobles during the French Revolution*. Oxford: Clarendon Press, 1981.

Hirsch, Jean Pierre, ed. *La nuit du 4 août*. Paris: Gallimard, 1978.

Hiver de Beauvoir, Alfred. *Histoire critique des institutions judiciaires de la France de 1789 à 1848*. Paris: Joubert, 1848.

Holtman, Robert B. *The Napoleonic Revolution*. Philadelphia: Lippincott, 1967.

Hufton, Olwen. *Bayeux in the Late Eighteenth Century*. Oxford: Clarendon Press, 1967.

Hunt, Lynn. *Politics, Culture, and Class in the French Revolution*. Berkeley: University of California Press, 1984.

Hyslop, Beatrice Fry. *A Guide to the General Cahiers of 1789*. New York: Columbia University Press, 1936.

———*French Nationalism in 1789 according to the General Cahiers*. Reprint ed. New York: Octagon Books, 1968.

Jaffé, Grace M. *Le mouvement ouvrier à Paris pendant la Révolution française*. Paris: Librairie Felix Alcan, 1924.

Kagan, Richard L. "Law Students and Legal Careers in Eighteenth-Century France." *Past and Present* 68 (August 1975): 38–72.

Kaiser, Colin. "The Deflation in the Volume of Litigation at Paris in the Eighteenth Century and the Waning of the Old Judicial Order." *European Studies Review* 10 (1980): 309–336.

Kelley, Donald R. *Historians and the Law in Postrevolutionary France*. Princeton: Princeton University Press, 1984.

Kessel, Patrick. *La nuit du 4 août 1789*. Paris: Arthaud, 1969.

Lacroix, Sigismond. *Le départment de Paris et de la Seine de 1791 à l'an VIII*. Paris: Société de l'histoire de la Révolution française, 1904.

Lanzac de Laborie, Leon de. *Paris sous Napoléon*. 8 vols. Paris: Plon, 1905–1913.

Lebègue, Ernest. *La vie et l'oeuvre d'un constituant: Thouret (1746–1794)*. Paris: F. Alcan, 1910.

Lefebvre, Georges. *The Coming of the French Revolution*. Princeton: Princeton University Press, 1947.

———*The French Revolution*. 2 vols. New York: Columbia University Press, 1962–1964.

———*Napoleon*. 2 vols. New York: Columbia University Press, 1969.
Lemercier, Pierre. *Les justices seigneuriales de la région parisienne de 1580 à 1789.* Paris: Edition Domat-Montchrestien, 1933.
Lepointe, Gabriel. *Histoire des institutions du droit public français au 19ᵉ siecle (1789–1914).* Paris: Montchrestien, 1953.
Levy, Darline Gay. *The Ideas and Careers of Simon Nicolas Henri Linguet.* Urbana: University of Illinois Press, 1980.
Loncle, Maurice. *L'ordre des avocats au Parlement de Paris aux XVIIᵉ et XVIIIᵉ siècles.* Abbeville: F. Paillart, 1910.
Lucas, Colin. "Nobles, Bourgeois and the Origins of the French Revolution." *Past and Present* 60 (August 1973): 84–126.
———"The First Directory and the Rule of Law." *French Historical Studies* 10 (1977): 231–260.
Mackrell, J. Q. C. *The Attack on 'Feudalism' in Eighteenth-Century France.* London: Routledge and Kegan Paul, 1973.
———"Criticism of Seigniorial Justice in Eighteenth-Century France." In *French Government and Society, 1500–1850*, ed. J. F. Bosher, pp. 123–144. London: Athlone Press, 1973.
Markham, Felix. *Napoleon.* New York: New American Library, 1963.
Mater, André. "L'histoire juridique de la Révolution." *Annales Révolutionnaires* 11 (1919): 429–458.
Matthews, George T. *The Royal General Farms in Eighteenth-Century France.* New York: Columbia University Press, 1958.
McManners, John. *The French Revolution and the Church.* New York: Harper & Row, 1969.
Méthivier, Hubert. *L'ancien régime.* 8th ed. Paris: Presses Universitaires de France, 1983.
———*L'ancien régime en France XVIᵉ XVIIᵉ XVIIIᵉ siècles.* Paris: Presses Universitaires de France, 1981.
Meynier, Albert. *Les coups d'état du Directoire.* 3 vols. Paris: Presses Universitaires de France, 1927–1928.
Mornet, Daniel. "Les renseignements de bibiothèques privées (1750–1780)." *Revue d'Histoire Littéraire de la France* 17 (1910): 449–496.
Mousnier, Roland. *Les institutions de la France sous la monarchie absolue, 1598–1789.* 2 vols. Paris: Presses Universitaires de France, 1974–1980.
Olivier-Martin, François Jean Marie. *L'organisation corporative de la France d'ancien régime.* Paris: Recueil Sirey, 1938.
Palmer, Robert R. "The Central Schools of the First French Republic: A Statistical Survey." In *The Making of Frenchmen: Current Directions in the History of Education in France, 1679–1979*, ed. Donald R. Baker and Patrick J. Harrigan, pp. 223–247. Waterloo, Ontario: Historical Reflections Press, 1980.
Paquin, Pierre. *Essai sur la profession d'avocat dans les duchés de Lorraine et de Bar au XVIIIᵉ siècle.* Paris: Paquin, 1961.
Péries, George. *La faculté de droit dans l'ancien Université de Paris (1160–1793).* Paris: L. Larose et Forcel, 1890.
Picot, Georges. *La réforme judiciaire en France.* Paris: Hachette, 1881.
Pinard, M. O. *Le barreau au XIXᵉ siècle.* 2 vols. Paris: Pagnerre, 1864.
Pocock, J. G. A. *The Machiavellian Moment: Florentine Political Thought and the Atlantic Republican Tradition.* Princeton: Princeton University Press, 1975.
Ponteil, Felix. *Napoléon Iᵉʳ et l'organisation autoritaire de la France.* Paris: A. Colin, 1956.
Popkin, Jeremy D. *The Right-Wing Press in France, 1792–1800.* Chapel Hill: University of North Carolina Press, 1980.

Pottinger, David T. *The French Book Trade in the Ancien Régime, 1500–1791.* Cambridge, Mass.: Harvard University Press, 1958.
Ramsey, John F. "The Judicial Reform of 1788 and the French Revolution." In *Studies in Modern European History in Honor of Franklin Charles Palm,* ed. by Frederick J. Cox, Richard M. Brace, Bernard C. Weber, and John F. Ramsey, pp. 217–238. New York: Bookman Associates, 1956.
Raynal, Jean. *Histoire des institutions judiciares.* Paris: A. Colin, 1964.
Régnier, Jacques. *Les préfets du Consulat et de l'Empire.* 3rd ed. Paris: G. Ficker, 1913.
Reinhard, Marcel. *Nouvelle histoire de Paris: La Révolution 1789–1799.* Paris: Hachette, 1971.
Robiquet, Paul. *Le personnel municipal de Paris pendant la Révolution: Periode constitutionelle.* Paris: D. Jouaust, C. Noblet, Maison Quantin, 1890.
Roblot, René. *La justice criminelle en France sous la Terreur.* Paris: Librairie générale de droit et de jurisprudence, 1937.
Rose, John Holland. *The Life of Napoleon I.* 2 vols. London: Macmillan, 1902.
Rousselot, Marcel. *Histoire de la magistrature français des origines à nos jours.* 2 vols. Paris: Plon, 1957.
———"Napoléon Ier et la magistrature." *Revue de l'Institut Napoléon* 70 (1959): 1–13.
———"Le premier consul et la magistrature." *Revue de l'Institut Napoléon* 111 (1969): 61–67.
Royer, Jean Pierre. *La Société judiciaire depuis le XVIIIe siècle.* Paris: Presses Universitaires de France, 1979.
Sagnac, Philippe. *La législation civile de la Révolution française.* Paris: Hachette, 1898.
Saulnier de la Pinelas, Gustave. *Le barreau du Parlement de Bretagne 1553–1790.* Rennes: Plihon, 1896.
Savant, Jean. *Les préfets de Napoléon.* Paris: Hachette, 1958.
Seligman, Edmond. *La justice en France pendant la Révolution.* 2 vols. Paris: Librairie Plon, 1901–1913.
Sevin, André. *Le défenseur du roi: Raymond de Sèze, 1748–1828.* Paris: Gabriel Enault, 1936.
Sewell, William H., Jr. "*Etat, Corps* and *Ordre*: Some Notes on the Social Vocabulary of the French Old Regime." In *Sozialgeschichte Heute: Festschrift für Hans Rosenberg zum 70. Geburstag,* ed. Hans Ulrich Wehler, pp. 49–68. Göttingen: Vandenhoeck & Ruprecht, 1974.
———*Work and Revolution in France: The Language of Labor from the Old Regime to 1848.* Cambridge: Cambridge University Press, 1981.
———"Ideologies and Social Revolutions: Reflections on the French Case." *Journal of Modern History* 57 (1985): 57–85.
Shennan, J. H. *The Parlement of Paris.* Ithaca: Cornell University Press, 1968.
Skocpol, Theda. *States and Social Revolutions: A Comparative Analysis of France, Russia and China.* Cambridge: Cambridge University Press, 1979.
———"Cultural Idioms and Political Ideologies in the Revolutionary Reconstruction of State Power: A Rejoinder to Sewell." *Journal of Modern History* 57 (1985): 86–96.
Stone, Bailey. *The Parlement of Paris, 1774–1789.* Chapel Hill: University of North Carolina Press, 1981.
Sydenham, Michael J. *The French Revolution.* New York: Putnam, 1965.

———*The First French Republic, 1792–1804.* Berkeley: University of California Press, 1974.
Taylor, George V. "Types of Capitalism in Eighteenth-Century France." *English Historical Review* 79 (1964): 478–497.
———"Noncapitalist Wealth and the Origins of the French Revolution." *American Historical Review* 72 (1967): 469–496.
———"Revolutionary and Nonrevolutionary Content in the *Cahiers* of 1789: An Interim Report." *French Historical Studies* 7 (1972): 479–502.
Thiry, Jean, baron. *Jean Jacques Regis de Cambacérès, archichancelier de l'empire.* Paris: Editions Berger-Levrault, 1935.
Thomas, Hubert. *Le tribunal criminel de la Meurthe sous la Révolution, 1792–1799.* Nancy: Georges Thomas, 1937.
Tudesq, André Jean. *Les grands notables en France, 1840–1849: Etude historique d'une psychologie sociale.* 2 vols. Paris: Presses Universitaries de France, 1964.
Tudesq, André Jean, and André Jardin. *La France des notables.* 2 vols. Paris: Editions du Seuil, 1973.
Tulard, Jean. *Nouvelle histoire de Paris: Le consulat et l'empire.* Paris: Hachette, 1971.
———*Napoléon ou le mythe du sauveur.* Paris: Fayard, 1977.
Vauthier, G. "L'épuration de la magistrature en 1808." *Revue des études Napoléoniennes* 15 (1919): 218–223.
Vignery, Robert J. *The French Revolution and the Schools.* Madison: State Historical Society of Wisconsin, 1965.
Villers, Robert. *L'organisation du Parlement de Paris et des conseils supérieurs d'après la réforme de Maupeou.* Paris: Recueil Sirey, 1937.
Viollet, Paul. *Histoire du droit civil français.* Paris: L. Larose and L. Tenin, 1893.
Wallon, Henri. *Histoire du tribunal révolutionnaire de Paris.* 6 vols. Paris: Hachette, 1882.
Walzer, Michael. *Regicide and Revolution: Speeches at the Trial of Louis XVI.* Cambridge: Cambridge University Press, 1974.
Wills, Antoinette. *Crime and Punishment in Revolutionary Paris.* Westport, Conn.: Greenwood Press, 1981.
Wilson, Arthur M. *Diderot.* New York: Oxford University Press, 1972.

Index

Abrial, André Joseph, 131, 132
Académie de Législation, 130, 134, 135, 136, 140–147, 150, 151, 152, 162–164, 166, 184
Académie Française, 28
Académie royale des belles-lettres, 11
Agier, Pierre Jean, 148
Agresti, Michel, 138
Aiguillon, duc d', 40
Alix, Jacques François, 97
Ameilhon, Hubert Pascal, 83
Angot, Pierre, 75
Annales de Législation et de Jurisprudence, 135, 137, 139
Artois, comte d', 20, 107
Association for Judicial Benevolence, 17
Attorneys, 2, 3, 5, 8, 12, 14, 19, 20, 24, 42, 44, 50, 52, 76–77, 78, 88, 125, 133, 153
Aubert Dubourg, Jean Jacques, 188
Audouin, François Xavier, 189
August 4, 1789, resolutions of, 33, 40–41, 42, 43, 44, 47, 49, 58
Auvray, Jacques, 97, 112
Avocats. *See* Barristers
Avocats ad honorem, 10
Avocats du Parlement, 8–9
Avocats en Parlement, 9
Avoués, 77, 78, 81, 82, 87, 95, 96, 99, 100, 124, 125, 126, 132, 133–134, 152–153, 176, 178, 185, 186

Babille, Laurent Jean, 119, 148
Bagges, Baron and Baroness, 15
Bailly, Jean Sylvain, 38, 39, 40, 61
Barère, Bertrand, 51
Barnave, Antoine, 53
Barristers, 3, 21, 24, 26, 46, 48, 50, 51, 56, 77, 78, 79, 96, 98, 99, 100, 103, 104, 122, 128, 132, 133, 152–153, 156, 158, 160, 194, 195; impact of Terror on, 105–110, 111; intellectual interests, 28–29, 30, 31; monopoly on pleading rights, 43, 44–45, 46, 47, 48–49, 52, 81; opposition to Directory, 127–129;

political activities (1789), 34, 35, 37, 40; professional functions, 2, 8, 18–19; pursuit of judgeships, 71, 74–75, 80, 86; reaction to abolition of Order, 69, 78, 80–81, 88–89, 93; social background, 23–24; unofficial coalition after abolition, 88, 96, 100, 109–110, 111, 114–116, 117, 118, 122–123, 128, 129, 130, 165, 167, 173, 175, 176–177, 182–183. *See also* Order of Barristers
Bâtonnier, 13, 25, 76, 160, 178–179, 180
Beaucousin, Christophe Jean François, 10
Beccaria, Cesare, 30
Bellart, Nicolas François, 78, 114, 116, 144, 156, 157, 176–177, 187, 190
Belliot, Etienne François, 97
Bergasse, Nicolas, 43, 45, 52, 61, 62
Berlier, Théophile, 150, 162
Bernardi, Joseph Elzéar, 142, 146
Berri, duc de, 191
Berryer, Pierre Nicolas, 7, 18, 20, 21, 55, 60, 63, 78, 90, 91, 95, 103, 106, 114, 116, 132, 135, 144, 173, 187
Berthelot, Jean François, 165
Béthune, comtesse de, 25, 26
Béthune, marquis de, 25
Bexon, Scipion Jérôme, 138, 156
Beytz, Joseph François, 125
Bigot de Préameneu, Felix Julien Jean, 11, 63, 133, 185
Billaud de Varennes, Jacques Nicolas, 20, 21, 92, 112
Billecocq, Jean Baptiste, 157
Bizet, Denis Alexis, 148
Blacque, Edme Jean, 144
Blanchard de la Valette, Claude, 30
Blondel, Jean, 20, 30
Bodson jeune, Joseph, 97
Bonaparte, Napoleon, 129, 130, 150, 154, 155, 156, 157, 160, 161, 162, 167, 169, 171, 172, 174, 178, 179, 180, 181, 182, 184, 190, 191, 197, 198

Bonnet, Louis Ferdinand, 55, 78, 114, 116, 144, 156, 157, 187
Boucher d'Argis, André Jean, 17
Boucher d'Argis, Antoine Gaspard, 30
Boucher de la Richarderie, Gilles, 80, 119
Boullay, Antoine Jacques Claude Joseph, 150
Boullemer de la Martinière, Jean Baptiste, 61
Bourrée de Corberon, Theodore Anne, 188–189
Boursault de Troncay, Charles, 108
Boys, Julien François, 106
Breton Club, 40
Briefs, 14–15, 18, 19, 22, 25, 28
Brissot, Jacques Pierre, 22, 23, 28, 44
Broglie, maréchal de, 25, 26
Bruguière, J. T., 135, 163, 164
Brunet, Jacques François, 128
Bulletin de l'Académie de Législation, 135
Bureau de paix et de conciliation, 51, 68

Cadoudal, Georges, 155
Cahier de Gerville, Bon Claude, 61
Caillau, Henri François, 165
Cambacérès, Jean Jacques Regis de, 116, 117, 131, 132, 157, 160, 161, 162, 167, 176–177, 179
Camus, Armand Gaston, 29, 30, 31, 35, 38, 63, 92
Carcenac, Antoine Jean Jacques, 97
Carpentier, Michel Jacques, 189
Carret, Michel, 152
Cathala, Marc Guillaume, 148
Cazalès, Jacques Antoine Marie de, 47
censors, 30–31
Central schools, 119–120, 134–135, 141, 151, 166
Certificat de civisme, 95, 96, 99, 102, 103, 110, 114
Chabroud, Jean Baptiste Charles, 49, 50, 51, 56, 63
Champeaux, 98
Champion de Cicé, Jérôme Marie, 72
Chaptal, Jean Antoine, 149
Chartres, 121
Châtelet, 9, 15, 17, 52, 71
Chauveau, Louis René, 61, 62, 145
Chauveau-Lagarde, Claude François, 107–108, 114, 128
Civil Code, 133, 139, 151
Civil Constitution of the Clergy, 68–69
Clement de Malleran, Louis Nicolas, 10
Clermont-Ferrand, 71
Clermont-Tonnère, Stanislas Marie Adélaïde, comte de, 45

Clerks (greffiers), 12
Club de Sainte-Chapelle, 74
Club de Valois, 74
Coffinières, Antoine, 189
Collet, Claude Nicolas, 108
Collot d'Herbois, Jean Marie, 112
Commissioner of the king, 65, 72–73, 81, 82–83, 85, 91, 93
Committee of Legislation, 91, 109, 113, 114, 117
Committee of Public Safety, 103, 109
Committee of the Constitution, 39, 43, 45, 46, 48, 50, 51, 52, 53, 54, 55, 61, 62, 76, 145
Committimus, 9, 47
Condillac, Etienne Bonnot de, 31
Confraternity of Saint Nicholas, 2, 3
Conseil judiciaire, 81
Constitution of 1791, 39, 40, 45, 52, 53, 58, 88, 90, 127
Constitution of the Year III, 117, 119, 121, 126, 127, 131
Constitution of the Year VIII, 131
Consulate, 130, 133, 134
Consultants, 19
Corporatism, 1, 31, 33, 49, 50, 56, 57, 58, 63, 88–89, 90, 125, 126, 150, 151, 160, 185, 191, 194, 195, 196, 197, 198–199
Council of State, 117, 131, 140, 158, 159, 160, 161, 162, 166, 167, 169, 171, 172, 177, 178, 179, 180, 181, 186, 190
Couthon, Georges, 93
Criminal courts, 80, 81–82, 86, 87, 96, 100, 102, 112, 117, 118, 131, 132, 133, 173–174, 175

Dalloz, Jacques François, 97, 98, 112
Danton, Georges Jacques, 20, 92, 93
Dassy, Claude André, 15
de Bonnières, Alexis Jules Benoît, 107, 128
Défenseur officieux, 76, 77, 78, 81, 82, 83, 86, 87, 96, 99, 100, 101, 102, 107, 108, 113, 134, 153, 167
Defermon, Joseph Jacques, 178
Delacroix, Jacques Vincent, 127
Delacroix-Frainville, Joseph, 60, 144, 182, 186
Delamalle, Gaspard Gilbert, 115, 156, 167, 182, 186
de la Metherie, Louis, 128
Delavigne, Jacques, 38, 40, 87, 182
Delvincourt, Claude Etienne, 165
Demeunier, Jean Nicolas, 46, 51
Derché, Jean Joseph, 189
de Sèze, Raymond, 11, 75, 95, 107, 128, 185
de Stassart, Godwin Joseph, 140

Dictionnaire de droit et de pratique, 30
Diderot, Denis, 30, 31
Dinocheau, Jacques Samuel, 76
Directory, 114, 115, 117, 118, 119, 120, 122, 123, 124, 125–126, 127, 128, 129, 130, 131, 132, 133, 149
Disbarment, 14, 15
Dodin, Paul Laurent, 14
D'Outremont, Anselme Joseph, 25
Duport, Adrien, 51
Duport-Dutertre, Marguerite Louis François, 20, 72, 73
Duveyrier, Honoré Marie Nicolas, 115

Écrivains, 18–19
Electors, 35–36, 39
Empire, 158, 168, 179, 192
Encyclopédie methodique, 10, 19, 21
Enghien, duc d', 155, 156
Enlightenment, 28–29, 30–31, 58, 197
Essai sur les réformes à faire dans notre législation criminelle, 30
Estates-General, 34, 35, 36, 37, 38, 39, 40, 59, 195–196; deputies to, 37–38, 113
Etat des travaux de l'Académie de Législation, 135

Ferey, Claude François Charles, 187
Ferey, François Placide Nicolas, 11, 115, 116, 176–177, 185
Ferrier, Claude Jean, 30, 91, 93
Ferrières, Charles Elie, marquis de, 41
Feudalism, 68
Feval, Louis François, 14
Foisy de Tremont, Denis, 108
Fondé de pouvoir, 100
Fourcroy, Antoine François, 143, 149, 150, 151, 152, 163
Fournel, Jean François, 54, 55, 56, 60, 63, 66, 69, 78

Gabaille, Ange Christophe, 187–188
Garde-meuble, 94
Garran de Coulon, Jean Philippe, 80, 95, 113
Gaultier de Biauzat, Jean François, 71
Gerbier, Jean Baptiste, 15, 21, 25, 26, 27, 28, 59
Gicquel, Charles Pierre Marie, 182
Godard, Jacques, 83, 92
Godard, Jean, 106–107
Godineau de Villechenay, Joseph Simon, 108
Gorguereau, François, 107
Government commissioner, 133
Grappe, Pierre Joseph, 146

Guyot-Desherbiers, Claude Antoine, 114

Hardi de Juine, Léon Pupil, 188
Hardouin de la Reynerie, Louis Eugene, 59
Hardy, Jacques Joseph, 83
Helvétius, Claude, 31
Henrion de Pansey, Pierre Paul Nicolas, 19, 120
Hom, Gilbert, 80
Hommes de loi, 70, 74, 75, 76, 78, 80, 81, 82, 83, 86, 87, 96, 99, 122, 124, 147, 148
Houard, David, 11
Hua, Eustache Antoine, 18, 22, 55
Hutteau, François Louis, 63

Jacobin Club, 100
Journal de Jurisprudence, 135
Judiciary, 41, 42, 43, 44, 45, 46, 47, 48, 49, 50, 51, 52, 54, 66, 77, 78–79, 84–86, 90–91, 93, 99, 102, 109, 111, 117, 119, 121, 122, 123, 130, 131, 132; elections to (1790), 71–72, 74–75; elections to (1793), 96–98; elections to (year V), 118, 128. *See also* Paris, courts
Justice of the peace, 52, 66, 68, 73–74, 80, 84, 93, 132

Lacretelle, Pierre Louis, 11, 29, 30, 92, 128
Lafayette, marquis de, 72
Lally-Tollendal, Trophime Gérard, comte de, 45, 46
Lambon, Nicolas, 25, 26, 27
Lamoignon, Chrétien François de, 8, 28, 34
Langlois, Jean Thomas, 127
Lanjuinais, Jean Denis, 51, 141, 143
Laujac, Bernard, 125
Laurent, François, 123
Lauze de Perret, Pierre Joseph, 174–175
Law: as societal principle, 41, 45, 56–57, 77, 104–105, 114, 126–127, 134, 161, 192; reform of, under Old Regime, 29–30
Law of 22 prairial, 99, 104, 105, 109
Law of 22 ventôse year XII, 130, 150–153, 154, 158, 159, 166, 168, 170, 171, 175, 183, 189
Law schools, 4, 7, 23, 69–70, 88, 102, 119, 141, 147, 149, 151, 158, 161, 162–163, 184; enrollments, 4; University of Besançon, 23; University of Caen, 70; University of Cahors, 5; University of Orléans, 70; University of Paris, 4, 10, 69, 88, 102–103, 162, 163, 164, 165–166, 186, 187; University of Reims, 5. *See also* Legal education, under Old Regime

Lebrun, Jean Baptiste Pierre, 162
Le Chapelier, Isaac René Guy, 46, 58, 63
Le Cointre, Gilles, 188
Lefebvre, Jean Baptiste François, 97
Lefebvre, Louis François Aubin, 135
Legal education, under Old Regime, 4, 5. *See also* Law schools
Legislative Assembly, 83–84, 85, 88, 91, 92, 94, 113
Legislative Body, 150, 151, 152
Lelievre, Jacques Mathurin, 97
Le Maire, Nicolas Eloi, 189
Lenoir de la Roche, Jean Jacques, 38
Le Paige, Louis Adrien, 29
Leprestre-Boisderville, Pierre François, 121
Le Roy, Louis, 12
Lesparat, Jean François, 182
Lettres historiques, 29
Linguet, Simon Nicolas Henri, 11, 15, 16, 25; disbarment of, 25–27
Locré, Jean Guillaume, 84, 113
Louis XV, 25
Louis XVI, 25, 26, 60, 72; overthrow of, 90; trial of, 94–95, 107, 156
Louis XVIII, 190
Lubin fils, Jean Jacques, 97

Mably, abbé de, 31
Mailhe, Jean Baptiste, 135
Maison de secours, 86–87
Malesherbes, Chrétien, 95
Maleville, Jacques de, 141
Mallarmé, Claude Joseph, 151, 152
Mallet, Etienne, 14–15
Marie Antoinette, 107
Martineau, Louis Simon, 52, 53, 54
Maugue-Massis, François Joseph, 108
Maultrot, Gabriel Nicolas, 29
Maupeou parlements, 8, 24–25, 26, 27, 34, 78
Maxims du droit public française, 29
Medical profession, 57, 126, 182
Melun, 121, 122
Mémoires de l'Académie de Législation, 135
Mercier, Sebastian, 122
Merlin de Douai, Philippe Antoine, 63
Mey, Claude, 29
Millet de Gravelle, Jacques Nicolas, 84, 85, 104
Ministry of Justice, 73, 81, 94, 117, 186
Mirabeau, comte de, 42
Mirbeck, Frédéric Ignace, 136
Mitouflet de Beauvois, Louis, 61
Montigny, Charles Claude, 198, 199
Montmorency, duc de, 106
Montpellier, 68
Morand, François, 138, 139, 142

Moreau, Jean Victor, 154–158, 160, 162, 169
Moreau, Simon Pierre, 187
Moreau de Saint-Méry, Médéric Louis Elie, 40
Morillon, Jean Baptiste Augustin, 188
Mounier, Jean Joseph, 45, 46
Muraire, Honoré, 117, 143, 178

National Constituent Assembly, 33, 34, 39, 40, 41, 42, 46, 47, 48, 49, 51, 52, 56, 57, 58, 59, 62, 63, 65, 66, 67, 70, 71, 75, 76, 78, 79, 82, 83, 89, 90, 92, 97, 194, 195, 196–197
National Convention, 92, 93, 95, 96, 99, 100, 106, 111, 113, 115, 119, 127, 128, 131
National Treasury, 78, 103, 106
Natural law, 29, 30
Nau, Jean Marc, 188
Necker, Jacques, 39
Noailles, vicomte de, 40
Notables, 195

Orateurs (plaidants), 18, 19
Order of Barristers; abolition, 33, 43, 50, 54–56, 63, 64, 65, 69, 70, 72, 73, 75–76, 80–81, 83, 88–89, 100, 149, 167, 183, 194, 196; charitable work, 16–17; criticism of, 16, 36–37; discipline within, 11–12, 13–14, 15, 16, 160, 184; entry into, 4, 6, 7, 11, 13, 16, 17, 24, 138–139, 146; independence, 3, 4, 16, 24, 160, 169; library, 17–18, 83, 100, 176; membership of clerics, 24; organization, 12–13, 18; prestige, 9–10, 69; privileges, 9, 24, 50, 54; relationship to Parlement, 24–25, 27, 28, 29, 36, 37; reorganization, 124–126, 150–153, 154, 158–162, 166, 167–173, 174, 177–190, 199. *See also* Barristers
Orléans, 66, 67, 70, 93
Orry, Nicolas, 86–87
Oudot, Charles François, 124, 125

Palais de Justice, 12, 117
Panis, Etienne Jean, 92
Papet, Charles Jean Baptiste, 157
Paré, Jules, 20, 21
Parfait Daupeley, Louis Isidore, 146
Paris; Appeals Court, 132, 133, 148; city of, 34, 35, 39–40, 52, 55, 158; courts, 52–53, 55, 63, 65–66, 66–67, 69, 71–72, 73, 78–79, 81, 84–85, 96, 97, 99, 100, 102, 104, 111–112, 115, 117, 118, 120–121, 148; municipal

Index

government, 60, 70–71, 84, 92, 97, 101, 103, 190; University of, 20, 69
Parisot, Jacques, 108
Parlement of Paris, 2, 9, 13, 14, 15, 16, 20, 21, 22, 26, 27, 28, 29, 31, 32, 34, 36, 37, 44, 52, 62, 65, 66, 71, 79, 80, 91, 99, 121; chambre des enquêtes, 18; Grand' chambre, 7, 18, 80; jurisdiction, 1, 7, 23, 66
Parlements, 43, 46, 50, 132; outside Paris, 11
Pasquier, Etienne Denis, 5
Pérignon, Pierre, 143
Perrin, Jean Baptiste, 152
Peuchet, Jacques, 138, 142
Philippeaux, Pierre, 93
Picasse, Louis, 188
Pichegru, Jean, 155
Pigeau, Eustache Nicolas, 138, 139, 165
Pison du Galand, Alexis François, 125
Pleading, 18, 19
Poirier, Jean Etienne, 144
Polverel, Etienne, 11
Popelin, Louis Auguste, 182
Portalis, Jean Etienne, 63, 117, 141, 143
Portiez (de l'Oise), Louis François René, 166
Privilege, 33, 41, 44, 45, 46, 47, 49, 50, 56, 57, 58, 63, 88, 114, 125, 126, 179, 191, 194, 195, 196, 197
Procureurs. *See* attorneys
Professions (professionalism), 31, 57, 77, 82–83, 93, 99, 100, 103–104, 105, 106, 115, 116, 122, 126–127, 134, 146–147, 160, 182, 197–198
Public prosecutor, 71
Pujoulx, Jean Baptiste, 122

Quesnel, Jacques, 122–123

Rabaut de Saint-Etienne, Jean Paul, 46, 47
Ratel, Gregoire Omer, 188
Raymond, Louis Claude, 93–94
Raynal, Guillaume, 31
Regnault de Saint-Jean d'Angély, Michel Louis Etienne, 117, 135, 143, 150, 158, 180
Regnier, Claude Ambroise, 63, 126, 144, 167–170, 171
Revolutionary Tribunal, 98, 99, 100, 101–102, 103, 104, 105, 107, 108, 109, 112, 113, 127
Rimbert, Louis Claude, 14, 21
Riou, François Marie Joseph, 124
Robin de Mozas, Louis, 11
Roederer, Pierre Louis, 47, 85
Rouen, 66, 67, 71
Rousseau, Jean Jacques, 31

Royal General Farm, 20

Saint-Vincent, Mme. de, 15
Sarradin, Jean Louis, 106
Sedillez, Mathurin Louis Etienne, 152
Seignorial courts, 12
Seminé, Guillaume, 97
Senate, 132, 133, 157, 175–176, 190
September massacres, 91–92, 113
Serpaud, Jacques, 106
Sieyes, Emmanuel Joseph, 38, 46, 51
Siméon, Jean Pierre, 108
Sublimity of the nation, 41, 42, 44, 45, 49, 56, 58, 59, 194, 196

Tableau des avocats, 7, 9, 13, 15, 16, 27, 123, 151, 152, 168, 170, 171, 172, 177, 179, 182–186, 189
Taillandier, Louis Auguste, 198, 199
Talleyrand, Charles Maurice, Archbishop, 46
Tallien, Jean Lambert, 93
Talon, Antoine Omer, 52
Target, Guy Jean Baptiste, 20, 25, 28, 35, 38, 42, 46, 61, 63, 92, 94, 95, 112, 135, 141
Testard, Pierre, 97
Teste, Jean Baptiste, 142
Thibaudeau, Antoine Claire, 116, 117
Thouret, Jacques Guillaume, 46, 47, 51, 52, 53, 63, 71
Toulouse, 2, 21, 74, 75, 162, 166, 194
Tournelle, 13, 86
Toutin, André, 97, 112
Treilhard, Jean Baptiste, 20, 63, 162, 177, 178, 179, 180
Tribunal de cassation, 79, 80, 115, 118, 132, 133, 147
Tribunate, 151, 152
Tronchet, François Denis, 25, 63, 76, 77, 92, 94, 95, 116, 133, 135, 167
Tronson-Ducoudray, Guillaume Alexandre, 94, 107, 127, 128
Troyes, 28, 34
Trumeau, Jean Antoine, 191

Université de Jurisprudence, 130, 134, 135, 136–140, 142, 143, 145, 146, 147, 150, 151, 156–157, 162–163, 166, 184

Vautrin, Claude Jacques, 108
Vermeil, François Michel, 30
Versailles, 121
Viefville des Essarts, Jean Louis, 48, 52
Vitasse, Angelique Françoise, 102
Voltaire, François Marie Arouet, 31
Vulpian, Jean Baptiste, 107

Harvard Historical Monographs

Out of Print Titles Are Omitted

1. W. S. Ferguson. Athenian Tribal Cycles in the Hellenistic Age. 1932.
3. J. B. Hedges. The Federal Railway Land Subsidy Policy of Canada. 1934.
9. Crane Brinton. French Revolutionary Legislation on Illegitimacy, 1789–1804. 1936.
11. C. S. Gardner. Chinese Traditional Historiography. 1938. Rev. ed., 1961.
21. O. H. Radkey. The Election to the Russian Constituent Assembly of 1917. 1950.
27. Marius B. Jansen. The Japanese and Sun Yat-sen. 1954.
31. Robert L. Koehl. RKFDV: German Resettlement and Population Policy, 1939–1945. 1957.
32. Gerda Richards Crosby, Disarmament and Peace in British Politics 1914–1919. 1957.
33. W. J. Bouwsma. Concordia Mundi: The Career and Thought of Guillaume Postel (1510–1581). 1957.
34. Hans Rosenberg. Bureaucracy, Aristocracy, and Autocracy: The Prussian Experience, 1660–1815. 1958.
36. Henry Vyverberg. Historical Pessimism in the French Enlightenment. 1958.
38. Elizabeth L. Eisenstein. The First Professional Revolutionist: Filippo Michele Buonarroti (1761–1837). 1959.
40. Samuel P. Hayes. Conservation and the Gospel of Efficiency: The Progressive Conservation Movement, 1890–1920. 1959.
41. Richard C. Wade. The Urban Frontier: The Rise of Western Cities, 1790–1830. 1959.
42. Harrison M. Wright. New Zealand, 1769–1840: Early Years of Western Contact. 1959.
44. Jere Clemens King. Foch versus Clemenceau: France and German Dismemberment, 1918–1919. 1960.
46. James Leiby. Caroll Wright and Labor Reform: The Origin of Labor Statistics. 1960.
47. Albert M. Craig. Chōshū in the Meiji Restoration. 1961.
48. Milton Berman. John Fiske: The Evolution of a Popularizer. 1961.
49. W. M. Southgate. John Jewel and the Problem of Doctrinal Authority. 1962.
50. Edward W. Bennett. Germany and the Diplomacy of the Financial Crisis, 1931. 1962.
51. Thomas W. Perry. Public Opinion, Propaganda, and Politics in Eighteenth-Century England: A Study of the Jew Bill of 1753. 1962.
52. Ramsay MacMullen. Soldier and Civilian in the Later Roman Empire. 1963.
53. Charles Montgomery Gray. Copyhold, Equity, and the Common Law. 1963.
54. Eugene Charlton Black. The Association: British Extraparliamentary Political Association, 1769–1793. 1963.
55. Seymour Drescher. Tocqueville and England. 1964.
56. Mack Walker. Germany and the Emigration, 1816–1885. 1964.
57. Stephen Lukashevich. Ivan Aksakov (1823–1886): A Study in Russian Thought and Politics. 1965.

58. *R. C. Raack.* The Fall of Stein. 1965.
59. *Charles T. Wood.* The French Apanages and the Capetian Monarchy, 1224–1328. 1966.
60. *James Holt.* Congressional Insurgents and the Party System, 1909–1916. 1967.
61. *Keith Hitchins.* The Rumanian National Movement in Transylvania. 1780–1849. 1969.
62. *Louis M. Greenberg.* Sisters of Liberty: Marseille, Lyon, Paris and the Reaction to a Centralized State, 1868–1871. 1971.
63. *Alan B. Spitzer.* Old Hatreds and Young Hopes: The French Carbonari against the Bourbon Restoration. 1971.
64. *Judith M. Hughes.* To the Maginot Line: The Politics of French Military Preparation in the 1920's. 1971.
65. *Anthony Molho.* Florentine Public Finances in the Early Renaissance, 1400–1433. 1971.
66. *Philip Dawson.* Provincial Magistrates and Revolutionary Politics in France, 1789–1795. 1972.
67. *Raymond Callahan.* The East India Company and Army Reforms, 1783–1798. 1972.
68. *Francis Godwin James.* Ireland in the Empire, 1688–1770: A History of Ireland from the Williamite Wars to the Eve of the American Revolution. 1973.
69. *Richard Tilden Rapp.* Industry and Economic Decline in Seventeenth-Century Venice. 1976.
70. *Hock Guan Tjoa.* George Henry Lewes: A Victorian Mind. 1977.
71. *Marjorie O'Rourke Boyle.* Rhetoric and Reform: Erasmus' Civil Dispute with Luther. 1983.
72. *Jon Butler.* The Huguenots in America: A Refugee People in a New World Society. 1984.
73. *William J. Callahan.* Church, Politics, and Society in Spain, 1750–1874. 1984.
74. *Michael P. Fitzsimmons.* The Parisian Order of Barristers and the French Revolution. 1987.